Brave New Workplace

Brave New Workplace

Designing Productive, Healthy, and Safe Organizations

Julian Barling

OXFORD
UNIVERSITY PRESS

Oxford University Press is a department of the University of Oxford. It furthers the University's objective of excellence in research, scholarship, and education by publishing worldwide. Oxford is a registered trade mark of Oxford University Press in the UK and certain other countries.

Published in the United States of America by Oxford University Press
198 Madison Avenue, New York, NY 10016, United States of America.

Library of Congress Cataloging-in-Publication Data
Names: Barling, Julian, author.
Title: Brave new workplace : designing productive, healthy, and
safe organizations / Julian Barling.
Description: New York, NY : Oxford University Press, 2023. |
Includes bibliographical references and index.
Identifiers: LCCN 2022028852 (print) | LCCN 2022028853 (ebook) |
ISBN 9780190648107 (hardback) | ISBN 9780190648121 (epub) | ISBN 9780197672686
Subjects: LCSH: Quality of work life. | Work—Social conditions. |
Multiculturalism. | COVID-19 Pandemic, 2020—Social conditions.
Classification: LCC HD6955.B345 2023 (print) | LCC HD6955 (ebook) |
DDC 306.3/6—dc23/eng/20220805
LC record available at https://lccn.loc.gov/2022028852
LC ebook record available at https://lccn.loc.gov/2022028853

DOI: 10.1093/oso/9780190648107.001.0001

Printed by Integrated Books International, United States of America

To my grandsons
Miles Quest Maxwell
and
Felix Landon Barling

Contents

Acknowledgments

One of the real delights of writing a sole-authored book is nearing the end and realizing that I could never have finished this by myself! So many people helped in so many ways, all of whom left me with a feeling of awe and deep gratitude. Writing a sole-authored book also offers the opportunity to publicly thank those who mean so much to me.

As any psychologist will tell you, what happens early on helps to set the stage for what happens many decades later. I was indeed fortunate to encounter three people who made a real difference to me in my high-school and university years. Hughie Wilson may have been my Latin teacher, but what he really taught me was that learning is fun, that there was so much more to be learned than what appeared in the rigid and limited school curriculum, and that it was OK to demand more of myself. Alma Hannon mentored me throughout fourteen wonderful years, first when I was a student and then a faculty member at Wits University. Alma taught me through her actions that it was not just OK to challenge orthodox thinking—but that social and scientific progress depended on all of us doing so. Jack ("Prof") Mann, my PhD supervisor and the long-time head of the Psychology Department at Wits, taught me the importance of thinking, speaking, and writing clearly and logically, as well as always being open to alternative, rival hypotheses. I know that without their presence and influence, my life would have been very different.

My role as an academic has enabled me to form the most wonderful personal and work relationships that flourish to this day. I was truly lucky to meet Dan O'Leary, Clive Fullagar, Steve Bluen, Bill Cooper, Ilona Kryl, Ruediger Trimpop, and Kevin Kelloway in the 1980s, and Mike Frone, Peter Bamberger, Mike O'Leary, Kate Dupré, and Nick Turner in the 1990s. I am indeed fortunate to have colleagues like Jana Raver, Christopher Miners, Nicole Robitaille, and Matthias Spitzmuller. I still miss the wonderful times I had with Rick Iverson, who died far too young. You have all helped me love everything I do.

Ever since I joined the Smith School of Business almost forty years ago, I consider myself blessed in having been able to supervise, and learn from, the most amazing graduate students. This offered me innumerable opportunities for discussions about productive, healthy, and safe work in both our formal weekly research group meetings, and countless one-on-one discussions. A huge thank-you to all the graduate students who have worked with me in the Smith School of Business: Amy Akers, Kara Arnold, Mark Beauchamp, Alyson Byrne, Stacie Byrne, Erica Carleton, Jennifer Carson Marr, Amy Christie, Anika Cloutier, Julie Comtois, Marie-Sophie Desaulniers, Inez Dekker, Heather Dezan, Angela Dionisi, Kate Dupré, Cecilia Elving, Milena Guberinic, Sandy Hershcovis, Kristy Holmes, Colette Hoption, Michelle Innes, Amanda Jane, Karen

Lawson, Manon LeBlanc, Catherine Loughlin, Rebecca Lys, Morrie Mendelson, Erin Reid, Jennifer Robertson, Kate Rowbotham, Niro Sivanathan, Cindy Suurd Ralph, Melissa Trivisonno, Kelsey Tulloch, Nick Turner, Julie Weatherhead, Alysha Williams, Barry Wright, and Anthea Zacharatos.

I am so grateful that Alyssa Grocutt, Shani Pupco, Michaela Scanlon, and Kaylee Somerville are working with me toward their graduate degrees. Thank you for the countless discussions about productive, healthy, and safe work, and the world at large. A special thank-you to Alyssa, Shani, and Michaela for reading and commenting on multiple chapters, and to Kaylee for her invaluable comments on the entire manuscript.

I eagerly look forward to many more years of research (and hanging out) with Alyson Byrne, Erica Carleton, Anika Cloutier, Kate Dupré, Mike Frone, Kevin Kelloway, Cindy Suurd Ralph, Melissa Trivisonno, Nick Turner, and Julie Weatherhead.

I am lucky to be surrounded by the most wonderful people at work. Annette Lilly has supported me in everything I do for twenty-five years, far longer than I deserve. Judith Russell manages to smile calmly every time I enter her office and makes me feel as if I really was welcome. Lisa Rodrigues answers every single one of my questions, as if I have never asked that exact same question many times before. Amy Marshall keeps my spirits up. Liane Wintle has accepted that I will never really learn PowerPoint, and continually covers up my skills deficits. Amber Wallace and April Wallace are wonderful colleagues, and patiently redirect my emails when I get them mixed up yet again. And without Jie Niu, the manuscript for this book would literally never have been submitted.

I have had the luxury of researching productive, healthy, and safe work for more than four decades. None of this could ever happened without considerable financial support from the Borden Chair of Leadership, the Monieson Centre, the Social Sciences and Humanities Research Council of Canada, and the Smith School of Business at Queen's University.

Kyle Wallace and Andrew Swain, from our school's IT helpdesk: thank you for suppressing the eye-rolls whenever I walk through your door.

A special thanks to Tony Sanfilippo, Suzanne Shephard, and Martin Korzeniowski for keeping me moving forward.

I count myself as lucky to have had Abby Gross of Oxford University Press in my corner throughout the writing of this book. This is the second time I have worked with Abby.* Abby understood that sometimes life gets in the way of progress on the book, and her patience and support helped ensure that this project came to fruition.

Last, to my family, I will be brief. Not because there is nothing to say; there is certainly more than enough to say! But Niro Sivanathan reminds us, in a wonderful TED

* Abby also served as the editor of my earlier book from Oxford University Press, *The science of leadership: Lessons from research for organizational leaders* (2014).

talk, that brevity is key to others remembering what you really want to say; clutter just detracts from your core message.[†,‡] So, to my wife, Janice, my children, Seth and Monique, and their partners, Steven and Stephanie: thank you for the joy you bring me, and the way in which you each, in your own different ways, strive to make the world a better place for all.

[†] Sivanathan, N. The counterintuitive way to be more persuasive. TED Talk video. Accessed August 11, 2022. https://www.ted.com/talks/niro_sivanathan_the_counterintuitive_way_to_be_more_persuasive?language=en

[‡] Let's be honest: only an academic would have references in the Acknowledgments section!

Abbreviations

BIPOC	Black, indigenous, and other people of color
BLM	Black Lives Matter
BLS	Bureau of Labor Statistics
CLT	charismatic leadership tactic (or behavior)
CSB	US Chemical Safety and Hazard Investigation Board
CSR	corporate social responsibility
EAP	employee assistance program
EQ	emotional intelligence
FDR	Franklin Delano Roosevelt
FTE	full-time employee
HBDI	Hermann Brain Dominance Inventory
HBR	Harvard Business Review
HPWS	high-performance work system
ILO	International Labor Organization
MBTI	Myers-Briggs Personality Inventory
MLB	Major League Baseball
NBA	National Basketball Association
NSC	National Safety Council
OCB	organizational citizenship behaviors
OSHA	Occupational Safety and Health Administration (the government agency responsible for worker health and safety)
PPE	personal protective equipment
PTSD	posttraumatic stress disorder
RODI	return-on-*development* investment
TMGT	too much of a good thing
UGC	user-generated content
WFH	work from home

1
Brave new workplace

Brave new work! If that has a familiar ring, it is no doubt because of Aldous Huxley's *Brave new world*.[1] Published in 1932, Huxley's classic novel depicted a dystopian society based on the principles upon which Henry Ford's assembly line was built: efficiency, mass production, conformity, predictability, and mass consumerism. *Brave new workplace* could not be more different. At its essence, *Brave new workplace* presents an optimistic picture of work that is productive, healthy, and safe. And each of the words, *brave*, *new*, *workplace*, conveys something very different about this perspective on work.

Brave: Moving toward productive, healthy, and safe work is not for the faint-hearted. Not because doing so involves enormous actions and interventions that border on the impossible. On the contrary, we see throughout the book that the scope of the changes that need to be made are manageable and, in some cases, surprisingly small. Instead, what requires bravery on the part of management is consciously choosing to step away from the status quo and doing things differently. We know that organizations like to benchmark their practices to those of their competitors. What I offer in this book instead is the opportunity to base those workplace practices on the best available evidence from organizational research, in some cases, decades of organizational research. Reiterating Peter Drucker's wise words, "You can either take action or you can hang back and hope for a miracle. Miracles are great, but they are so unpredictable."[2] To this I add that they are also altogether too infrequent as a strategy for organizational success!

New: Some people would have us believe that there is nothing about work today that is new, as seen in the title of Sarah Kessler's 2017 article, "We've been worrying about the end of work for 500 years."[3] But then the world was turned upside down by the COVID-19 pandemic in 2020 and 2021, changing ... well, time will tell what will change. *Brave new workplace* is not a book prophesying exactly how work and society will change in the near or mid-term future. By and large, doing so amid great social upheaval must surely result in predictions that are premature at best and simply wrong at worst. But consistent with Fareed Zakaria's observation that major events such as the Great Depression, World War II, or the attacks of 9/11 caused some of the most momentous social changes of the last century,[4] it is safe to say that work and workplaces will change. What we cannot yet know is the direction, pace, or extent of those changes. What we do know is that what people seek from their work, namely high-quality leadership, job autonomy, a sense of belonging, being treated fairly, opportunities for growth and development, meaningful work, and safe work,

Brave New Workplace. Julian Barling, Oxford University Press. © Oxford University Press 2023.
DOI: 10.1093/oso/9780190648107.003.0001

is unlikely to change. Understanding and recognizing these basic human needs will enable organizations to confront new challenges and build productive, healthy, and safe work.

Work: There are countless books, talks, webinars, and the like that advocate changing aspects of individuals to improve our work lives and productivity: EQ,[5] growth mindset,[6] lean in,[7] mindfulness,[8] resilience,[9] ... the list goes on. The underlying premise of these techniques is that workplaces will become more productive if we can just make people psychologically stronger. Alternatively, approaches such as EAPs wait for individuals to be harmed in some way, and then offer some form of counseling or support to treat the problems after they emerge.[10] Taking this a step further, I have always wondered about the wisdom and morality of offering people such help, and then sending them back to the same, unchanged workplace. Sir Michael Marmot highlights the inherent foolishness in this approach. He opens his book *The health gap: The challenge of an unequal world* by asking, "Why treat people and send them back to the conditions that made them sick?" (2015, 1).[11] Why would we expect to see any lasting change?

In sharp contrast, *Brave new workplace* takes you down a very different path that is consistent with the core tenets of primary prevention initiatives. The core goal is to give people access to the kind of workplaces and working conditions that will help them thrive and succeed, and prevent work-related stress and suffering from emerging in the first place. Perhaps no one has articulated this approach better than Christina Maslach. Commenting on the problem of burnout, among other things, she reminds us that "if you're really going to try and make a dent in the problem and get to a better place, you're going to have to not just focus on the people and fix them, you have to focus on the job conditions and fix those as well."[12]

Toward productive, healthy, and safe workplaces

All that being said, perhaps the most important decision is the first decision to do what you can to build a productive, healthy, and safe workplace. In the immortal words of Peter Drucker, "You can either take action or you can hang back and hope for a miracle." And, alas, he reminds us, "Miracles are great, but they are so unpredictable."

Seven distinct but interrelated work characteristics trigger productive, healthy, and safe work. These characteristics are depicted in Figure 1.1, and they are high-quality leadership, job autonomy, a sense of belonging, fairness, growth and development, meaningful work, and safe work.

Two assumptions are fundamental to this approach to productive, healthy, and safe workplaces. First, as Christina Maslach reminds us, productive, healthy, and safe work is realized by creating optimal work environments in which people can flourish, not by making people more resilient so that they can withstand damaging and destructive workplaces. Second, optimal work environments are composed of

Fig. 1.1 The seven work characteristics of a productive, healthy, and safe workplace

high-quality leadership, autonomy, a sense of belonging, fairness, opportunities for growth and development, meaningful work, and safe work.

Having said that, an important word of caution. Organizations do not need to implement all seven characteristics to change the way people view their work environments. On the contrary, a fundamental assumption of this approach is that small changes are enough to create productive, healthy, and safe workplaces. This is evident throughout the book, but most notably in two different sections in each chapter. First, each chapter showcases an intervention that exemplifies how the *small* things we choose to do create meaningful change in the long term. Second, while it may seem odd, each chapter also examines whether you can have too much of each characteristic. As examples, we will consider whether work can enable so much autonomy, or be so meaningful, that it backfires on employees and organizations.

Accepting that organizations do not need to implement all seven characteristics, where would you start if you wanted to move toward a productive, healthy, and safe workplace? The answer is anywhere, and there are two reasons for this. First, there is simply no research suggesting that any of the seven characteristics is more effective than the others. Thus, decisions as to where to start can be guided by local realities, which include current strengths and weaknesses of the organization and its leaders, as well as any particular resource considerations. Second, employees actively and continuously scan their workplaces and evaluate management actions (and inactions) accordingly.[13] Employees then respond positively irrespective of whether management introduces initiatives to enhance high-quality leadership, autonomy, belonging, fairness, growth and development, meaningful work, or safe work.

Another important assumption is that the seven characteristics are interrelated rather than stand-alone best practices. For example, granting employees more autonomy in their work can be beneficial. However, doing so without first providing them with the training (an essential aspect of growth and development) would not only be pointless but also one of the most dangerous things you could do in your organization. Similarly, providing employees with training is a waste of scarce resources if they do not also have autonomy to use the skills they learned. Accordingly, changes to meaningfully integrated "bundles," that is, interdependent characteristics such as autonomy and growth, would likely bring the greatest benefits to organizations and their members. On the contrary, trying to change all seven characteristics would overwhelm employees, resulting in less productive, healthy, and safe workplaces.

Last, the characteristics that lead to productive workplaces, as one example, could also lead to healthy and safe workplaces. This runs counter to the assumption in many organizations that they have a choice: either a productive *or* a healthy/safe workplace. Many organizations believe that the factors that lead to productivity (e.g., compensation) do not affect safety, and that factors that result in employee well-being (e.g., EAP programs, vacation) have no effect on productivity. Despite being widespread, this assumption is not supported in reality. For example, granting employees autonomy enhances well-being and work attitudes (see Chapter 3),[14] offering training improves commitment to the company (see Chapter 6),[15] and performance-based pay (negatively) affects safety (see Chapter 8).[16]

An evidence-based approach to productive, healthy, and safe workplaces

Think about the last time you visited your family doctor. My guess is that you assumed that whatever tests they ordered, diagnoses they made, or treatments they prescribed were based on the best and most current scientific knowledge available. If that is the case, you may be horrified to learn that this is not necessarily so. Earlier estimates suggested that about 15 percent of medical decisions follow the most recent medical or scientific knowledge.[17] And this was despite the fact that David Sackett and his colleagues at McMaster University in Canada had earlier developed what they called "evidence-based medicine," which they defined as "the conscientious, explicit, and judicious use of current best evidence in making decisions about the care of individual patients."[18] Since then, numerous other professions such as policing,[19] education,[20] and firefighting[21] have followed suit.

The field of management has fared no better than medicine. In fact, some estimates suggest that only about 1 percent of HR managers deliberately use research-based knowledge to guide their everyday workplace decisions.[22] Whatever the many reasons for this situation,[23] the consequences for organizational functioning are potentially disastrous: for example, organizations continue to adapt forced ranking systems in performance management, use stock options for compensation and motivation, and benchmark against other organizations—despite considerable evidence showing that such techniques are ineffective at best and harmful in more situations than we might care to acknowledge.[24]

Thus, a major goal of this book is to bring findings from the enormous body of management research to current and aspiring organizational leaders and management professionals in a way that can help guide their everyday decisions and behaviors. Invoking Sackett and colleagues' definition of evidence-based medicine, my goal is that this book helps management bring the "the conscientious, explicit, and judicious use of current best evidence in making decisions about healthy, safe and productive work," one step closer. In doing so, this is not another how-to book offering easy and prescriptive linear solutions to complex problems. Instead, the essence of this evidence-based approach acknowledges and respects the intelligence, experience, integrity, ingenuity, and flexibility of organizational leaders and managers who want to make their workplaces more productive, healthy, and safe for all.*

While adopting an evidence-based approach, it is tempting just to focus on the latest scientific advances. Nonetheless, we will not allow society's fascination with the most recent scientific research to obscure decades-old "classics" from which invaluable lessons can still be drawn. This approach will also remind us that the knowledge about how to make work productive, healthy, and safe has been with us for decades.

Taking an evidentiary approach also means that some topics that you might have expected to see in this book are given short shrift. For example, even though the Myers-Briggs Type Indicator (the MBTI) is extensively used in organizations around the world, it is barely mentioned again. The reason for this is that despite its enormous popularity, there is simply no credible evidence that it enhances the practice of management in any way.[25] Also, despite widespread concern that employees belonging to different so-called generations (e.g., baby boomers, Gen-X millennials) behave differently in organizations, there is simply no evidence that these categorizations mean anything or that people in these supposed categories have different needs at work.[26]

Similarly, having seen the model of productive, healthy, and safe work in Figure 1.1, you might already be asking—but what about compensation? Without delving into decades of research, we can say that with the exception of people who have to work for abysmal wages,† evidence does not support the notion that compensation is directly or meaningfully tied to productive, healthy, and safe work. Several sources support this idea. First, in their groundbreaking research, the Gallup organization identified twelve factors that contribute to a great workplace—but found no role for compensation!‡ Second, in his fascinating *Harvard Business Review* article, "Six dangerous myths about pay," Jeffrey Pfeffer concludes that one of the biggest myths about pay is that people are primarily motivated by money. The reality, Pfeffer reminds us, is that "people do work for money, but they work even more for meaning in their lives.

* At the same time, it is important to note that each chapter represents a sample of existing research on the topic. Given the sheer amount of research that has been conducted, this book is not meant to be an exhaustive (and exhausting) review of all the available research on the topic. Instead, what is reflected in each chapter are the findings most able to guide management decisions and behaviors.

† Given that the US federal minimum wage is $7.25 per hour, and the number of people engaged in gig work is increasing, the number of people affected in the United States is rising.

‡ In contrast, as will be seen later, no fewer than three of their twelve factors were directly related to growth and development!

In fact, they work to have fun. Companies that ignore this fact are essentially bribing their employees and will pay the price in a lack of loyalty and commitment" (112).[27] An even harsher reminder comes from Ed Lawler. Lawler illuminates some reasons why compensation typically fails to yield its hoped-for benefits: "Many organizations end up using an enormous amount of time to allocate small amounts of money to individuals based on an uncertain assessment of performance in the hope that performance will improve ... [I]t is a kind of corporate fantasy ... that takes time, effort and resources but has few ... positive outcomes" (210–211).[28,§]

Ideas about productive, healthy, and safe workplaces go back almost a century

My journey of learning about productive, healthy, and safe work began decades ago when I was an undergraduate studying what was then called industrial psychology. My time working as a researcher in the gold mines in South Africa while I completed my master's degree heightened my curiosity. My research focused on the application of Maslow's theory of motivation in an apartheid-riddled, dangerous work environment in 1975. Since then, I have been privileged to learn about productive, healthy, and safe workplaces from many different sources: Research I have conducted, roles I have held such as chair of the Ontario Advisory Council on Health and Safety and the editor of the *Journal of Occupational Health Psychology*, students I have encountered in executive MBA courses and executive education programs, involvement with many organizations, and innumerable discussions with wonderful colleagues and graduate students. Part of what I learned is that new ideas have appeared almost every decade over the past hundred years, many of which still guide our thinking about productive, healthy, and safe work today as you will see throughout the book. Allow me to introduce you to some of the ideas and the people behind them.[29]

The immense contribution of Marie Jahoda started with the publication *Marienthal: The sociography of an unemployed community*.[30] This groundbreaking book presented findings from her research on the effects of unemployment in the Austrian town of Marienthal.[**] Marienthal had thrived economically and socially for decades but was hit by massive unemployment in 1929. Based on what she learned from her many interviews with unemployed workers, Jahoda developed a theory of the psychological meaning of both employment and unemployment. Jahoda's theory was influential for at least two reasons. First, Jahoda posited that it is not simply the presence or absence of employment or unemployment that affects people. Instead,

§ Nonetheless, aspects of compensation that are implicated in issues such as fairness or financial insecurity will be woven into relevant chapters.

** In her obituary for Marie Jahoda, Rhoda Unger (2001) notes that this book was initially published without naming the three authors because the publisher feared that the authors' Jewish names would attract negative attention. Despite this precautionary step, "most of the copies of the first edition were burned because of its authors' origins" (Unger, 2001, 1040).

it is the quality of the employment and/or unemployment experience that is critical. Second, Jahoda showed that employment has both manifest and latent functions. The manifest function of employment is to provide sufficient financial resources. The latent function of employment is to provide the time structure, social contact, collective purpose, status, and activity that are essential for psychological well-being and mental health. Remarkably, Jahoda herself was active fifty-five years later, as is evident from her review of the effects of economic recessions on psychological well-being in 1988.[31] How influential is Jahoda's work? Well, her notion of unemployment and employment guided research on the effects of unemployment in the 1970s, 1980s, and 1990s in the United States, United Kingdom, and Australia, and I would also venture to say that Jahoda may be the second most famous social scientist of the 20th century. After all, how many other social scientists could boast of having a rock band named after them? Well, the eclectic rock band Nojahoda[32] took their name from Jahoda's work on mental health (saying that they had an absence of mental health).[††]

The 1940s saw the initial publication of Maslow's theory of self-actualization,[33] after which Maslow continued developing his theory until his death in 1970. It took about ten years for organizational theorists to question whether Maslow's theory could be useful in industry, even though initially this was of no interest to Maslow. Intrigued by this interest, Maslow took a sabbatical in 1962 and worked at Non-Linear Systems, a technology company in California. Whilst at Non-Linear Systems, he kept a daily diary that was published as *Eupsychian management: A journal* in 1965,[34] a book that Peter Drucker later said was "by far Maslow's best book."[35] Eighty years later, discussions about motivation in organizations are still guided by Maslow's hierarchy of needs. In fact, his theory is so well known that the mere mention of his hierarchy of needs probably has you visualizing a pyramid with his five needs, starting at physiological needs and extending through to the pinnacle, the need for self-actualization. If you can visualize his model, this is one of several other ironies about Maslow's theory. Possibly because it is so widely known, it has also suffered from widespread misinterpretation. As but one example, Maslow himself never created a pyramid to depict the hierarchy of needs—what Todd Bridgman and colleagues refer to as "management studies' most famous symbol."[36] An even bigger irony is the fact that despite the attention it has received, very little research was conducted investigating the application of Maslow's theory within organizations. Of the research that was conducted, the results were disappointing at best.

Nonetheless, Maslow's theory is critical for thinking about brave new work. A core assumption that underpinned his entire theory was that only psychologically healthy individuals (which he equated with self-actualized individuals) would reach their full potential and be capable of high performance. In addition, while research findings have not been kind to the usefulness of self-actualization within organizational settings,[‡‡] other needs in the hierarchy such as the need for safety and security and

[††] Read on to find out who might be the most famous social scientist of the 20th century, and why.

[‡‡] One practical reason for this is the very nature of self-actualization, which Maslow described so: "A musician must make music, an artist must paint, a poet must write, if he is to be ultimately happy. What a

a sense of belonging are foundational to understanding productive, healthy, and safe work.

How influential is Maslow's theory? It still influences management thinking, and has also been applied in other areas such as education, child development, and clinical psychology. In fact, I would suggest that Maslow is the most widely known psychologist of the 20th century. Yes, Marie Jahoda had a rock band named after her. But do you know of any other psychologist who had a hotel named in their honor? The Maslow Hotel in Sandton, South Africa, was named after Maslow to reflect the hotel's mission of catering to the well-being of its guests.[37]

As we enter the 1950s, production methods in coal mining in England were changing. Until then, coal mining involved doing a unified, whole task in which skilled mineworkers were granted autonomy over their work. But no more. To improve productivity, work was becoming ever more mechanized with miners only performing small fractions of the whole job. In addition, workers were now more isolated from each other, though they did work in small interdependent groups. Psychiatrist Eric Trist and Ken Bamforth, a former coal miner with eighteen years of experience, soon noticed that high levels of anxiety, anger, and depression were coupled with major disruptions in social-support systems.[38] Trist and Bamforth concluded (1951, 41) that it was "difficult to see how these problems can be solved effectively without restoring responsible autonomy to primary groups within the system and ensuring that each of these groups has a satisfying sub-whole as its work task and some scope for flexibility in work pace." This realization would affect how theorists and practitioners (largely in the United Kingdom and Europe) thought about work in general, and autonomy more specifically, for decades.

Focusing on the individual job rather than the entire social system as Trist and Bamforth had done, Frederick Herzberg was responsible for one of the most widely known developments in organizational thinking in the 20th century.[39] This was most likely due to his classic *Harvard Business Review* article in 1968, "One more time: How do you motivate employees?" In pre-internet times, people would gain access to *HBR* articles by purchasing a hard copy. In reprinting his article in 1987 to mark the journal's sixty-fifth birthday, the editors of *HBR* noted that in the twenty years since its publication in 1968, Herzberg's article had sold 1.2 million copies,[§§] three hundred thousand more than the next most popular article. Based primarily on semistructured interviews with about two hundred engineers and accountants in the United States, Herzberg insisted in this article that work motivation and performance can only be enhanced by enriching people's jobs,[***] which involves granting people

man can be, he must be." While probably true (as we will see in Chapter 7), a question that is often raised is, what happens if you find yourself in an organization that does not need musicians, painters, artists, or poets?

[§§] And the number of people who read the article would have been even greater, as the 1.2 million does not include those who shared the copy they had bought, or who read it in the journal.

[***] Herzberg also referred to job enrichment as vertical job loading.

responsibility for their own work, allowing them to use their skills, providing challenge, and recognition. In turn, enriched jobs provide opportunities for psychological growth and development.

Evaluating the impact of Herzberg's ideas is complicated. Herzberg insisted that benefits and compensation do not affect motivation and performance. Yet as we have already seen, organizations around the world remain fixated on compensation in the hope of influencing motivation. Despite this, even though Herzberg was never an organizational scientist and did not explain why enriched jobs would result in higher motivation and performance levels, others took up the mantle, ensuring his enduring indirect influence. Eight years after the publication of Herzberg's *HBR* article, Richard Hackman and Greg Oldham systematized many of Herzberg's ideas with the publication of their *job-characteristics model*.[40] Their model explains how facets that Herzberg had identified as critical for job enrichment influence the psychological experience of work, and that it is the psychological experience that affects work motivation and performance. Hackman and Oldham's ideas spurred considerable research over the next several decades, with very encouraging results. Many of the central ideas in their model (e.g., autonomy, task identity and significance, feedback, and meaningful work) feature prominently as antecedents of productive, healthy, and safe work.[†††]

Starting in the late 1970s, two different groups of researchers drew attention to the importance of feeling in control of your work. Working together, Robert Karasek, an architect by training, and Töres Theorell, a clinical and research cardiologist, initially developed the "demand-control" model, which at its core is a model of healthy work.[41] They proposed that unduly demanding work need not result in negative personal effects if employees enjoy some control over their work, such as the ability to refuse additional work with no fear of repercussions.[‡‡‡] Working separately at first, Sir Michael Marmot, an epidemiologist, initiated a massive study of the working conditions of 17,500 UK civil servants. Now known as the "Whitehall" studies, this research continues today and clarifies why social class is positively associated with life expectancy and negatively associated with early mortality. Essentially, ever-increasing levels of social status influence longevity by giving people access to resources, most critically, autonomy and social control.[42] These ideas apply equally in organizations, and explain a seemingly counterintuitive phenomenon. Many CEOs and top-level executives justify their enormous salary packages as reasonable compensation for the long hours, stressors, and challenges they face on the job. Yet studies consistently show that life expectancy is much higher in executives than blue-collar workers, with the difference sometimes reaching ten years.[43]

Last, starting in the 1980s and moving into the 1990s, Peter Warr developed his "vitamin model" to explain how many work characteristics (e.g., opportunities for

[†††] Notably, Hackman and Oldham also saw no need to include compensation in their model.
[‡‡‡] Karasek and Theorell subsequently extended the model to include the role of support as a way in which people could cope with overdemanding work.

control and interpersonal contact, physical safety) influence mental health.[44] Warr suggested that we should think of work characteristics as vitamins. Some vitamins have linear effects on physical health; for example, the more vitamin C or E you take, the better your health. In contrast, small doses of vitamin A and D are beneficial, but very large doses can be toxic. In the same way, high doses of some work characteristics such as autonomy may cause stress or anxiety, and a "one-size-fits-all" model of work characteristics would not be appropriate. If Warr is correct, two practical implications follow. First, in cases where workplace characteristics parallel vitamin A or D, implementing small changes might not only be the most efficient strategy but also the only productive, healthy, and safe strategy. Second, questions about *which* workplace changes should be made need to be supplemented with how *much* change would be optimal. Warr's ideas will guide us as we consider whether each of the seven work characteristics can be "Too Much of a Good Thing" (TMGT) in some circumstances.

Organization of the book

The next seven chapters appear in the following sequence. We start with leadership (Chapter 2), but not because leadership is the most effective of all the characteristics leading to productive, healthy, and safe work. Indeed, I know of no compelling evidence to suggest that this is the case. Instead, the story starts with leadership because someone in the organization has to decide to move toward productive, healthy, and safe work, and that takes real leadership. Autonomy (Chapter 3), belonging (Chapter 4), fairness (Chapter 5), growth (Chapter 6), meaningful work (Chapter 7), and safety (Chapter 8) all follow in alphabetical order, again to emphasize that each of the seven characteristics has an equal place in the model.

To enhance the consistency and readability of the book, the chapters largely follow the same sequence.[§§§]

- Each chapter opens with comments and observations about the nature of the particular characteristic.
- We then examine the attitudinal, performance, and well-being benefits that emerge when organizations get it right.
- We follow with an evaluation of what happens to work attitudes, work performance, and employee well-being when organizations get it wrong.
- We then consider how it is that the work characteristic exert their positive or negative effects.

[§§§] The one exception to this consistent structure/sequence is the chapter on safety. The reason for this is that there is a considerable body of research investigating what happens when safety is an issue at work, but precious little that I know of directly investigating the attitudinal, performance, and well-being benefits of getting it all right. Relatedly, there is no research investigating whether high levels of safety can have negative effects (i.e., the TMGT phenomenon). Accordingly, those sections do not appear in Chapter 8.

- Large bodies of research show how gender and culture influence each of the seven work characteristics, and we examine the role of gender and culture in each chapter.
- Following the idea that small changes make a big difference in the long term, we consider what is often referred to as the TMGT phenomenon in the organizational sciences—whether it is possible to have "too much of a good thing" with respect to any of the seven different work characteristics.
- Each chapter also describes an example of an intervention that was implemented and rigorously evaluated; the goal in doing so is to demonstrate that implementing each of the work characteristics is doable. Before going any further, a clarification on what is meant by an "intervention" is warranted. No, we are not referring to the kinds of family interventions you might see on TV where people intervene when other family members are descending into a bad place, often due to an addiction. The kind of interventions that will be described involve a carefully planned process in which one group in the organization receives a new program (e.g., leadership training). Conclusions as to whether the program worked are based on a comparison with a separate group that has not (yet) received the program, with measurements on the outcome of interest taken after the program is delivered, often several weeks or months later.
- Each of the seven characteristics raises unique issues for productive, healthy, and safe work. For example, what is the implication of autonomy (Chapter 3) for whether and how organizations should implement electronic performance monitoring? Similarly, knowing what we do about meaningful work (Chapter 7) raises questions about "dirty work." Finally, data about the relative risk of unsafe work for different demographic groups make the consideration of young workers crucial (Chapter 8).
- Last, I end each chapter with a section entitled "In case you are not yet convinced" in which I solidify the arguments made in the chapter, sometimes by reiterating what was said, other times by introducing additional information.

I look forward to meeting up with you again in Chapter 9, where we consider some remaining challenges as we move toward productive, healthy, and safe work. In the meantime, my hope is that as you move through the book, you come to appreciate what it takes to build productive, healthy, and safe workplaces, and the many benefits that employees and their organizations enjoy from high-quality leadership, a sense of autonomy, belonging, fairness, opportunities for growth and development, meaningful work, and safe work. Last, and by no means least, I anticipate that by the end of the book, you will know that productive, healthy, and safe workplaces are well within reach.

2
Leadership

Please help others rise. Greatness comes not from a position, but from helping build the future. We have an obligation to pull others up.
—Indra Nooyi, former President and CEO, Pepsico, Inc

The story about brave new workplaces necessarily starts with leadership, and not because leadership is more effective than autonomy, belonging, growth, fairness, meaningfulness, or safety. Indeed, despite my involvement in organizational and leadership research for several decades, I have yet to see compelling evidence showing that leadership is any *more* effective than any of the other characteristics. Then why start with leadership?

Because the brave new workplaces of the future literally must start with high-quality leadership. As we will see, autonomy, belonging, fairness, and the other characteristics are integral to a productive, healthy, and safe workplace, but someone must commit to introduce and integrate these characteristics into the fabric of the organization. As organizations around the world emerge from the pandemic, it will be courageous leaders who create the conditions that empower their employees and prepare their organizations for productive, healthy, and safe work.

The nature of leadership

The leadership literature is overflowing with different theories and approaches. Ambidextrous leadership! Authentic leadership! Charismatic leadership! Ethical leadership! Leadership-member exchange theory! Servant leadership! Transformational leadership! There are simply so many leadership theories competing for our attention that deciding where to start in explaining the nature of high-quality leadership is a daunting task.

I have selected transformational leadership as the exemplar for high-quality leadership because it is the most widely studied leadership theory since 1990.[1,2,*] As a

* However, we should not confuse popularity and effectiveness. Although transformational leadership remains the most popular theory among researchers inasmuch as it is the most frequently studied, there is no compelling evidence to suggest that it is necessarily any more effective than any of the other major leadership theories (e.g., servant leadership, leader-member exchange).

Brave New Workplace. Julian Barling, Oxford University Press. © Oxford University Press 2023.
DOI: 10.1093/oso/9780190648107.003.0002

result, the following discussion of leadership is rooted in the best-of-leadership research. Developed initially from the ideas of presidential historian and Pulitzer Prize–winner James McGregor Burns[3] and eminent scholar and researcher Bernie Bass,[4] transformational leadership comprises four separate components: idealized influence, inspirational motivation, intellectual stimulation, and individualized consideration. Of course, these particular names mean very little to all but groups of dedicated researchers. Greater clarity about the nature of transformational leadership is possible if we think of idealized influence as ethical leadership, inspirational motivation as inspirational leadership, intellectual stimulation as forward-looking or developmental leadership, and individualized consideration as relational leadership.[†] Taken together, then, the best of leadership is about behaving ethically, being inspirational, focusing on the future, and developing employees. When leaders do so, they meet the challenge posed to all leaders by Indra Nooyi, former CEO of Pepsico: help others rise and build a better future for all.

One corollary of this approach to leadership is that, as Indra Nooyi's observation reminds us, it is about a set of behaviors rather than a position. As a result, the best of leadership is not limited to those fortunate few who occupy the C-suite in organizations. On the contrary, as a tour around any organization will confirm, the very best of leadership happens at all levels of the organization, as is evident throughout this chapter.

The many benefits of transformational leadership

There is a mountain of evidence on the wide-ranging positive effects of transformational leadership. Indeed, if anything, the challenge is not what to include but what to omit from this discussion. Perhaps the best way to capture the wide-ranging effects of transformational leadership is to focus on its effects on employees' work attitudes, work performance, and well-being.

Workplace attitudes

While often demeaned as "the soft stuff" and therefore less important to organizations, employee attitudes cannot be summarily dismissed. The reason for this is that work attitudes play a major role in generating the outcomes organizations cherish.[5] For example, loyalty or commitment to the organization, fairness, and trust in management all motivate attendance, the retention of most valued employees, higher levels of sales performance, service quality, workplace safely, and organizational

[†] Nonetheless, the vast majority of researchers study transformational leadership as a single dimension, and we follow this convention.

citizenship behaviors (OCB).‡ We limit our focus in this section to two attitudes, namely employees' commitment (or loyalty) to the organization and their trust in management.

Leadership plays a significant role in organizational commitment, which is evident when employees are proud to be members of their organization, happy to tell others that they are members, and want to help their organization be successful. In one study, CEOs' transformational leadership predicted the organizational commitment of 210 top-level executives of organizations listed on the Fortune 500 in Turkey.[6] Importantly, the effects of transformational leadership on commitment extend throughout organizations. In our own research in the commercial banking environment in Canada, subordinates whose branch managers received transformational-leadership training subsequently had higher levels of organizational commitment.[7] Other research shows that all forms of high-quality leadership play a substantial role in the development of employees' commitment to their organization.[8,9]

Given the massive changes over the past two decades toward part-time, temporary, or contract employment, is high-quality leadership still relevant to employee loyalty in precarious work environments? One study provides an optimistic answer. Researchers analyzed responses from 126 temporary employees who had been with the same health care and medical research organization in the United States for at least one month.[10] After accounting for possible factors that could influence employee commitment such as age, gender, and length of tenure with the organization, supportive leadership behaviors resulted in a sense of pride in being associated with the organization and a desire to remain with the organization, that is, greater commitment to the organization. Thus, despite questions as to whether it is even possible to secure the commitment of temporary employees, high-quality leadership offers organizations one way of attracting the commitment of those employees with the most tenuous formal ties to the organization.

Importantly, the effects of transformational leadership go beyond strengthening the bond between employees and their organizations. Again, focusing on the highest levels of the organization, an intriguing study of 304 executives from top management teams in 152 firms in Vietnam highlights the role of trust in understanding how CEO transformational leadership affects firm performance.[11] Consistent with the notion that leadership primarily exerts indirect effects on outcomes (which will be discussed later), higher levels of CEO transformational leadership were associated with more trust in the top management team. This is important because trust in the top management team then influenced employees' performance. Research conducted in both the United States and Canada confirms the link between transformational leadership and trust in management.[12] A good place to end this section is with a reminder

‡ Organizational citizenship behavior (OCB) is a term used throughout the book. OCBs are discretionary (rather than required by a performance contract or collective agreement) and contribute to the functioning and success of the organization. Citizenship behaviors take various forms, such as helping others when not required to do so, participating in non-work activities of the organization, and respecting others.

from noted author Stephen Covey. In his book *The speed of trust: The one thing that changes everything*, Covey suggests that when trust exists, for example, within organizations or between leaders and followers, it pays dividends.[13] Alternatively, when leaders create distrust with their followers, it imposes a tax on organizations.

Work performance

For those concerned that work attitudes are of little importance to organizations, knowing about the effects of transformational leadership on performance might be more persuasive. John Antonakis and his colleagues illustrate the economic value of high-quality leadership to organizations.[14] Given that organizations routinely devote considerable time, effort, and money to ensuring that their compensation systems are effective, how much added value might leadership offer? Unlike studies of compensation and leadership in isolation, Antonakis et al. contrasted the effects of charismatic leadership and two different forms of compensation, namely fixed wages and piece rates, on work performance. In their research, 120 temporary workers stuffed 30,000 envelopes to help Birmingham Children's Hospital with a fundraising campaign. One group received a regular fixed wage of £6.31 for 4.5 hours of work, in addition to standard motivation speech. The piece-rate group received the same basic wage as well as a bonus of £0.12 for each envelope that exceeded the 220 target; in other words, this group received performance-based compensation. The third "charismatic" group received the fixed wage, and for them the standard motivation speech was replaced with a speech that was similar in content but delivered in a more charismatic manner. Despite the widespread organizational emphasis on compensation as a primary motivator, charismatic leadership was as effective as the piece-rate or performance-based compensation in achieving higher performance. More importantly, charismatic leadership was also more cost-effective than performance-based compensation. While the researchers suggest that caution is appropriate as this is the first study to make this comparison, the effectiveness and cost-effectiveness of charismatic leadership is demonstrated.

Some studies have focused on the important question of whether CEO transformational leadership affects organizational outcomes more broadly. Christian Resick and colleagues investigated whether CEOs of major league baseball teams influence organizational performance. Publicly available data going back a hundred years indicate winning percentages, manager turnover, fan attendance, and external ratings of team managers' influence. Ratings of the CEOs' transformational leadership styles were provided by external raters who read biographies of the CEOs.[15] Resick et al.'s analyses showed that CEO transformational leadership was associated with team-winning percentage, fan attendance, and managers' influence.[§]

[§] The finding that CEO transformational leadership was not associated with manager turnover might seem surprising. However, one possibility is that the best of leadership entails encouraging your employees

Maike Jensen and her team took a more nuanced approach in their study of forty-two of the largest US and European publicly traded companies.[16] Specifically, they investigated whether the four dimensions of CEO transformational leadership affected operating-profit margins, net-profit margins, and returns on assets (ROAs) over four years. Similar to Resick et al., data on transformational leadership were derived from reputable news sources, namely the *Financial Times*, *Guardian*, and *Economist*, as well as *Forbes* and *Fortune* magazines, which were all merged with financial data available from Thomson Datastream. CEO inspirational motivation predicted net-profit margins and ROAs. In addition, CEO intellectual stimulation predicted operating-profit margins and ROAs, suggesting that facilitating followers' creativity and providing them with opportunities to problem-solve enhance firm performance.

As important as the effects of CEO leadership might be, they are not limited to financial outcomes. David Waldman and his team questioned whether the effects of CEO transformational leadership extend to organizations' involvement in activities that support corporate social responsibility (CSR).[17] After statistically controlling for company factors that could influence CSR involvement, such as company profit and size, CEO tenure, and R&D intensity, CEO intellectual stimulation (but not charisma) predicted strategic-focused CSR.

Taken together, these studies point to the importance of high-quality leadership in work performance and organizational functioning.

Well-being

"Well-being" almost defies definition. As Sir Cary Cooper laments, we cannot even agree on how it should be spelled! Hyphen, or no hyphen? For our purpose, we follow the elegant description provided by Bob Merberg: "In simple terms, well-being can be described as judging life positively and feeling good."[18] So, can high-quality leadership improve employee well-being?

The answer is yes! In separate samples of 319 Canadian health care workers and 146 service workers, Kara Arnold and colleagues showed that transformational leadership helps employees find meaning in their work; having meaningful work then enhances employee well-being.[19] In subsequent research by Kevin Kelloway and colleagues, transformational leadership enhanced employees' trust in leadership, and being able to trust one's leader positively affected employee well-being.[20] Studies conducted among Dutch eldercare employees by Karina Nielsen and colleagues add to our understanding, showing that transformational leadership helps employees enjoy

to grow and develop, and sometimes that might mean supporting them when they seek better opportunities elsewhere.

higher levels of self-efficacy,[21,**] more opportunities for development, and greater role clarity, all of which result in improved well-being.[22]

Despite findings such as these, Alissa Parr and colleagues caution that the benefits of transformational leadership may not be universal.[23] They document the growing number of employees diagnosed with autism spectrum disorder (ASD), pointing out that adults with ASD have attributes such as reliability, trustworthiness, and attention to detail that would make them valuable employees. At the same time, the anxiety that is common in ASD employees might lead them to respond negatively to leadership behaviors such as inspirational motivation that rely heavily on emotions, abstract ideas, and collaborative action. The results of their study showed that inspirational motivation was indeed associated with higher levels of anxiety among adult employees with ASD, reminding us that any leadership initiatives focused on enhancing employee well-being need to be implemented with considerable forethought and sensitivity.

Establishing that high-quality leadership benefits employee well-being is consistent with growing interest in employee well-being by organizational decision-makers and scholars. But as my colleague Anika Cloutier and I have noted, something is missing from this discussion, and that is a parallel focus on leaders' well-being.[24] Leaders' well-being is no less important to leaders themselves, their families, and their organizations, and it cannot not be taken for granted. On the one hand, if as Indra Nooyi insists, leadership is indeed about helping others rise, the authentic pride leaders might feel from lifting up their employees could enhance their own well-being. On the other hand, the cognitive and emotional demands of engaging in high-quality leadership may take its own toll on leaders. Some studies have tried to understand the seemingly contradictory effects of enacting high-quality leadership on leaders' own well-being.

Klodiana Lanaj and her colleagues posited that engaging in transformational leadership would benefit leaders for several reasons.[25] For example, showing enthusiasm and positive facial expressions could benefit the leader through biofeedback cycles. In addition, watching followers' positive emotions could spark emotional contagion.[††] To investigate this, Lanaj et al. conducted two studies with different samples of executive MBA students in the United States. In both studies, engaging in transformational leadership was associated with leaders experiencing positive moods. They replicated these findings in a separate study, which showed that treating others politely and with respect helped leaders replenish emotional resources that are critical for dealing with demanding situations.[26]

However, the story does not end here, and some research has explicitly investigated whether the cognitive, emotional, and relational demands of high-quality

** Based on the influential research of psychologist Albert Bandura, self-efficacy reflects people's beliefs that given appropriate effort, they will be able to perform the required behavior.

†† Emotional contagion is a process whereby emotions and emotional expressions spread to people close by; it is often reflected in statements such as "misery loves company."

leadership tax leaders' emotional resources,[27] thus both helping and hurting leaders' well-being.[28] Joanna Liu and colleagues collected data from 79 US leaders and 217 US followers each week for six weeks. What this study showed was that enacting transformational leadership benefitted positive mood (e.g., being enthusiastic and excited) and work engagement, but at the same time exerted a toll on negative mood (e.g., being upset and distressed) and emotional exhaustion.

Clearly, the primary beneficiaries of transformational leadership are employees. The picture becomes more complex when we focus on leaders' own well-being, an issue that researchers will no doubt return to in the future.

When leadership goes awry

So many people go to work each day only to confront poor leadership, and this is reflected by the considerable attention among the lay public, management practitioners, and researchers, as well as in popular movies and other media, to the nature and effects of bad leadership. In this section, we discuss the consequences of two extremes of bad leadership, namely abusive supervision and passive leadership.

Ridiculing employees, breaking promises, lying, taking credit for their work, gossiping about them, or putting them down! These are just some of the behaviors that Ben Tepper included in the notion of abusive supervision—"the sustained display of hostile and nonverbal behaviors, excluding physical contact" (178).[29] These behaviors do not necessarily occur frequently, but they are sustained over time. Seemingly the opposite of abusive supervision is laissez-faire or passive leadership, and the knowledge that some leaders do very little is hardly new: Robert Blake and Jane Mouton's managerial grid explicitly included passive management more than fifty years ago, calling it an indifferent or impoverished leadership style![30] With the appearance of Bass' transformational-leadership theory some twenty years later,[31] laissez-faire leadership involved procrastination, abdication, avoidance, and denial especially when action was needed. In trying to understand the effects of passive leadership, we are faced with a problem: much less research has been focused on passive leadership than abusive leadership, possibly driven by the widespread but erroneous belief that as long as leaders just do nothing, nothing bad will happen. But as we will see, this is just wishful thinking.

Work attitudes

It will come as no surprise that studies confirm that the demeaning and demoralizing nature of abusive supervision is overwhelmingly destructive.[32] As examples, in one study of 480 sales employees in China, abusive supervision was associated with lower levels of loyalty to the company, with the diminished loyalty resulting in poorer sales performance.[33] Similarly, abusive supervision experienced by 198 frontline hotel employees in China resulted in poorer customer service by these employees.[34] Among 458 employees in a transportation company in Taiwan,[35] abusive supervision was associated with ambiguity as to what was required for good job performance, and dealing with the ambiguity resulted in burnout.

But leadership does not have to be overtly bad to take a toll. For Timothy Hinkin and Chester Schriesheim, passive managers neglect the basics of management, namely rewarding positive performance and punishing poor performance.[36] To illustrate, imagine you had just finished some work that you knew was of a very high standard and went well beyond the normal requirements of the job. In fact, your work was so good you believed you deserved some attention from management—and then none was forthcoming. Or imagine that the quality of your work was so poor that you knew that a visit from management was warranted—but, again, nothing happened.[‡‡] Given how these two different situations might leave you feeling, it is perhaps not surprising that passive leadership is associated with feeling less satisfied with your leader and viewing your leader as less effective. The consequences of passive or laissez-faire leadership are uniformly negative,[37] exemplified by lower organizational commitment,[38] job dissatisfaction,[39] and poorer work attitudes.[40]

Work performance

Faced with the demeaning and demoralizing nature of abusive supervision, most employees don't just stand idly by; they respond in different ways that hurt work performance. Robert Sutton, author of the entertaining and thoughtful *Good boss, bad boss*,[41] highlights "malicious compliance," which involves deliberately doing exactly what your abusive or incompetent boss demands, knowing fully that it will lead to failure and expose their incompetence, as one overlooked consequence. Malicious compliance reminds us that simply doing what you must can never be enough for organizations to succeed. Instead, organizations need employees who willingly go well beyond the minimum performance levels necessary to keep their jobs.

A different response to abusive supervision is to choose to withdraw from the organization.[42]While turnover can be costly to organizations, the effects of abusive supervision might be even worse if employees choose to stay. There is also strong evidence that some employees seek retaliation following incidents of abusive supervision—in their minds, it is now "payback time," and they feel justified in whatever they do. In one study on 427 US employees, experiencing abusive supervision was associated with deviant behaviors such as deliberately embarrassing or being rude to the supervisor or fellow coworkers, or taking property home without permission.[43] Importantly, the authors of this study also showed that deviance targeted at the supervisor was even greater when employees believed that their supervisors deserved the mistreatment.

‡‡ Hinkin and Schriesheim refer to the former as "reward omission," and the latter as "punishment omission."

The negative effects of passive or laissez-faire leadership on work performance belie the belief that just doing nothing might be the safest option; moreover, negative effects are even present at the highest levels of the organization. In their study of seventy-nine high-tech firms in the United States and Ireland, Patrick Flood and colleagues showed that passive leadership among CEOs hurt the effectiveness of the top management team.[44] The effects of laissez-faire leadership are also more widespread. For example, laissez-faire leadership is negatively associated with the learning climate in the organization, perhaps because the presence of laissez-faire leadership puts more demands on employees who then believe that they do not have enough time for learning.[45]

No less important is the fact that laissez-faire leadership can imperil employee safety. Kevin Kelloway and colleagues showed that when leaders disengage and abdicate their responsibilities for safety, employees focus less on safety issues. In doing so, they compromise not only their own safety but also likely that of others around them.[46] Going beyond physical safety, Anders Skogstad and his colleagues demonstrated that laissez-faire leadership creates a climate in which bullying can flourish.[47] This is important, because being bullied results in productivity losses, partially through its effects on depression.[48] As Irish political philosopher Edmund Burke reminds us, "The only thing necessary for the triumph of evil is that good men do nothing."

Thus, both abusive supervision and passive leadership exert negative effects on performance. But is one worse than the other? After all, the belief endures that as long as you just do nothing, no harm will result? Findings from Thomas Fosse et al.'s meta-analysis[§§] are instructive: abusive supervision and passive leadership exerted equally negative effects on work attitudes, work performance, and well-being.[49] As a result, they describe both abusive supervision and passive leadership as "destructive leadership," a term that derives less from the nature of leadership behaviors than from their harmful effects.

Well-being

Not surprisingly, numerous studies affirm that abusive supervision and passive leadership have negative effects on well-being. For example, Yucheng Zhang and Zhenyu Liao's meta-analysis confirms that abusive supervision negatively affects different aspects of employees' psychological and physical well-being, such as anger, anxiety, depression, and emotional exhaustion.[50] Later research showed that abusive supervision also hurts the quantity and quality of employees' sleep.[51]

[§§] In many places, we discuss findings from meta-analyses. Simply stated, a meta-analysis is a single study that statistically combines the results of many other studies on the same topic and enables statistical conclusions to be drawn from multiple prior studies.

What is perhaps more surprising is that engaging in abusive supervision also hurts abusive leaders themselves. In separate samples from a private organization and a large state-owned company in China, engaging in abusive supervision left some leaders thinking about how poorly they had treated their employees, with these invasive thoughts still present at least two weeks after the abusive treatment.[52] The researchers also showed that in the United Kingdom leaders ruminate after enacting abusive supervision even if they justify the abuse as a response to employees' poor performance. Thus, contrary to what many people might believe, enacting bad leadership is bad for the leaders, too, especially because ruminating at work is enough to keep you awake at night.[53]

The effects of abusive supervision are so pervasive they can even threaten the well-being of unintended bystanders. Keren Turgeman-Lupo and Michal Biron investigated the extent to which abusive supervision stays with employees after work, specifically whether it could affect how safely you drive home after work.[54] In their study, 216 employees from a large electronic manufacturing plant completed questionnaires about abusive supervision and dangerous driving behaviors before and after work, twenty-four months apart. Abusive supervision had negative effects on commuting violations in both time periods. Findings such as these suggest that the negative effects of abusive supervision can extend beyond the workplace: rumination and the resultant emotional aftermath of abusive supervision leave people unable to concentrate on driving safely, possibly endangering innocent bystanders.

While we often hear employees wishing that they could see less of their leaders, passive leadership also hurts well-being. Robert Caplan and Kenneth Jones' findings from the mid-1970s showed that not having a clear idea of your leaders' expectations was associated with follower anxiety.[55] Research since then has shown that passive leadership predicts employee depression,[56] and based on a national probability sample of 2,467 US employees, passive leadership also indirectly affected employees' fatigue and mental health.[57]

How does leadership work?

What we have seen so far is that leadership "works"! High-quality leadership benefits employees and their organizations, while abusive and passive leadership harms them. But how does this happen? Simply having a high-quality leader does not mean you wake up each morning and decide to do amazing work. Nor does having an abusive leader mean waking up each morning and refusing to leave your bed. The process in both cases is much more psychologically nuanced. As we shall soon see, the effects of good and bad leadership are invariably indirect (and sometimes referred to as a "downstream" effect), and good and bad leadership indirectly shape the way in which we experience our work.

Leadership exerts indirect effects

The most direct and immediate effects of leadership are not the outcomes that organizations covet, such as increased sales performance or service quality. Instead, studies consistently show that high- (and poor-) quality leadership changes how followers view themselves, their work, and their relationships with their leaders.[58] These same views shape follower behavior: followers with positive beliefs about themselves, their work, and their leaders usually want to do amazing work and help their organizations succeed.[***]

Karoline Strauss and colleagues highlighted the importance of the way in which employees view themselves in a study of 196 employees in an Australian public sector organization.[59] Supervisors' transformational leadership behaviors directly affected employees' self-efficacy beliefs. In turn, employees' self-efficacy beliefs affected individual and team proficiency and proactivity. This effect is not limited to transformational leadership. In other research, leader-member exchange,[60,†††] as well as empowering,[61] ethical,[62] and visionary leadership,[63] also positively affected organizational outcomes by raising employees' self-efficacy beliefs. It was employees' self-efficacy beliefs that positively affected customer satisfaction and employee sales performance.

High-quality leadership affects not only the way people feel about themselves but also how they view their work. One important goal for many managers is employee work engagement. In one study of seventeen nursing supervisors and 364 nurses in a large Portuguese hospital, nursing supervisors' transformational leadership resulted in nurses enjoying higher levels of self-efficacy, which eventually resulted in greater involvement in organizational citizenship behaviors.[64]

High-quality leadership also benefits the leader-follower relationship, for example, by encouraging greater trust in the leader. Trust in a leader should never be taken lightly; after all, trust requires that followers are willing to leave themselves vulnerable at the hands of their leaders, even though they cannot constantly monitor their leader's behavior.[65] One study focused on the indirect effects of leadership on the extent to which team members were willing to share task-appropriate information, knowledge, and ideas, all of which require trust.[66] After all, you cannot compel employees to share information; employees will do so if they trust their leaders and peers.[67] In a study of 102 hotels properties in the United States, Abhishek Srivastava et al. confirmed this, showing that higher levels of empowering leadership were associated with employees being more willing to share information, which in turn resulted in

[***] This is often referred to as a "mediation" effect, a term we use in other chapters. Simply stated, a hypothetical example of mediation would be that transformational leadership influences job performance through its effects on affective commitment; in this case, the effects of transformational leadership on job performance go through affective commitment. Affective commitment functions as the "mediator."

[†††] Leader-member exchange reflects the quality of the relationship between leaders and their employees.

improved financial performance (in this case, revenue based on room rentals relative to other local establishments).

Zhi-xia Chen and Hong-yan Wang's research on 630 employees in public and private organizations in South China shows that negative leadership works the same way.[68] Abusive supervision lowered employees' self-efficacy beliefs and trust in their supervisors, both of which hurt employees' job performance.

The indirect way in which leadership exerts its effects helps to explain why we almost never see leadership exerting immediate effects. Whether we are considering the best or the worst of leadership, it takes time for followers to see themselves, their work, and their relationship with their leaders differently. Only then will employees want to change their behaviors and perform at the highest levels that benefit their organizations.

Leadership shapes the way you experience your work

Consider what happened to a colleague of mine when thinking about how leadership "shapes" the way in which we experience our work. At the time, she was a faculty member at a university with policies that provided generous parental leave. When she learned she was pregnant, she arranged with her dean to take six months' leave. Soon thereafter, she learned she was having twins. She told her dean about the twins and asked if she could access the full year of parental leave that the policy permitted. Not only did her dean immediately say yes, he told her he would bring her sabbatical forward so that in effect she could take two years. At the same time, her husband taught in a different faculty at the same university governed by the same family-friendly policies. When he approached his dean and told him he wanted to access his parental benefits, the dean immediately explained that no one else in the faculty had ever taken any paternal leave. My colleague's husband knew exactly what he was being told—and chose not to take any parental leave.[‡‡‡] Yes, organizations may have policies in place, but leadership behaviors and decisions shape the way in which those policies are interpreted, implemented, and experienced.

Peng Wang and Fred Walumbwa's study on family-friendly workplace policies provides scientific support for this story. Their study took place in the banking sector in China, Kenya, and Thailand, with 186, 110, and 179 employees, respectively.[69] As expected, having access to a range of childcare benefits such as on-site childcare service, subsidies for childcare, flexible work schedules, and personal and family leave was associated with higher levels of employee commitment and retention. More importantly, the benefits of these childcare benefits were more pronounced in the presence

‡‡‡ Technically speaking, the dean's behavior functioned as a *moderator*, a term that is widely used in the literature and that appears in this book. Whether the policy would result in parental leave actually being taken was dependent on (or moderated by) the leadership behavior of the particular dean.

of transformational leadership. An important lesson from these findings is that even the most progressive workplace policies need support from leaders.

Transformational leadership also shapes the experiences of top management teams. Justin Jansen and colleagues investigated the effects of senior teams on organizational ambidexterity—the ability to run the organization in the present while preparing it for the future. Their study took place among 305 senior team members and eight-nine executive directors in Dutch branches of a Fortune 500 global banking company.[70] Social integration among senior team members only influenced organizational ambidexterity in branches where levels of CEO transformational leadership was high. As the authors conclude, it takes transformational leaders to create the conditions under which socially integrated teams will be willing to go against the tendency to limit divergent perspectives, and have open and conflictive debates that can lead to organizational ambidexterity.

TMGT: Can we have too much good leadership in organizations?

Despite the popular belief that leaders should be inspirational at all times with all people, this is neither possible nor necessary. It is not possible because most leaders are simply not physically close to their followers most of the time; in the globalized workplace, they may not even be in the same country or time zone. Never was this more evident than during the pandemic, with so many people—leaders included—working from home. But being inspirational all the time is also not necessary: faced with a leader who was inspirational all the time, employees would likely be totally overwhelmed. And as evidenced by Alyssa Parr and colleagues' research, not all employees respond positively to inspirational forms of leadership.[71] Thus, the leadership challenge concerns not whether you can sustain wonderful leadership all the time with all your employees. Instead, the best of leadership is about moments, about whether you can do the *right thing at the right time with the right person*. We see this clearly in stories about wonderful leaders and in the results of scientific research.

Jon Meachem, a US presidential historian, asks how it was that the seemingly non-charismatic George H.W. Bush Sr. became president in 1988.[72] His answer? Bush Sr. had already served as vice president for eight years, director of the CIA for a year, ambassador to the United Nations for two years, and ambassador to China for fourteen months. In all these roles, Bush made a habit of sending people thank-you cards when they did something out of the ordinary, leaving a trail of people very positively disposed toward him. When it came to the presidential election, Meachem maintains that "George Herbert Walker Bush became president one thank-you card at a time."

It is not just politicians who go to great lengths to do the smallest things to show their gratitude. Doug Conant, the former CEO of Campbell Soup, deliberately looked for success stories involving employees across his company's global workforce and would spend an hour a day personally writing them thank-you notes. Indra Nooyi even sent letters to the parents of executives: "It dawned on me that all of my executives who worked for me are also doing a damn good job, but I'd never told their parents what a great job [they] had done for them." As author and consultant Tom Peters reminds us so compellingly, it is not only lower-level employees who respond well to small acts of appreciation; rather, "we're all suckers for it."[73]

Anecdotal stories are always heartwarming, but does hard-nosed research back them up? The answer is yes! In one study, Adam Grant and Francesca Gino were interested in what motivates fundraisers given that their work is monotonous, and they face frequent rejection and occasional rudeness. All fundraisers in their study were effectively working in a call-center operation, and received performance feedback at the end of the workday.[74] As part of this study, the director of fundraising visited twenty of these employees. In addition to receiving their regular feedback, the director told them, "I am very grateful for your hard work. We sincerely appreciate your contribution to this organization." Sixteen words! Yet this small expression of gratitude was enough to double the number of calls made in the next week for those who had been thanked (with no meaningful change in performance for fundraisers who received performance feedback but no gratitude).

This effect was no flash in the pan. A separate study by Gino and Grant reinforces the benefits of the smallest expressions of gratitude. Seventy-nine student participants helped another student edit a letter he had written. Someone working with the researchers then arrived, introduced himself by name ("Eric"), and engaged in frivolous conversation. To the students assigned to receive gratitude, Eric simply added, "Thank you for your feedback," and left; the others received no gratitude after small talk. All students were then asked to edit a second letter, but they could leave whenever they wanted. Remarkably, those who had been thanked with a mere five words spent an average of 22.8 minutes editing the letter, compared with the 19.8 minutes spent by their counterparts—a difference of almost 14 percent in response to only five words of gratitude![§§§]

We learn from these studies that it is the little things that leaders do that affect their followers so deeply. Why then don't more leaders engage in these small behaviors more often? Amit Kumar and Nicholas Epley conducted four studies that provide intriguing answers to this question.[75] Participants in their studies wrote letters expressing gratitude to someone they knew. The researchers then contacted the recipients to get their reactions. It turns out that the writers significantly underestimated how positively recipients would feel about their expressions of gratitude and overestimated how uncomfortable recipients would be. What these findings suggest is that leaders do not shy away from these small acts because they do not know they an element of leadership; after all, most leaders know that listening, caring, developing,

[§§§] In one of the ten most watched TED talks of 2021, Niro Sivanathan explains why. He shows that the same message is more persuasive when written briefly instead of embedded in a longer statement. Essentially, irrelevant material dilutes the main message, because with longer messages, people tend to weigh all of the information they hear instead of prioritizing key information (https://www.ted.com/talks/niro_sivanathan_the_counterintuitive_way_to_be_more_persuasive) and so forth are an integral part of leadership. Instead, leaders chose not to engage in these behaviors because they did not appreciate just how powerfully they affect their followers. These implications are important because not only did the writer's gratitude positively influence the letter's recipient, but the writer experienced better mood simply by writing the letter. Separately, Erica Boothby and Vanessa Bohns' research confirmed that people underestimate how much small acts of gratitude and kindness on the part of leaders might mean to others, and as a result they express gratitude less frequently. In addition, their study also showed any apprehensive anxiety about complimenting others generally dissipates after giving a compliment.[76]

Changing direction, if it only takes small amounts of gratitude to exert meaningful outcomes, how bad does leadership have to be to exert its negative effects? In a series of cleverly designed experiments, Christine Porath and Amir Erez showed that a single expression of rudeness is enough to hurt performance and well-being.[****] As one example, eighty-two undergraduate students participated an experiment appropriately titled "Does rudeness really matter?"[77] Upon arriving at the scheduled room, students in the control group were simply told that the location of the study had changed and given directions to the actual location. Things were very different for those in the experimental group: those randomly "assigned" to rudeness. After knocking on the door and entering the initially scheduled room, the person inside told these students:

> "Can't you read? There is a sign on the door that tells you that the experiment will be in room YYY. But you didn't even bother to look at the door, did you? Instead, you preferred to disturb me and ask for directions when you can clearly see that I am busy. I am not a secretary here, I am a busy professor." (1188)

Once they made their way to the "correct" room, all students completed questionnaires, and the findings were clear-cut: students who experienced the relatively mild act of rudeness solved fewer anagrams correctly, were less creative, less helpful, and had worse mood than their counterparts who did not experience rudeness. They also showed a greater desire for revenge. And the effects of a little rudeness get worse. First, the anagram task required students to reassemble the letters "remdue." One appropriate response would be the word "demure." Yet those exposed to rudeness were nine times more likely to transpose this to "murder"![78] Second, a separate study showed that even *witnessing* rudeness was enough to hurt routine and creative performance, expanding the negative effects of rudeness beyond the targets of the rudeness themselves.[79] Porath and Erez are correct: We don't need massive amounts of rudeness to hurt people—even a little rudeness goes a long way!

[****] In this respect, rudeness differs from abusive supervision, which is defined as the sustained use of abusive behaviors over time (Tepper, 2000).

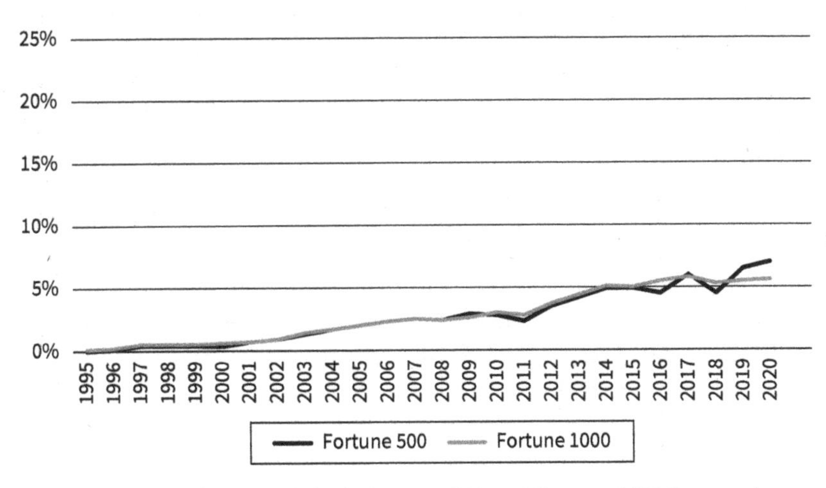

Fig. 2.1 Percentage of women CEOs in Fortune 500 and Fortune 1000 Companies, 1995–2020.

Gender and leadership

Gender looms large in all aspects of leadership, such as who becomes a leader in the first place, "leadership styles" (or behaviors) exhibited by men and women once they attain leadership positions, and leadership effectiveness. Indeed, the intersection of leadership and gender is a fascinating and important issue for employees and leaders, organizations, and society.

When Canadian Prime Minister Justin Trudeau assumed office, he famously explained why 50 percent of his cabinet members were female with a simple "Because it's 2015."[80] Yet it is now 2021, and women are still substantially less likely to be in leadership positions than men, with this discrepancy worsening the higher up you go in organizations. Remarkably, in the United States, only 7.4 percent of the top Fortune 500 companies had a female CEO in 2020—and that was only because of an unusual (but uneven) increase in the past four years! Put another way, the percentage of women CEOs of Fortune 500 companies has more than doubled over the past decade, but that is because only 2.4 percent of Fortune 500 companies had female CEOs in 2010 (see Figure 2.1). The sheer lack of diversity at the top of organizations is more apparent when we realize that only three CEOs of Fortune 500 companies in 2020 were women of color, and there was not one African American woman CEO.[††††]

[††††] And these gender differences go well beyond CEOs. Former Australian Prime Minister Julie Gillard and former Nigerian Finance and Foreign Minister Ngozi Okono-Iweala devote an entire chapter of their remarkable book, *Women and Leadership: Real lives, real lessons*, to a discussion of the way in which gender-based bias pervades our private and public sector organizations as well as the global institutions that influence all our financial systems.

The question as to what this all means remains. While some articles lead with optimistic headlines (e.g., "The number of female CEOs in the Fortune 500 hits an all-time record"[81]), a more sober and realistic interpretation is called for. A series of studies conducted by Oriane Georgeac and Aneeta Rattan shows that when people overestimate the degree to which women enjoy equal access to opportunities, such as top-level leadership positions, they tend to be more accepting of other forms of gender discrimination such as pay inequity.[82] Indeed, a study of the largest 1,500 companies in the United States showed that in companies with a female CEO, women in top management teams earned less than they would have had they worked for a male CEO. The authors of this study suggest this occurs because having a female CEO signals an organization's commitment to diversity, the result of which is that the organization can afford to pay other women less.[83]

The situation is more mixed when it comes to gender composition of boards of governance (addressed more fully in Chapter 9). The percentage of Fortune 500 board seats occupied by women went from 9.6 percent in 1995 to 16.9 percent in 2013.[‡‡‡‡] But at the same time, only 4 percent of all board chairs were women, and women of color held only 3 percent of all board positions. All this is important because board gender composition affects organizational functioning. As one example of this influence, National Football League teams in the United States with boards that had a critical mass of women (defined as two or more women at the VP level or above) suffered fewer player arrests for crimes that were more serious than traffic violations.[84]

Even when women do make it to the top of organizations, the barriers do not disappear. Quite the contrary. Karen Lyness and Donna Thompson compared the experiences of 51 female and 56 male executives in the financial-services sector who were similar in terms of age, pay level, ratings of performance, and potential.[85] Female executives enjoyed less satisfaction with future career opportunities and had less authority, as well as fewer stock options and international travel opportunities. Yes, this study was reported in 1977, but the phenomenon persists. After holding factors such as firm size, profitability, leverage, and dividend yield constant, one recent study by Vishal Gupta and colleagues showed that women CEOs were more likely to be the target of threats from activist investors than their male counterparts.[86] Based on a very large US sample of 2,390 different organizations between 2000 and 2014, a subsequent study by Gupta et al. showed that female CEOs were about 45 percent more likely to be fired than male CEOs.[87] More troublingly, while male and female CEOs were equally likely to be dismissed when firm performance was poor, female CEOs were much more likely to be dismissed than their male counterparts when organizations are doing well. These findings suggest that CEO dismissal is invariably a function of poor firm performance for male CEOs. However, female CEOs' tenure seems to be governed by a different set of rules.

‡‡‡‡ For those of you doing the math in your heads—that's an increase of 7.3 percent over an eighteen year period, or again, 0.4 percent per year, enough to get us to gender parity just before the turn of the next century.

The long-term implications of these findings should give us cause for concern. What do young females learn when they look up and dream about their future, as all children do? A fascinating study from the University of Waterloo in Ontario shows that when young female undergraduates are subtly reminded of gender stereotypes, they are less motivated to seek and assume leadership roles. But when these female undergraduates were explicitly told that there are no gender differences in leadership effectiveness, they were as interested in assuming leadership roles as their male counterparts.

The value of being exposed to positive female role models is evident in an unusually large-scale and innovative study of some five hundred villages in India, involving fifteen households in each village and all members of the household.[88] As part of a national-policy initiative, some villages only had women run in local elections once or twice, and in the remaining villages men or women could stand for election. Young girls who had been exposed to a female head of the village council across two election cycles were more motivated to stay in school longer and more interested in pursuing a career. In addition, both mothers and fathers showed higher aspirations for their daughters, and fathers were now far more interested in their daughters assuming leadership positions. However, these effects only emerged in villages where women held the leadership role for two consecutive terms, an important lesson for organizations designing mentorship programs. Evidently, the mere presence of female role models is insufficient. Instead, long-term exposure to female role models is critical if role-modeling is to have an effect.

Given the substantial gender differences in terms of who has access to leadership positions, you might think that there must surely be a sizable body of data showing that men engage in more effective leadership behaviors and outperform women in terms of leadership competence and effectiveness. To the contrary! Where gender differences do exist in leadership behaviors, women tend to have an advantage, for example, in terms of transformational leadership.[89,§§§§] In a more recent analysis, Jack Zenger and Joseph Folkman compared the ratings from 360-degree feedback of thousands of male and female leaders across nineteen different leadership behaviors (see Table 2.1).[90] Contrary to what many might believe given the preponderance of male leaders in top positions, females scored significantly higher in no fewer than seventeen of the nineteen positive behaviors!

Last, discrimination against females holding senior leadership positions become even more perplexing when evaluating the effects of leaders' gender during the COVID-19 pandemic. Supriya Garikipati and Uma Kambhampati compared the caseload and COVID-19 death rate of all 194 countries for which data were available until May 19, 2020. To increase the validity of their findings, they carefully matched countries of

§§§§ Caution must be exercised in interpreting these findings. In no way do they suggest that all women, for example, exhibit more transformational leadership than all men. What these findings do suggest, however, is that on average women tend to have an advantage with respect to transformational leadership.

Table 2.1 Women are rated better than men on key leadership capabilities

Leadership capability	Percentile score	
	Women	Men
Bold leadership	53.2	49.8
Builds relationships	53.2	49.9
Champions change	53.1	49.8
Collaboration and teamwork	52.6	50.2
Communicates powerfully & prolifically	51.8	50.7
Connects to the outside world	51.6	50.3
Develops others	54.1	49.8
Develops strategic perspective	51.1	51.4
Displays high integrity, honesty	54.0	49.1
Drives for results	53.9	48.8
Establishes stretch goals	52.6	49.7
Innovates	51.4	51.0
Inspires and motivates others	53.9	49.7
Leadership speed	51.5	50.5
Practices self-improvement	54.8	49.6
Resilience	54.7	49.3
Solves problems and analyzes issues	51.5	50.4
Takes initiative	55.6	48.2
Technical or professional expertise	50.1	51.1

Data taken from Zenger, J., & Folkman, J. (2019).

similar size and socio-demographic indicators.[91] The results were startling: the number of cases was substantially higher, and deaths twice as high, in male-led countries.[*****] Remarkably, Kayla Sergent and Alexander Stajkovic replicated these findings in the fifty states of the United States, the District of Columbia, and the four US territories using data until May 5, 2020.[92] They accounted for factors that might explain any gender differences in leader effectiveness such as governors' age, tenure, and political affiliation, and whether there was a mask mandate, stay-at-home order, or statewide curfew. Still, states with female governors suffered far fewer COVID-19 related deaths, and this difference was even more pronounced in states that imposed early stay-at-home orders.

The authors of both these studies conducted further analyses that help explain why these differences emerge, and they teach us a lot about female leadership. Contrary to

***** The gender differences are probably even greater than those reported. At the time of the study Taiwan had a female prime minister and very few COVID-19 fatalities, but Taiwan could not be included in the analyses as the World Bank includes Taiwan in Chinese data.

stereotypes that males are more likely to "take charge," Garikipati and Kambhampati showed that countries with female leaders acted more quickly, and more decisively, by imposing lockdowns sooner, and used coronavirus tests more frequently. In addition, qualitative analyses on all governmental briefings from thirty-eight governors in the United States showed that female governors were more willing to share their feelings, and were more empathic about their citizens' job and financial concerns. Again, defying gender stereotypes, female leaders expressed greater confidence than their male counterparts throughout the pandemic, as evidenced by Rhode Island Governor Gina Raimondo telling her residents, "I am confident that by working together and sharing our best ideas, we will be much, much more likely to get it right for the citizens of our state" (776).

While there will be a lot more to learn about leadership during the pandemic in the years to come, there is an urgency about the lessons from these two studies. We need to revisit our ideas about what leadership behaviors are most effective in general, and especially during turbulent times. More practically, we need to remember that the leadership behaviors that differentiated male and female governors, namely confidence, decisiveness, and empathy, are well within the reach of standard leadership-development interventions.

Cross-national influences on leadership

Perhaps one of the most influential events of the 20th century was globalization. This global shift is relevant when discussing organizational leadership, because different social, economic, and political conditions may facilitate and favor different forms of leadership. As one example, people in countries facing economic uncertainty are more likely to prefer dominant rather than prestigious leaders.[93,†††††] The possible effects of globalization on leadership is also of some theoretical interest. Bernie Bass argued that with very few exceptions, the ideas underlying transformational leadership are universally applicable across national contexts—was he correct?[94]

Differences in the level of leadership

There would appear to be no research investigating whether the levels of transformational leadership differ across different countries. However, Carmen Lai Yin Leong and Ronald Fischer shed some light on cultural influences on transformational leadership based on their meta-analysis of fifty-four independent samples from eighteen countries.[95] They showed that transformational leadership scores were higher in

††††† Dominance and prestige are different approaches that leaders use to gain status and influence. Dominant leaders tend to use power and intimidation, while prestigious leaders gain influence by demonstrating their knowledge and treating others with respect.

societies which valued individual mastery and egalitarian values. Given the role of cultural values in shaping leadership, the authors recommend that expatriate leaders need to understand that local cultural values can shape followers' expectations about what leadership behaviors are appropriate. Thus, leaders from North America working in countries such as India, Taiwan, or China need to appreciate that employees may be somewhat less responsive to transformational leadership.

Turning our attention to negative forms of leadership, Mackay et al.'s extensive meta-analysis of 112 research studies involving 38,527 participants in thirteen countries showed clear cross-national differences on abusive supervision.[96] The lowest levels of abusive supervision occurred in Belgium (average = 1.47), Canada (average = 1.53), and the United States (average = 1.68). In contrast, the highest scores emerged in China (2.06), Taiwan (2.13), and the Philippines (2.17). While precise explanations must await further analyses, one observation is that levels of abusive supervision are highest in countries where there are fewer external restraints (e.g., legislation or unionization), and in culturally "tight" societies in which autocratic rules suppress dissent and transparency, with citizens enjoying fewer rights.[97] This may have important implications for organizations everywhere: abusive supervision may be less likely to occur in situations typified by procedural fairness (see Chapter 5).

Differences in the function of leadership

A somewhat separate question is whether leadership exerts different effects in different countries or cultures. Earlier, we saw how leadership affects work attitudes, work performance, and employee well-being. Intriguingly, the magnitude of these effects is shaped to some extent by cultural and national characteristics.

Mert Aktas and his colleagues were curious as to whether cultural tightness—exemplified by survey questions such as "In this country, if someone acts in an inappropriate way, others will strongly disapprove," and "People in this country almost always comply with social norms"—would influence beliefs about effective leadership behaviors.[98] Data collected from 6,823 participants from twenty-nine countries showed that autonomous leadership, which emphasizes self-reliance by the leader, was likely to be viewed as more effective in culturally tight countries. In contrast, charismatic leadership and team leadership, which rely on collaboration and the challenging of assumptions, were viewed as less effective in culturally tight societies.

While interesting, these findings only speak to which leadership styles are *perceived* to be effective. Marcus Crede and colleagues conducted the largest study to date of the actual effects of transformational leadership on diverse aspects of work performance across different cultures. The findings from their analyses of 57,000 people from thirty-four countries are intriguing yet somewhat counterintuitive. Transformational leadership exerted weaker effects on employee performance in North America and Western European countries, the very countries in which this particular leadership theory was developed and much of the earlier research conducted.[99]

Crede et al. provide an intriguing explanation for this finding. They suggest that employees in these countries have become skeptical about leadership in general, and transformational leadership in particular, because of prior negative experiences with leadership. In contrast, Crede et al. suggest that because employees in African, Middle Eastern, South American, and some southeast Asian countries were less likely to expect transformational leadership, its effects were more pronounced. As they state in their article, "Leaders with a compelling vision, who live their values, who challenge assumptions, and who take an active interest in the lives of their subordinates may be so unexpected in some countries as to create a sense of delight and wonder when it does occur" (151).

Thus, while we should be tentative in concluding that any leadership theory is "universal," the evidence to date has not uncovered countries or cultures in which transformational leadership is ineffective or counterproductive.

Interventions to enhance high-quality leadership

One of the most common questions management practitioners ask is whether leaders are "born or made," and this is a fascinating question. As the famous behavioral psychologist B.F. Skinner noted, we tend to stand in awe of the inexplicable.[100] And what could be more inexplicable than why some leaders are so elevating and encouraging but others so bad and belittling. This is not simply a question of idle curiosity; the answer has personal and practical consequences. After all, believing that wonderful leadership is something that some lucky people are born with would be a good reason not to put effort to improve leadership behaviors or attempt to become a leader in the first place. Moreover, if management decision-makers believe that leaders are born that way, they would likely rely on selecting the right person—a notoriously difficult endeavor[101]—and be less inclined to invest the time and money necessary to develop leadership. Fortunately, developing leadership behaviors is a lot less complicated than many might believe.

Skeptics may be surprised to learn just how many successful leadership interventions exist. Christina Lacerenza and her colleagues located no fewer than 335 examples of some form of leadership training, and the conclusion from their meta-analysis is worth reiterating: "leadership training is substantially more effective than previously thought" (1686).[102] Add to this the fact that, as evident in Chapter 6, leadership-development initiatives are cost-effective as well.[103] As one telling example, let's consider a question about which many people are skeptical—is it possible to develop charismatic leadership behaviors?

According to John Antonakis and his colleagues, leaders are viewed as charismatic when they engage in specific verbal and nonverbal "tactics" (or behaviors). Verbal tactics include the use of metaphors, stories, and anecdotes, sharing the sentiments of the collective, setting high expectations, and communicating confidence. Verbal tactics also include the use of contrasts, lists, and rhetorical questions. The nonverbal tactics convey passion through gestures, facial expressions, and tone of voice.[104]

Antonakis et al. report on two different interventions in which they successfully taught charismatic leadership behaviors.[105] In the first, thirty-four middle managers from a relatively large Swiss company participated in the intervention as they were interested in their own leader development, and were then either randomly assigned to a group that would receive the intervention or one that would serve as the control group. Training took place at a company facility, an important feature as on-site leadership training maximizes training effectiveness.[106] Managers in both groups completed 360-degree assessments before the training, which lasted five hours. The effectiveness of charismatic leadership was emphasized first, with the twelve charismatic-leadership tactics introduced and reinforced through video clips from movies such as *Dead Poets Society* and *True Blue*. Participants then worked in dyads to create a short charismatic speech, and one person from each dyad delivered the speech to all participants. Thus, all participants either received or gave feedback based on the 12 CLTs. After the training, all participants received feedback based on their initial 360-degree assessment, and one week later, met with a coach to discuss their feedback, set leadership goals, and develop and discuss a leadership plan. Participants also received the audio and transcripts of Martin Luther King's "I Have a Dream" speech and Jesse Jackson's speech to the 1988 Democratic National Convention, both widely viewed as exemplars of charismatic leadership.

The intervention worked! Individuals who received the charismatic leadership intervention were rated by their followers as significantly more charismatic than those who did not, even after accounting for participants' age, gender, and pre-training charisma scores. Moreover, leaders who had received the charismatic leadership training were rated as more trustworthy, competent, influential, and likable by their followers.

The researchers conducted a second, somewhat different study to confirm these findings. The forty-one participants in this second intervention were (mostly part-time) MBA students at a Swiss public university. One week before the training, the researchers asked participants to prepare and deliver a four-minute speech to their staff aimed at resolving a major organizational issue. The content of the training was very similar to their first study, but lasted for a total of twenty hours and took place over seven weeks. Six weeks after the training, participants were asked to deliver the same speech again. The content had to remain the same, but they could shape the speech differently based on what they had learned. Participants were even asked to wear the same clothes as they had during the first delivery to ensure that the ratings were focused on the delivery and not extraneous factors. Again, the training worked. Participants used significantly more CLTs after the training, 2.1suggesting that charismatic leadership behaviors can be learned. Just as importantly, changes in charismatic behaviors (an indication of how much they had learned) again predicted follower ratings of leaders' trustworthiness, competence, influence, and likability. Taken together with a recent study replicating the effectiveness of this same intervention in a face-to-face setting in the United States,[107] we can conclude that charismatic leadership behaviors can indeed be learned.

One issue regarding leadership-development initiatives is that timing matters. Most leaders are promoted to ever-higher positions in the organization before they are offered significant leadership-development opportunities.[108] This practice is always perilous, and the pandemic has exposed just how perilous. Offering leadership training is unlikely during crises when organizations can ill afford to have their leaders absent, but it is also not advisable. Leaders and their organizations will benefit most from providing these developmental initiatives before crises hit, and during downtimes when leaders' absence would be felt less keenly.[109]

A special case: Leadership during (and after) the pandemic

Whether it was politicians hosting near-daily press conferences, news media updating the numbers of infections or deaths, or incessant debates in social media about PPE and vaccinations, people everywhere have been reminded on an almost daily basis of the threat to their health and lives since the start of the COVID-19 pandemic. This is especially relevant to leadership. One way in which people cope with the worst physical and existential threats is to coalesce around charismatic leaders. This effect is magnified when an existential threat is perceived as externally generated, as feelings of in-group identity and solidarity would be heightened and attributed to the actions of the charismatic leader.[‡‡‡‡‡]

Researchers have investigated the effects of what psychologists call "mortality salience," that is, awareness of the inevitability of one's mortality, and its relevance to leadership.[110] In one study appropriately titled "Fatal attraction,"[111] the researchers used an experimental technique in which one group of participants were reminded of their inevitable mortality, while the second group were not exposed to mortality salience at all. The effects of being reminded of one's potential mortality were then assessed on how participants evaluated three different leadership styles: charismatic, relationship-oriented, and task-oriented leadership. Enthusiasm for and evaluation of the charismatic leaders were significantly higher when participants were reminded of their mortality. However, this was not the case for either of the other two leadership styles. In fact, there was lower enthusiasm for the relationship-oriented leader who emphasized the importance of personal responsibility. The researchers also asked participants which of the three leaders they would vote for if an election took place. Once mortality salience had been induced, there was a massive increase (almost 800 percent) in votes for the charismatic leader. In contrast, being reminded of

‡‡‡‡‡ If this is indeed the case, Rudy Giuliani's leadership following the attacks of 9/11 must be attributed, at least partially, not only to his actions but also to the overriding needs of people everywhere.

one's mortality produced no change in votes for the task-oriented leader, and an unexpected decline in votes for the relationship-oriented leader.

Intriguingly, the media play a role in the attraction to charismatic leadership during such crises. Faced with mortality salience themselves, journalists coalesce around charismatic leaders. As Steve Rendell noted following the attack on 9/11, "On September 11, 2001, with George W. Bush in hiding for much of the day, mainstream journalists were desperately looking for a man on horseback. For many, that man would be New York City Mayor Rudolph Giuliani."[112]

Other research has asked how uncertainty and ambiguity shape the effects of leadership during crises. David Waldman and colleagues' research highlighted how environmental uncertainty influences the effectiveness of the charismatic leadership behavior of 131 CEOs of Fortune 500 companies.[113] As expected, the effects of CEO charismatic leadership behaviors on net-profit margins was greatest when environmental uncertainty was high (i.e., environmental changes were perceived as dynamic, risky, rapid, and stressful). Studies on charisma among fifty-four CEOs in the Netherlands,[114] and the intellectual-stimulation dimension of transformational leadership in forty-two US and twenty-nine Canadian CEOs,[115] also showed that uncertainty and ambiguity heightened the effectiveness of leadership. Importantly, the effects of CEO charisma on company performance emerged for the next four years, suggesting that high-quality leadership during the pandemic may be critical to how well companies do *after* the pandemic. Across all these studies, leadership exerted its strongest effects when it mattered most.

When trying to understand why this might be the case, Bernie Bass, who has arguably had more of an influence on how we understand leadership than anyone else since the 1950s,[116] speculated that during times of crisis, employees became "charisma hungry."[117] Based on observations of and experience with leaders since the onset of the COVID-19 pandemic, I believe we can now extend this. I suggest that during their worst moments, employees look to their leaders for consistency, calm, clarity, and compassion, which as we see reflects the idealized influence, inspirational motivation, intellectual stimulation, and individualized-consideration dimensions of transformational leadership.

When ambiguity and uncertainty are rampant, as they were during the pandemic, people see events in their environment as less predictable and less controllable. In times like these, employees prize leaders who consistently choose to do what is right. These leaders behave with the honesty, integrity, and humility that confirms that they value others, all of which reflect idealized influence. Leaders build trust and respect when they tell the truth no matter how bad the situation,[118] as former US President Franklin Delano Roosevelt (FDR) did in his first inaugural speech during the Great Depression, and Churchill did in especially perilous days in 1940 and 1941. Learning from Winston Churchill and George Orwell during the 1940s, Thomas Ricks suggests that what enabled Churchill to be victorious over tyranny and Orwell to write *1984*, one of the 20th century's great works of literature, was that they both worked "diligently to discern the facts of the matter, and then use[d] ... principles [such as the truth] to respond" (265).[119] Leaders build trust when they act with integrity, as Don Carty, CEO of American Airlines, did soon after 9/11, when he announced twenty thousand layoffs and said he would forgo *all* compensation for the rest of 2001. Contrast that with the Pfizer CEO, who sold $5.6 million of his stock on the same day in 2021 the company announced favorable news about the vaccine.[120]

How important is consistency? At the start of the pandemic, many national and state-level leaders publicly promised that their actions and decisions would be guided only by the health of their citizens. As the pandemic persisted, many of these same leaders gave increasing and even greater weight to economic factors in their decisions, only to find people turning against them as they seemed to abandon their principles. Extensive research by Tamar Kreps and her colleagues might explain why this would happen[121]: people respond negatively when leaders move away from a moral position, even if they agree with the change. Moreover, even though leaders who can justifiably point to external factors that required their leadership change are regarded as courageous, they are still viewed as hypocrites, a damning evaluation for any leader. Clearly, people expect that the moral positions taken by their leaders will be stable across time; anything less, according to Kreps et al., is viewed as hypocritical flip-flopping. This again helps to explain the outrage toward CEOs who announced pay cuts at the start of the pandemic,[122] only to receive hefty bonuses and stock awards a year later.[123]

Transparency is also critical. After all, the consistency that derives from integrity and humility would matter little if all remains hidden from others. Thus, the best leaders are transparent. In practical terms, they "show up." New Zealand Premier Jacinda Ardern was widely praised for the way in which she "showed up" during crises, whether during the pandemic or the terrorist attack in 2019 on the mosque in Christchurch. Showing up also demonstrates a leader's concern for others,[124] and gives leaders the opportunity to establish for themselves how their employees are doing and what they need.[§§§§§]

In the best of times, inspirational motivation is all about "firing people up." In contrast, history tells us that during turbulent times inspirational motivation is often about calming people down.[125] During the turmoil of the 1930s, FDR reached out to the nation during his famous fireside chats and conveyed calm and reassurance during dreadful circumstances. As one American remarked, "I never saw him—but I knew him. Can you have forgotten how, with his voice, he came into our house, the President of the United States, calling us friends?" (90).[126] Starting in 1935, Eleanor Roosevelt did this when she reached out to millions of Americans through her nationally syndicated column, "My day."[127] Calming people down was just as true for employees during the pandemic, given elevated levels of anxiety and depression.

§§§§§ Showing up is a necessary but insufficient condition for effective leadership. A leader can show up and still mess up; but it is unlikely that a leader could excel during a crisis without showing up in the first instance.

Leaders themselves also need to remain calm. This is no easy feat, given that they too can become agitated, short-tempered, and overcontrolling of others when they experience mortality salience or face ambiguity and uncertainty. Clementine Churchill provided a vivid lesson of how leaders need to rise above the turmoil in a letter to husband Winston on June 27, 1940.[128]

> "One of the men in your entourage (a devoted friend) has been to me and told me that there is a danger of your being generally disliked by your colleagues and subordinates because of your rough sarcastic and overbearing manner... Higher up, if an idea is suggested... you are supposed to be so contemptuous that presently no ideas, good or bad, will be forthcoming.... My Darling Winston—I must confess that I have noticed a deterioration in your manner; and you are not so kind as you used to be... It is for you to give the orders... Therefore with this terrific power you must combine urbanity, kindness, and if possible Olympic calm."

And then she reminded him, "Besides you won't get the best results by irascibility and rudeness."

Faced with the confusion and chaos of the early days of the pandemic, people sought clarity from their leaders. Leaders exemplify intellectual stimulation when they help employees regain clarity by challenging their own assumptions and anxieties, separating facts from fear, and envisioning an optimistic and realistic future. History again provides compelling examples of leaders who did this. Returning to FDR, one goal of his many fireside chats was to explain complicated issues such as the banking crisis that threatened the nation during the Great Depression, in ways that people could readily understand. "He did not want Americans to be confused at such as critical time" (91).[129] A story about Barack Obama reinforces the importance of leaders bringing clarity to people. While at Harvard Law School, one of Obama's fellow students predicted that he would be president of the United States one day. When challenged on why she might say that, she responded that she had never met anybody who could take such complicated material and explain it to others with such clarity.

Compassion, concern, and listening are at the heart of individualized consideration. As difficult as this is for might be for leaders during "normal" times, these behaviors became even more important during pandemics, especially when opportunities for interpersonal interactions are limited because of physical distancing. Yet another leadership lesson for the pandemic can be gleaned from FDR's fireside chats. Historian Arthur Schlesinger Jr. tells us that FDR would write his speeches gazing "at a blank wall, trying to visualize the individuals he was seeking to help: a mason at work on a new building, a girl behind a counter, a man repairing an automobile, a farmer in his field."[130] Perhaps leaders could benefit by putting themselves in their followers' shoes while gazing at them during yet another Zoom meeting? British Columbia's Chief Medical Officer Bonnie Henry had unique qualifications to head up the COVID-19 response, having led Toronto's response to the SARS outbreak in

2003. She noted that one of the major lessons she had learned was empathy, tearing up during one press conference when announcing the initial COVID-19 outbreak in long-term care homes in her province. She later became synonymous with empathy and kindness, ending her press conferences, "This is our time to be kind, to be calm and to be safe." This statement brought such comfort to so many that it was eventually "hung in windows, painted on streets, printed on T-shirts, stitched on shoes, folded into songs and stamped on bracelets."[131]

A special case: Leader personality

At this stage you might well be asking yourself, we have reached the end of the chapter on leadership, and still not a word about the role of personality? Let me explain why.

Regarding the question of who becomes a leader and why, decades of research confirm that some personality characteristics, most notably extraversion, conscientiousness, and being open to new experiences, are consistently associated with leader emergence.[132] However, there are several important nuances regarding these findings. First, we should not confuse consistency with strength of these associations. Yes, there is tendency for people who score higher on extraversion, conscientiousness, and openness to new experiences to become leaders, but there are many exceptions to the rule. Second, personality is not the only game in town with respect to who attains a leadership position. Instead, it is only one of numerous factors that are at least equally implicated in leader emergence, such as gender, race, current and prior socioeconomic status, intelligence, leadership experience, motivation to lead, and even just the sheer quantity of time applicants for leadership positions spend talking.[133] Thus, hanging your hat solely on personality in leadership-selection competitions could result in poor decisions. Third, leadership selection is notoriously difficult anyway,[134] especially as we go higher up in the organizational hierarchy.

A separate issue is predicting why some leaders are successful, and others not. Susan Cain, author of the wonderful book *Quiet*, notes how most people believe that extraversion is a precondition for successful leadership. But is it that simple? After all, the notion that any personality trait by itself accounts for leader effectiveness ignores the multitude and complexity of factors, such as the external regulatory environment, macroeconomic factors, organizational constraints, and even followers' psychology, that are at play.[135] In what might be the most important study on the topic, Adam Grant and colleagues questioned the "extraverted leadership advantage"—the notion that extraverted leaders hold a clear advantage across leadership situations.[136] They note that employee proactivity is important for organizational success, but that not all leaders will be receptive to proactive behaviors by their employees. Based on research showing that higher-quality interpersonal interactions require a balance (rather than a similarity) between characteristics such as dominance and assertiveness, or obedience and compliance, they asked whether the dominance and assertion involved in both extraversion and proactivity might create conflict.

Going against widely held beliefs about the importance of leader extraversion, Grant et al. predicted that group performance would be highest when extraverted leaders were paired with less proactive employees and proactive employees were paired with less extraverted leaders. They tested this notion among fifty-seven store leaders and 374 employees of a nationwide US pizza delivery company. After controlling for factors which usually influence profitability (e.g., proximity to a university campus), stores were most profitable when low extraverted leaders were paired with proactive followers, or extraverted leaders were paired with less proactive followers. They also replicated these findings in a laboratory study, reinforcing the possibility that leaders' extraversion might even detract from their effectiveness under some conditions.

We should also be concerned with the misuse of personality in organizations, which is most glaring when it comes to popular but wholly unscientific questionnaires such as the Myers-Briggs Personality Inventory[137] (the MBTI) or the Hermann Brain Dominance Inventory (the HBDI).[138] Given that personality is relatively stable, to pass the most basic tenets of scientific credibility, tests such as these should provide the same results when testing the same person over different time periods. Yet they fail to do so. As Adam Grant points out, up to 75 percent of people who retake the MBTI are given a different personality type, with about 50 percent of people who retake the test receiving a different personality type *within five weeks*. Even more troubling, there would appear to be no meaningful link between the MBTI types and transformational leadership.[139]

The organizational implications of these findings are far-reaching. Personality has its role, but it is not as dominant an issue in leadership as is widely believed. Arguably, in their efforts to ensure high-quality leadership, organizations would do a lot better by devoting more attention and resources to leadership development than relying on personality-based leadership selection.

Conclusion

In case you are still not convinced

The overwhelming majority of organizations already take leadership seriously. Nonetheless, critically re-evaluating longstanding practices may help to ensure that organizations are populated with the very best leaders.

First, some organizations prioritize external applicants for leadership positions to introduce fresh perspectives. However, doing so may be a mistake. A study by Saul Fine and his colleagues of 568 officer trainees in the Israeli Defense Forces showed that unsuccessful applicants in leadership-selection competitions subsequently engaged in more misconduct, including verbal and physical aggression, theft of equipment or supplies, neglect of work activities, and insubordination.[140] Moreover, these negative effects endured for six months! Clearly, if employees were good enough to make it to the final rounds of these competitions, organizations need do what they can to help them remain valuable employees.

Second, we now know that leadership-development initiatives work and that the ingredients are for effective interventions. They should include feedback, multiple delivery methods and opportunities for practice, and training that is spaced over different days. Moreover, training should take place on-site and in-person (rather than via the internet). When these conditions are met, the initiatives are effective—participants learn more, transfer what was learned in the program to their work, and achieve better results.[141] Thus, the best organizations will ensure that they wisely use evidence-based data in guiding the development of the current and future generations of leadership.

Third, organizations can no longer afford to exclude women from the pool for the next generation of organizational leaders, nor be biased against them when they do become leaders. Successful organizations of the future will be those that voluntarily choose to create environments that respect, reward, develop, and promote male *and* female leaders. Doing so will create a larger and richer pool of talent from which to draw their future leadership, and these are the organizations that will attract and retain high-quality women leaders. Both social justice and optimal organizational functioning demand that the time for debate about gender and leadership is over. Still, this awareness remains the tip of a very precarious iceberg. Questions about leadership opportunities for people in the LGBTQ community, people of color, and religious minorities have yet to be confronted by organizations in any meaningful way—after all, only three of the Fortune 500 CEOs in 2020 were people of color, and there were no Latino or Black CEOs in this auspicious group. These are the issues that successful organizations must confront and conquer in the future.

To conclude, the overwhelming majority of organizations take leadership seriously, but some might say too seriously. We need to avoid what James Meindl and colleagues termed "the romance of leadership"[142]: the overwhelming tendency to ascribe all organizational success (and failures) to extraordinarily good (or bad) leadership. Yes, leadership is important, but organizational success is equally reliant on motivated and healthy employees. In the ensuing chapters, we see how employees' needs for autonomy, belongingness, growth, fairness, meaningful work, and safety play equally critical roles in the pursuit of productive, healthy, and safe workplaces.

3
Autonomy

Steve Kerr coached the Golden State Warriors to five consecutive NBA championships between 2014 and 2019. Yet in February 2018, he was struggling to influence his players when the Warriors recorded only three wins in six games. His players were tired of hearing from him, and he was tired of hearing himself as well. On the morning of the game against the Phoenix Suns, Kerr decided that he would allow his players to take full responsibility for coaching that day and during the game that evening. The result? A convincing 40-point victory by the Golden State Warriors, 123-89.[1]

Just how much do people want autonomy? We are often told that one of the most formidable human motives is the need for power. Yet, one study contrasted the need for power vs autonomy across nine different studies conducted in the United States, India, and Europe, confirming that gaining autonomy was more important to participants than gaining power.[2] Indeed, when people gained autonomy, their need for power subsided. Evidently, freedom from constraints imposed by others was more important than the ability to place constraints over others.

The nature of job autonomy

The idea that people might respond well to job autonomy is by no means new.[*] As we see in Chapter 1, Frederick Herzberg highlighted the importance of job control for job satisfaction, work motivation, and well-being in his famous study on two hundred accountants and engineers in Pittsburgh more than sixty years ago.[3] Ten year later, Herzberg popularized these ideas in his article "One more time: How do you motivate employees?"[4] In 1976, Richard Hackman and Greg Oldham extended these ideas in their model that suggested that together, job autonomy, task identity, task significance, skill variety, and job-related feedback all result in work motivation.[5] Over the next four decades, employees reported an increase in job autonomy, yet still experienced less job autonomy than the other four job characteristics over this same period.[6] Clearly, granting autonomy to employees at work does not necessarily come easily to many managers.

By the 1980s, questions about the benefits of control started to emerge, for example, in public debates over whether mothers of young children should be employed or homemakers. In one study based on her doctoral dissertation, Inge Stafford showed

[*] Throughout this literature, the terms *autonomy* and *control* are used synonymously, as are *job autonomy* and *work autonomy*.

Brave New Workplace. Julian Barling, Oxford University Press. © Oxford University Press 2023.
DOI: 10.1093/oso/9780190648107.003.0003

that the actual role someone held (whether as homemaker, job holder, or "careerist") was unimportant for self-esteem. What was important was being in the role that you wanted—whatever that role, and having that luxury was associated with higher self-esteem.[7] Separate research indicated that new mothers who preferred to be employed but were stuck in the homemaker role were mildly clinically depressed, but mothers who were employed or homemakers by choice were not.[8] At the same time, I conducted with a study with Clive Fullagar and Jenifer Marchl-Dingle in South Africa in which we examined the effects of an employment status–preference mismatch on elementary schoolchildren's behavior.[9] What we learned was that the children of mothers who were in a role they did not choose were more immature and less attentive than those whose mothers enjoyed an appropriate status-preference match. Across these three studies, therefore, what people did during the day and where they did it was less important than whether they had some control over what and where they did it. These early lessons have important insights for today's workplaces.

As the COVID-19 pandemic began in March 2020, major global organizations almost fell over each other in the rush to announce work-from-home (WFH) policies, with some even announcing that these policies would stay in place until at least the end of 2021.[10] Yet aspects of these policies limit autonomy for many. What we likely now[†] have is large numbers of people who work from home but who wish that they could be back in their regular workplaces, and many people stuck in their regular places of work who wish they could be working from home. Understanding the full effects of working from home during the pandemic will not be easy. We will need to weigh the benefits, which range from less time, stress, and pollution associated with commuting, against rising inequality for those who cannot work from home and must still work in retail stores, manufacturing, or distribution centers. Complicating this evaluation is the need to separate the effects of where people work (at home vs the traditional "office") from the extent to which they had any control over decisions about where they work. (We return to many of these issues throughout the book.)

What do we mean by job control or job autonomy? Perhaps the most important lesson for management and employees alike is that, as see throughout this chapter, job control is not an "all-or-none" issue. It is not about either granting employees total control or granting none at all. Instead, nuance is critical. As Herzberg suggested in this 1969 article, it was about "granting *additional* authority to an employee" (59, italics added). One personal experience shaped my appreciation for this. Toward the end of the 1980s, I served as the chair of Ontario's Advisory Committee on Occupational Health and Safety. At the time, the committee was considering legislation that would grant employees the right to stop work they deemed to be unsafe. Unsurprisingly, this controversial legislation left management and employees deeply divided, with management concerned that the legislation would open the door to widespread work stoppages. Eventually, the legislation passed, and no evidence emerged that employees

[†] Early February 2022.

abused the right to stop work. What was evident, however, was that just having the right to stop work resulted in significant increases in morale—even if that right was not exercised. Knowing that you could do so if needed was the critical factor. What I learned was that employees are not asking for total control over their workplaces; all they want is the right to exert appropriate control when necessary.

Nuance is again critical in understanding job control because employees distinguish between different aspects of the job over which they might want some control. Three categories of control include method control, scheduling control, and decision-making control.[11] Method control involves the extent to which employees have some choice over the procedures used in their job: literally over *how* they do their jobs. Scheduling control itself is nuanced, because it involves control over *when* people do their work, or even the sequence in which different tasks are undertaken. Last, decision-making control, sometimes referred to as criteria control, reflects the extent to which employees have *input* into the criteria used when evaluating their work.

Given the uptake of WFH policies at the start of the pandemic, I expect that one additional dimension of autonomy will become of great importance in a postpandemic environment: "locational autonomy." What we have seen already in this chapter is enough to predict that any benefit for productivity or well-being from working from home may not materialize unless employees have some input into decisions about working from home postpandemic, rather than feeling that they have been "sent home" or were "forced" to go to the office.

The benefits of workplace autonomy

Work attitudes

Publication of Hackman and Oldham's *Job Diagnostic Survey* in 1975 provided researchers with a questionnaire to investigate the many attitudinal outcomes of workplace autonomy, so much so that by 1988, Paul Spector was able to meta-analyze findings from eighty-eight studies.[12] Spector's research confirmed that the more workplace autonomy people experienced, the more satisfied they were with the work they did, as well as their supervision, opportunities for promotion, and growth at work. Workplace autonomy was also associated with greater motivation and attachment to the organization.

More recent research has addressed the effects of different aspects of job autonomy. Telecommuting is relevant right now as it speaks to the issue of locational autonomy. In one meta-analysis of forty-six studies that involved 12,883 employees,[13] having the opportunity to telecommute resulted in higher levels of job satisfaction, less workplace stress, higher intentions to remain with the organization, and higher job performance. What is especially important in a postpandemic environment is the positive effects of telecommuting were primarily a function of increased employee control.

Flexible work schedules provide an opportunity to understand the effects of scheduling control. Research on flexible work schedules dates back to at least 1973 when the US government introduced flexible work schedules in an attempt to deal with the oil boycott following the Yom Kippur War, which had created huge commuting problems. Fortunately for researchers, the US government mandated that the effects of any flexible schedules introduced be rigorously evaluated.[14] As a result, Boris Baltes and his coresearchers meta-analyzed results from twenty-nine studies on this topic in 1999.[15] What they found was that being involved in some form of a flexible work arrangement was associated with higher levels of job satisfaction and satisfaction with the schedule more specifically. What was unexpected, however, was that the greatest benefits (e.g., for satisfaction) emerged from less (rather than more) flexible programs. In considering why this would be the case, Baltes et al. offered two explanations. First, greater flexibility might be offset by management trying to impose other controls, nullifying any benefits of the control offered by flexibility. Second, greater flexibility might reduce the number of interactions with colleagues if schedules no longer overlap—an important issue that will be discussed further in Chapter 3. Whatever the reason, this is yet another reminder that employees are not seeking total control over their work. Instead, small, meaningful changes in working conditions make a big difference to employees' everyday work experiences.

One final aspect of Baltes et al.'s research is worth noting. Flexible work schedules had greater benefits on absenteeism than on job satisfaction or supervisor-rated performance. This result is not unexpected; after all, the purpose of flexible work schedules is to allow people opportunities to better balance work and nonwork responsibilities. The implication for management is clear: gaining the benefits of work autonomy is not dependent on offering all forms of autonomy, nor on offering full flexibility. Instead, the type and level of autonomy offered should be tied closely to the desired work outcomes.

Work performance

Spector's early research also pointed to a strong effect of workplace autonomy on work performance and choosing to remain with the organization,[16] findings which have been replicated consistently. As but one example, Zhen Chen and Anne Marie Francesco showed in a large sample of employees in a pharmaceutical manufacturing company in China that *choosing* to remain a member of the organization was associated with working conscientiously and informally helping new employees learn about the work environment.[17] In contrast, employees who felt they had no option but to remain with the organization worked less conscientiously, and were less willing to go above and beyond normal work to help their organizations. The fact that these findings emerged in a sample in China speaks to their generalizability of the need for some level of autonomy.

The benefits of workplace autonomy extend to safety performance. Despite the efforts of employees, labor unions, organizations, and governments, rates of occupational injuries and fatalities remain stubbornly high.‡ Given the gravity of workplace safety for employees, their families, and their organizations, understanding the causes of workplace injuries has long been the focus of social-science research. While earlier research concentrated on the effects of factors such as the "accident-prone personality," safety training, substance abuse, health and safety committees, ergonomics, and even compensation,[18] we now know job autonomy affects different aspects of safety performance.

In an earlier study, we investigated the effects of what we referred to as high-quality work on injuries.[19] In our research, high-quality work reflected a combination of autonomy and extensive training because it would make little sense to offer extensive training if people could not use newly learned skills; similarly, it could be dangerous to offer greater autonomy with no additional training. Poor quality work predicted the severity of injuries as measured by the number of workdays lost because of the injury. These results are noteworthy, as they are based on a large random sample of employees from the 1995 *Australian Workplace Industrial Relations Survey*, and the findings were consistent across a range of industries.

Nonetheless, the unique effects of autonomy remain somewhat unclear as autonomy was only one part of high-quality work. Fortunately, other studies focused explicitly on job autonomy. Sharon Parker and her colleagues contrasted the effects of autonomy, work overload, supportive supervision, training adequacy, job security, and communication quality on compliance with safety rules and procedures.[20] Taking all these work factors together in their study of 161 employees in two plants of a glass manufacturing company in England, only autonomy and communication quality affected safe working. Their study went further, however, showing that job autonomy affects safety because it results in higher levels of commitment to the organization, which motivated employees to work more safely.

Despite the importance of these findings, organizations that wish to excel in terms of safety need employees who are willing to do more than just comply with safety regulations; they need employees who are willing to go beyond the minimal requirements of safety regulations. Job autonomy plays an important role in this respect too. In a sample of 179 physicians working within various hospitals in Pakistan, job autonomy again predicted compliance with safety regulations. Perhaps more importantly, autonomy also predicted physicians' willingness to do more than the minimal required by safety regulations. As one example, they were also more willing to promote safety in their organization.[21] A similar effect emerged among 334 railway workers in the United Kingdom, in which higher levels of job autonomy prompted employees to believe that their personal safety role included the safety and well-being of their coworkers.[22]

‡ The terms *workplace* and *occupational injuries* are used interchangeably throughout.

Parker et al.'s explanations as to why job autonomy affects safe working sheds more light on why autonomy is invaluable at work. According to them, job autonomy enables people to decide for themselves whether procedures and rules are important and act accordingly. In addition, granting employees some autonomy over their own work signals to them that their judgment is respected by the organization.

Well-being

Research has consistently demonstrated that job autonomy benefits well-being. Two large-scale studies highlight the lessons that can be drawn. First, Ronald Fischer and Diana Boer were intrigued by an important question: if you wanted to enhance national well-being, would you be best advised to provide people with more money or more autonomy?[23] They conducted three studies to answer this question, using data on 420,599 people from sixty-three nations. Despite the attention devoted to increasing economic status to enhance well-being, and the continuing focus on compensation as a dominant form of work motivation, the degree to which people have opportunities to make personal choices best predicted well-being. Supporting the need to rethink the importance of economic status or wealth, Fischer and Boer's research demonstrated that where financial factors do play a role, it is by increasing the number of choices people have to shape their lives.

Second, Daniel Wheatley's study of a nationally representative UK sample that collected information via face-to-face and telephone interviews highlights the well-being benefits of control over tasks, pace of work, how the work is done, and schedule control.[24] As expected, both job and schedule control had positive effects on different aspects of subjective well-being, including job, leisure, and life satisfaction. Some of the findings provide more nuance. First, the findings were gendered. Even though management typically enjoys more autonomy than others in the organization, professional women had lower levels of scheduling control than other women in the sample. Second, as might be expected, managers enjoyed the highest levels of job and schedule control, but this is something of a managerial paradox. Likely driven by fear of losing control over their employees who might misuse any autonomy they have, managers are often reluctant to offer similar levels of autonomy to their employees. This likely explains why employees who enjoy greater method and scheduling autonomy are more satisfied with their supervisors.[25] Regardless, helping managers appreciate that their employees share the same motivations and fears as themselves remains a significant challenge for management education.

When autonomy is lacking

The discussion thus far has focused on the diverse benefits of job autonomy for employees and their organizations. The benefits of autonomy become even more apparent when we understand what happens to work attitudes, work performance, and well-being when job autonomy is limited or, worse still, lacking.

Work attitudes

A robust test of the effects of low autonomy emerges from work in which external control is an overriding concern. "Service work," with its frequent demand that "the customer is number one," would be a good place to start. Implied within service work is the expectation that satisfying customers is the major priority and that employees' needs are secondary. To ensure that customers are the first priority, employees would have to suppress their own emotional needs, necessitating what organizational researchers refer to as "surface acting," that is, subduing or faking your own emotions to satisfy others.

The daily work of bus drivers in large metropolitan areas embodies the need for surface acting, which at its core is inconsistent with employee autonomy. As Brent Scott and Christopher Barnes point out, bus drivers have personal contact with each passenger who enters the bus: they take passengers' fares, provide transfer tickets, answer questions about schedules and stops, and engage in conversations with passengers—who might be sad, frustrated, or angry.[26] As a result, Scott and Barnes surveyed sixty-eight bus drivers before and after each shift each workday for two weeks. The more bus drivers engaged in surface acting (e.g., faked a good mood) during the day, the more likely they were to report being irritable, distressed, and upset at the end of their shift, and the more likely they were to think about psychologically withdrawing from their jobs (e.g., daydreaming, thinking about being absent or quitting).

The negative effects of surface acting on work attitudes are not limited to bus drivers. Ute Hülsheger and Anna Schewe meta-analyzed the effects of surface acting among 23,574 participants from ninety-three studies.[27] Higher levels of surface acting were associated with lower levels of organizational commitment and job satisfaction.[§] Surface acting was also associated with lower levels of customer satisfaction. One explanation for this is that the psychological and cognitive energy used in bottling up your own emotions affects the ability to provide the quality of customer service that leads to customers' satisfaction.

Last, varying levels of job autonomy are built into different organizational processes or systems. To cope with increased external demand, one company in the United Kingdom instituted lean production and assembly lines, both of which reduce autonomy in the pursuit of productivity.[**] Compared with technical staff for whom there were no changes in work process (and thus no change in autonomy), both lean production and assembly lines had negative effects on employees' organizational

[§] Surface acting was also negatively associated with psychological well-being.
[**] That company also introduced workflow formalization and standardization, but this is of no concern here.

commitment and feelings of job anxiety, effects that were still present three years later.[28] Most importantly, these effects emerged at least in part because both lean production and assembly lines resulted in a loss of job autonomy (which was worse for employees working in the assembly line). One lesson learned from this study is that organizational systems and policies shape employee autonomy.

Work performance

Faced with low levels of autonomy, the most obvious, short-term (albeit inappropriate) coping response might simply be to withdraw from the organization, and there are studies showing that this does indeed happen. For example, in one study of more than a thousand randomly selected Dutch truck drivers, low levels of autonomy in 1998 increased employees' feeling of fatigue and need for recovery, and these two manifestations of psychological strain resulted in employees quitting the organization over the next two years.[29]

Nonetheless, I start this discussion with a different form of withdrawal, namely absenteeism, for two reasons. First, most employees who endure low levels of autonomy simply do not have the luxury of quitting and seeking more favorable conditions elsewhere. Second, and more costly from an organizational perspective, enduring low levels of autonomy but staying is likely more costly to the organization than quitting. This was made clear to me by Ben Hamper, author of the highly acclaimed memoir *Rivethead: Tales from the assembly line*. A former line worker at the General Motors plant in Michigan, Hamper tellingly describes what work is like when you are controlled by the clock.[30] After reading *Rivethead*, I invited Hamper to guest lecture to my MBA classes, and he did so for several years. During one class, a student got visibly frustrated with Hamper and blurted out, "If you disliked it so much, why didn't you just quit?" To which Hamper responded, "Oh I did! I just never left the organization."[††]

Understanding the causes of medically certified absenteeism has long been a target of research in Europe and the Scandinavian countries, and several studies implicate job autonomy. In one study of almost four thousand Finnish forestry employees, Ari Väänänen and colleagues showed that low levels of job autonomy predicted long (between four and twenty-one days) and very long (more than twenty-one days) absence spells for men over the next twenty-one months.[31] Notably, although males and females did not differ in levels of autonomy, females experienced almost 50 percent more days of absence than their male counterparts, suggesting that women's absences are likely a function of a greater number of factors (e.g., family responsibilities) than is the case for males. A separate study confirmed the effects of low job autonomy on sickness absence.[32] Again accessing company absence records, municipal workers in

[††] This story amply demonstrates that the notion of "quiet quitting," heralded as a new organizational phenomenon in 2022, was anything but new.

a single town in Finland who experienced low job control in 1991 suffered a 30 percent increase in sick leaves of more than three days over the next six years, compared to those who enjoyed higher levels of job control. These findings are noteworthy because, unlike much of the absenteeism research in which absence is self-reported, absence data were obtained from company records in both these studies.[33]

But absence is not the only response to unfavorable working conditions. One course of action could be to work with their organizations to improve the quality of work. When employees do so and their attempts fail, they typically do not just give up. Instead, they seek other solutions, and longstanding research confirms that one response is to turn to unions to resolve their issues. While historically the most significant distal cause of unionization was dissatisfaction with pay, supervision, and safety,[34] feeling that you lack influence in your job now also motivates people to seek help from a union. In one study of fifty-nine production workers in the United States, greater dissatisfaction with the amount of job-related independence resulted in significantly more votes for a union in a certification election.[35] Similar findings emerged in a study of voting by 112 university faculty members in a certification election, with dissatisfaction with the independence in their jobs and a lack of opportunities to be creative resulting in a greater likelihood of a pro-union vote.[36] More recently, some employees of vaunted high-tech companies such as Alphabet have turned to unions because of what they saw as an inability to get the organization to take their grievances seriously.[37] The effects of feeling frustrated about autonomy does not stop with voting for a union. Once members of a union, employees who believe that they should have greater input into workplace decisions are also more likely to file grievances[38] and to go out on strike.[39]

A very different way in which to understand the effects of low autonomy would be to focus on situations in which leaders engage in micromanagement, a management "style" that centers around excessive and unreasonable control of employees. You can understand just what micromanagement means by a story shared by orchestra conductor, leadership consultant, and author Itay Talgam about Riccardo Muti. Having conducted La Scala, the Chicago Symphony Orchestra, the Philadelphia Orchestra, the Philharmonic Orchestra in London, and the Salzburg Whitsun Festival, Muti is highly acclaimed yet someone who prefers to maintain strict control. After having the opportunity to play with Muti, a concert master was asked by a colleague how it was. His response? "It was fine. It could have been better, but he wouldn't let us" (89).[40]

In perhaps the first micromanagement study about fifty years ago, Robert Day and Robert Hamblin investigated the effects of what they called "close supervision" on twenty-four groups of undergraduates.[41] Close supervision resulted in lower levels of productivity and aggressive feelings toward the supervisor among students who scored lower on self-esteem. Thirty years later, Greg Oldham and Anne Cummings investigated the triggers of, and obstacles to, creativity at work among 171 design or manufacturing engineers, toolmakers, and technicians in two manufacturing plants.[42] Overcontrolling supervision exerted negative effects on employees' creativity as measured, for example, by the number of written patent disclosures and general performance. Overcontrolling supervision was also associated with the extent to which employees thought about and took initial steps to quit the organization.

More recent studies show similar effects. Research Kate Dupré and I conducted showed that prison guards who felt that they were overcontrolled responded with increased levels of psychological aggression against their supervisors.[43] Lest we think aggressive responses are unique to people working within prisons, graduate students who felt their work was too tightly controlled by their research supervisors in a university setting targeted their supervisors with psychologically aggressive behaviors, such as sharing damaging information about them or being spiteful toward them.

Last, a study in a very different context showed the same negative effects. Together with Amy Akers and Darren Beiko, we studied the effects of surgeons' overcontrolling leadership behaviors on surgical teams during 150 surgeries in Canada.[44] Yet again, higher levels of overcontrolling leadership (as rated by two trained observers who watched all the surgeries) were associated with team members feeling that they were less competent and effective during the surgery.

Well-being

Might low job autonomy be enough to compromise well-being? A very large body of research has set out to answer this question, so much so we will limit this discussion to one aspect of physical well-being (namely, coronary heart disease), and one of psychological well-being (namely, depression).

One of the most important initiatives of the past fifty years in understanding the effects of workplace conditions on health in general, and coronary heart disease in particular, is the Whitehall studies[‡‡] initiated by Sir Michael Marmot. Whitehall I started in 1967 and surveyed 17,500 male civil servants in the United Kingdom for the next ten years. Whitehall II began in 1985 and follows 10,308 civil servants (a third of whom are women).

One large-scale study used data from 6,895 male and 3,413 female civil servants in Whitehall II to understand whether workplace factors predict new instances of coronary heart disease five years later.[45] As job control decreased, angina, severe chest pain, diagnosed heart attack, and other coronary events, all increased. Because it remains possible that it is not the lack of autonomy that is at play but personal factors such as age, employment-grade level, Type A behavior, competitiveness, evidence of a psychiatric disorder, negative affect, or angry or unassertive coping techniques, the researchers reanalyzed the data in a separate study statistically controlling for all these personal factors.[46] The negative effects remained: the odds of males with the lowest levels of job control subsequently experiencing a diagnosed or suspected coronary event was at least 30 percent higher than those enjoying the highest levels of

‡‡ This initiative took its name from the headquarters of the civil service in the United Kingdom.

autonomy. Notably, the risk of a coronary event for females experiencing similarly low levels of autonomy was at least 60 percent higher than for males.

Confidence in any findings is increased when they are replicated by independent researchers using different methods in different settings. George Bishop and colleagues' intensive research study on 118 police officers in Singapore confirms the effects of low autonomy.[47] They tracked officers' heart rate and blood pressure using ambulatory blood-pressure monitors every thirty minutes throughout their regular workdays. At the same time these measurements were taken, the officers reported on the amount of autonomy they had in prior the ten minutes. Lower autonomy was associated in real time with higher levels of diastolic and mean arterial blood pressure. Moreover, the negative effects of low autonomy were exaggerated during periods of high work demands. Findings from both these studies are credible because the researchers controlled for personal factors that could have affected coronary events, such as body mass index, and in the latter study, whether the police officers were sitting, standing, or smoking.

Changing focus, could a lack of autonomy compromise psychological well-being? Amanda Cooklin and her team were interested in whether poor-quality employment influences new mothers' postpartum depressive symptoms.[48] Cooklin's team had access to data from 1,300 employed mothers of an infant less than a year old. Even after statistically accounting for factors that contribute to depression, such as having had a prior depressive episode, marital dissatisfaction, or low levels of social support, low job control was associated with a 39 percent increase in experiencing depressive symptoms. Supporting the notion that the link between low autonomy and depression is not limited to one country, low autonomy also predicted depressive symptoms in a sample of 1,739 experienced Dutch employees working across a wide variety of industries.[49]

While important, these two studies focused on subclinical level of depression, leaving open the question of whether low levels of control can lead to clinically diagnosed cases of depression? Hilde Mausner-Dorsch and Willian Eaton addressed this question, and their study deserves close attention as it was based on a US sample of 1,920 adults with depression diagnosed by trained personnel during one-on-one interviews.[50] A lack of job control was the strongest predictor of all levels of depression, but the negative effects of low autonomy were greatest for clinically diagnosed cases of depression.

Last, access to timing and scheduling autonomy might be especially important during the COVID-19 pandemic, because people working remotely might find their work more closely monitored than usual. Bin Wang and colleagues' research during the pandemic in China showed how employees experienced different forms of remote monitoring, including being required to keep their camera on while working.[51] Their research also showed that autonomy remains important during the pandemic. Among 522 employees working from home, having some job autonomy was associated with lower levels of loneliness and emotional exhaustion, and higher levels of life satisfaction.

How does autonomy exert its effects?

Autonomy exerts indirect effects

Just as leadership exerts its performance effects indirectly, so too does job autonomy. In the case of leadership, we already saw that the best of leadership initially helps employees think more highly of themselves, appreciate just how important their work is, and value their relationship with their leaders.[52] Each factor in turn then motivates employees to perform at superior levels. In much the same way, job autonomy and control exert indirect effects on important employee and organizational outcomes.

Arnold Bakker and colleagues' research provides one explanation as to how autonomy is associated with higher levels of attendance. Their survey of 214 nutrition production employees in the Netherlands showed that having job control was reciprocated by employees with greater loyalty to the organization.[53] In turn, employees with higher level of company loyalty engaged in fewer bouts of absenteeism and fewer workdays lost. Stated differently, people appreciate companies that offer them opportunities for autonomy, and are proud to be members of organizations that do so. Feeling proud to be a member of an organization has consequences; in this case, motivating people to physically attend work.

But there is more than one pathway from autonomy to valued work outcomes. Cynthia Thompson and David Prottas were interested in how job autonomy spills over into the family.[54] Using a sample of 2,810 employed adults in the United States, they also showed that the effects of job autonomy were indirect. In this case, job-related autonomy resulted in people feeling that they had more control over important issues in their lives. In turn, feeling more control over your life had positive effects on family functioning, life, and family and work satisfaction. An additional benefit was that feeling more general control was linked with a lower likelihood of quitting the organization.

Other studies add to the notion that any effects of job autonomy on desirable work outcomes are indirect. One possibility is that providing autonomy to employees signals that they are trusted, which results in higher levels of well-being. In line with this, a survey of 714 employees of an electrical engineering and electronics company in the Netherlands showed that job autonomy increased employees' optimism, work-related self-esteem, and self-confidence, all of which led to higher work engagement and lower of emotional exhaustion.[55] A separate study showed that having some control in one's job was viewed as being procedurally fair, and the sense of procedural fairness resulted in lower anxiety and depression.[56]

Autonomy shapes the way you experience your work

A separate line of research has focused on whether having job autonomy shapes the way in which we experience other aspects of our work, such as work stress. In their widely researched "job strain" theory, Robert Karasek and Töres Theorell suggest that having control over how we do our work, or scheduling of our work,[§§] is essential if we are to effectively deal with demanding, stressful work. Arnold Bakker and his team found support for this idea in a higher education institution in the Netherlands with more than a thousand employees. Job autonomy reduced the negative effects of work overload, demanding work, and work-family interference on the emotional exhaustion and cynicism dimensions of burnout.[57] In other words, the negative effects of negative working conditions were much lower for employees experiencing higher levels of autonomy.

Similar effects emerge across different countries and contexts. One study focused on the effects of lunch breaks among seventy-eight administrative staff and their coworkers at a US university, all of whom completed surveys each day for ten consecutive workdays. While people routinely look forward to lunch breaks as a way to recover from demanding or even boring work, lunch breaks only reduced fatigue at the end of the workday for employees who felt they could use the lunch hour as they wanted.[58] Similar effects for job control were obtained in South Korea. YoungAh Park and Sooyeol Kim studied seventy-one call-center employees, an occupation rife with customer mistreatment.[59] For employees who enjoyed little job control, mistreatment by customers was associated with being upset, irritable, sad, and distressed that same evening. However, for call-center operators who reported having more job control, customer mistreatment had no such effects. Given the number of call center-employees across the world, and hence the number of employees vulnerable to customer mistreatment, findings like this should not be easily dismissed.

Social scientists invariably place more faith in results from laboratory-based research, and a laboratory study with eighty experienced Colombian bus drivers in a simulated bus driving task again illustrates how job control shapes the experience of demanding jobs.[60] Half of the drivers were assigned randomly to drive on a route that only made three stops to pick up passengers in their preassigned plan; the others were assigned to a more demanding route and made seven stops. Within each of these two groups, half the drivers experienced low autonomy in that their route was timed and they could not contact the control room with questions. In contrast, those granted autonomy had no preassigned time limit and could contact the control room with questions. Yet again, any negative effects of job demands on three physiological indicators of stress (e.g., breaths per minute), feelings of pressure or tension, and interest or enjoyment were significantly lower among drivers who had more job autonomy.

[§§] What they refer to as "decision latitude."

To date, most of the research on the moderating effects of autonomy have focused on how it buffers the negative effects of work stress. Some research has now investigated if autonomy shapes how people experience high-quality leadership.[61] Judith Volmer and colleagues' interest in this question was partially stimulated by counterintuitive findings showing that high-quality leadership does not always result in increased creativity by followers. Based on data from 144 manufacturing employees of a global high-tech firm in Germany, high-quality leadership did not benefit creative work when job autonomy was low. What this suggests is that high-quality leadership by itself may not always be enough; employees need to be allowed by their leaders to behave in ways that result in superior levels of performance.

Changing focus, leadership researchers have been very interested over the past twenty years in the negative effects of abusive supervision, including behaviors such as ridiculing employees, putting them down in front of others, and being rude.[62] Perhaps not surprisingly, exposure to abusive supervision is consistently associated with poor psychosomatic health.[63] However, this negative effect is not inevitable[64]: In one study of 170 employees and their supervisors in Portugal, abusive supervision only affected psychosomatic complaints for employees with low levels of autonomy; there were no negative effects for their counterparts who enjoyed higher levels of autonomy. Essentially, enjoying higher levels of job autonomy was enough to suppress the negative effects of abusive supervision.

Gender and job autonomy

The intersection of gender and autonomy has certainly attracted research attention, and the findings have important practical implications. As just one example, Tarani Chandola and colleagues examined the link between control at home and gender inequities in cardiovascular health outcomes.[65] Using data from 7,470 participants in the Whitehall II studies, the way in which gender shapes the link between control reported at home and health becomes apparent. The amount of control men reported at home, measured sometime between 1991 and 1993, had no effect on medically diagnosed cardiovascular incidents some six year later. In contrast, women who felt a lack of control at home experienced worse cardiovascular health.

Despite the importance of these findings, there is very little research comparing the levels of job-related autonomy for men and women. Some studies show that men tend to experience higher levels of job control than women. In their study of 1,482 men and 1,350 women in South Korea who engaged in manual work, men enjoyed higher level of job control than did women.[66] Similar findings emerged in a large-scale, nationally representative study of 1,948 mothers and 2,164 fathers in Australia.[67] Complicating the picture, however, no differences emerged among 400 male and 400 female members of the Australian Institute of Management.[68]

We do know a lot more about how gender shapes the way in which job control is used in the workplace, primarily from the research of Karasek and Theorell's job-strain model. The results of these studies consistently show that gender does not affect how job control (or "decision latitude" in their terminology) affects work attitudes or well-being.[69] What this means is that job control is equally important for males and females, reiterating the importance of job control for all employees.

Culture and job autonomy

Differences in the level of autonomy

Studies differ somewhat as to whether differences exist in levels of autonomy across different countries.*** Alicia Grandey and her colleagues found no differences in job autonomy between 101 employees in the United States and 95 employees in France, all of whom worked more than sixteen hours per week in a job that required some contact with the public.[70] Man and Lam focused on team (rather than individual) autonomy in US and Hong Kong branches of one of the largest banking and financial-services institutions in the world.[71] Again, no differences emerged in the level of autonomy. One of the reasons Man and Lam's findings are noteworthy is that they are based on a relatively large sample of 178 teams from the United States and 224 from Hong Kong, with between four and seven members in each team.

Other research has contrasted levels of autonomy in the United States with other countries. In one study of 332 university employees in the United States, and 302 in China,[72] employees in the United States reported significantly higher levels of autonomy than their counterparts in China. Similarly, 120 American managers perceived higher levels of workplace control than a comparable group of 207 Iranian managers.[73] These findings are consistent with Lakshmi Narayanan et al.'s analyses of work-control beliefs: 133 clerical employees in a US university viewed the lack of work control as a more significant source of stress than a comparable group of 130 employees in India.[74]

Yet this is not the end of the story, so let's change focus slightly. Charles Mueller and Tor Wynn were interested in how much *value* people from different countries place on job autonomy. Based on 12,426 employees in Canada and the United States, 3,844 in South Korea, and 1,433 in Kenya, Mueller and Wynn showed that consistent with the strong individualism ethic in the United States, job autonomy was more highly valued in the US-Canada sample than in both South Korea and Kenya.[75] As a result, what we learn from these studies is that employees in North America value job autonomy more than in other countries, and tend to enjoy higher levels of job autonomy in their work.

*** The extent to which research on autonomy and job control has been conducted from a North American perspective is evident in the studies discussed in this section: invariably, most studies involve a comparison of the United States and at least one other country.

Differences in the function of autonomy

A separate and perhaps more important question is whether job autonomy functions differently across diverse countries or cultures. Stated somewhat differently, might characteristics specific to certain countries or cultures strengthen or weaken the effects of job autonomy? As we will see, findings from countless studies show consistently that job autonomy is of far greater importance within individualistic cultures, which prioritize individual rather than collective needs and accomplishments.

To date, one of the most ambitious studies investigating the universality of job control on well-being at work surveyed 5,153 employees in no fewer than twenty-four distinct geopolitical entities.[†††] Findings from this study confirmed the effect of cultural characteristics on work control.[76] For example, the benefits of work-control beliefs on physical well-being were greater in the United States than in ten of the twenty-four countries investigated. Moreover, control beliefs had no effect on physical well-being in a further seven countries. In separate research, the effects of discretion (i.e., method control) on the satisfaction of frontline hotel employees were more pronounced in Canada than China.[77]Thus, the effects of job autonomy differ across counties, throwing into question any notion of universality. Just why this is the case will soon be clear.

Liu and colleagues examined other ways in which culture shapes the effects of autonomy in their research on university employees.[78] First, enjoying higher levels of autonomy was associated with less employee vs supervisor conflict in the United States, but not in China. Second, job autonomy reduced the negative effects of supervisor conflict on well-being in the US sample, but intensified the negative effects for their Chinese counterparts. What these findings suggest is that having some degree of control at work is especially important for US employees, and may even be sufficient to serve a health-enhancing role—with all these findings suggesting that having control at work is more important in individualistic societies.

While between-country comparisons are interesting, they provide limited information as they ignore potentially important cultural differences between people within countries. As a result, research by Boris Cendales and Viviola Ortiz warrants attention. Based on the assumption that people within the same country can differ in terms of their individualism, they studied how individualism shapes the effects of work stress on anxiety, depression, and psychosomatic symptoms. The sample for their study included 283 firefighters, 134 bus drivers, and 102 administrative employees in Columbia.[79] As they had predicted, higher levels of job control did indeed lessen the negative effects of work stress, but only for employees with higher individualistic beliefs. In contrast, high levels of control worsened the negative effects of work stress for employees who scored higher in terms of collectivist beliefs.

††† More details about this large-scale initiative are available at: http://shell.cas.usf.edu/~pspector/cisms.html

Similar effects emerged in other countries. For example, using data from 7,310 employees in different European countries, feeling overqualified was associated with poorer well-being for respondents with low levels of job autonomy, while no such effect emerged for respondents high in job autonomy. Presumably, enjoying some level of job control provides people with opportunities for dealing with job stressors resulting from being overly qualified. However, these benefits only emerged for employees within individualistic cultures; job autonomy again exerted no beneficial effects for respondents from more collectivistic societies.[80]

These studies show that when it comes to job autonomy, culture matters. Cultural factors shape how much employees value autonomy, the amount of job autonomy afforded to employees, and in turn, how that autonomy affects work performance. As Man and Lam succinctly conclude, "Simply put, individualists enjoy their autonomy more than collectivists" (995).[81]

TMGT: Can we have too much autonomy in organizations?

Given the pervasive benefits of job-related autonomy for job performance and well-being, should management just keep increasing employees' autonomy? Peter Warr was one of the first to caution that this may not be appropriate.[82] To explain why not, he compared autonomy and other job characteristics to vitamins. Vitamins are essential for physical well-being, but for some vitamins, this is true only to a certain point, beyond which they offer no further benefit. Just as importantly, increasing levels of other vitamins can be detrimental to physical health. Vitamins C and E, for example, have what Warr called a "constant effect," meaning that you could not extract further benefits at higher levels. In contrast, an overdose of vitamin A or D could prove to be toxic (what Warr called the "additional decrement"). Job autonomy, he suggested, functions in the same way as vitamin A or D.

Some research has tested Warr's notion that you can have too much autonomy, and the findings are mixed. De Jonge and colleagues studied experienced Dutch employees working within a wide variety of industries, and found no support for the notion that higher levels of autonomy are harmful.[83] However, evidence for a harmful effect of high levels of autonomy has emerged since then. Bettina Kubicek and colleagues conducted two separate studies investigating the effects of job control among registered nurses, nursing assistants, and orderlies working in multiple eldercare facilities.[84] Employees with lower and higher levels of job control in their first study experienced more burnout and lower levels of work engagement. Their second study went further, showing that the negative effects of high levels of job control were maintained sixteen months later. Nonetheless, Kubicek et al.'s study only focused on the effects of overall job control.

Barbara Stiglbauer and Carrie Kovacs clarified this effect by examining the effects of different forms of job autonomy on personal well-being. As can be seen in Figure

3.1, the negative effects of higher levels of autonomy were strongest for method autonomy (e.g., "The job allows me to decide on my own how to go about doing my own work"), and weakest for decision-making autonomy ("The job allows me to make a lot of decisions on my own").[85]

Studies that focus only on well-being cannot adequately convey the full extent of potential negative effects of too much autonomy. Jackson Lu and his team broadened their focus from employee well-being to employee creativity and unethical behaviors.[86] Across several studies in Israel and the United States, they showed that job autonomy can be a double-edged sword. High levels of autonomy were associated with more creative performance. At the same time, they were also associated with more unethical behaviors. The reason for this is that high levels of autonomy removed the organizational constraints from some people that enabled them to behave unethically. However, this was not necessarily the case for everyone. Higher levels of autonomy were less likely to result in unethical behaviors for employees who placed a high value in having autonomy.

Taken together, these findings provide some guidance for organizations that might be reluctant to offer ever-increasing amounts of autonomy to their employees, or managers who fear that doing so would result in a loss of control. Not only do the data suggest that it is not necessary to offer very high levels of control to employees, but doing so might even be detrimental to employees and their organizations.

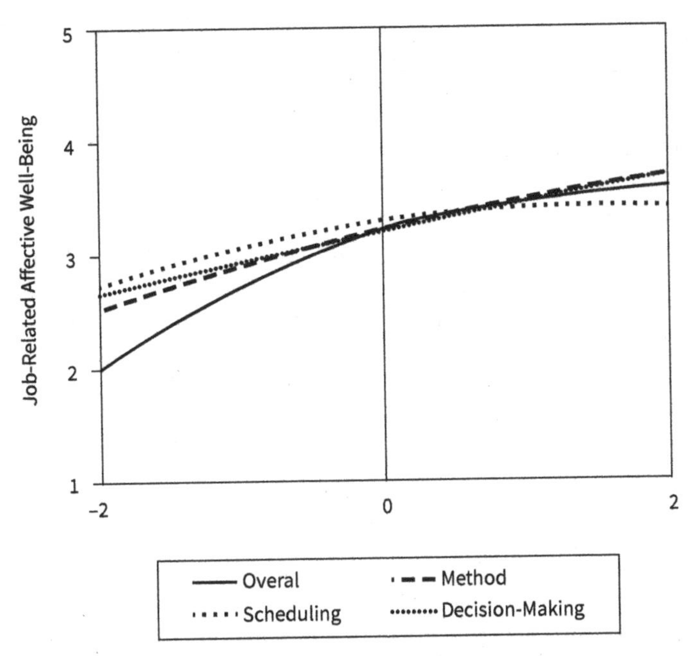

Fig. 3.1 Relationship between different forms of autonomy and well-being.
Republished with permission from American Psychological Association—Journals from Stiglbauer, B., & Kovacs, C. (2018). The more, the better? Curvilinear effects of job autonomy on well-being from vitamin model and PE-fit theory perspectives. *Journal of Occupational Health Psychology, 23*(4), 520–536; permission conveyed through Copyright Clearance Center, Inc.

Interventions to enhance workplace autonomy

Just knowing that job control or autonomy are associated with widespread organizational outcomes would matter little to organizations if they have no way to enhance employee autonomy. Fortunately, numerous interventions exist to demonstrate that organizations can indeed increase job autonomy.

One intervention implemented by Toby Wall and his colleagues at the University of Sheffield provides numerous lessons.[87] They worked together with a single department of a large electronics company in the United Kingdom that assembled circuit boards for mainframe and microcomputers. There were seven computer-controlled machines, three of which caused most of the operational problems requiring significant employee monitoring and involvement. Consistent with prevailing management practices at the company, operators were required to inform a supervisor when a problem emerged, which would trigger help from a specialist engineer—a time-consuming process. Underlying this management practice was the belief that rectifying equipment problems was too important or too complex to entrust to employees, a signal that would not have escaped employees' notice.

During the twenty-day intervention, management, worker representatives, and one of the researchers jointly decided to redesign the process to give operators more control over the work process. Critically, all this new process involved was that when machine problems emerged, operators would have fifteen minutes to fix the problem themselves. If they could not, they would call their supervisors. All operators then attended an intensive training programing to provide the skills and knowledge to help them meet their new responsibilities (a critical precursor to autonomy that will be discussed further), after which the new system was introduced. Thus, the goal of the intervention was to replace the "specialist control" with an "operator control" model. After the twenty-day intervention, performance data were collected each day for fifty days, together with surveys assessing employees' psychological well-being completed at the end of the fifty-day period.

If the intervention was successful, the "operator system" should result in fewer equipment downtimes, especially for high-variance (i.e., operationally complex) machines. The intervention worked well: downtime for high-variance machines was reduced from approximately fifty to thirty minutes for each eight-hour shift worked. In practical terms, the reduction in downtime allowed for an extra ten hours of production per week. What makes these findings even more important is that these effects were maintained twelve months after the intervention, meaning that the organization gained an additional ten hours of production each week for one year. All that was required was allowing employees fifteen minutes to fix problems with their equipment rather than having to call an "expert."

But these were not the only benefits gained from the intervention. Operators were also more satisfied with the way in which they carried out their work under the operator-control system. Despite the additional responsibilities they now had for their machines, they felt less, not more, job pressure. Later studies would confirm that greater autonomy at work is associated with lower levels of job-related anxiety and depression.[88]

Last, an unintended benefit emerged from the move to an operator-control system that all too often goes unnoticed. Despite their initial opposition to the change, specialist engineers now had an average of ten hours each week when they would not be repairing equipment, during which they could concentrate on more demanding and arguably more important tasks in the factory.

Thus, Wall et al.'s intervention offers important lessons for management. First, the shift to an operator-oriented system did not happen until all employees had received training to ensure that they had the skills required to benefit from their newfound autonomy. After all, it would make very little sense to offer additional autonomy without first ensuring that people have the skills to use their autonomy; indeed, in some situations, not doing so first could be nothing less than dangerous. Similarly, organizations that excel in training would likely see no benefits unless employees have opportunities to use the new knowledge they had gained. Second, the symbiotic relationship between autonomy and training reminds us that none of the seven components of productive, healthy, and safe work considered in this book should be thought of as a stand-alone best practice. Instead, implementation of any of the seven components usually requires the implementation of some others to be successful.

Job autonomy: The special case of electronic performance monitoring

By their very nature, some management practices allow while others limit autonomy. Earlier, we saw how both lean production and assembly lines can limit autonomy,[89] and we now turn our attention to electronic monitoring, a practice favored by management for a long time. Charlie Chaplin's classic 1936 movie, *Modern Times*[90] provides a great description of how electronic surveillance is by no means a recent phenomenon; it even predated the dark and dystopian vision of George Orwell's *1984*.[91] *Modern Times* opens with a scene involving electronic performance monitoring. We see sheep being herded into a pen, immediately followed by dozens of male workers streaming down narrow corridors into a factory. At exactly the same time, we become aware of the president of the Electro Steel Corporation sitting in his office, struggling with a jigsaw puzzle and reading the newspaper. He is interrupted by his secretary, who brings his medication. After taking his medication, he presses some buttons on a machine on his desk, and swivels around to face a giant screen on the wall behind him, on which he watches workers on the shop floor in real time. And that was in 1936! Fifty years later, Barbara Garson noted in her intriguing book *The Electronic Sweatshop* how technological progress was deskilling work and stripping autonomy from workers—even highly skilled workers, such as those in the Joint Chiefs of Staff in the US military.[92] A more modern incarnation of electronic monitoring would be gig work, an increasingly important segment of the labor market with gig workers making up at least 10 percent of the US labor market prepandemic.[93] Ethnographic research now shows that despite the push to see gig work as a way of promoting individual freedom and autonomy, longtime Uber and Lyft drivers report feeling controlled by algorithms and swamped in exhausting work schedules over which they have very little control.[94]

The extent to which employees are subject to electronic monitoring is also apparent in the modern long-distance trucking industry. Long-distance truck drivers are everywhere. The US BLS estimates that there were 1,871,700 long-distance truck drivers in 2016, and that this number is expected to grow by 6 percent by 2023,[95] a trend that may be bolstered by the surge in online shopping that started during the pandemic. On the one hand, Finn Murphy, a self-employed long-distance trucker talks glowingly in his delightful book *The Long Haul* about the freedom of being on the road in the 1980s and 1990s, when the only performance monitoring he experienced was an occasional call from head office.[96] Contrast that, on the other hand, with interviews with long-distance truck drivers at highway truck stops across the United States some three decades later and it is apparent how pervasive electronic monitoring has become.[97] One truck driver provided this string of electronic messages (168):

12:57 pm	Firm: Are you headed to delivery?
1:02 pm	Firm: Please call.
2:33 pm	Firm: What is your ETA to delivery?
2:34 pm	Firm: Need you to start rolling.
2:34 pm	Firm: Why have you not called me back?
3:25 pm	Driver: I can't talk and sleep at the same time.
3:37 pm	Firm: Why aren't you rolling? *You have hours* and are going to service fail this load.
3:44 pm	Firm: *You have hours* now and the ability to roll—that is a failure when you are sitting and refusing to roll to the customer.
3:51 pm	Firm: Please go in and deliver. We need to service our customers. Please start rolling. They will receive you up to 11:30. Please do not be late.
4:14 pm	Driver: Bad storm. Can't roll now.
4:34 pm	Firm: Weather Channel is showing small rain shower *in your area*, 1–2 inches of rain and 10 mph winds???

And all this occurred while the driver was taking a legally authorized sleep break!

However, even though laboratory[98] and field research[99] show that electronic performance monitoring usually results in higher levels of stress, lower productivity, and poorer mental well-being, we are now well past the point where the solution is to simply eliminate electronic monitoring. As a result, Jeffrey Stanton's research is important for several reasons. First, with the number of people involved in remote work already increasing as a result of the COVID-19 pandemic, we can expect to see an increase in electronic monitoring. Second, Stanton's extensive research suggests that *how* electronic performance monitoring is implemented is critical.

One lesson from Stanton's research is that negative effects are reduced when the implementation of electronic monitoring is viewed as procedurally fair (see Chapter 5), for example, when employees viewed the monitoring as consistent across people and the knowledge gained about work performance as objective and unbiased.[100] A second lesson is that any negative effects of electronic performance monitoring were diminished by giving employees the ability to exert some control over the monitoring system.[101] Thus, even when management practices might limit autonomy, supervisors should still grant employees some control over the system. Third, potential benefits arising from the information obtained were compromised when electronic performance monitoring was viewed as less interpersonally fair than traditional forms of performance monitoring.[102]

These findings have significant practical implications. While managers may not always decide whether electronic monitoring systems will be implemented, they do have some control over how they are implemented and the way in which information obtained is used. And these are the factors that will largely determine whether electronic monitoring helps, or hurts, organizations and their employees.

Conclusion

In case you are not yet convinced

First, the fact that managers limit employees' access to job control, as well as do what they can to retain as much control for themselves, is ironic. After all, managers enjoy more control in the workplace than others, even more than people holding professional jobs.[103] In addition, even though the reason management often give for withholding is to be more effective and demonstrate control, Roshni Raveendhran and Cheryl Wakslak's research shows that opposite is the case.[104] Across three studies, subordinates viewed micromanaging behaviors as ineffective, not reflecting leadership, and as revealing an underlying insecurity by the managers.

Second, the pandemic resulted in a significant shift toward working from home. The number of Canadians working from home doubled between February 1, 2020, and May 29, 2020,[105] and this happened in the United Kingdom as well (and we will return to this topic in Chapter 9).[106] Despite the fact that the move to remote work resulted in an increase of about 2.5 hours of work per day in the United Kingdom, United States, Canada, and Austria,[107] managers worry that employees will be less productive when they cannot watch them. As a result, the move to remote work at the start of the pandemic coincided with an increased interest by management in technologies to monitor work remotely.[108] By the end of 2020, Microsoft had already issued an apology for crossing a line in the way in which their software offered management opportunities for invasive surveillance.[109] With many organizations already continuing with remote or hybrid work options, successful organizations will do so in ways that enhance rather than limit job autonomy. As Jeffrey Pfeffer reminds us, the paradox of these monitoring initiatives is that they make managers trust their employees less. Yet only when we stop watching them so actively will we learn the full extent to which they can be trusted.[110]

Third, in a world in which the effects of many interventions are short-lived, the opposite may be true with job autonomy. In the intervention that shifted from a specialist to an operator-oriented system, performance benefits were maintained one year later. In a different intervention in which nursing and clerical staff had increased opportunities to participate in decision-making,[111] not only were the benefits evident three and six months later, they *increased* over time.

Fourth, when it comes to job autonomy, what happens at work does not necessarily stay at work. When parents gained more autonomy at work in an early study on blue-collar employees, they reported positive changes in their parenting at home.[112] As examples, one father of four children disclosed that "I have a 16 year old son and I use some of the things we do at work with him instead of yelling" (81). A mother who was a machine operator noted, "I say things to my (8-year-old) daughter that I know are a result of the way we do things at work. I ask her, 'What do you think about that?' or 'How would you handle this problem?' I . . . deal with her the way I deal with people at work" (81–82). A similar spillover from work to parenting is evident in a recent study of 120 working-class families in the United States in which both parents were employed in the twelve months after childbirth.[113] Mothers' and fathers' job autonomy was associated with lower levels of what the researchers called "parent overreactivity" (e.g., "When I'm upset or under stress, I am picky and on my child's back"). These benefits are important, because less parental reactivity in the first year of the children's lives was associated with better social and academic outcomes during first grade.

Fifth, the rise of and expansion of "the gig economy"[114] must give some pause for concern given what we know about the many benefits of job autonomy. While flexibility is often touted as a major benefit of gig work, this flexibility primarily goes to management. As Sarah Kessler, the author of *Gigged*[115] who spent a month doing gig work for her research points out, "Despite the oft-repeated promise of the gig economy, in fact I have no control over when I work, because the only way to get gigs is to be available sporadically and often without much notice."[116]

Last, ask people if they agree with the statement that "nobody knows the job as well as the person who does it!" My experience is that you will get nearly unanimous agreement. Yet when I ask leaders attending executive development sessions or executive MBA students what this means for their own leadership, that agreement soon fades. While the clear implication of this statement is that we should do what we can to grant people autonomy to do *their* jobs,[‡‡‡] doing so is not as easy. Knowing that what is required is small increments in autonomy, and that large increases can even be counterproductive, may encourage management to ensure that employees also get to enjoy the control necessary to thrive at work.

‡‡‡ That is, after they have received the requisite training.

4
Belonging

Individuals looking to improve their business practices have often turned to Tom Peters' classic *In Search of Excellence* (or any of his other nineteen best-selling business books[1]), for the very best advice on how to run their businesses and organizations. Yet sometimes people are selective in the advice they choose to follow or to ignore, even from Tom Peters. One overlooked nugget from Tom Peters is that we should "read more novels and fewer business books" because "relationships are really all there is."* In this chapter, we will now see why it is time to heed Peters' wise counsel and give serious consideration to the role of workplace relationships, so frequently disparaged as "the soft stuff."

The nature of belonging

Even though Maslow's emphasis on the need for belonging is widely recognized in management circles, many people might be surprised to know that his interest went well beyond "belonging." As he stated in his seminal paper in 1943, "If both the physiological and the safety needs are fairly well gratified, then there will emerge the *love and affection and belongingness* needs" (italics added).[2] Yet somehow, a focus on love and affection was lost in the management literature. This is an important omission, as it may have contributed to the scant attention paid to the role of work relationships in fulfilling people's need for belonging. The Gallup organization certainly appreciates the importance of relationships. From decades of consulting and research,[3] they learned that one survey item, namely "I have a best friend at work," consistently predicts employee engagement, talented teams, and great workplaces[4] Because of negative responses to the word "best" from some employees, Gallup initially changed the item to a "close" or "good" friend, or just deleted the word entirely. The result? Without the term "best" friend, the item no longer distinguished between the most and least productive workgroups. Moreover, across multiple surveys Gallup conducted, only 20 percent of employees strongly endorsed the item on their survey "I have a best friend at work." Extrapolating from these data, they could show that if 60 percent of respondents had endorsed this item, we could have expected 36 percent fewer safety incidents, 7 percent more engagement by customers, and 12 percent

* Tom Peters, quoted in Charles Handy's (1994) *The empty raincoat: Making sense of the future* (126). London: Hutchinson.

Brave New Workplace. Julian Barling, Oxford University Press. © Oxford University Press 2023.
DOI: 10.1093/oso/9780190648107.003.0004

higher profitability, reminding us of just how important high-quality social relationship at work are for employees and their organizations. Despite this, the percentage of employees who say that had a close friend at work has been decreasing since 1985.[5]

Complementing these Gallup findings, we learnt from our own research that one the three core reasons people love their jobs is high-quality or intimate social relationships with coworkers. As a school janitor told Oprah Winfrey on her show in 2003, "I love my job because I come into contact with so many wonderful people."[6]

To illustrate the importance of high-quality personal relationships at work in this chapter, I examine what happens when people enjoy positive relationships at work. I also use examples from two different streams of research that show what happens when high-quality personal relations are missing, either because of workplace ostracism or belonging needs being thwarted.

Going beyond relationships with other people at work, employees also feel a sense of belonging or commitment to their organization. For more than forty years, researchers have investigated the effects of people's commitment to their organization. Starting in the early 1980s, John Meyer and Natalie Allen distinguished between different types of commitment to the organization, namely affective and continuance commitment.[7] Integral to the notion of belonging is the feeling of *affective commitment*. Affective commitment reflects feelings of an emotional attachment to, and identification with, the organization. Placing affective commitment in a wider context, research identifies an affective attachment to the organization as one key reason why people love their jobs.[8] More specifically, people who enjoy a strong emotional attachment are more likely to stay with the organization, but importantly, they do so because they *want* to.

Unlike affective commitment, sometimes employees choose to stay with the organization because of the costs of leaving, or because there are no alternative opportunities available to them, and Meyer and Allen called this *continuance commitment*. People with high levels of continuance commitment also remain with the organization, but they do so because they feel they *have* to, rather than *want* to. In that sense, people with high levels of continuance commitment feel stuck or trapped, which does not fulfil the need for belonging and reflects a poor relationship. Throughout this chapter, our discussion focuses primarily on the benefits of affective commitment. In some cases, we examine the consequences of continuance commitment as well, because understanding the effects of staying for the wrong reasons can sometimes be just as informative.[†]

To reiterate, affective commitment involves feelings of an emotional attachment and identification with an organization, whereas continuance commitment emerges because of a lack of available alternative or the costs of leaving. These two forms of attachment are so fundamental that their effects go beyond the workplace. One

[†] Meyer and Allen also include retaining membership of the organization out of a sense of obligation as a third component of commitment, which they referred to as "normative commitment," but this is of little relevance to our discussion.

example of this is the existence of continuance commitment in marital relationships. The absence of a universal health-insurance system in the United States leaves many people dependent on their spouses or partners for their health insurance, and it illustrates how the lack of available alternatives might lead to harmful decisions, such as staying in a marriage when you would rather be elsewhere. In an enormous study of 17,388 married people over four years, Heeju Sohn showed that people whose only health insurance came from their partners were significantly less likely to get divorced. Perhaps predictably, this effect was worse for females, given pay inequities that so many women continue to face.[9] Although Sohn's primary lessons from these findings relate to health-policy issues, they highlight how continuance commitment in the form of a lack of available alternatives can lead to bad decisions.

The benefits of belonging

Workplace attitudes

Consistent with Robert Cialdini's reciprocity principle that people feel an obligation to return favors, often with interest,[10] we can expect that when people believe that the organization meets their needs, they will want to reciprocate. In their research, Kyle Ehrhardt and Belle Rose Ragins investigated what happens when people feel that their need for positive relationships at work, what they referred to as relational attachment, were fulfilled.[11] In one of their studies, strong feelings of relational attachment among 312 full-time employees in the United States predicted affective commitment to the organization, citizenship behaviors, and work engagement one year later. Separate analyses based on 224 staff at small colleges in the United States showed that relational attachment fulfilment also predicted life satisfaction and affective commitment to the organization four weeks later.

There is also a very large literature focusing on the link between affective commitment and work attitudes, almost too large to summarize for this discussion. Suffice it to say that affective commitment is consistently and positively associated with career commitment, citizenship behaviors that help the organization, less work-family conflict, wanting to remain a member of the organization, fewer absences, as well as pay, coworker, supervisor, and promotion satisfaction.[12]

Work performance

I was once involved with an organization that had just taken on a new CEO. After the customary walk-about on day one, his first impression was that people were largely disengaged from their work. Having also noticed that many people kept family photos on their desks, he concluded that this must be the source of distraction. Consequently, he issued an edict: all pictures of family members were to be removed.

I always wondered just how negative that was; more than a decade later, we have a research-based answer to this question.

In a series of studies, Ashley Hardin and her colleagues turned the question away from the effects of organizational attachment to an organization, and showed that feeling closely attached to others, such as family members or close friends, can reduce unethical behavior at work.[13] Hardin et al. posited that being at work prompts people to focus on economic justifications for their decisions. However, having photographs nearby of people with whom they are emotionally close (such as family) reminds them that they are part of something valuable that transcends the organization, inspiring greater motivation to behave ethically. In one of Hardin et al.'s studies, the researchers counted the number of pictures of family and close others, while 181 supervisors rated the extent to which employees engaged in unethical behavior such as padding expense reports. Having photos of close others in their immediate work environment was associated with less unethical behavior. Greater confidence in this result is appropriate for at least two reasons. First, Hardin et al. showed that it was not just a matter of having pictures in general. Only photos of family members had this effect; having photos of the environment or other nonclose people did not influence unethical behavior. Second, other research shows that simply being together with someone close, such as a marital partner or child, led people to rate moral values as being more important.[14] That being said, maybe what the CEO really should have done is encourage more family photos?[‡]

Ehrhardt and Ragin went beyond work attitudes and investigated the effects of relational attachment on absenteeism and turnover.[15] Higher levels of relational attachment at work was associated with lower levels of absenteeism and turnover over the next year. Findings such as these emphasize the importance of high-quality, personal relationships at work given the financial costs associated with absenteeism and withdrawal.

Turning our attention from relational attachment with others to affective attachment to the organization, John Meyer and colleagues investigated the effects of affective commitment on the job performance of sixty-five unit managers of a food-service organization across Canada.[16] Each unit manager filled out a survey on their own commitment. Separately, their supervisors and district managers completed performance appraisals on the unit managers, which provided information on unit managers' training and management of their followers, verbal communication, and success in customer and public interactions. District managers also rated how promotable unit managers were, an important issue for organizational success given the constant need for leadership succession. Unit managers with higher levels of affective

[‡] Sometimes, real-life steps in and validates research. During his inauguration speech in 2019, Ukrainian President Volodymyr Zelensky humbly advised the people of Ukraine, "I would very much like for you to not have my portrait in your offices. No portraits! A president is not an icon, nor an idol. A president is not a portrait. Put photographs of your children there, instead. And before making any decision, look them in the eyes." Dowd, M. (March 5, 2022). Zelensky and Trump: Two performers, one hero. *New York Times*. https://www.nytimes.com/2022/03/05/opinion/zelensky-ukraine-trump.html

commitment received more positive performance appraisals and were evaluated as more promotable by their district managers.

The benefits of satisfying the need for belonging extend to new venture performance. Li-Qun Wei and colleagues theorized that the need for belonging among 152 new venture founders across China would have two important consequences. First, their need for belonging would initially predispose them to form their own communities that communicate and cooperate in resolving their needs.[§,17] Second, involvement in these communities would then lead to new venture success as measured by growth in sales, return on assets, and the extent to which they could fund the new venture from profits. Wei et al.'s assumptions were supported. Fulfilling single founders' need for belonging indirectly affected new venture performance two years later, when new founders established these cooperative communities. What make these findings even more important is that these effects were substantially stronger in the earlier stages of product development, arguably when their beneficial effects may be most important.

Well-being

Maslow's primary focus was always on how fulfilling the basic needs, including the need for love, affiliation, and belonging, affected mental health. Does fulling these needs through work and organizations offer the same benefits? Research focused at the individual and organizational level would say yes. Turning again to Ehrhardt and Ragins' research, relational attachment with others is associated with thriving and flourishing at work, as well as general happiness. Unsurprisingly, given what we know about leadership (see Chapter 2), the benefits of belongingness extend to relationships with leaders, inasmuch as experiencing a high-quality relationship with your leader is associated with better psychological well-being.[18]

Might some of these benefits be lost if people work remotely? Despite the seeming simplicity of the question, the answers are not straightforward. Research on how workplace interruptions, which seem to occur so naturally when working in close proximity to others, might be a "blessing in disguise" serves as one example.[19] Acknowledging that workplace interruptions hurt work performance and job satisfaction, Harshad Puranik and colleagues remind us that interruptions also create chance connections between people at work which can satisfy the need for belonging. To investigate this, they surveyed 111 US employees for 15 consecutive workdays. Both interruptions and feelings of belonging at work (expressed in survey items such as "since arriving at work, I felt connected to others") were measured each day at midday, with satisfaction assessed toward the end of the workday. Although interruptions left employees feeling more drained, these chance interactions also resulted

§ A process known as the *tertius iungens* orientation.

in greater feelings of belonging, which led to led to higher levels of job satisfaction toward the end of the workday. As we move toward an environment in which remote work is more prevalent, the concern about the benefits that might be lost from chance interactions will need to be carefully balanced against gains that might be achieved from fewer interactions.

Somewhat similar results emerged from research by Jessica Methot and her colleagues.[20] They found that "small talk" at work about nonwork-related topics—the kind of chats that allow for sharing information about any topic, from hobbies to family matters, but which also enable sharing of ideas that inspire creativity and innovation, were a mixed blessing. Although small talk disrupted concentration at work, it also had a positive effect on emotions and well-being. Together with Puranik et al.'s research, these results help to explain the findings from surveys conducted by R/GA (rga.com).[21] The agency's talent experience team conducted employee surveys in the first six months of the pandemic, and the results were generally positive: employees were satisfied with remote working, and at the time, 30 percent of managers thought that employees were more productive because they worked from home. Six months later, the situation was not as positive. Aside from difficulties in integrating new hires remotely, and the fact that employees were working much longer hours and experiencing the inevitable Zoom fatigue, one of the "pain points" identified by employees was "a lack of spontaneous interactions with colleagues."

Moving away from high-quality relationships, Coissard and colleagues studied the effects of feelings of belonging to the department (rather than the organization) on psychological well-being among 444 hospital employees in France.[22] Feelings of belonging to the department were associated with higher levels of personal fulfillment and lower levels of burnout. Shannon Currie and her colleagues focused on affective commitment in an intriguing context, namely 444 Canadian military personnel returning from a tour of duty in Afghanistan.[23] Currie et al. investigated whether feeling emotionally attached to the army upon return would mitigate any negative mental health consequences of having been deployed. Their findings reveal an intriguing role for affective commitment: feeling more affectively attached to the military postdeployment was associated with fewer posttraumatic stress symptoms, which then predicted fewer increases in alcohol consumption upon return from deployment.

Last, as I write this, I am working from home and have been doing so for twenty-four long months. Before the pandemic, I had never used Zoom. Now on most workdays, I use Zoom for meetings for at least a few hours each day, and most days, experience what I call "Zoom gloom" by the end of the day. Intriguingly, Andrew Bennett and his colleagues have now shown that the fatigue we experience from overuse of videoconferencing is real.[24] Videoconference fatigue is all about being worn out, with some aspects inherent in videoconferencing being more exhausting than others, such as the attention needed because fewer visual cues are available. As one participant in their study said about videoconference meetings: "Tired of being in them, extra tired after being in them" (334).

Their findings also offer some practical advice for avoiding this fatigue and remaining more connected to others as organizations continue to rely on remote work and individuals are compelled to use videoconferencing. First, timing matters. Longer meetings later in the afternoon are particularly draining, suggesting that people working remotely pay careful attention to how they schedule videoconferencing meetings. Second, one of the ways people protected themselves from fatigue during meetings was by using the mute option, but this could reduce the effectiveness of their participation. Intriguingly, people who felt they belonged did not need to use the mute function to avoid fatigue. The researchers suggest that enhancing employees' feelings of belonging during videoconferencing sessions (e.g., by creating opportunities for social chitchat) could go a long way to reducing videoconference fatigue and enhancing meeting productivity.

When belonging goes awry

There are at least two ways in which the feeling of belonging can go awry, and we will examine the effects of both. First, instead of being fulfilled, people's need for belonging are sometimes frustrated. To reflect this, researchers have introduced the notion of "thwarted belongingness," which captures situations in which the need to belong is greater than the actual experience of belonging and hence remains unfulfilled. Employees can also feel ostracized at work. Feeling ostracized may be worse than thwarted belonging because ostracism implies an intentional act by others to keep you apart from the group. Second, as noted earlier in this chapter, people can remain members of the organization for the wrong reasons,[25] such as when they are deeply dissatisfied yet choose to stay either because they risk losing too much (e.g., pensions, seniority) if they leave, or because of a lack of available alternatives. As such, we move from the bright side of affective commitment to an examination of the dark side of continuance commitment.

Work attitudes

Understanding the effects of telecommuting[**] could be informative, because more time spent telecommuting leaves fewer opportunities for meaningful personal contact with others at work. Any research findings on telecommuting could be especially

** Telecommuting predates remote work by about fifty years. Telecommuting was introduced by NASA scientist Jack Niles in 1972, who was working remotely on a complex scientific project for NASA. Part of Niles' motivation was to ensure he did not contribute to commuting problems amid oil and gas shortages. Use of the term *telecommuting* vs *remote work* seems more a matter of the timing (i.e., 1970s vs 2020) and proximal cause (i.e., oil and gas shortages vs public health consideration) for their implementation, rather than any meaningful or substantive difference. The history of telecommuting. *Allied.* https://www.allied telecom.net/the-history-of-telecommuting/

relevant given the endless list of major organizations (e.g., BP, Spotify, 3M, Twitter) that have already announced early in the pandemic that a mix of partial and fully remote work will become the norm.

In the larger context of 20 million people in the United States already involved in telecommuting by 2000,[26] Timothy Golden and John Veiga studied the effects of telecommuting on job satisfaction among 321 employees of a large US high-tech firm.[27] The more people telecommuted, the greater their job satisfaction. Intriguingly, this benefit only emerged for up to fifteen hours of telecommuting per week; telecommuting more than that yielded no further benefits. A later meta-analysis clarified this, showing that any benefits on coworker satisfaction turned negative at 2.5 days per week of telecommuting.[28] Presumably, the greater the amount of time spent telecommuting, the less time available for face-to-face interactions at work. The lesson from these studies is not whether we can specify the exact number of hours after which the benefits of telecommuting plateau, but rather that negative effects should be expected when telecommuting starts to limit interpersonal interactions. Going forward, findings like these provide guidelines about the successful implementation of remote work.

Feeling that you are intentionally being ostracized by others could trigger feelings of resentment. A recent meta-analysis of workplace ostracism confirms this is the case and points to the different ways in which the harmful effects of ostracism play out.[29] First, feeling ostracized is associated with lower job satisfaction and perceptions of unfairness in the organization. Given this result, it is not surprising that feeling ostracized at work is also associated with lower affective attachment to the organization, effects which lasted for at least six weeks.[30] Second, given the uncomfortable feelings aroused by ostracism, one logical response would be to do what you can to exit the situation, and studies consistently show that feeling ostracized at work is associated with thoughts about quitting the organization.[31]

Last, as evident from the meta-analysis by Meyer et al., continuance commitment is negatively associated with dissatisfaction in myriad forms: pay, peer, promotion, supervision, and in terms of overall work.[32] Clearly, staying in the organization when you would rather be elsewhere has a negative effect on work attitudes. Faced with employees who have announced that they wish to exit the organization, this would question widespread organizational strategies to try and keep these employees leaving by offering additional compensation if no changes are made to organizational conditions.

Work performance

"If you can't join them, beat them"! This title from a study conducted by Jean Twenge and colleagues more than twenty years ago provided early insight into just how negative the performance-related consequences of thwarted belonging might be.[33] Underlying their five experiments was a considerable body of research already showing that social exclusion is consistently associated with aggressive behaviors by children, adolescents, and adults. In several of Twenge et al.'s ingenious studies, students first filled out a standard personality questionnaire, and then wrote an essay either for or against abortion. Students then evaluated what they thought was another student's essay that provided the opposite perspective; in reality, these other essays had been written by the researchers. After that, students received false feedback about their own essay. Some were led to believe that based on their personality, they would be alone in the future. For example, these students were told:

> "You're the type who will end up alone later in life. You may have friends and relationships now, but by your mid 20s most of these will have drifted away. You may even marry or have several marriages, but these are likely to be short-lived and not continue into your 30s. Relationships don't last, and when you're past the age where people are constantly forming new relationships, the odds are you'll end up being alone more and more."

The others were told that their belongingness needs would be satisfied (e.g., "You're likely to have a long a stable marriage ... the odds are you'll always have friends and people who care about you"). The third group received no feedback about relationships but were informed that their personality suggested that they might experience misfortune in the years to come (e.g., "You're likely to be accident prone later in life.... Even if you haven't been accident prone before, these things will show up later in life, and the odds are you will have a lot of accidents").

All students then received negative feedback on their essays that presumably came from the other participant, which included the comment, "One of the worst essays I have read." Last, students were informed that the other student had applied for a very competitive position as a research assistant, were asked to be open-minded and evaluate that student on a 1–10 scale in terms of friendliness, and indicate whether they personally would hire them. The results across these studies were unambiguous. Students who were led to believe that their belongingness needs would be thwarted in the future rated the other person significantly lower (25.78 out of 100[††]) than those who believed their needs would be satisfied (51.56 out of 100) or that they would suffer misfortune (56.30 out of 100).

In an extension of these studies, students took part in a group game and then received false feedback: They were either told "I have good news for you—everyone else chose you as someone they would like to work with," or "I hate to tell you this, but no one chose you as someone they wanted to work with." Those who felt rejected acted significantly more aggressively against the person who they believed had rejected them.

[††] These data are from Twenge et al.'s study one.

These studies show that when students suspect that their needs for belonging are being thwarted, they do not sit idly by. Instead, they reciprocate. In these studies, students evaluated those who threatened their belonging needs much more harshly when they believed they were applying for a job; and when given the opportunity, acted much more aggressively toward them. More importantly, these experiments made it clear that the negative responses were not a function of *any* bad news. After all, there were no negative responses to learning you would suffer general misfortune, only to learning that you would be alone. Thus, the results from Twenge et al.'s research are important and startling—but do they generalize to real-world organizations?

This is an important question. While responding to social exclusion with aggression might be understandable in a laboratory, it could be self-defeating at work where cooperation and coordination are essential for effective performance. Yet one study shows that these negative and self-defeating effects do carryover to work contexts.[34] In phase one of this study, employees from a Dutch clinical laboratory completed surveys assessing their feelings of actual and desired belonging. In phase two, supervisors provided ratings of how much employees engaged in behaviors that hurt themselves or helped the team. The findings were somewhat ironic: people who felt their belonging needs were not being met were more likely to engage in behaviors that undermined themselves in the eyes of their team members, likely increasing the possibility that they would be further excluded from the team.

A different response to being shunned at work would be to accept the implicit message and quit, resulting in higher levels of turnover. Jane O'Reilly and her team tested this proposition among 858 employees of a large Canadian organization.[35] Employees who felt ostracized were more likely to quit the organization within the next three years. A comparison of the negative effects of ostracism vs bullying on turnover highlights just how negative ostracism is. Even though we know that workplace bullying leads to turnover among healthcare workers,[36] the effects of ostracism on turnover were much higher than bullying behaviors such as teasing, embarrassing, demeaning, and humiliating others.

Several studies confirm that the harmful effects of thwarted belonging do not stop at individuals who feels left behind. First, Longqi Yang and colleagues conducted an ingenious and large-scale study testing the effects of moving to remote work during the pandemic.[37] Based on the premise that moving to remote work could stifle the fulfilment of social and belonging needs, they used data from all 61,182[‡‡] Microsoft employee in the United States for the three months before a work-from-home mandate was imposed by the company on March 4, 2020, and the three months that followed the transition to remote work. Given the importance of social and collaboration networks for productivity, their findings should give some pause for concern. Remote work decreased the number of different groups that employees were connected to, the time employees spent in cross-group collaboration, and the extent of collaboration

‡‡ The only exclusions were senior leadership or teams dealing with what the company regarded as especially sensitive data.

between members of different groups. As the researchers observe, collaboration networks became more siloed, which they suggest would limit employees' ability to access new information. Intriguingly, these findings are consistent with a survey of 4,363 professional in the United States that was conducted by LinkedIn between May 22 and June 4, 2021.[38] When asked why they would return to work, the most frequent response (63 percent) was for in-person collaboration.

Second, Liu-Qin Yang et al. questioned whether feeling thwarted would leave people less willing to engage in behaviors that would help the members of the team that excluded them, and extended this to safety-related behaviors that could place the entire team in jeopardy.[39] In their study of 520 frontline employees engaged in the production of hazardous electrical transformers and switchgears in China, employees who felt their belonging needs were thwarted were less likely both to comply with existing safety standards and to expend any extra effort to enhance safety in the workplace. Thus, feelings of thwarted belonging by one employee could compromise the safety of entire teams.

Changing focus, what happens to performance when you feel stuck or trapped in the organization for all the wrong reasons? We already read about Meyer et al.'s research on sixty-five unit managers of a food-service organization, which showed the benefits of affective commitment for job performance and promotability. Their study also had employees complete a survey assessing continuance commitment, allowing for a comparison of the effects of the two forms of attachment.[40] The effects for continuance commitment were reversed: employees who felt that they stayed in the organization because of a lack of available alternatives or the costs associated with leaving received lower job performance and promotability ratings from their managers. Studies such as these serve as an important reminder that it is not *just* belonging to the organization that it important. *Why* one belongs is what makes the difference!

Well-being

Feeling your belonging needs are thwarted can hurt well-being. Tyler Stillman and his colleagues conducted several experiments with undergraduate students, all of which showed that social exclusion resulted in questioning the meaning of one's life.[41] Feeling a lack of belonging at work also has physical effects and is associated with somatic symptoms such as stomach problems and headaches one week later.[42]

Going beyond thwarted belonging, Yang Chen and Shuang Li focused on the effects of workplace ostracism on an issue of growing importance to organizational scholars and practitioners alike, namely sleep quality.[43] This study is important, as it identified one way in which ostracism exerts its negative effects. Specifically, feeling ostracized left employees unable to disengage psychologically from work. Instead, it left them thinking and worrying about work much of the time, and it was this rumination that interfered with sleep quality. Given the importance of sleep quality to overall physical and psychological well-being (and job performance), the widespread effects of workplace ostracism become difficult to ignore.

Belonging to the organization for the wrong reasons also hurts well-being. While research on the topic is somewhat limited, one small-scale study in Canada showed that continuance commitment was associated with lower self-esteem and lower self-efficacy beliefs[§§] among sixty employees of a food-products organization.[44] A larger study of 1,396 nurses from Hungary, Italy, the United Kingdom, and the United States extended these findings, showing that continuance commitment, which leaves people feeling stuck or even trapped, was also associated with anxiety.[45]

John Meyer and colleagues took the issue of affective and continuance commitment a step further. Instead of looking at the effects of continuance commitment in isolation, they developed six different commitment profiles that reflect peoples' standing on affective, continuance, and normative commitment.[***] From our perspective, the profile of most interest is people whose continuance commitment is dominant (i.e., high in continuance commitment and low in the other two dimensions[†††]).[46] Findings from 402 employees working in different Canadian organizations revealed that psychological well-being and positive affect (e.g., feeling interested, excited, proud) were lowest among this continuance dominant group, as well as the "uncommitted" (i.e., low on all three commitment dimensions) groups. Taking account of all three commitment dimensions simultaneously provides a more nuanced understanding of the harmful effects of feeling attached to the organization because you feel you have to rather than because you want to.

Last, this discussion would not be complete without considering how the pandemic, with its prolonged and mandated stay-at-home orders and increased numbers of people working from home, has affected loneliness and well-being. Returning to the issue of personal relationships at work, Stephanie Andel and her colleagues conducted an intensive study of 265 US employees who responded to surveys each week for eight consecutive weeks.[47] The first questionnaires were distributed on March 20, 2020, shortly after the declaration of the global pandemic. A major focus of their study was the frequency with which the participants were engaged in telecommuting over the past week as it reflects the amount of time isolated from coworkers. Their study showed that the more employees engaged in telecommuting, the higher the feelings of work-related loneliness, which then resulted in depressive symptoms. Findings like this are important because workplace loneliness indirectly affects individual and team performance.[48]

[§§] Self-efficacy reflects the belief that given sufficient effort, you can be successful in what you are doing.

[***] Normative commitment refers to employees' belief that they have an obligation, including a moral obligation, to remain members of the organization.

[†††] The other profiles are "uncommitted" (low commitment on all three dimensions), "moderate commitment" and "low-moderate commitment" (on all three dimensions), "fully committed" (high commitment on all three dimensions), and "affective/normative dominant" (but low on continuance commitment).

Thus, an appropriate way to conclude is with a thought from Sherry Turkle, who has studied the intersection of technology, mental health, and relationships for four decades. If the pandemic has taught us anything, Turkle reminds us, it is that people need people and people need relationships.[49]

How does belonging exert its effects?

Belonging exerts indirect effects

So far, we have seen that feelings of belonging at work enhance work attitudes, work performance, and well-being, while thwarted belonging and ostracism hurt these same outcomes. Feelings of belonging also transmit the effects of leadership on these important outcomes. One reason for this is that leadership behaviors, as well as organizational policies and practices, provide implicit and often unintentional signals to employees as to whether they are valued and part of the group or organization, and they then respond in kind. Research on the effects of high-quality and uncivil leadership illustrate this. One study used data from 247 supervisor-employee dyads working in a high-tech products organization in Canada to investigate the effects of positive leadership. They showed that servant leadership was associated with greater satisfaction of relatedness needs in the first phase of their research.[50] Two months later, employees who were satisfied with their relatedness needs received higher ratings on their citizenship behaviors from their supervisors. Higher satisfaction with relatedness needs was also associated with maintaining above-average attendance. Separately, Sandy Hershcovis and colleagues hypothesized that because they are taken by employees as signals that they are valued less and not a part of the group or organization, uncivil or hostile leadership behaviors would threaten their well-being.[51] Remarkably, Hershcovis and colleagues showed that one instance of supervisor incivility was enough to threaten feelings of belonging and to set this chain in process.

Yaping Gong and colleagues go further in clarifying how affective commitment to the organization transmits the effects of different types of HR systems on firm performance.[52] To do so, Gong et al. contrasted the roles of affective vs continuance commitment and differentiated between performance and maintenance-oriented HR systems. Performance-oriented HR systems include practices aimed at fulfilling employees' higher-order needs, such as participation in decision-making. By contrast, maintenance-oriented HR systems focus on fulfilling extrinsic needs such as security and recognition. Findings based on 2,148 managers from 463 Chinese organizations showed that performance-oriented HR practices affected profit, sales, and asset growth, as well as market share and labor productivity, through affective, but not continuance, commitment. In contrast, maintenance-oriented HR practices were associated with continuance commitment, but continuance commitment had no effects on firm performance. The fact that this study was based on managers rather than employees should not be overlooked. Feelings of belonging are not just important for employees; they affect people throughout all levels of the organization.

Last, one study on the effects of workplace ostracism by a supervisor on employee creativity further illustrates how these effects emerge.[53] The study was based on the idea that ostracism by a supervisor impedes the very purpose of leadership, which is to provide employees with the resources needed for job performance, promote a culture characterized by trust, intergroup cooperation, and creative psychological engagement, all of which facilitate creative performance. In phase one of this study, 308 financial-products salespeople provided ratings of the extent to which they were ostracized by their supervisors. Two months later, employees reported on access to task resources and opportunities for creative engagement. After another two months elapsed, supervisors rated employees' creative performance. Their findings supported the indirect effects of supervisor ostracism. Being ostracized by a supervisor hurt creative behaviors by limiting access to necessary resources and opportunities for creative behaviors.

Feeling you belong shapes the way you experience your work

There are so many examples of how affiliation and attachment shape our lives outside of the organization. Sebastian Junger, journalist and author of *The perfect storm: A true story of men against the sea*, illustrates this idea in asking searching questions about war.[54] Why is it that some people who return safely from life-threatening wars choose to go back? Why did many people who lived in underground railway stations during the bombing of London claim afterwards that they missed the communal living, even though more than forty thousand civilians died during the war? Why it is that PTSD rates following wars have differed across time, and now differ dramatically between countries? Citing scientific studies, the answer to Junger may be straightforward: "the problem doesn't seem to be the trauma on the battlefield so much as re-entry into society." In Junger's telling, soldiers return to societies that lack the closeness, cooperation, interpersonal reliance, and loyalty that marked their lives on the battlefield, and Currie et al.'s research on Canadian soldiers returning from Afghanistan supports this.[55] As one specific example, Junger asks why the PTSD rate in Israel is only 1 percent, vastly lower than other countries that have fought modern wars. Junger suggests that because most members of the society have military experience and their wars take place close to home, reintegration into society is made easier.[‡‡‡]

Feelings of belonging shape organizational experiences as well. One of the most stable findings on work and well-being is that excessive workplace demands can

‡‡‡ Intriguingly, Junger questions whether the reflexive comment, "Thank you for your service," on meeting a member of the military in the United States reinforces just how psychologically and geographically distant combat veterans remain.

hurt well-being; Wladislaw Rivkin and his colleagues were interested to see whether feelings of belonging might buffer these negative effects.[56] In an intricate study, sixty people working in Germany first completed a survey assessing their affective commitment to the organization. For each of the next ten workdays, they completed questionnaires about workplace demands that taxed their self-control by midday. They then completed additional surveys about their feelings of emotional depletion and need for recovery each evening. The findings from this study are compelling. For people who felt a sense of affective attachment to the organization, daily work demands had no effect on emotional depletion or the need for recovery. In contrast, for those with a low sense of attachment, daily demands assessed at midday were associated with greater depletion and need for recovery that same evening. Rivkin et al. conclude that organizations should do what they can to strengthen employees' affective commitment as a way of enhancing employees' well-being. However, this blanket conclusion may be premature. As we see later in this chapter, affective commitment can sometimes be counterproductive.

Feelings of belonging within the organization also shape the effects of management practices on company productivity. To test this, Kamal Birdi et al. studied management practices and productivity among 308 UK companies over a twenty-two-year period.[57] Two management practices—namely empowering people by pushing responsibility down to the level at which the work is conducted and extensive (rather than skill-specific) training (which we will discuss in Chapter 6)—enhanced productivity. More importantly, the benefits of empowerment and extensive training were greatest for employees in highly functioning teams in which members worked interdependently and could allocate work tasks among team members, practices which would clearly signal to members that they belonged in that team.

Similar findings from a study of 216 autonomous business units in Chile reinforce this explanation. Employees provided evaluations of the use of different HR practices[§§§] and their own affective commitment.[58] In addition, unit managers provided information on customer satisfaction, product/service quality, and work unit productivity. Again, the benefits of all five HR practices on business-unit performance were greater for employees higher in affective commitment.

Gender and attachment to the organization

Dating back decades, we have been told that people respond to external threats with the "fight-or-flight response." Further entrenching the idea that this as a normal human reaction is the claim that it is a physiological response. About twenty years ago, Shelley Taylor challenged this idea.[59] Taylor pointed to a long body of research showing that faced with stress, women are more likely to respond with caregiving and

[§§§] The practices included the type of selection methods used, performance evaluation and training, job descriptions, compensation and incentives, and empowerment practices.

affiliation, and that this was a function of different oxycontin responses to stress in males and females. As a result, Taylor and her colleagues suggested that the fight-*or*-flight response is more characteristic of males, while women are more likely to exhibit a "tend-*and*-befriend" response to stress. Subsequent research has supported the notion that women are more likely to use a tend-and-befriend response to stress.[60] Given this, might women be more predisposed to seek attachment to organizations than men?

Despite the seeming appeal of Taylor's idea, and the ubiquity of work stress, results regarding gender differences at the level of affective commitment to organizations are mixed. Some earlier research showed that affective commitment was higher among men.[61] However, a more recent meta-analysis of thirty-three studies shows mixed results: where significant gender differences did emerge, men showed higher affective commitment in sixteen of the studies, with women showing higher commitment in fourteen.[62] What this suggests is that there are no individual or biobehavioral factors that predispose men or women to experience higher levels of attachment to the organization. Instead, any differences in the level of affective commitment between men and women are likely a result of the local context.

Where gender does play a role is in the development of affective commitment. One study of 531 elementary school teachers from thirty schools in Malaysia showed that principals' distributed leadership, which emphasizes sharing formal and informal leadership responsibilities between principals, assistant principals, and head teachers, was associated with teachers' affective commitment to change.[63] However, this effect was much stronger for female teachers. Other studies find similar gender effects. For example, a separate study of 522 knowledge workers in Malaysia showed that the benefits of a knowledge-sharing culture on affective commitment were greater for women. At the same time, the negative effects of unfair promotion practices on affective commitment were greater for females as well.[64] DuckJung Shin and colleagues' study of 6,320 employees from 104 small and medium-sized retail businesses in Spain showed that opportunities to engage in professional development, receive relevant information about profitability and costs from the organization, and participate in decision-making were all associated with employees' affective commitment.[65] In each case, the effects were again stronger for females.

Jayasingam et al. offer one explanation for this gender effect. They suggest that because women have historically been subjected to less favorable working conditions than men, such as gender-based salary gaps and access to leadership positions, women respond more favorably to organizations that provide positive working conditions. In turn, women then reciprocate by offering their loyalty and commitment to the organization.

Culture and affective attachment to the organization

Differences in the level of affective attachment

To understand whether affective commitment to the organization differs across countries and regions, John Meyer and colleagues conducted a meta-analysis on surveys collected from no fewer than 433,129 individuals from more than fifty countries.[66] The average affective commitment score across countries was 58.4 percent, and ranged from a low of 43.4 percent in Finland to a high of 68.8 percent in Israel. In order to make sense of the differences across so many countries, Meyer et al. classified each country into one of the nine different geographical regions and compared scores from the different regions to those in the United States. Affective commitment was lower in countries in Germanic Europe and Latin America than the United States, and higher (in ascending order) in Confucian Asia, Eastern Europe, the Middle East, and Southern Asia than the United States.[****] Meyer et al. suggested that two different cultural dimensions explain these findings. First, affective commitment is higher in societies characterized by embeddedness, reflecting the extent to which people's meaning in life comes from social relationships and identification with the larger group and its values.[67] Second affective commitment to the organization is lower in societies that emphasize the importance of its members seeking emotionally positive experiences, what Schwartz refers to as autonomy orientation.

Meyer et al. then examined whether country or regional characteristics influence continuance commitment. To do so, they used survey data from 199,831 people across forty-four countries. Two features of the findings were noteworthy. First, the range of continuance-commitment scores across countries was much lower than that seen for affective commitment, extending from a low of 48.9 in Australia to a high of 57.5 in the Netherlands. Second, none of the differences in continuance commitment between countries or regions was explained by cultural values. One probable reason for the difference between affective and continuance commitment is that affective commitment arises from a pride in being identified with the values of the organizations, while continuance commitment is instrumental in nature, as a result of which individuals' values are less important.

Differences in the function of affective attachment

There is no shortage of research investigating the effects of belonging in different countries. As examples, studies based in China show that feeling that you are a part of the organization results in engaging in safety behaviors that help others[68] and higher

[****] Sub-Saharan Africa and Latin America were not included because of insufficient data for analysis.

levels of work engagement.[69] Likewise, higher levels of affective commitment to the organization were associated with lower levels of employee theft among 120 employees and their supervisors in South Korea.[70] In contrast, research from China shows that workplace ostracism is associated with lower family satisfaction and higher work-family conflict,[71] as well as behaviors that hurt the organization such as intentionally working more slowly, surfing the internet, being rude or argumentative to others, or covering up mistakes.[72]

Thus, while this only reflects a small sample of the many studies conducted, the question is not whether belongingness is important in some countries but not others. Instead, the issue is whether the effects of belonging on organizational outcomes might be stronger in some countries or cultures than others. Meyer et al.'s research showed that the effects of affective commitment on citizenship behaviors, job performance, and thoughts about staying with the organization were stronger outside of North America.[73]. However, no regional differences emerged in the effects of affective commitment on other organizational outcomes in their study of 50,146 employees, suggesting that the benefits of affective commitment are not strongly affected by country or regional differences.

Akanksha Bedi was interested in whether and how national culture shapes the effects of workplace ostracism.[74] Bedi's research was based on the notion that harmony, interdependence, and strategies that de-emphasize conflict in resolving interpersonal conflicts were more likely to be valued in collectivist-oriented cultures. In contrast, individual self-fulfillment would be a greater concern in individualistically oriented cultures. As a result, she expected that any effects of workplace ostracism would be worse in individualistic cultures because of greater sensitivity to individual mistreatment. Bedi's study of 27,968 employees provided some support for her argument. In general, workplace ostracism harmed citizenship behaviors directed at helping the organizations, and the negative effects were worse in individualistic than collectivistic cultures.

Taken together, therefore, any effects of affective commitment may be stronger in collectivist cultures. This fact should not be surprising given the affiliative nature of affective commitment, and should alert management in collectivist societies to the added benefits that might accrue to higher levels of affective commitment.

TMGT: Can we have too much belonging in organizations?

Earlier thinkers such as Maslow and Alderfer prioritized belonging as a critical step in attaining mental health, and as we see in this chapter, a greater sense of belonging to a team or the organization fosters better well-being. But are there situations in which positive relationships, or strong feelings of belonging to a team or an organization, exert negative consequences?

An earlier study of the effects of work-family conflict on marital satisfaction among fifty-one employed mothers in Canada suggests that this might be the case.[75] As the researchers had expected, experiencing work-family conflict was associated with marital dissatisfaction three months later. Unexpectedly, however, receiving high levels of support from family members who cared about you worsened the effects of work-family conflict on marital dissatisfaction. Other studies taking a different approach have uncovered similar findings. For example, Ehrhardt and Ragins showed that providing levels of support that exceed those needed are experienced as intrusive and hurt relational attachment in the organization.[76]

Several explanations help us make sense of these counterintuitive findings. Very high levels of support can be intrusive,[77] foster dependence on the source of the support, and be demotivating.[78] In addition, the benefits of support from others are optimal when they are reciprocated.[79] These explanations have considerable implications for organizational decision-makers: obtaining the benefits of supportive behaviors at work is not just a function of how much support is received. Instead, we need to match the belonging needs of the people involved to the amount and type of support provided.

Research on how people react when they see close colleagues treated unfairly also questions whether we can be too connected to others at work. Joel Brockner and colleagues posited that witnessing others being treated unfairly in terms of compensation when they are laid off could hurt the witnesses' affective attachment, especially if witnesses identified closely with the people being laid off.[80] The results of their study of 504 salesclerks or store managers were clear-cut. Postlayoff affective-commitment scores for employees who identified with people who were laid off and treated unfairly averaged 68.2. Commitment scores for all others were greater than 90.[††††] A subsequent study of 1,600 employees and managers in a large US manufacturing company extended these results, showing that close personal contact with people who were laid off resulted in greater sickness absences among managers and professionals.[81] Yes, watching someone close to you being treated unfairly is enough to make you feel sick.

Other studies point to other circumstances under which high levels of organizational attachment can hurt well-being. In two different studies in the United States, experiencing workplace incivility predicted burnout two months later, and this effect was more pronounced for people who scored higher in affective commitment to the organization.[82] In other research, the effects of incivility on negative mood and guilt were worse for employees with higher levels of affective commitment.[83]

Dana Kabat-Farr and colleagues offer two explanations for these counterintuitive effects. People who feel attached to their organizations are less likely to minimize acts of incivility, and more likely to blame themselves for destructive behaviors such as incivility. In addition, employees with higher levels of affective attachment may feel

†††† The three groups (and their scores) are low compensation and high identification (90.47), high compensation and high identification (99.3), and high compensation and low identification (98.93).

more disappointed when leaders in their organization behave badly, leaving themselves vulnerable to burnout and negative mood.

Some research has gone beyond personal relationships and examined "multiplex relationships" at work, where employees have both personal and business relationships with the same person. Multiplex workplace relationships are widespread, making this an important topic.[84] Moreover, research from LinkedIn suggests that multiplex relationships are valued by employees.[85] In the survey conducted by LinkedIn discussed earlier in this chapter, 4,362 US professionals were asked why they would return to the workplace amid the pandemic. The two most frequent responses offered was "collaborating on work in person"; 63 percent) and "socializing with colleagues and clients"; 62 percent). Research by Jessica Methot and her colleagues in the United States suggest that multiplex relationships may, in their words, be a mixed blessing."[86] The positive emotions and trust engendered by multiplex relationships were associated with higher ratings of work performance by supervisors. At the same time, the effort involved in maintaining multiplex relationships can be emotionally draining and detract from work performance.

While acknowledging that sharing important information for work performance would be easier in multiplex relationships, Shah and colleagues suggested that this was an instance of TMGT. Having too few multiplex relationships would limit work performance. At the same time, too many multiplex relationships could be overly demanding and have diminishing returns on work performance.[87] To test this, Shah et al. conducted different studies in the United States with corporate employees of an international bank, and with middle managers in a part-time MBA program. The results of these two studies are clear and depicted in Figure 4.1. Too few multiplex relationships are associated with poorer performance. The optimal number of multiplex relationships lies somewhere between five and seven, after which multiplex relationships bring diminishing returns to work performance. The reasons for these diminishing returns include the mixed and sometimes conflicting goals of emotional and

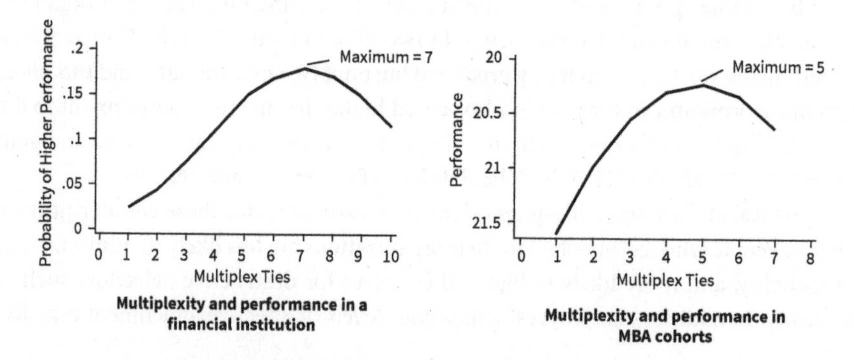

Fig. 4.1 Effects of multiplex relationships on performance.

Republished with permission from Sage Publications Inc. Journals, from Shah, N.P. et al. (2017). Examining the overlap: Individual performance benefits of multiplex relationships. *Management Communication Quarterly, 31*, 5–38; permission conveyed through Copyright Clearance Center, Inc.

instrumental relationships that can create tension and detract attention from work-related issues. In addition, the cognitive and emotional energy required to maintain each additional multiplex relationship may not exceed the benefits they provide.

More recent research paints an even darker picture, suggesting that belonging to a team or an organization can become so important that people choose to suspend their better judgment and behave in unethical ways. One study investigated whether employees who were highly committed to the organization might be more willing to comply with directives of dubious ethical intent. In an experiment with 107 secondary-school teachers from Germany, teachers who were highly committed to the organization were more likely to follow discriminatory directives from management during a hiring simulation, by favorably evaluating and selecting applicants from a demographic group clearly preferred by their school principal.[88] A second study with 169 secondary school teachers in the same German state explained why they would do this. Essentially, higher commitment to the organization predisposed teachers to be more submissive to organizational authorities. When they were then asked to choose which of four teachers should be hired, those teachers were more willing to abide by managers' discriminatory preferences.

Even though these findings do not suggest that highly committed employees or managers consciously behaved unethically, they do have important implications for organizations and their leaders. First, as the researchers emphasized, leaders must be aware that loyalty can be a "double-edged sword."[89] Second, leaders must be made aware of how even harmless or ambiguous directives can be misinterpreted by highly committed employees, and of the ethical ramifications of this. At the same time, highly committed employees should be reminded that the best expression of their loyalty is not blind or silent obedience. Instead, these employees should be actively encouraged and rewarded for engaging in what US civil rights icon John Lewis referred to as "good trouble," which would include speaking up in ethically fraught situations for the organization's benefit.[90]

Interventions to enhance affective commitment

Choosing which organizational intervention to showcase in the chapters on leadership and autonomy presented a challenge—which of the many that have been conducted should be left out? Choosing an intervention to illustrate how to enhance affective commitment poses a different challenge. A search of the literature and conversations with colleagues suggests that no interventions exist that directly target employees' affective commitment to the organization. However, we know that different forms of high-quality leadership are associated with affective commitment.[91] One meta-analysis of 102 studies yielded a significant link between transformational leadership and affective commitment; a separate analysis of 45 studies yielded positive associations between charismatic leadership and affective commitment.[92] Thus, we turn to an intervention I conducted with my colleagues Kevin Kelloway and Tom

Weber (see Chapter 2) that showed the indirect effects of transformational leadership training on sales performance.[93] In that study, the effects of transformational leadership on sales performance were transmitted through employees' affective commitment.

In this project, managers from nine bank branches were assigned randomly to receive the transformational-leadership training, and their employees were unaware they were doing so. Managers from eleven other branches were unaware of the project at the time, as were employees of all twenty branches. More details on how we conducted the training, and our rationale for doing so, are available in a separate article I wrote with Kevin Kelloway.[94]

Prior to the transformational leadership training, all employees from the twenty branches completed surveys assessing their affective commitment to the organization. Employees were also asked to complete feedback surveys on their managers' transformational leadership and were told that this was part of their managers' normal evaluation. Managers from the nine branches then received one full day of group-based training about transformational and transactional leadership. To begin, participants identified the best and worst leaders they had ever encountered, and the instructor related these different behaviors to the appropriate transformational- or transactional-leadership dimensions. After that, the group received a more formal presentation and discussion of transformational leadership and its known effects from research. Throughout the day, participants were placed into groups where they could discuss and role-play the different behaviors, and toward the end of the day, they returned to their groups and set goals for their future behaviors. At the conclusion, participants were encouraged to maintain contact with other managers who had received training to continually discuss ideas, successes, and frustrations.

The day after the training, each participant who had received the leadership training received one-hour of coaching based on employees' pre-training 360-degree feedback, with the coaching couched in terms of the transformational leadership behaviors discussed during the training. These meetings were repeated once a month for the following three months, at which stage the program was concluded. The idea for these individual booster sessions was taken from clinical psychological treatments and is discussed in *The science of leadership*.[95]

The intervention worked! Branch managers who had received the leadership training and booster sessions were rated by their employees as higher on transformational leadership than those who did not receive training. More importantly, the changes in transformational leadership behaviors resulted in significantly higher levels of affective commitment for employees in the nine branches whose managers had received the training. In turn, improvements in employees' affective commitment then resulted in increased sales performance. Thus, while it does not seem feasible to set up interventions that directly target affective commitment, targeting the foundations of affective commitment such as high-quality leadership may be enough to bring about changes in affective commitment necessary for better organizational functioning.

As evident elsewhere in this book, changing performance-oriented management practices such as autonomy or participation in decision making (see Chapter 3) and extensive training (see Chapter 5) could have the same effects on affective commitment.[96] However, the effort, cost, and resources required for systemic changes in management practices may outweigh those of one day of group-based leadership training and four one-hour booster sessions.

A special case: Does it matter whether my manager thinks I am committed or not?

So far, we have seen that commitment matters—positive relationships with others, and affective attachment to the organization, influence employees' work attitudes, work performance, and well-being. In contrast, feeling ostracized and continuance commitment exert negative effects on work attitudes, performance, and well-being. Some researchers have asked a related but different question: does your manager's perceptions of your commitment make a difference? This is an important question. Managers continually use formal (e.g., 360-degree feedback) and informal (e.g., first- and second-hand conversations) information to make important decisions about employees' pay raises, team and task assignments, and promotability decisions. What if these decisions are influenced not just by employee performance, but also by managers' perceptions of their employees' commitment? Findings from this research offers some important lessons.

In one study, Lynn McFarlane Shore and colleagues surveyed 231 managers and 339 of their employees, all of whom worked for the same large multinational organization in the United States.[97] The first issue Shore et al. investigated was what information managers use in developing their perceptions of employees' affective and continuance commitment. Employees who were viewed by their managers as complying with normal job requirements, and voluntarily helping the organization, were viewed as having higher levels of affective commitment by their managers. In contrast, being older, having spent more time in the current job and organization, and having more education, which may signal to management that employees may have difficulty finding jobs elsewhere, led managers to see them as having higher levels of continuance commitment.[98]

Shore et al. then investigated whether managers' perceptions of their employees' affective and continuance commitment make a difference. As they had expected, the more managers believed employees exhibited affective commitment, the more highly managers rated their potential and promotability one year later. The effects of managers' perceptions of continuance commitment were reversed. The higher managers rated employees on continuance commitment, the lower they rated the employees on promotability and potential. Moreover, the more managers thought their employees were motivated by continuance commitment, the less likely they were to satisfy requests from those employees for issues such as salary increases and access to training and feedback.

Ted Shore and colleagues returned to this question just over a decade later. Again, they first sought to uncover why managers would see some employees as high in affective or continuance commitment, and others not.[99] Based on data from 490 leader-follower dyads from a US commercial building supply company, high-performing employees were seen by their managers as being affectively committed to the organization. In contrast, low-performing employees were seen by their managers as having high levels of continuance commitment. As in their earlier study, demographic factors such as age and length of tenure in the organization were again associated with managers believing that employees had higher levels of continuance commitment.

Of greater practical importance, however, managers behaved differently toward employees based on whether managers thought that employees were motivated by affective or continuance commitment. Employees whose managers thought they were higher on affective commitment were more likely to be rewarded for good performance and less likely to be punished for reasons unrelated to performance. In contrast, employees' whose managers thought they were higher on continuance commitment were less likely to receive rewards for good performance and also more likely to be punished for reasons unrelated to performance.

What these two studies tell us is both interesting and important. Managers' beliefs as to whether their employees feel affectively attached to the organization stem from actions taken by employees, such as their citizenship behaviors and job performance. Moreover, signals as to whether employees have available alternatives predict managers' perceptions of continuance commitment. Once formed, these managerial perceptions are of considerable consequence for employees, as they shape how managers respond to employees and how managers rate their employees in terms of potential and promotability.

Conclusion

In case you are still not convinced

First, a sense of belonging is clearly important for employees, and affective commitment is important to both employees and organizations. A concern right now is that both may be threatened by enormous social change brought about by the COVID-19 pandemic. While it is too soon to have studies from which we can know more about these effects, research on how the Great Recession influenced affective commitment is instructive.[100] Based on representative samples of 2,354 US employees pre- and 2,322 employees post-recession, affective commitment declined significantly after the Great Recession. In practical terms, the number of employees who said they were uncommitted increased by 5.5 percent after the Great Recession. Given that the COVID-19 pandemic caused more personal dislocation, job initial losses, and greater disruption to the global financial system than the Great Recession, optimistic predictions about postpandemic productivity may be premature given the role of affective commitment in employees' work performance and well-being.

Second, organizations need to consider complex relationships. Typically, organizations devote considerable time and effort to developing work relationships, for example, high-functioning teams. In contrast, social or emotional relationships at work are invariably ignored, if not actively discouraged, by management. Shah et al.'s research on multiplex relationships discussed earlier in this chapter suggest that this approach may be shortsighted[101]: in both their studies, work-focused relationships by themselves did not result in better work performance. One explanation for this is that the real value of information sharing within team is only realized within the trusting environments that typify high-quality interpersonal relationships.

Third, what does affiliation and belonging look like in the gig economy in which companies like Uber, Uber-Eats, Lyft, Handy, Rover, or Postmates[‡‡‡‡] are proliferating, with no decrease expected? All these companies share a key characteristic: work is controlled centrally by an app but conducted locally by isolated individuals. In many respects, work in the "gig economy" is moving in the opposite direction of traditional workplaces that fulfilled the sense of belonging. Prepandemic estimates suggested that by 2000, 10 percent of the US labor force relied on gig work for their primary income,[102] and up to 35 percent were involved in some gig work in 2020.[103] One study using semistructured interviews and a survey of 679 gig workers in the Philippines, Malaysia, Vietnam, Kenya, Nigeria, and South Africa, showed that the methods of control central to the management of gig work resulted in social isolation, as well as working long, irregular and unpredictable hours. The social disruption, sleep problems, and exhaustion that ensued compromised possibilities for social interactions outside of work and presumably at work as well.[104]

Fourth, COVID-19 has exposed just how extensively inequality pervades our organizations and workplaces. Public and private sector leaders must now ensure that opportunities for affiliation and belonging are equally available to all employees. Employees from underrepresented minority groups have long found themselves excluded from higher-status social groups at work, restricting opportunities to reap the benefits of affiliation and belonging.[105] As business models change, it behooves organizations to ensure that opportunities for inclusion, belonging, and attachment are available to all their members.

Last, remote working has already increased and will likely continue to do so.[§§§§] Given what we now know about the importance of belonging and attachment, organizations would do well to consider not only what might be gained from remote work but also what might be lost. In the immortal words of folksinger Joni Mitchell,

‡‡‡‡ With the latter three being app-based "Uber-style" companies for house cleaning, pet sitting and delivery/couriers, respectively.

§§§§ A partial list of companies using some form of remote work would include Amazon, Facebook, Google, Mastercard, Microsoft, Nationwide Insurance, Nielsen, REI, Reuters, Salesforce, Spotify, Twitter, Uber, and Zillow.

"You don't know what you've got till it's gone."[106] As one example, it is sometimes easy to take for granted how workplaces relationships and attachments play a crucial role in our larger social lives. Political scientists Diana Mutz and Jeffery Mondak remind us that in families, neighborhoods, or voluntary associations, people seek out others who are like themselves. In contrast, workplaces offer opportunities for "cross-cutting" political discussions with people with hold very different beliefs and perspectives.[107] Another reminder of the importance of a sense of belonging at work comes from John Seabrook's searching article "Has the pandemic transformed the office forever?"[108] After surveying the work-related changes brought about by the pandemic, and questioning what the world of work will look like, he describes a tour of his former workplace:

> Following the new one-way directional signage, I eventually came to my desk. I booted up my virtual desktop, thinking I might take advantage of the rare quiet and privacy to actually do some work in the office. But I couldn't concentrate. I missed my colleagues. Whether walled, open, or cloud-based, an office is about the people who work there. Without the people, the office is an empty shell.

5
Fairness

Just how important is a sense of fairness in the workplace? Perhaps we can learn a lesson from a large-scale study of UK employees on the effects of fairness on cardiovascular health. We discuss this study later in the chapter; suffice it to say that perceptions of unfair treatment by a supervisor negatively affected cardiovascular health. The investigators, a group of medical researchers and epidemiologists, concluded that the reason people care so deeply is because of the message that fair or unfair treatment sends to employees. Being treated fairly signals to employees that they are valued and enjoy high status in the organization. In stark contrast, being treated unfairly "may be a source of oppression, deprivation and distress" (Kivimäki et al. 2005, 2250).[1]

The nature of fairness

The sense of fairness and unfairness is ubiquitous. When toddlers are as young as sixteen months, they reward adults for distributing resources fairly.[2] And it is not just toddlers. Even some animals have a strong preference for fairness. An intriguing study conducted by Sarah Brosnan and Frans de Waal two decades ago (and reported in the prestigious journal *Nature*), showed that even monkeys reject unfair pay.[3] Essentially, two capuchin monkeys were placed side by side in identical test chambers so that they could watch each other. Both monkeys performed the same task (returning a small rock to the experimenter) to receive a reward. For one monkey, the reward was a quarter of a cucumber slice. For the other, the reward was a grape—which is valued more highly by capuchin monkeys. The results were immediate and startling: after only a few trials, the monkey receiving the cucumber slice tried to throw it at the neighboring monkey and rattled the test chamber, seemingly trying to get out. After continuing to receive cucumber slices, the monkey tried to throw it back at the experimenter. Brosnan and de Wall conclude that like human beings, capuchin monkeys "seem to measure reward in relative terms, comparing their own rewards with those available, and their own efforts with those of others" (299).*

Feelings about fairness are indeed pervasive, including in organizations, and organizational scholars have studied workplace fairness for almost fifty years. As a

* Parts of this remarkable experiment can be seen at: de Waal, F. (April 2018). Moral behavior in animals. https://www.ted.com/talks/frans_de_waal_moral_behavior_in_animals

Brave New Workplace. Julian Barling, Oxford University Press. © Oxford University Press 2023.
DOI: 10.1093/oso/9780190648107.003.0005

result, we now have a very good understanding of the nature of organizational fairness. But before going any further, we need to make an important clarification: are we discussing fairness or unfairness? I can only imagine that you have heard others discuss how unfairly they have been treated at work far more often than you have people talking about how fairly they have been treated. Staying with the focus of the book, however, which is on the psychological needs of employees, our focus will be predominantly on fairness.

Moreover, you have probably heard the words *fairness* and *justice* used interchangeably; and this is certainly true within the organizational literature. Barry Goldman and Russell Cropanzano remind us, however, that these two terms are not interchangeable.[4] To simplify their discussion, organizational *justice* refers to what is objectively stated in the organizations' regulations and whether organizations adhere to those regulations. In contrast, *fairness* refers to how employees feel about those regulations and how they are implemented. Taking this framework, we can see that events can be "just" but felt to be "unfair," and even unjust events might be perceived as "fair." In this chapter, we are concerned with peoples' perceptions of fairness.

There are four different dimensions of fairness. *Distributive fairness* was the first to attract scholarly attention in the mid-1970s. Unlike pay satisfaction, which signals satisfaction with the *amount* of pay received, perceptions of distributive fairness reflect the belief that outcomes are appropriate given the personal effort required or, as in the case with the capuchin monkeys, relative to the efforts and rewards of others.

Distributive fairness helps us understand why some people feel so strongly about others' pay. Take the case of CEO compensation. Tim Steiner, the CEO of Ocado, an online grocery and technology company in the United Kingdom, was paid £58.7 million in 2019.[5] This was a staggering 2,605 times more than the average of company employees. For reference, the average ratio of CEO pay to that of the typical employee for retail companies in the United Kingdom is 140:1, which itself is larger than the ratio for CEOs of British FTSE100 companies, which is "only" 73:1. And these ratios have consequences. In a carefully designed experiment, Niklas Steffens and colleagues showed that employees find it difficult to identify with CEOs who receive substantially higher compensation than their counterparts and, in turn, view the CEOs as less charismatic.[6]

The idea of comparing your efforts and rewards with others loomed large during the COVID-19 pandemic. Employees of many large retail organizations received some hazard pay during the first wave of the pandemic, often ranging between $1–$3 per hour. Yet this amount was arbitrarily stopped within months despite their organizations enjoying unprecedented profits because of the pandemic. The issue for essential workers was that their effort remained the same in an environment of considerable risk, yet the reward was arbitrarily reduced[7] in a way that defied all the criteria necessary for procedural fairness.

Procedural fairness exists when employees believe that they have some influence over the way in which organizational policies are established. Gerald Leventhal and his colleagues identified six criteria for procedural fairness.[8] These criteria included consistency in application across time and people, bias suppression by decision makers, policies and procedures that are based on accurate information, procedures existing to challenge bad outcomes, the fact that all those affected by a policy had input, and that basic moral and ethical standards are met.†

Procedural fairness helps explain why politicians dealing with the COVID-19 pandemic encountered public opposition regarding a lack of information regarding school openings at the start of the summer of 2020. Many people accepted that politicians could not know the final decision until just before the school semester. What would probably have satisfied the public was knowing the procedural criteria that would be used in making those decisions (e.g., consistency, informational accuracy, ethicality). Without this information, they were predictably distressed.

The notion of *interactional fairness* was introduced about a decade later, and comprised four criteria, namely justification, truthfulness, respect, and propriety. Shortly thereafter, Jerald Greenberg differentiated between interactional fairness (interpersonal sensitivity) and informational fairness (availability, timing, and accuracy of information).[9]

Distinctions between distributive, procedural, interactional, and informational fairness are important because they tend to have different causes and consequences. As examples, procedural fairness predicts willingness to comply with rules, informational fairness predicts positive evaluations of leaders, and interactional fairness is associated with collective self-esteem.[10] Yet at the same time, employees do not always make finite judgments between these four dimensions of fairness. Instead, people tend to make more global evaluations of whether they are treated fairly—or unfairly.[11]

Last, we cannot underestimate the importance of transparency in employees' evaluations of all forms of fairness. By itself, transparency improves the quality of organizational processes, leadership, and management. Why? Secrecy enables us to hide poor process and bad leadership in the shadows of the organization. But when you know that what you do will be apparent to all, poor process and bad leadership are no longer options. In contrast, achieving fairness in a way that is not visible is not worth the considerable effort involved. After all, it makes little sense to struggle to ensure fair process in organizations if employees are none the wiser; as Joel Brockner cautioned, "it's not enough for executives to *be* fair, they also have to be *seen* as fair" (128).[12] The need for transparency might explain why employees often respond negatively to what is now referred to as "pay secrecy," i.e., systems followed by most US organizations in which both the criteria guiding decision-making about employees' pay and the amount different employees are paid are kept secret. Not surprisingly, within pay-for-performance systems, pay secrecy has negative effects on employee performance.[13]

† Technically, these criteria were referred to as consistency, bias suppression, information accuracy, correctability, representation, and ethicality, respectively.

The benefits of fairness

Work attitudes

There is no shortage of studies showing the beneficial effects of workplace fairness on workplace attitudes. By 2001, Jason Colquitt and his colleagues could already meta-analyze 183 studies that had investigated workplace fairness.[14] In general, their analyses showed that the different dimensions of workplace fairness were all related to work attitudes, such as job satisfaction, organizational commitment, trust in management, organizational citizenship behaviors, and intentions to quit the organization.

Even stronger support for the role of fairness would emerge if it helped organizations and employees in troubled times, such as during layoffs when the sense of fairness might be seriously threatened. In one series of studies, Brockner et al. investigated the effects of procedural-fairness perceptions about the way in which layoffs were implemented among so-called victims, survivors, and "lame ducks" (employees who knew that they would be laid off in the future but remained in the organization in the interim).[15] Across all three groups, the lesson was clear. Believing that the layoff was implemented fairly, which involved sufficient prior notification with the layoff and then handled sensitively, largely spared employees from any negative effects. Moreover, if employees believed the layoffs had been handled fairly, they retained positive attitudes toward the organization.

A different study by Brockner and colleagues further advances our understanding of the benefits of perceived fairness. In this particular study, they surveyed 150 full-time employees who had survived a layoff in a financial-services organization occurring six months earlier.[16] Employees' pre-layoff commitment to the organization was not hurt if they believed that the downsizing was implemented fairly. A more important lesson from this study is reflected in the subtitle of their article "The higher they are, the harder they fall." Any negative effects of procedural unfairness were greatest for those whose pre-layoff commitment levels were the highest, surely the employees you would want to hurt the least.

This line of research demonstrates that organizations that pay close attention to procedural fairness in implementing layoffs will limit any damage resulting from the layoff. But procedural fairness may also be important in implementing other change initiatives. One current challenge is effectively establishing remote work policies during and after the pandemic. Whether employees feel they were treated fairly during the development and implementation of these policies will likely shape how they respond. Leventhal et al.'s six criteria of procedural fairness, namely consistency, bias suppression, information accuracy, correctability, representation, and ethicality, could serve as a useful guide to management throughout this process. The pace with which organizations have moved to implement remote work policies highlights the critical role of these criteria.

Work performance

Thus, perceptions of fairness can buffer the negative effects of disruptive organizational events such as layoffs on negative work attitudes. But could fairness perceptions guard against any negative effects on work performance? Fortunately, studies on different organizational initiatives provide answers to the questions.

John Schaubroeck and colleagues conducted an interesting study in a manufacturing plant in the United States.[17] Management was concerned that employees' work attitudes had worsened about a year after the company implemented a pay freeze. Together with a consultant and the researchers, they designed an intervention to see if they could reduce any negative effects of the financial security that had resulted. Half the employees were randomly assigned to receive the procedural-fairness intervention that was based on Leventhal et al.'s six criteria. As part of an ongoing workshop, these employees learned that the organization had been under considerable financial pressure a year earlier, leaving management with a dilemma. They could either introduce layoffs for some or a pay freeze for all. They were told that management had considered all employees' concerns and chose to avoid layoffs, that the pay freeze applied to all organizational members, and that management did what they could to implement the policy fairly. The findings from this study are instructive: even though the intervention did not reduce employees' actual financial hardship, employees' attachment and intentions to remain with the organization were significantly higher among those who received the explanation.

Mary Konovsky and Russell Cropanzano turned their attention to employee drug testing, a controversial workplace practice that frequently elicits very negative responses.[18] Employee drug testing was routine following workplace safety incidents, chronic absenteeism, or marked changes in the quality of work performance in the privately owned US pathology lab they studied. Employees strongly opposed drug testing. However, the more employees believed that procedural fairness was adhered to in implementing drug testing, the better their annual work performance appraisal and the more they wanted to remain a part of the organization.[‡]

One possible response to these two studies is that organizations have changed so much since they were conducted in the 1990s (e.g., the rise of gig work in the late 2010s), that employees might have lower expectations of being treated fairly.[19] If that is the case, any negative effects of unfairness might now be reduced. Recent research by Hai-jiang Wang investigated the effects of feelings of job insecurity, a chronic issue for employees given the rise of short-term and temporary work contracts and gig work. In two studies conducted at different insurance companies in China, job insecurity had no effect on employees' general job-performance ratings or sales

‡ Both studies just discussed also showed positive effects of procedural justice on workplace attitudes.

performance when employees had favorable perceptions of overall fairness in their organization.[20]

Well-being

We know that fairness is good for the organization. But do employees enjoy any personal benefits? You have probably heard some people claim that their work is so stressful they will have a heart attack, but is there any truth to such claims? To answer this question, Kivimäki et al. studied whether supervisory unfairness predicts new instances of heart disease over time.[21] As part of the remarkable Whitehall II project established by Sir Michael Marmot in 1985,[22] 6,442 male public sector participants had an extensive medical examination and then completed wide-ranging surveys between 1985 and 1988. Assessments of coronary heart disease were conducted several years later, enough time for any health and cardiac consequences to emerge.

Like all research from the Whitehall II project, the researchers first statistically excluded variables that might themselves affect cardiovascular health and therefore complicate any conclusions about the effects of fairness. These included personal factors such as ethnicity, marital status, educational and employment level, and health-status indicators such as cholesterol levels, BMI, hypertension, smoking, alcohol consumption, and physical activity level. What did they find? Employees initially experiencing higher levels of perceived fairness at work had a 30 percent lower risk of onset of new instances of heart disease nine years on. This finding is made even more compelling because the sense of fairness required for this effect was well within the reach of most organizations. Specifically, participants' perceptions of fair treatment were derived from five questions (2246)[$]:

- Do you ever get criticized unfairly?[**]
- Do you get consistent information from line management (your superior)?
- Do you get sufficient information from line management (your superior)?
- How often is your superior willing to listen to your problems?
- Do you ever get praised for your work?

Importantly, these are not isolated findings. Studies in many different countries on other aspects of health, including mental health, show that workplace fairness has similar benefits.[23] The lessons from these studies are clear: people are remarkably sensitive to the way in which they are treated by their supervisors and respond accordingly.

In the leadership chapter, we asked whether engaging in transformational leadership affected leaders themselves. We now end this section by asking whether treating

[$] Each question was responded to on a four-point scale: 1 = never, 2 = seldom, 3 = sometimes, 4 = often.
[**] Scores on this item are reverse-coded, so that high scores reflect fairness.

others fairly benefits leaders themselves. Russell Johnson and colleagues addressed this question in their study of 82 managers who were completing an executive MBA program on a part-time basis. For ten days, managers completed surveys at work every morning and afternoon.[24] Like the research on leaders' well-being, the results are not straightforward. Expressions of interpersonal fairness by leaders were associated with the leaders experiencing better well-being. In contrast, procedural fairness resulted in leaders feeling depleted and unfocused. The probable reason for this is that procedural fairness poses a different set of emotional and cognitive challenges, requiring leaders not only to interact with others but also to deal with organizations, for example, in seeking input from others prior to decision-making and providing opportunities for others to appeal decisions.... This may help explain why in the words of Jerald Greenberg, organizational fairness "may be common sense... but obviously not common practice" (8, 9).[25] Given the attitudinal, performance, and well-being benefits resulting from fairness, organizations would be well-served in doing what they can to remove obstacles to fair treatment for all employees and creating a culture in which those who do treat others fairly are appropriately recognized and rewarded.

When fairness is lacking

But what happens when employees sense that fairness is lacking? Most people expect that they should be treated well by others as part of a larger social contract and take for granted that this right extends to the workplace. From a psychological perspective, receiving fair treatment is important because it signals to people that they are respected by others. How do people respond when this expectation is violated at work? In his delightful book about his life as a long-haul trucker, essential work that we take for granted as we learned during of the COVID-19 pandemic, Finn Murphy has one answer. In relaying many stories of deep disrespect by customers, Murphy reminds us (and his customers),[26] "If we don't get a modicum of respect, well, ... we will preserve our dignity one way or another (128)," and he tellingly recounts some of the creative ways in which people packing and moving our furniture can restore the balance of fairness.[††] As Finn Murphy may have warned us, employees' work attitudes, work performance, and well-being all suffer in the face of workplace unfairness.

Work attitudes

David Jones proposed that the moral and emotional hurt resulting from unfairness leaves employees wanting to respond in some way; common comments such as

[††] See pages 128 and 129!

"payback time," "getting even," and "firing back" reflect this need to restore an equitable level of fairness.[27] Jones further suggested that the desire to respond to the injustice would be targeted specifically toward the source believed to be responsible. Thus, feelings of interpersonal mistreatment would be associated with desires for revenge against the immediate supervisor, while feelings of procedural injustice would predict desires for revenge against the organization. Results based on responses from 424 employed students in Canada strongly support Jones' suggestion. Interpersonal (but not procedural) unfairness resulted in longing for revenge against the supervisor, while procedural (but not interactional) unfairness predicted the desire for revenge against the organization.

The notion of target-specific revenge as a response to mistreatment is supported by an intriguing study by Michelle Inness and her colleagues.[28] They studied 105 "moonlighters" in North America, i.e., people who had one primary job but also worked a secondary job. In each of these two jobs, people reported to a different supervisor. As Jones might have predicted, feeling you had been treated unfairly in one job resulted in psychological aggression against that supervisor but not against the supervisor from the other job.

Findings such as these provide some guidance for management. First, it is often tempting to dismiss unacceptable behaviors by employees as the result of personal failures of integrity. These results suggest otherwise: the target-specific nature of the response to unfairness indicates that the solution may well rest with management. Second, despite the considerable financial resources, time, and effort that management devote to ensuring compensation is appropriate (which was reflected in Ed Lawler's powerful observation in Chapter 1‡‡), distributive unfairness had no effect on the desire for revenge against either the supervisor or the organization in Jones' study.[29]

Thus, management may be well advised to allocate as much, if not more attention, to interpersonal and procedural fairness.

Work performance

Perceived unfairness has widespread negative effects on so many aspects of work performance. As one example, facing unfair treatment, one response might simply be to leave the organization,[30] the effects of which would be heightened if the most productive employees were those choosing to leave. However, I focus primarily on employee theft because it is one of the most substantial forms of loss through theft by organizations,[31] and the way management typically responds to employee theft often

‡‡ As a reminder, "many organizations end up using an enormous amount of time to allocate small amounts of money to individuals based on an uncertain assessment of performance in the hope that performance will improve.... it is a kind of corporate fantasy ... that takes time, effort and resources but has few... positive outcomes" (210–211).

exacerbates the problem. For example, acting on the assumption that employee theft occurs because of dishonest employees, management often confront employee theft with the use of integrity tests, an approach that may be misguided at best.

The destructive effects of unfairness are dramatically illustrated in Jerald Greenberg's study of three geographically distinct plants of a manufacturing organization in the US Midwest.[32] Before the study, the parent organization had experienced the loss of large manufacturing contracts in two of the plants; a third plant experienced no losses. Rather than opting for layoffs to deal with the situation, the organization chose to cut payroll by 15 percent for *all* employees (up to and including the VP) for ten weeks in the two plants directly affected by the loss of the contracts. No pay cuts were necessary in the third plant. A senior company executive delivered the news about the pay cuts to employees in the two different plants. Both plants received the same information, but the information was deliberately delivered differently. In the first, which Greenberg called the *adequate-explanation group*, news of the pay cuts was delivered with respect and remorse. The company VP delivered the news in person, stayed for an hour afterwards, and answered all questions sensitively. In contrast, while employees in the *inadequate-explanation group* received the same information about the pay cuts, it was delivered in a way that displayed neither respect nor remorse: the meeting and question-and-answer session lasted only fifteen minutes. Thus, any differences in the way in which the two groups responded could be tied to differences in interpersonal unfairness rather than distributive, procedural, or informational fairness.[§§]

The primary focus of Greenberg's analysis was on differences in theft between the three groups ten weeks before the pay cut, the ten weeks during which the 15 percent pay cuts were in effect, and a ten-week period after pay levels returned to normal. Clear conclusions about the harmful effects of interpersonal unfairness were possible because the company's accounting department routinely kept weekly data on employee shrinkage. The results were dramatic and can be seen in Figure 5.1.

As expected, employee theft remained the same across the three time periods within the plant that experienced no pay changes throughout the study. Similarly, there were no differences in employee theft between the three groups before the announcement. But all that was soon to change. During the pay cuts, theft increased by about 50 percent among employees who suffered a pay cut but were treated with as much fairness as possible. But employee theft almost tripled among employees who received the same pay cut but were treated unfairly.[***] To pursue a point made earlier, while we may want to attribute the employee theft to the employees themselves, what happened after normal pay levels were resumed defies such an explanation: employee theft returned to their earlier levels as soon as pay was restored to its normal level. The best explanation for these findings is that while there is no good way to give bad news, even small levels of interpersonal unfairness have very significant effects. To reiterate

§§ Pay in the third group was unchanged, making them an ideal control group.

*** Intriguingly, identical findings emerged for turnover.

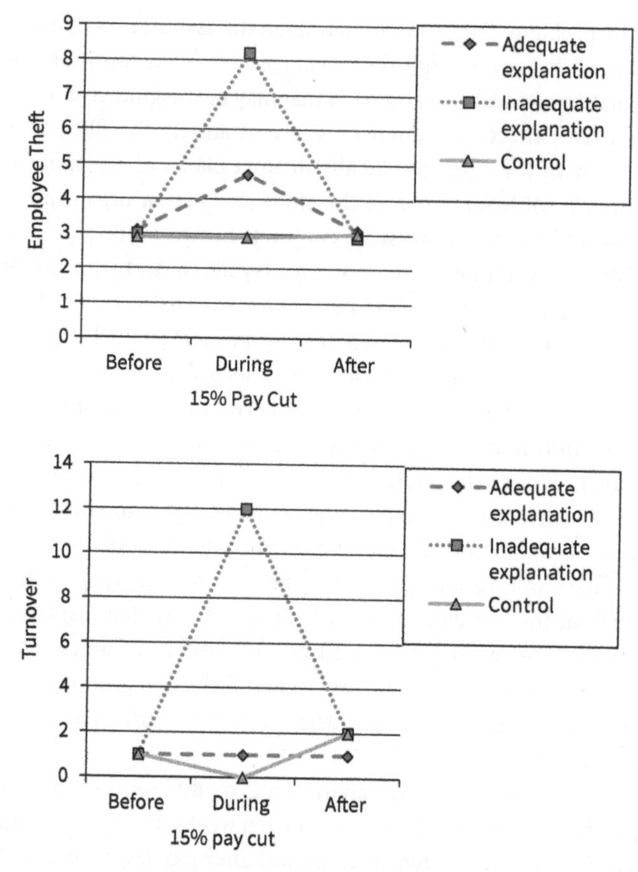

Fig. 5.1 Effects of perceived injustice on employee theft and turnover.

Copyright © 1990 by American Psychological Association. Reproduced with permission. Greenberg, J. (1990). Employee theft as a reaction to underpayment inequity: The hidden cost of pay cuts. *Journal of Applied Psychology, 75*(5), 561–568

a point made earlier, the lesson from this research is that people are remarkably sensitive to the way in which they are treated and are likely to respond accordingly.

Field studies such as this can be influenced by environmental factors that could influence the findings. As a result, Greenberg conducted a laboratory-based study among 103 university students who participated in a one-hour task that required them to complete clerical tasks for which they would receive $5.00.[33] After forty-five minutes, the experimenter told all participants that they had to stop. Half were told that they would still receive the full $5.00, but the others learned that they would only receive $3.00. Among this group, some students received explanations that emphasized fairness, while the explanations the others heard were unfair. The experimenter then announced he had to leave immediately to start another session, placed $10.42 on each table, asked participants to take the amount they were allowed (either $5.00 or $3.00), and then left. What did Greenberg find? On average, participants who were treated fairly (i.e., paid $5.00) took exactly $5.00. In the group that were told they should take $3.00, those who felt they were treated unfairly took an average of $4.07, i.e., 34 percent more than they were allowed! Given these findings, Greenberg, appropriately titled his article, "Stealing in the name of justice."

Employee theft can take many forms, and a different study focused on more than a thousand employees in Michigan who had been diagnosed with repetitive-motion injury by a company physician. While we might expect that the severity, duration, and level of impairment resulting from the injury would be the only reasons people file workers' compensation claims, this was not the case.[34] Even after taking the severity of the injury into account, feeling that you had been poorly treated by a supervisor was a salient factor in whether injured employees filed a compensation claim. Like Greenberg, the authors capture this phenomenon in the title of their article, "Claiming in the name of justice," and the lesson is unambiguous. Injured workers believe that they are entitled to fair treatment. In the absence of that fairness, they can be remarkably creative in how they ensure they receive what they believe they deserve, whether it be through employee theft or worker-compensation claims.

Is it possible that such responses are limited to lower paid employees? Probably not. In early 2010, comedian Conan O'Brien was publicly humiliated by his employer, NBC. At the time, his show had the most prized evening time slot on the network. Soon afterwards, his show was bumped to a much less favorable time slot to accommodate his rival, Jay Leno. When asked how he would respond, Conan O'Brien explained, "Everyone wants to know what my plans are. All I can say is I plan to keep putting on a great show night after night while stealing as many office supplies as humanly possible. I'm going to rob this place blind."[35] O'Brien's pride in the quality of his work remained intact, but the psychological need for "payback," to reciprocate what he saw as unfair treatment by his leaders and somehow level the playing field, was overpowering.

Taken together, the organizational lessons are enormous. First, the negative effects of unfairness are dramatic and immediate. But as we saw in Greenberg's study in the three manufacturing plants, so too are the benefits of restoring the sense of fairness. Second, employee theft is not necessarily a moral failure on the part of dishonest employees. Instead, employee theft (and retaliation more generally), is more likely a predictable response to feeling unfairly treated and disrespected, and the psychological need to redress the perceived imbalance. Thus, addressing issues of employee theft may benefit more from interventions aimed at enhancing fairness than initiatives aimed at selecting honest employees.

Well-being

"My boss makes me sick!" is something that most all of us have heard friends or colleagues say, or perhaps it is something that even we have said before. But is there any truth to such a statement? For better or for worse, there is now a large body of evidence suggesting that work can indeed make you sick, and one of the major reasons is feelings of interpersonal fairness.

We saw earlier in the Kivimäki et al. study how workplace fairness lowered the risk of future heart disease. But does the experience of unfairness increase the risk? One study based on a much smaller sample of fifty-seven women working in a long-term eldercare facility in Finland suggests that it does: the risk for blood pressure problems was 3.8–5.8 times higher in employees who experienced mistreatment.[36]

Importantly, the effects of feeling treated unfairly at work go way beyond cardiovascular problems. Could your boss "drive you to drink"? As part of one study in Finland, 24,196 male and female employees completed surveys during 2000–01, and again in 2004.[37] Males and females who experienced unfairness at the hands of their supervisor were significantly more likely to be involved in heavy drinking three to four years later. These finding are especially credible given the rigorous statistical controls imposed that exclude the possibility that the results are a result of participants' age, gender, marital status, socioeconomic status, initial levels of work stress, or psychological distress.

Similarly, might there be any truth to the idea that your boss can hurt your mental health? Based on a subsample of more than eighteen thousand participants from this same Finnish study and almost five thousand employees from a different study in Finnish hospitals, Jaana Ylipaavalniemi and her team showed that believing that one's supervisor acted unfairly predicted subsequent depression.[38] This finding is especially important as the depression was diagnosed by qualified physicians.

One study is of particular relevance as it examined the effects of informational unfairness during the early days of the COVID-19 pandemic.[39] For that study, 265 US employees completed surveys each week for eight weeks starting on March 20, 2020, when ambiguity and uncertainty levels would undoubtedly have been very high. At times like that, receiving accurate information from your supervisor would be of the utmost importance. What the researchers found was that a lack of informational unfairness, for example, whether employees believed supervisors had been open and honest about issues related to COVID-19, was associated with feelings of work-related loneliness and depressive symptoms. The lessons from this study go beyond organizations and surely question whether the misinformation and disinformation spread during the pandemic had any negative effects on broader public mental health.

To conclude, two findings that recur throughout this section are worth reiterating. First, we do not need to see substantial expressions of fairness (or unfairness) to see their benefits (or costs), as evident in the research by Kivimäki et al. on cardiovascular health or Greenberg on employee theft. Second, when employees do respond to acts that they believe were unfair, their responses are typically target-specific. This is important, as it implies that they are reacting to the unfairness, and however inappropriately from an organizational perspective, trying to restore what they see is an equitable balance.

How does unfairness exert its effects?

We have already seen from Greenberg's study on employee theft that feeling you have been treated unfairly can result in immediate effects.[40] As we shall soon see, fairness (and unfairness) also exerts important indirect effects as well.

Fairness exerts indirect effects

Think about a day at work when you were treated unfairly by someone in authority. Many people find it very difficult to just let it go. The unfairness of it all, and why you did not respond differently, probably swirl around in your head again and again. If this describes your response, you are not alone. Ruminating about workplace unfairness is one reason why feeling that you have been treated unfairly indirectly affects well-being.

Eib and her team isolated the role of rumination in understanding the lingering effects of workplace unfairness in their study of 782 employees of a nationwide Swedish accounting firm.[41] Feeling mistreated resulted in increased rumination, as expressed in employees' responses to questions such as "Work rarely lets me go, it is still on my mind when I go to bed," and "My work is on my mind even on the weekends." In turn, rumination predicted poor mental health for those employees who felt less in control of events in their lives. One reason why rumination plays such an important role is that it effectively lengthens the psychological experience of the unfair event. Even though the incident itself is over, ruminating about it keeps it alive psychologically, as a result of which it can still exert negative effects. This really is important: following some incidents, employees have reported being mentally preoccupied with the unfairness for years![42]

Zhenyu Yuan and colleagues also focused on the role of rumination following mistreatment, but their research takes an unexpected twist. Instead of focusing on the target, they focused on the perpetrator of the mistreatment.[43] Dispelling the notion that people who mistreat others must surely be inconsiderate and uncaring at best, mistreating others during the day resulted in rumination that same night. This finding is even more credible as it emerged in separate samples in the United States and China. Unsurprisingly, ruminating at night was associated with supervisors' insomnia. Nonetheless, knowing that your supervisor lies awake at night ruminating and sleepless may be cold comfort to employees who themselves are awake after being mistreated at work.

Still, rumination is not the only reason why unfairness exerts long-term negative effects. Other emotions caused by feeling you have been treated unfairly are equally important. In one study of 332 junior police officers in two German states,[44] officers who believed their performance appraisals had been conducted unfairly from a procedural, interpersonal, and distributive perspective reported frustration, anger, and anxiety. In turn, these negative emotions resulted in them behaving unethically, for example, fabricating or exaggerating work results, and deliberately expending less effort on important tasks. Importantly, the reports of unethical behaviors came not only from coworkers but also from employees themselves. When people feel they have been mistreated, they feel little shame in telling others how they intend to "get even."

Physiological factors also explain the negative consequences of being treated unfairly. Liu-Qin Yang and colleagues argued that being treated unfairly signals to people that they are neither respected nor valued. In turn, this activates cortisol activity.[45] Increased cortisol activity is important, as it is implicated in impulsive and risk-taking behaviors, and lower self-control, all of which are linked with aggression and deviant behavior. To investigate this process, Yang et al. randomly assigned sixty-eight undergraduate students to be treated patiently and politely, or impatiently and impolitely. Their laboratory-based experiment showed clearly that faced with interactional unfairness, it was the increased cortisol activity that led to deviant behaviors such as theft and deliberately disobeying legitimate instructions.

Fairness shapes the way people experience their work

Workplace fairness also shapes how we experience our work more generally. We know that knowledge sharing between employees is critical for optimal organizational functioning, and whether employees choose to do so depends to some extent on how that are treated at work.[46] One study investigating this took place among 606 frontline nurses from thirty distinct hospital departments in a hospital in the United States, a context in which not sharing vital information could literally prove fatal.[47] Overall, higher levels of identification with the workgroup and professional commitment or pride were associated with sharing information on patient safety. Going deeper into the data for this study, there were no negative effects on sharing patient-safety information for employees who experienced low identification with the group and low professional commitment if they worked in any of the thirty departments that had better procedural-justice climates.[†††]

A different study produced similar findings. Yochi Cohen-Charash and Jennifer Mueller investigated the effects of feeling envious at work—a largely unstudied yet common and difficult experience.[48] Workplace envy is an important issue for management, because one way people deal with feelings of envy is to harm those they envy, mistakenly believing that doing so might reduce their negative feelings and restore a sense of balance or equity with the person they envy. Several lessons emerge from this study of 188 employed individuals in the United States. First, experiencing envy was associated with attempts to interfere with the job performance, and to harm the reputation, of the envied person. Second, this effect was much stronger if

[†††] Justice climate was measured as the average of individual members' procedural fairness score within each department.

the envied person was believed to have gained their advantages unfairly. Third, and equally importantly, feeling envious did not lead people to harm those they envied—if they believed that those they envied deserved any advantages they had gained.

Gender influences on fairness

Given the enormous body of research on the intersection of gender and leadership, it is surprising that the intersection of gender and fairness has attracted so little research. This is an important omission considering that interpersonal fairness is gender-typed. As we saw in Chapter 2, women are expected to behave in ways that exemplify interpersonal fairness, such as treating others sensitively, kindly, and with concern—burdens that do not necessarily extend to men.[49] Suzette Caleo conducted four experimental studies that investigated how gender affects perceptions of procedural and interactional justice violations.[50] Not surprisingly, women who were perceived to have violated interactional fairness expectations by being impolite or uncaring toward subordinates received worse performance evaluations than men who exhibited the exact same behaviors. However, unlike interactional fairness, procedural fairness was not gender-typed. There were no gender differences in the way in which men and women were punished for violations of procedural fairness. One probable reason for this is that people hold their organizations responsible for procedural fairness but their supervisors responsible for interactional fairness. While the results of this study are certainly interesting and in line with studies on gender and leadership, a lot more needs to be learned about the intersection of gender and fairness.

Cultural influences on fairness

Fascinating research by psychologists Marie Schäfer and colleagues' highlight why the cross-cultural generalizability of organizational fairness is so important. Their research was not conducted in organizations but still shapes the way we might think about cultural influences in organizations. They studied three groups of four-to-eleven year-old children from three very different cultural groups. The first two groups were from very small, rural, and isolated communities in northern Namibia and north-central Kenya, respectively.[51] Status and authority in the Namibian community play limited roles. Instead, communal sharing is critical both economically and socially, and personal relationships are important. As a result, community members place great importance on equal and balanced distributions between community members. In contrast, the community in which the Kenyan children lived was based on an age-based hierarchy. Tradition dictated that elders in the community made decisions about the distribution of work roles and resources, even extending to elders being involved in family decision-making and conflict resolution. A common feature of these two communities is that most exchanges, whether social or economic, take place between members who likely know each other. The third group consisted of German children who went to elementary or nursery schools in the same neighborhood of a small town. Unlike the Namibian and Kenyan children, the German children would be less likely to have enjoyed sustained or meaningful peer relationships. Schäfer et al.'s research was based on the premise that children within the three different groups will have internalized different cultural values, resulting in different distributive choices.

Children within each cultural group in this study were assigned to play a game with one other child. What the researchers were interested in was whether sharing rewards with the other child at the end of the study was based on merit (i.e., performance during the game) or equality. The results from this study were unambiguous. Merit drove decisions by the German children as to how to share the outcomes of the game. In sharp contrast, decisions about distributive fairness by children from the gerontocratic Kenyan community and the egalitarian Namibian community was driven more by equality principles, with merit being much less important. These findings justify the title of the article, "Fair is not fair everywhere," and raise the intriguing question: if culture influences fairness perceptions during childhood, might this extend to fairness perceptions at work?

Cultural differences in the level of fairness

Based on an extensive study of 12,426 employees from the United States and Canada, 3,844 in South Korea, and 1,443 employees in Kenya, Charles Mueller and Tor Wynn provide a framework for understanding why distributive fairness is valued differently across cultures.[52] They proposed that their US-Canadian sample would be more individualistic, whereas the Confucian doctrine would leave the South Korean sample characterized more by collectivism. As a result, the US-Canadian sample should value merit-based rewards and promotions, whereas seniority would be more highly valued in South Korea. Separately, as a developing nation still influenced by the vestiges of British rule, Kenyans should favor seniority rather than merit. As expected, distributive fairness was valued more highly in the US-Canadian sample than the South Korean sample, which in turn valued distributive fairness more highly than the Kenyan sample. These findings highlight how individualism and collectivism influence the extent to which people cherish distributive fairness.[‡‡‡] One last finding warrants mention: although there were different influences on distributive fairness between the three groups, distributive fairness was valued equally in these groups.

Cultural differences have been shown to affect the level to which other dimensions of workplace fairness are valued across several different countries. Zhou Jiang and colleagues contrasted procedural and distributive fairness among university employees

‡‡‡ The original study did not report analyses of significant differences between these three groups. I conducted these analyses based on the data from Table 4.

in Australia, China, and South Korea. As expected, given the more individualistic nature of Australian society, Australian employees rated procedural and distributive fairness more highly than their counterparts in China or South Korea.[53] Separately, with the United States higher on individualism and lower on power distance than in Bangladesh, distributive fairness, perceptions were higher in the United States than Bangladesh in Afzalur Rahim et al.'s study.[54]

What do these findings mean? Certainly, cultural characteristics exert modest but significant effects on perceptions of workplace fairness. However, aside from the study by Mueller and Wynn, most other studies are based on relatively small samples, leaving conclusions somewhat tentative. A more important lesson from these studies is that despite any modest differences in why people value fairness in countries and cultures, levels of workplace fairness were high enough in all contexts to for us to conclude that the need to be treated fairly is universal.

Cultural differences in the effects of fairness

While any differences in fairness perceptions across cultures are interesting, the bigger question is whether there are cultural differences in fairness' effect on organizational outcomes. In a large meta-analysis of 190,000 employees in thirty-two different countries and regions, Ruodan Shao and colleagues examined whether individualism, power distance, masculinity, and uncertainty avoidance influence the strength of any effects of fairness on organizational outcomes.[55] Perceptions of supervisory (or interactional) fairness and overall organizational fairness were positively associated with work attitudes, work performance, and reports of leadership quality in Shao et al.'s research. Moreover, their findings confirmed the importance of cultural characteristics, as all these effects were greater in individualistic vs collectivist countries, low- vs high-power distance countries, feminine vs masculine countries, and high- vs low-uncertainty countries.

As part of their research on workplace unfairness, Jordan Robbins and colleagues contrasted the strength of the effects of workplace unfairness on employee well-being in the United States vs elsewhere.[56] Consistent with Hofstede's characterization of the United States as individualistic, Robbins et al. expected that employees' well-being in the United States would be more sensitive to any effects of unfairness. The role of individualism was supported. The effects of workplace unfairness on physical health (e.g., hypertension, body mass index), unhealthy behaviors (e.g., smoking, excessive drinking), mental health (e.g., subclinical depression, anxiety), burnout, and stress were at least one-third higher in the United States than the data from all countries combined.

One implication of all these findings should be highlighted. Across these studies, it is not simply that there are differences *between* countries in workplace fairness. Instead, organizations need to be aware that values such as individualism and collectivism *within* countries also influence the level and functioning of workplace fairness perceptions.

TMGT: Can we have too much fairness in organizations?

Experiencing fairness has clear benefits for individuals and the organizations for which they work. But is there is a limit to just how much fairness is needed to get the benefits? J. Stacy Adams' notion of *overpayment inequity* might help us understand this issue. Overpayment inequity describes what happens when people believe that they are paid more than they deserve.[57] An intriguing laboratory study conducted by Lawler and his colleagues a few years after Adams introduced the idea provided an initial answer to the question. Even when performance benefits did emerge as a result of overpayment inequity, they were short-lived, as people who were overpaid offset the overpayment by increasing their perceptions of how qualified they thought they were for the job.[58]

Two more recent studies provide a nuanced perspective of any positive effects of overpayment inequity. In the first, Jerald Greenberg worked with a large insurance company in the United States that was refurbishing the offices of the underwriting department. As a result, most employees needed to be reassigned to different workstations for two weeks.[59] The organization agreed that assignments to workstations would be made randomly, creating the ideal conditions for a research study. Employees were either reassigned to a higher- (e.g., in terms of desk size, occupant space) or lower-status office, with some workers assigned to remain in their current office. As part of its normal operations, this organization collected weekly performance measures on all underwriters. The results of this study were clear. During the reassignment, employees who had been randomly assigned a higher status office (and thus experienced positive inequity because they had done nothing to deserve the newfound status) increased their work performance. Additional support for the effects of overpayment inequity emerges because employees assigned to a lower status office, and who therefore experienced negative inequity, decreased their performance. Employees in the control group did not change their performance. Two additional findings are especially noteworthy. First, like the earlier studies by Greenberg and Lawler, any effects on job performance dissipated soon after employees returned to their original offices. Second, any positive changes in job performance following overpayment inequity were less than corresponding negative changes in job performance following underpayment inequity. This is consistent with a stable finding in the social sciences, namely that that negative effects of bad events are more powerful than the positive effects of good events.[60]

A second study clarifies the performance changes that might follow over- or underpayment inequity. Joseph Harder studied the effects of objective inequity on job performance using sports data from MLB and the NBA in the United States.[61] These are ideal contexts for understanding overpayment inequity. Performance data are meticulously maintained by professional sports organizations, and salary is based on pay-for-performance in both these contexts. However, performance in baseball is more independent, and basketball more interdependent. Over- and underpayment inequity motivated different types of behaviors. Underrewarded individuals played more selfishly. Basketball players who were underrewarded attempted more shots but scored fewer points, and performance suffered. In contrast, overrewarded players became significantly more team-oriented, which is beneficial in a context like basketball where team success rests on interdependent performance. As a result, the answer to the question of whether you can be too fair, in this case by overpaying people based on their performance, is nuanced. Any benefits that do emerge may be short-lived and not as great as the negative effects of underpayment.

Interventions to enhance workplace fairness

Can we enhance perceptions of workplace fairness? Researchers have implemented several interventions to do so, and we discuss three very different interventions in this section.

Over the years, James Pennebaker has shown that just writing about our psychological problems can be an effective intervention, so much so that doing this is now known as the "Pennebaker effect."[62] One intervention examined whether Pennebaker's victim-centered expressive-writing intervention might benefit employees who had experienced unfairness at work. In this study by Laura Barclay and Daniel Skarlicki,[63] all 101 participants had experienced unfairness from a manager and were assigned to one of four groups. Each of these groups wrote about their (a) emotions, (b) thoughts, or (c) both emotions and thoughts about the unfairness for twenty minutes every day for four days. A fourth group wrote about a trivial topic and served as a comparison. As expected, the intervention was effective and wide-ranging. Employees who wrote about their emotions *and* thoughts experienced better psychological well-being, less anger, and fewer intentions to retaliate against the manager. They were also more likely to believe that the problem had been resolved. This intervention is also cost-effective, as it reduced anger and intentions to retaliate in only four twenty-minute sessions. Nonetheless, the drawback of initiatives such as this is that while they help employees feel better, the effects are likely not sustained once employees are sent back to the same situation in which the unfairness occurred in the first instance. As Barclay and Skarlicki themselves note appropriately, despite their benefits, secondary interventions like these do not "absolve the organization or managers of their responsibilities to treat employees fairly in the first place" (519).

That is the role of primary interventions—initiatives that focus on preventing unfairness from occurring in the first instance. Daniel Skarlicki and Gary Latham were perhaps the first organizational researchers to design an intervention to enhance fair treatment by supervisors.[64] Eleven local union leaders representing 274 members of the Public Service Alliance of Canada, Canada's largest public sector union, took part in their fairness intervention; nine different local leaders representing 307 members served as a control group. The training took place in four three-hour sessions conducted over a three-week period. Following best practice for training programs,[65] all sessions included lectures, case studies, group discussions, and role-playing exercises. The first session focused on Leventhal et al.'s six principles of fairness identified earlier (consistency, bias suppression, and so on).[66] The second session dealt with ways in which members could influence the local union's decision-making process. The third session focused on how local leaders could improve interactional fairness with their employees, with the final session concentrating on managing perceptions of fairness. Participants practiced what they had learned between sessions to augment the extent to which the material learned in the workshops would be transferred to their workplaces.

The intervention worked! Union leaders who had received the training were rated by their members as significantly higher on procedural and interactional fairness than those who did not receive the training. Moreover, union leaders' improved fairness resulted in higher levels of prosocial behaviors by union members. As examples, these members now attended more voluntary union meetings outside of normal work hours and volunteered to serve on union committees, behaviors that are critical to a union's effectiveness. Importantly, the benefits of interventions like this are not limited to the union context: in a separate study, Greenberg showed that even an eight-hour version of a similar training program was sufficient to change employee ratings of nursing supervisors' interactional fairness in organizations that were facing pay cuts.[67]

A third intervention highlights the need for fairness to be integrated into the way in which all organizational initiatives are implemented. Michael Johnson and colleagues investigated how an absence-control program might affect two different forms of absenteeism, namely casual or unscheduled absenteeism, such as unexcused absence and informal personal leave, vs legally protected leave for personal medical needs, or the medical needs for close family members.[68] Implementation of absence-control programs is an ideal context in which to understand the costs of unfairness, because believing that absenteeism was dealt with unfairly is a frequent reason why employees resort to arbitration to restore the balance of fairness.[69] Over two years, absence data were recorded every three months on 1,019 employees of a large, unionized automobile-parts manufacturer in the United States. The absence-control program itself was not unusual. Progressively harsher discipline (e.g., starting with written reprimands and culminating in a dismissal after the sixth absence) was administered for poor attendance, coupled with rewards (e.g., preferential parking spaces) for good attendance records. As intended, the policy reduced casual absenteeism. At the same time, employees who believed the absence-control policy was implemented unfairly increased their legally protected absences, suggesting that employees who believed the process was unfair found a way of "getting even" with the organization that was not punishable. The implication for organizational interventions more broadly is clear and critical: irrespective of the content of the initiative, the likelihood that it will achieve its goals depends in large part on how fairly it is implemented.

Special case

Fairness trajectories

Imagine you and I were completing a questionnaire about your experience of unfairness at work. One item on interactional fairness might ask, "My supervisor treated me with respect,"[70] and gives you the option of responding on a ten-point scale, where 1 = Strongly disagree, 5 = Neither agree nor disagree, and 10 = Strongly agree. After thinking about it, you and I both respond with a "5." The way in which much research is currently conducted, where researchers take a static snapshot, you would be forgiven for believing that we feel the same about how fairly we had been treated.

However, this is not necessarily the case. Imagine that a year ago, you had responded with a "10" to this question, six months later your response was 7.5, and now it is 5. In contrast, assume I had responded with a 1 to this question a year ago, six months later I recorded 2.5, and now I also respond with a 5. If this were the case, our current experience would likely be very different. You might be quite despondent about your treatment, while I could be quite optimistic about the future. As a result, even though we now both have the same response to this question, our future behaviors might differ substantially. This basic idea was supported by a study conducted by Mika Kivimäki and his team[71]: using data from the 10,308 UK civil servants who were part of the Whitehall II study, negative changes in feelings of fairness at work increased the risk for poorer health two years later, but favorable changes in feelings of fairness reduced this risk.

Two recent studies provide more support for the importance of understanding trajectories of fairness. In one study, John Hausknecht and colleagues surveyed 523 employees in a range of occupations four different times over a one-year period.[72] Improvements over the year in all four fairness dimensions resulted in job satisfaction, commitment to the organization, and intentions to remain with the organization. In contrast, declining feelings of fairness over the same time period predicted dissatisfaction, poorer commitment, and intentions to leave the organization. These findings are especially important, as changes in fairness and unfairness were better predictors of the outcomes than perceptions of fairness measured once at the end of the year.

A separate study examined procedural and distributive fairness changes over four years in an even larger sample of 4,348 employees in 278 branches of a large US bank.[73] The specific focus of the study was the effects of changes in fairness on prosocial helping behaviors and employee retention one year later. Positive changes in procedural fairness predicted both prosocial workplace behaviors and employee retention one year later. In contrast, positive changes in distributive fairness predicted prosocial workplace behaviors but had no effects of organizational retention.[§§§] These findings align with those of Hausknecht et al. When all four fairness dimensions were considered together in their study, changes in procedural fairness were the best predictor of the distal outcomes.

A hallmark of these three studies is that fairness was either increasing or decreasing steadily over lengthy time periods. Fadel Matta and colleagues were interested in the effects of more sudden changes in interpersonal fairness over shorter time periods given that they are common. In two different studies in the United States,[74] the benefits of interpersonal fairness on team pride and cooperative behaviors were greatest when day-to-day variability in fairness was low. The probable reason for this is that rapid changes in perceptions of interpersonal fairness would create uncertainty, and these findings have important practical implications for leadership training. While it is obviously important for leaders to understand the benefits of interpersonal fairness, it is just as important to help leaders appreciate the benefits of short-term consistency.

The findings of these four studies have intriguing implications for management practice that both go beyond workplace fairness perceptions. Hausknecht and colleagues highlight that organizational surveys will be most useful when the questions asked go beyond a single snapshot and instead delve into trends and changes over time. The importance of this suggestion is not limited to fairness perceptions. Obtaining information about changes in employee attitudes (e.g., commitment, trust) and experiences (e.g., autonomy, meaningfulness) might well provide invaluable information to organizations.

Special case

The vicarious experience of fairness

One intriguing lesson learned from the large literature on workplace aggression and violence is that you do not need to be the direct target of any aggression to be affected.[75] Instead, just witnessing workplace aggression against others can affect the witness, not only because of any moral objections against violence but also because it signals to witnesses how they could be treated in the future. The same is true for unfairness in the workplace. Simply witnessing others being targeted unfairly can affect witnesses negatively. This has major implications for everyday organizational functioning, because far more people learn about unfairness at work from watching or even hearing about what happens to others rather than personally experiencing it themselves. For example, more people watch or hear about others getting laid off than get laid off themselves, exposing them vicariously to incidents that potentially violate

§§§ This latter finding is important, suggesting that despite widespread beliefs to the contrary, issues involving pay are not always the best predictors of organizational turnover.

procedural and interpersonal fairness. Extrapolating from renowned psychologist Albert Bandura's influential social-learning theory,[76] while personally experiencing unfairness would have the greatest negative effects, seeing or even hearing about incidents involving unfairness could be enough to trigger negative reactions in witnesses. A program of research by Sandy Hershcovis illustrates some of the effects of witnessing unfairness at work.

In an initial study, thirty-seven nurses, doctors, and administrative staff of an emergency department in an urban hospital in the United Kingdom recorded unfair interactions that they witnessed over several days. Remarkably, this resulted in 509 pleasant and no fewer than 495 unpleasant interactions.[77] But the importance of this study goes beyond isolating how frequently people witness unfair interactions. Witnessing interpersonal unfairness also left employees feeling emotionally drained, and these effects were even stronger for witnesses who took the perspective of the target of the unfairness.

Employees who witness organizational unfairness do more than internalize their response; they also set out to punish perpetrators. In a separate study, Tara Reich and Sandy Hershcovis showed that employees who witnessed uncivil treatment evaluated the perpetrator more negatively, and when they had the power to do so, punished them with less desirable work allocations.[78] However, when given the opportunity to exact personal punishment against the instigator in this laboratory-based research, witnesses chose not to do so. The implication is that the punishment is meant to restore a balance of fairness, not to cause undue personal harm.

The news, however, is not all bleak! Watching workplace unfairness can also motivate witnesses to respond positively. Hershcovis and Namita Bhatnagar investigated how people respond when they watch another customer treating an employee unfairly.[79] Because people generally do not want to see others being mistreated, the researchers expected that witnessing a customer mistreating an employee would motivate people to do something to restore a balance of fairness. Data from observations of actual customer-server interactions in a fast-food restaurant (and two laboratory-based studies) showed that people who watched another customer mistreating an employee left significantly higher tips than those who witnessed no mistreatment. Presumably, they were trying to restore the balance by righting a perceived wrong. However, there was one important exception: if employees responded negatively to the rude customer, they were unlikely to receive higher tips, perhaps because doing so left witnesses believing that the balance of fairness had been restored.

Another way of dealing with seeing mistreatment would be to confront the perpetrator. In practice, however, this occurs infrequently, and Hershcovis and colleagues set out to understand why not. In a series of studies, whether witnesses choose to confront perpetrators depended on how much power witnesses feel they themselves have.[80] Witnesses were more likely to intervene when they felt a general sense of power as well as the specific power to influence the perpetrator.

Despite the negative effects of exposure to unfairness, there is room for optimism because organizational policies could limit the damage. A classic early study

by Bandura[81] helps us understand how children learn aggression from others.****
Preschool children watched an adult model act aggressively toward a bobo doll. Children were then assigned to groups that saw the adult model either be rewarded, rebuked, or receive no consequences for the aggression. Only the children who watched the adult model be rewarded or receive no consequences later acted aggressively toward the bobo doll. In contrast, children who had seen the model rebuked for the aggression acted less aggressively toward the bobo doll. These results have profound implications for organizations. Organizations are not powerless in the face of mistreatment. Having policies that punish acts of mistreatment, including sexual harassment[82] and workplace aggression,[83] sends clear signals to perpetrators, witnesses, and other employees about which behaviors are valued in the organization and which are unacceptable.

Conclusion

We need to take workplace fairness more seriously

Despite what we have learned about the nature and effects of organizational fairness, it is not unusual for managers to be dismissive when they hear employees complain about unfairness. Doing so would be a big mistake for several reasons. First, the consequences of unfairness on work attitudes and performance, as well as employee well-being, are often greatest on the most valuable employees. As one more example from research with manufacturing employees and in a laboratory setting, the negative effects of interactional unfairness on organizational citizenship were greater for employees who were more closely attached to the organization.[84] Moreover, it is not just employees who respond to fairness or unfairness; leaders do too. One study of 211 leaders in a Chinese high-tech manufacturing facility showed that leaders who felt that they were treated unfairly engaged in significantly more self-interested rather than team-focused behaviors.[85]

Second, it is not only procedural, interactional, informational, and distributive justice that exert these effects. Perceptions of organizational fairness as a whole also shape how people respond to these individual fairness dimensions. In a study of 355 US employees, after being treated unfairly regarding performance, compensation, promotion, or reasons for a layoff, employees were more willing to forgive and less likely to seek revenge if they people believed that were treated fairly in general.[86] Intriguingly, this effect was even more pronounced for employees who were more focused on others' needs rather than their own.

Third, not all employees remain silent in the face of unfairness. If employees choose to voice their dissatisfaction and they are not heard, they may consider whether their

**** Fascinating video footage of the original 1961 study is available at: The brain: A secret history—emotions; Bandura Bobo Doll Experiment. https://www.youtube.com/watch?v=zerCK0lRjp8

collective voice through labor unions would resolve the issues.[87] Historically, people turned to unions when distributive fairness and occupational safety were threatened. More recently, employees are turning to unions when issues surrounding procedural unfairness (e.g., complaints about sexual harassment, racism) are ignored, even in vaunted organizations such as Amazon or Alphabet and its subsidiaries such as Google.[88]

Fourth, exactly what postpandemic workplaces will look like is not yet known. What is apparent is that "inequality was bad and the COVID-19 pandemic is making it worse."[89] This increase in inequality is crucial: one meta-analysis of over fifty thousand participants from thirty-six countries showed that the negative effects of unfairness on work outcomes are heightened under conditions of greater inequality.[90] A separate meta-analysis of 30,275 employees across thirty-one countries found that the effects of unfairness on employee performance and organizational citizenship were greater when socioeconomic conditions, such as the weak rule of law and income inequality, were bad.[91] With rising concerns about inequality, organizations need to be sensitive about the effects of global societal issues on perceptions of fairness within organizations.

Thus, taken together, fairness is central to organizational functioning and employee well-being, and there is room for optimism. Any external turbulence heightens the benefits of fairness within organizations. Precisely because people are so sensitive to the way in which they are treated, they respond quickly to even small acts of fairness (and unfairness), as evidenced in the research on cardiovascular health and employee theft. Moreover, the effects of restoring fairness can be dramatic,[92] highlighting opportunities for organizations and leaders to facilitate the move to productive, healthy, and safe work.

6
Growth

Richard Branson perfectly captured the challenge facing organizations regarding employee growth and development: organizations need to take all reasonable steps to help their employees acquire the skills and knowledge that make them the envy, and even the target, of all their competitors. At the same time, organizations need to create the conditions, such as high-quality leadership, autonomy, belonging, fairness, meaningful work, and safety that would ensure that their employees would simply not want to be anywhere else.[1] In doing so, Branson reminds us of the interrelated nature of each of these seven dimensions.

The nature of growth and development

Focusing on employee growth within organizations is by no means new. As with any idea, however, trying to trace its origins back to one specific person is hazardous. Nonetheless, it is safe to say that in building on Maslow's basic-needs theory, Clayton Alderfer was one of the first to explicitly point some fifty years ago to employees' need for growth in the workplace[2] with his existence, relatedness, and growth (ERG) theory.* A few years later, Richard Hackman and Greg Oldham recognized employees' need for growth in their influential model of work motivation.[3]

Initiatives to foster employee growth and development start even before people join organizations. As we saw from Beamen et al.'s study among adolescents living in villages throughout India (see Chapter 2), role-modeling can significantly impact growth and development before people ever assume their first job.[4] Once members, the number and variety of formal initiatives or programs increase. When we think of training, we probably think of programs designed to teach specific skills, and these programs are the bread and butter of traditional HR departments. Other training initiatives focus more broadly. For example, cross-training teaches team members the skills needed by one another.[5] Extensive training initiatives, epitomized by access to university degrees with fees reimbursed, occur less frequently but go further, teaching employees skills that they may only need in the future.[6] Similarly, 360-degree feedback, performance appraisals, mentoring and (executive) coaching are routine in

* "Growth" needs encompass Maslow's needs for self (vs other) esteem and self-actualization.

Brave New Workplace. Julian Barling, Oxford University Press. © Oxford University Press 2023.
DOI: 10.1093/oso/9780190648107.003.0006

many organizations. Taken together, all these practices are integral parts of what today is often referred to as human capital development.

Several factors highlight the practical importance of fulfilling employees' needs for growth and development. First, global consulting company Deloitte even points to the extent to which their own members have opportunities for learning and development as one of the top ten reasons to join their own organization.[7] Second, fully three of the twelve items in the Gallup survey on what makes a great workplace focus on growth and development. These three items are "There is someone at work who encourages my development," "In the last six months, someone at work has talked to me about my progress," and "This last year, I have had opportunities at work to learn and grow." For anyone concerned that the resources required to achieve employee growth might be too costly, these three items make clear that we are not talking about daily investments in employees but opportunities in "the last six months" or "this last year." Moreover, these items also show that growth and development are no longer synonymous with promotion. Now, growth and development can occur within your job.

The benefits of growth and development

So why would some companies choose to invest in human capital development but others not? One clue is how they strategically view people in the organization. Think of your own organization: are people viewed as assets or as costs? After all, we do what we can to invest in our assets, and it makes sense to do what we can to keep our costs to a minimum. While this might seem simplistic, this thinking might play a large role in whether organizations have a culture of growth and development, or not (an issue we will take up in in the conclusion to this chapter).[8]

Workplace attitudes

Organizations invariably use human capital development programs to enhance performance. Yet as we will see, socialization, training, feedback, mentoring, and executive coaching bring other benefits to organizations as well.

Socialization[†] into the organization can be formal, for example, when it is offered by the organization with all newcomers exposed to the same information. Socialization can also be informal, with learning taking place through interactions with colleagues at work, as a result of which newcomers receive different information. Clive Fullagar and his colleagues contrasted the effects of formal and informal socialization among 305 members of the National Association of Letter Carriers, a large labor union in the

[†] Socialization is also frequently referred to as "onboarding."

United States.[9] Findings from this study were clear-cut: formal socialization had no effects on members' commitment to the union one year later. In contrast, informal socialization affected both union commitment and engagement in the union one year later.[‡] These findings are especially interesting for at least two reasons. First, they echo many of the similar benefits of personal relationships at work we see in Chapter 4. Second, as organizations embrace remote work, one of the significant issues they will need to overcome is onboarding employees, a task made more difficult in remote work environments.

Research on training in organizations has existed for more than a century and received an early boost by practical needs arising in World War I[10]; today, organizations spend billions of dollars each year on training.[11] As a result, we have a rich understanding of the nature and benefits of training, extensive practical lessons for organizations, and simply too many articles to summarize meaningfully in this chapter. But here is one lesson: while the primary goal of training remains the development of skills and knowledge, we also see many benefits to work attitudes.

One large-scale meta-analysis showed that employees' belief that training programs were available had a positive effect on their affective commitment and job satisfaction.[12] A separate study of 165 retail employees of a petroleum company in Singapore revealed that access to training was a better predictor of job satisfaction than autonomy, skill variety, and specific-task feedback.[13] One reason for these findings is that the availability of training opportunities signals to employees that their organizations are willing to invest in their development. While these findings are important, a more nuanced understanding of the value of training requires that we go beyond considering simply whether or not organizations offer training.

Training breadth, the extent to which employees receive training for different skills or activities, is important in its role in the development of role-breadth self-efficacy.[§] In one study of a manufacturing facility in the United Kingdom, ninety-four employees completed a survey on the breadth of training in which they had been involved.[14] This included whether they had received training in management or leadership skills, team building, communication, any form of on-the-job training, technical or maintenance training, vocational training, or health and safety training in the past eighteen months. Greater breadth of training during the prior eighteen months was associated with higher levels of role-breadth self-efficacy, which is critical in dynamic work organizations.

As anyone who has ever attended any form of training will tell you, some training is worth attending and, sadly, some not. Scott Tannenbaum and colleagues investigated what happens when the training needs of newcomers to the organization are met.[15] They focused on 666 new naval recruits in the United States, asking them about their

[‡] Informal socialization practices included receiving a personal invitation to attend a union meeting, a personal introduction by the shop steward, or help by a union member in solving a work problem.

[§] Role-breadth self-efficacy reflects employees' beliefs they can successfully go beyond traditional, narrowly prescribed roles.

training expectations within an hour of starting their jobs (to ensure that early socialization experiences did not affect their expectations). Eight weeks later, after the completion of the training, they asked the recruits whether the training had met their expectations. The direct effects of the training were evident: the degree to which the training fulfilled newcomers' needs was associated with their belief that they could deal with the physical and skill-based challenges of the job. Perhaps just as importantly, feeling that training fulfilled their needs, and the amount newcomers learned, influenced posttraining organizational commitment. Simply stated, when employees see their organizations invest in their growth and development, they repay the organization with their commitment. Findings such as these are important, because as Tannenbaum et al. point out, these new trainees "will carry those attitudes with them into the workplace" (767).

An intriguing experiment conducted by Niklas Steffens and colleagues points to the effects of feedback on future growth and development.[16] Steffens et al. deliberately manipulated the feedback participants received regarding their future leadership potential. One group were told they were not seen as having any potential to fill a vacant leadership position, while those in a second group were told that they were viewed as having leadership potential and would likely fill the next available leadership position. A third group received no information about leadership potential.** Receiving positive feedback about their leadership potential positively affected not only leadership ambition but also resulted in an increase in affective commitment to the organization. Presumably, people want to be members of organizations that are optimistic about their futures.

Unlike the long history of training in organizations, mentoring can "only" be traced back to the late 1970s and early 1980s,[17] and the goal has primarily remained the same since then: personal and professional growth, as well as career advancement.[18] Merely having a mentor is associated with higher levels of affective commitment to the organization, and this effect is greater for internal mentors, presumably because of their local knowledge of the organization's norms and values.[19] But it is not just the presence of a mentor that matters. A study of 560 employees from US Fortune 500 companies showed that the developmental advice and role-modeling provided by the mentor, and satisfaction with the mentoring relationship, all predicted job satisfaction and affective commitment. Even when the supervisor was the mentor, higher levels of mentoring activity were positively associated with affective commitment and with wanting to remain a member of the organization.[20]

Executive coaching is ubiquitous. Countless organizations offer their senior members access to executive coaches, and many others access executive coaching independently. The 2016 *ICF Global Coaching Study* estimated that there were 53,000 professional coaches across the world, and total revenue from coaching in 2015 was $2.356 billion.[21] In 2009, the average hourly fee for coaches was estimated to be $237,

** As is the case in all the research considered throughout the book, the authors obtained ethical approval before conducting this study.

with some coaches reputedly earning as much as $3,500 per hour. Thus, the question of whether executive coaching "works" looms large!

There is enough research from which we can conclude that executive coaching positively influences work attitudes. Tim Theebom and colleagues meta-analyzed eighteen different studies in which professionally trained executive coaches from outside of the organization provided the coaching.[22] Receiving executive coaching was associated with higher levels of job and career satisfaction, and organizational commitment, matching the findings from a subsequent meta-analysis.[23] Whether organizations or individuals are responsible for the cost of the coaching, it is comforting to know that is it not the number of sessions but the type of coaching that makes a difference. Theebom et al.'s results point to the superiority of solution-focused executive coaching, and Jones et al.'s analyses suggest that the effects of coaching on work attitudes was stronger for internal than external coaches. Presumably, like mentoring, internal coaches' greater appreciation of the local context and culture might enable them to offer more guided direction in the coaching.

Last, Maria Kraimer and colleagues showed that participation in formal developmental activities and career mentoring influenced employees' perceptions of whether their organization supported developmental activities in a US Fortune 500 company.[24] In turn, believing that the organization supported developmental activities reduced turnover. However, further analysis showed that this effect only held for employees who believed they could match their work assignments and career interest in the organization. The lesson from these findings is that it makes little sense to provide training if the organization does not create opportunities for employees to use the skills they have acquired. Indeed, investing in training and then limiting opportunities to use newly acquired skills hastens the turnover of the most skilled and valuable employees.[25]

Work performance

Human capital initiatives such as individual, team, and extensive training, feedback (especially 360-degree feedback), and executive coaching, are used routinely to improve performance in organizations. Of all these initiatives, training has been the focus of more research than any of these other practices. An early meta-analysis of 39 studies conducted between 1952 and 1982 already pointed to the effectiveness of managerial training.[26] Findings from research since then continue to show widespread positive effects of training in organizations.

One frequent target of training is safety performance. Michael Burke and colleagues meta-analyzed ninety-two studies that investigated different aspects of training on safety knowledge and safety performance.[27] They classified training as to whether it was highly engaging (i.e., required hands-on training, simulations, or behavioral modeling) vs less engaging (i.e., based on lectures, reading material, or video presentations). Not surprisingly, highly engaging training was significantly more effective in terms of safety knowledge acquired through the training and subsequent safety performance. In addition, highly engaging training was more effective in promoting safety knowledge and safety performance in more hazardous situations. Stated somewhat differently, safety training that requires active participation can help to ensure it is effective when most needed.

While much training research has investigated the effectiveness of individually based training, Ashley Hughes and colleagues meta-analyzed the effects of team training in health care.[28] Despite the added complexity involved in team training, the training worked. Team training influenced how much participants learned, whether they transferred what they had learned back to the workplace, patient outcomes such as length of non-ICU stay, and even patient mortality. Moreover, team training was effective irrespective of the training method (e.g., information, demonstration, or practice), whether training took place in multi- or single-discipline teams, with students or clinicians, or in units involving patients of different health status.

Extensive training goes beyond the acquisition of specific skills targeted at a single job, and instead targets broad-based skills that would be useful to employees and the organization in the future. In a sample of 308 companies in the United Kingdom, extensive training and empowerment were the only significant predictors of company productivity.[††] One reason extensive training might be effective is that it signals to employees that they have a long-term future in the organization, as a result of which employees expend more effort in their own development.[‡‡]

Feedback, especially 360-degree (or multisource) feedback, is a mainstay of many organizations, and has been studied for close to fifty years. An early meta-analysis showed that feedback was associated with higher levels of performance and lower levels of absenteeism.[29] However, recent studies offer a more nuanced understanding of the effectiveness of multisource feedback. For example, James Smither and colleagues' meta-analysis of twenty-four longitudinal studies shows that by itself the effects of multisource feedback are modest.[30] More troublingly, some research even suggests that a third of feedback interventions decrease performance.[31] Possible reasons for this include the fact that negative feedback is less likely to be seen as accurate or useful and more likely to lead to negative reactions,[32] neither of which would necessarily motivate positive change. Instead, the effects are more positive when employees are receptive to the feedback, believe that they can change the targeted behaviors and set goals to do so, and enact the required behaviors to make the necessary changes.

Without suggesting that organizations do away with external feedback—an impractical suggestion to say the least, several studies offer interesting ideas as how to improve the design and delivery of single or multisource feedback. First, instead of time-based feedback, such as annual performance reviews, "after-event reviews" like

†† They chose not to focus on profitability because it is affected by factors other than employees' inputs.

‡‡ In contrast to extensive training and empowerment, teamwork, total-quality management, just-in-time techniques, advanced manufacturing technology, and supply-chain partnering had no effects of company productivity.

those that occur in aviation and health care (e.g., surgery, ICU) contexts might be more effective. Scott Tannenbaum and Christopher Cerasoli's meta-analysis of forty-six after-event reviews showed that performance was 25 percent higher after the review, and that improvement occurred in medical and nonmedical contexts.[33]

Second, a study of 209 engineers in the United States showed that feedback resulted in fewer costs, less overtime required to complete tasks, and higher levels of organizational commitment over the ensuing nine months. More importantly from our perspective, feedback was more effective when it was self-generated (i.e., employees compared their achievements against goals they had set) rather than derived from a formal external source. Therefore, organizations would do well to provide opportunities for self-determined feedback. Third, Luthans and Peterson showed that the benefits of 360-degree feedback in a small US manufacturing plant were enhanced when feedback was coupled with coaching.[34]

We can also have some confidence that executive coaching delivers on its promises. Jones et al.'s meta-analysis showed that executive coaching resulted in better leadership and technical skills and competencies.[35] Theebom et al.'s meta-analysis established that executive coaching enhanced sales quantity, supervisor ratings of job performance, and high-quality leadership.[36] Separately, a study of 281 executives participating in a program offering both 360 multisource feedback and coaching resulted in significant improvement in leadership effectiveness.[37] As is apparent throughout this chapter, an important lesson from this is the importance of combining different human capital initiatives rather than treating them separately as stand-alone programs.

Well-being

Training initiatives frequently focus on leadership development. Recall from Chapter 2 that leadership training is effective, so effective that Lacerenza et al. concluded from their meta-analysis that "leadership training is substantially more effective than previously thought" (1686).[38] The benefits of leadership training, however, go well beyond skills and behaviors learned by leaders, so much so that Kevin Kelloway and I suggested that providing training for leaders is one of the proactive steps organizations can take to enhance employees' well-being.[39] A series of studies by Leslie Hammer and her colleagues provide intriguing support for this idea.

Hammer et al. developed a three-part training program to improve supervisors' supportive behaviors, with some surprising well-being benefits. The first component of their program comprises a one-hour computer-based module that outlines how supervisors can support employees and their families. In the second, supervisors set goals focused on the newly learned behaviors and receive daily email reminders to track these behaviors. Finally, trainees can access supplementary activities, such as online discussions. Various studies have shown the well-being effects of supportive supervisor training. In one study, 144 US military veterans whose supervisors had received the training reported feeling more relaxed six months after the training.[40] A second study of 250 US employees showed that the effects of this specific training program go beyond employees themselves: nine months after the training, supportive supervisor training resulted in employees *and* their spouses enjoying higher levels of relationship quality.[41] In addition, people who experienced higher levels of stress pre-training enjoyed better relationship quality and engaged in more positive parenting nine months following the training.

Receiving feedback does more than provide knowledge and information; it can also enhance well-being. David Holman and his colleagues conducted a one-day, off-site program in a UK health insurance and healthcare company designed to change several job characteristics, one of which was the amount of feedback employees received.[42] The program was successful. The more feedback employees received in the three months following the intervention, the better their well-being.

Turning our attention to mentoring, Jae Uk Chun analyzed the effects of a seven-month formal mentoring program for white-collar professionals from nine companies in Korea.[43] Mentors and protégés met for at least 1.5 hours twice a month during the program, and the researchers focused on the effects of mentors' career support, psychological support, and role-modeling. At the end of the program, protégés experienced better well-being, but it was solely a result of career coaching. What is perhaps more interesting is that Chun et al. were just as interested in the effects on mentors themselves. What they learned was that providing mentoring to others resulted in improved well-being for the mentors themselves, and it was the role-modeling function of mentoring that was responsible for this effect. The fact that both mentors and protégés benefitted gives organizations added reasons for implementing formal mentoring programs in their organizations.

Last, Anthony Grant and colleagues investigated the effects of executive coaching after forty-one executives of a major public health agency in Australia received leadership training and 360 feedback.[44] Once the participants completed the training and had received feedback, half the participants were randomly assigned to receive four coaching sessions over ten weeks from executive coaches external to the organization.[§§] Executives who received the four coaching sessions later enjoyed greater resilience and well-being and less depression than those who only received training and feedback.

The results of this study offer two lessons with which to end this section. First, the addition of only four coaching sessions made a difference to participants' well-being, again showing that huge resources are not required to achieve important personal benefits. Second, added benefits accrue when more than one developmental initiative is offered.

§§ Random assignment to groups is important in studies like this, as it is widely regarded in the social and organizational sciences as the best way to provide robust answers to research questions.

When growth and development go awry

The idea that the pandemic changed work is difficult to dispute (especially after working in my basement for most of 2020 and 2021). However, this is not the first time we have heard that work has changed. Dire predictions of a similar nature seem to surface every decade or so. As Sarah Kessler perhaps said it the best, "We've been worrying about the end of work for 500 years."[45] But real changes have taken place. Many people may not even remember that a normal or standard day's work for most people during the last half of the 20th century consisted of a full-time job that had a predictable, cyclical Monday through Friday, 9–5 work schedule, punctuated by public holidays and vacations. The arrival of globalization, organizational restructuring, lean and mean practices, diminishing social-safety nets, and automation all ensured that by the end of the 20th century less than a third of people in the United States and Canada enjoyed what we might now think of as the luxury of a standard workday.[46] In its place, a wide variety of "alternative work arrangements" have emerged, including part-time work, temporary employment, self-employment, home-based employment, moonlighting, job sharing, outsourcing, and seasonal and migrant employment.[47] Twenty years later, we must add on-call work, agency employment, gig work, and the pressure to move to a four-day work week to this list.[48,***]

Several features of these new work arrangements are readily apparent. First, after close to a century of expanding employee rights and protections, each of these new arrangements transfer control for work rules and decisions back to management, limiting the amount of control employees exert over their work and their lives. This shift of control away from workers is evident in a recent analysis of US employees conducted by economists Lawrence Katz and Alan Krueger[49]: by 2015, 79.6 percent of temporary-help agency employees with temporary jobs preferred a permanent job but could not get one. Similarly, 44.7 percent of on-call workers would have preferred a job with regularly scheduled hours but could not get it.[†††] We can also see a pattern in the number of hours of work. For some time, some people have been working more hours and wishing they were working fewer, yet at the same time, more people have been working fewer hours and wishing they were working more. All this has surely been made worse during the COVID-19 pandemic. Some people working in finance and professional, scientific, and technical services have seen an increase in their work hours. Others, for example, those in industries such as accommodation, arts, travel, and food services, saw their hours slashed, if not entirely eliminated.[50] In many countries, the unemployment rates following the onset of the pandemic were greater than

*** I deliberately exclude shift work, which has been with us at least since Thomas Edison's invention of the light bulb in 1879.

††† This was not the case for independent contractors, 83.7 percent of whom reported that they would prefer to work for themselves.

those during the Great Recession of 2008, and remained higher than they were at the beginning of 2020 for about a year following the onset of the pandemic.[51]

Second, the proliferation of these different work arrangements is part of a larger trend in which management has weakened their commitment to stable, predictable, and long-term employment. In its place, management now prefer the flexibility that contract work, agency work, or gig work offer to them. One huge implication of this is that employee development and growth will be of little importance to organizations that rely on a transient labor force. Indeed, it would make little sense for such organizations to invest financial resources in a workforce that could soon be working for the competition. To paraphrase the title of Benson et al.'s article ("You paid for the skills, now keep them") discussed earlier in this chapter,[52] this new model is best reflected in the notion, "If you are not going to keep them, why pay for their skills?"

As a result, we should expect to see fewer initiatives targeting employee growth and development under these new work arrangements. One study using Finnish data from a large representative sample of traditional full-time, voluntary and involuntary part-time, and voluntary and involuntary temporary workers bears this out.[53] Full-time employees believed they had greater access to employer-funded training than those under temporary or part-time contracts, and they were correct. They did indeed participate in more employer-funded training opportunities. Moreover, while overall opportunities for skill development increased from 1997 to 2008, full-time employees enjoyed greater access to employer-funded training. Last, employees who were involuntarily employed on a temporary or part-time basis had less involvement in employer-funded training, fewer possibilities to learn and grow at work, and fewer career possibilities than those who chose to work on a temporary or part-time basis. To quote directly from the researchers, "the type of job contract matters for workers' skills development opportunities" (789).

One final point about terminology. To date, the term *alternative work arrangements* has usually been used in a purely descriptive, non-judgmental way to differentiate it from traditionally stable, predictable, permanent, full-time employment. With the realization that there are clear status differences at play, researchers, policy-makers, and labor activists now frequently prefer the term *precarious employment*, which reflects what Jamie McCallum calls "the perpetual instability," "volatility," and "unpredictability" (38)[‡‡‡] inherent in alternative work arrangements.[54] The implications of this trend should be seen in light of findings showing that believing that training opportunities were available to you is associated with higher levels of job satisfaction and organizational commitment.[55]

‡‡‡ McCallum notes that the increasing number of people who find themselves involved in such work now have their own name, the "precariat," a reference to Karl Marx's proletariat.

Work attitudes

So what do we know about the effects of thwarted growth and development needs? Early research already pointed to differences in work attitudes between permanent and contingent workers, with permanent employees enjoying more positive attitudes.[§§§] As one example, a study of professional workers in Singapore showed that people on contingent contracts expected less from their organizations, engaged in less organizational citizenship, and scored lower on affective commitment than those on permanent contracts.[56] The one exception was independent contractors, 83.7 percent of whom reported that they would prefer to work for themselves. This study serves as a reminder that even professional and high-skilled workers can find themselves in an array of alternative work arrangements, and that their status does not protect them from any negative effects of alternative work arrangements.

Most of the research on the effects of different work arrangements has focused on job satisfaction, with a meta-analysis of seventy-two studies showing that contingent workers report lower levels of job satisfaction than permanent workers.[57] Just as importantly, significant differences in job satisfaction also existed among different types of contingent workers. For example, both agency and direct-hire workers were less satisfied with their jobs than full-time employees. However, contractors were no less satisfied with their jobs than permanent employees, a finding that emerged in the Singapore study just discussed and in a representative sample of Australian employees.[58] Other research helps to explain why independent contractors respond differently. Any differences between the work attitudes of part- and full-time employees,[59] as well as different alternative work arrangements,[60] are largely a function of whether employees choose that work arrangement[61]; when people choose to work under any of these alternative arrangements, the negative effects are minimized. The fact that most contractors prefer to work for themselves[62] explains why their satisfaction scores are similar to those of full-time employees.

However, alternative work arrangements need not be negative, as is apparent from research by Victor Haines and colleagues. They statistically constructed groups of people holding either "good" or "bad" part-time jobs in Canada.[63] Employees in good part-time employment had more work hours and supervisory responsibilities, higher pay, and greater flexibility in choosing the sequencing of their work tasks, the speed of their work, and importantly, how they do their work. They also enjoyed higher household income. Haines et al. showed that employees in good part-time jobs enjoyed higher levels of job satisfaction (and better health) than those in bad part-time jobs. Thus, organizations that choose to use alternative work arrangement might avoid negative effects if employees maintain some control over working hours and

[§§§] Contingent work is defined by the absence of either an explicit or implicit contract for long-term employment or a minimum number of hours that could vary dependent on the needs of the organization.

schedules, some autonomy about the way in which they do their work, and opportunities for growth and development.

Employees who are assigned to work organizations on a temporary basis through agencies face some ambiguity. The agency is responsible for their salary and some human resource services, and as a result, employees could develop affective commitments to the agency. At the same time, how the host organization and its supervisors treat them could influence their affective commitment to the organization, resulting in dual commitment to two different organizations. One study investigated these dual commitments among ninety-eight contingent workers from different agencies who had been assigned to work at the same US Fortune 500 company.[64] Temporary employees who were affectively committed to their agency were rated as lower in commitment to the organization by their managers. These results have meaningful consequences for contingent workers. As we saw in in Chapter 4, managers rated employees as higher in potential[65] and were more likely to reward them for good performance if they believed they were highly committed to the organization.[66] As a result, temporary workers who feel an attachment to their employing agency may put themselves at a disadvantage for future work prospects in the organization in which they currently work.

Work performance

Organizations that strategically limit their investment in temporary employees' growth and development compromise their capacity for high performance. As one example, Nele de Cuyper and colleagues compared the job performance of 430 call-center workers who were on permanent vs temporary contracts working in the same organization in Portugal.[67] Satisfaction with customer relationships, a frequent goal of organizations, differed between the two groups. Specifically, the quality of customer relationships, and the quality and quantity of information provided to customers, were higher among permanent than temporary workers.

Other research has examined why such differences emerge, and three studies focusing on different aspects of performance are especially informative. First, Clint Chadwick and Carol Flinchbaugh investigated the effects of part-time workers on companies' financial performance in an enormous sample of 85 percent of all private sector companies in the United States that had more than twenty employees.[68] They based their analyses on the percentage of part-time workers in each company. While the average was 7.5 percent, a small number of companies made much greater use of part-time workers. Company financial performance was assessed by subtracting production and labor costs from total annual sales, which provided a measure of each company's gross operating margin.

What the results initially showed was that a lower proportion of part-time workers was associated with higher company performance. In contrast, a higher proportion of part-time workers resulted in lower company performance. More importantly, the

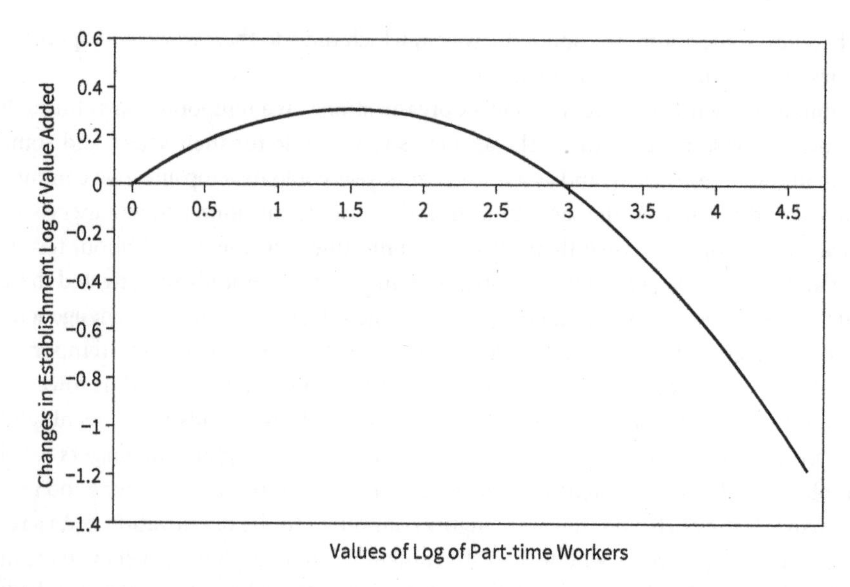

Fig. 6.1 Relationship between proportions of part-time workers and establishment value added.

Republished with permission from Sage Publications Inc. Journals, from Chadwick, C., & Flinchbaugh, C. (2016). The effects of part-time workers on establishment financial performance. *Journal of Management, 42*, 1635–1662; permission conveyed through Copyright Clearance Center, Inc.

researchers could pinpoint at what point the effects of part-time workers changed. Specifically, the positive benefits of part-time employees stop at about 3.2 percent of the total workforce, at which point the negative effects start to emerge (see Figure 6.1).**** From one perspective, organizations that use very small proportions of part-time workers probably do so because of the unique skills that these part-time workers offer, as a result of which the part-time workers enjoy higher status within the organization. In contrast, when the proportion of part-time workers increases, interactions between part-time and full-time employees would enable part-time employees to see that they are treated unequally, and relationships with full-time employees would be harmed. Findings like this could help organizations make constructive use of part-time employees.

Second, extending Chadwick and Flinchbaugh's research, Liat Eldor and Peter Cappelli explored the effects of agency temps on business performance in 270 retail service stores of a single chain in Israel.[69] The same agency provided temp workers for all stores, and all temp workers were paid an hourly wage that was different from full-time employees in the same store. In contrast to prevailing views about the benefits of temporary workers, higher proportions of temp workers in the store resulted in members of the regular workforce thinking that the status of the workplace had declined,

**** Note that the figure of 1.5 in Figure 6.1 reflects the logged value, which is equivalent to 3.2% of the companies' workforce.

which was associated with lower identification with the organization by the regular workforce.[††††] In turn, lower identification with the organization predicted poorer service quality as was assessed independently by secret shoppers, as well as fewer sales of private-label items, which would be of greatest financial benefit to the store.

Eldor and Cappelli also focused on management initiatives that could limit the negative effects of high proportions of temp agency workers. When store managers provided clarity as to why agency temp workers are used and set up activities to integrate regular and temporary workers, any negative effects of agency temp workers on service quality and sales performance were reduced. Nonetheless, Eldor and Cappelli's conclusion still needs to be taken seriously before organizations move to blended workforces: "The results are the opposite of the prevailing view of both economics scholars and executive managements that using agency temps improves business outcomes" (842).

Third, a large body of research links alternative work arrangements and safety performance.[70] Ioannis Anyfantis and George Boustros studied the effects of part-time employment on occupational safety incidents during the sudden and protracted financial crisis that started in Greece in 2009.[71] To cope with the financial crisis, many companies converted full-time employees to part-time status—against the wishes of the employees. Thus, there was overall decrease in full-time employment while the number of people holding part-time jobs increased significantly. Despite the decrease in full-time employment, the number of occupational safety "accidents"[‡‡‡‡] increased very significantly. The authors suggest that this occurred because part-time employees receive less safety training and have less access to safety professionals. David Collinson's qualitative analysis of safety on an oil rig in the North Shore would support this. His analyses showed that the lack of investment in contract workers even extends to safety equipment.[72] Not only did contract workers in his study receive lower pay, their safety equipment was of a lower standard than that provided to full-time workers. In some cases, it ended up being the discarded clothing of full-time workers, again highlighting the varied consequences of investing less in employees.

†††† Identification with the organization was reflected in survey items such as "When I talk about [name and location of the store], I usually say "we" rather than "they," and "When someone praises [name and location of the store], it feels like a personal compliment" (850). Thus, organizational identification is somewhat similar to affective commitment to the organization.

‡‡‡‡ In general, my preference is to steer clear of the term "accidents." What are frequently described as "accidents" defy the definition of being accidental, inasmuch as they were neither random nor unpredictable. This is a distinction that makes a difference! Using the term "accident" suggests that management had no control over these events, which is invariably not the case. However, I use the term "accidents" in this case because it is the term used in the article, and it is unclear whether the authors actually meant "injuries" or "accidents" (i.e., events).

Well-being

It might sound simple today, but a primary lesson Marie Jahoda took from her research on unemployment in Marienthal, Germany in the 1930s, was just how essential work is for mental health.[73] What we now know, however, is that not all work has the same value for mental health. As a result, we will consider the effects of different forms of precarious employment such as part-time, temporary, contract, and involuntary work arrangements on well-being.

Yuko Kachi and colleagues studied the effects of being engaged in precarious employment on the risk of serious psychological distress in a large representative study of middle-aged employees in Japan.[74] Men engaged in part-time work, temporary agency work, or contract employment were much more likely to develop symptoms of psychological distress over the following four years. Yet no negative effects emerged for women in precarious employment. The authors attribute this to prevailing gender stereotypes in Japan that prize men as breadwinners but view women as homemakers. As a result, the authors assume that many women holding precarious work choose to do so, which would limit any harmful effects.

While interesting, Kachi et al.'s research provides a static analysis of precarious employment. With the economic instability that followed the Great Recession of 2008, many people found themselves moving in and out of employment. A key question, therefore, is what would happen to employees whose employment status changed over time. One study using a large nationally representative sample of Korean employees investigated the effects on depressive symptoms of losing a full-time job and moving into precarious employment between 2008 and 2013.[75] Employees who went from full-time to precarious work suffered significantly more new symptoms of severe depression, and this was equally true for males and females. Unfortunately, the opposite was not the case: there was no decrease in severe depressive symptoms for employees who moved from precarious to full-time employment.

Most research treats the different types of precarious employment as if they occur in isolation, which is probably unrealistic. For example, while some people may be employed for regularly scheduled, full-time hours on a short-term contract, others might have been assigned by an agency to work for an organization on a part-time basis with irregular hours. In their meta-analysis, Torkel Rönnblad and colleagues compared the effects of working in a single form of precarious employment to simultaneously working in multiple forms.[76] Exposure to multiple forms of precarious employment was more detrimental to mental health than any single dimension alone. These findings are important, given that they probably capture the lived reality of many people in precarious employment.

One additional study explains why precarious employment has a negative effect on mental health. As we saw in Chapter 3, job autonomy provides a foundation for mental health. Kauhanen and Nätti's study of Finnish workers showed that full-time employees enjoy greater job autonomy and security than both voluntary and involuntary part-time and temporary employees.[77] There were also differences in autonomy and security among the different alternative work arrangements. Specifically, employees in *involuntary* part-time or temporary work had less job autonomy and security than their counterparts who did so voluntarily.

These are not isolated findings. By the mid-1980s, research had already shown that mothers having little control over whether they worked part or full-time experienced more depression[78] and parenting problems.[79] Thus, while precarious work is associated with poor work attitudes, work performance, and well-being, why people choose to be involved in different work arrangements is critical. This has important practical implications as organizations implement new remote work policies: having large groups of people working remotely who wish they could be in the office, or large groups working in the office who wish they could be working from home, may undo many of the intended benefits of remote working arrangements. We also need to ensure that those who can choose to work from home do not become a new privileged elite, while those who do not have the luxury to do so do not become even more disadvantaged while at work.

How do growth and development exert their effects?

Growth and development exert indirect effects

The idea that training exerts indirect effects on valued organizational outcomes should not be a surprise. In one study with 384 supervisor-employee dyads working for two different Chinese manufacturing firms, the researchers investigated how training affects later task performance.[80] One month after employees reported on their training experiences, employees completed a work-engagement survey. At the same time, their supervisors rated the quality and efficiency of their work, and the extent to which they had accomplished their work goals. Findings from this study showed that training worked by raising employee engagement, and it was this engagement that boosted employee performance. Hughes et al.'s large-scale meta-analysis of the effects of team-based training extends this notion.[81] While team training had moderate effects on patient well-being and organizational outcomes, team training again exerted indirect effects. Initially, team training provided new knowledge and skills. People then took what they have learned in training and transferred the knowledge and skills back to the workplace. Only then did patient well-being and organizational outcomes improve.

Feedback is no different, in that the information conveyed during feedback is not enough by itself to directly affect work performance. Instead, how people respond to feedback affects its use and effectiveness. Research by Frank Belschak and Deanne den Hartog on eighty-six employees of a large for-profit research company in Holland showed that it was employees' emotional responses to feedback that influenced their affective commitment, citizenship behaviors, and intentions to remain with the organization.[82] A similar pattern of findings emerged in a study of feedback and employee well-being in ninety-nine employees in Germany, Austria, or Switzerland.[83] In this case, the perceived fairness of the feedback was associated with higher quality employee-leader relationships, which in turn resulted in higher levels of well-being and intentions to remain with the organization. An additional finding from Belschak and Den Hartog warrants close attention. Negative feedback delivered publicly resulted in harmful behaviors such as purposefully wasting company time, ignoring your boss, or doing your work incorrectly, presumably because negative feedback delivered publicly breaches principles of interactional fairness. Taken together, these studies remind us of the importance of fairness perceptions, and how the basic tenets of fairness should structure how feedback is delivered if employees are to benefit from performance feedback.

Even the effects of ethical role models are indirect. In two studies in the United States, Tunde Ogunfowora and colleagues investigated how leaders' ethical role-modeling affects employees' morally courageous behaviors.[84] In both studies, leader role-modeling encouraged employees to take on greater moral responsibility for their own actions and behaviors, and increased their sense of obligation to act morally. In turn, both moral responsibility and the obligation to act in a moral manner influenced employees' morally courageous behaviors. One lesson from this research is that organizations need to look to their leaders' ethical behaviors if they are interested in what Ogunfowora et al. refer to as employees' morally courageous behaviors.

Last, any effects of mentoring are indirect. Research on 733 substance-abuse counselors in the United States focused on diverse components of the mentoring relationship.[85] The sponsorship, exposure, and visibility aspects of mentoring signal that mentors publicly back their protégés, which resulted in protégés viewing the organization as more supportive. In turn, believing that the organization was supportive resulted in higher levels of job satisfaction, affective commitment, and employee retention. In contrast, challenging assignments arising from mentoring do not signal that the organization cares for protégés and was unrelated to perceived organizational support. Similarly, the counseling, acceptance, confirmation, and friendship aspects of mentoring were unrelated to perceived organizational support, likely because they signify care and support from the mentor, not the organization. Thus, Baranik et al.'s research explains why some aspects of the mentoring relationship indirectly influence work attitudes, and for optimal effectiveness, highlights the need to tie specific components of mentoring with particular desired outcomes.

Growth and development shape the way you experience your work

In all our discussion of training, one factor we have not yet discussed is whether the training is mandatory. Of course, in some contexts such as occupational safety, training has to be mandatory to fulfil legal requirements. Does it make a difference whether people attend training voluntarily or not? Based on a representative sample of 486 Australian nurses, Joanna Carlisle and colleagues showed that the indirect effects of training effectiveness on task performance was greater when attendance was voluntary.[86] Notwithstanding findings such as these, mandatory training also signals to employees that the organization believes that the training is important,[87] and all these factors need to be considered in designing effective training programs.

Belle Rose Ragins and her colleagues highlight how mentoring shapes the effects of racial discrimination on employees' affective commitment and work stress (e.g., insomnia, absenteeism).[88] In two separate studies in the United States, greater exposure to racial discrimination was associated with lower affective commitment, and more insomnia and stress-related absenteeism. However, these negative effects were substantially lower if employees enjoyed a high-quality mentoring relationship. The unique role of the mentoring relationship is underlined, because high-quality relationships with supervisors or coworkers did not exert a similar effect. While the onus clearly remains on organizations to ensure discrimination-free workplaces, Ragins et al.'s findings highlight the widespread benefits that accrue to organizations that promote high-quality mentoring relationships.

Like mentoring, research on coaching relationships has focused mostly on their direct or indirect effects. Ellen van Oosten and colleagues offer a different role for executive coaching in their study of eighty-five senior leaders of a US-based Fortune 500 financial services firm.[89] All eighty-five leaders participated in a two-day leadership-development program aimed at improving emotional and social intelligence. After completion of the program, they all received two individual coaching sessions via the phone. The first coaching session focused on helping leaders develop their personal vision, and they reviewed their 360-degree feedback during the second session. As expected, the leadership-development program worked. Van Oosten et al. went further, showing that the effects of the leader-development program on leaders' work engagement and career satisfaction were even stronger for executives who had enjoyed a high-quality relationship with the coaches. These findings again point to the benefits of implementing more than one human capital initiative at a time.

Gender, growth, and development

Do men and women enjoy equal access to developmental opportunities in organizations? Given that organizations provide fewer developmental opportunities for people doing precarious work, perhaps the first question is whether gender differences exist in access to precarious employment. The answer to this question seems clear-cut. For example, data derived from the *Contingent Work Supplement* in the United States on alternative work arrangements in 1995, 1997, 1999, 2001, 2005, and 2017 showed that the proportion of women in precarious employment in the United States vastly exceeded that of men.[90] In addition, women were substantially over-represented in part-time work. This could have troubling consequences. If women do end up receiving fewer developmental opportunities, this could then spill over into fewer opportunities for leadership selection and promotion for women, which is already a serious issue (see Chapter 2). After all, advancing people in whose development you have invested makes sense. So too does denying advancement and promotion to those who have not received the developmental opportunities.

Given the role of performance reviews in employee growth and development, the fact that gender differences emerge in the performance-review process are concerning. Shelley Correll and colleagues highlight how women are treated unequally in performance evaluations in a study of 208 technical employees (of whom 80 were women) in a large technology company in Silicon Valley.[91] First, consistent with the gender differences in leadership (see Chapter 2), women were rated as more helpful and communal in performance reviews, but did not benefit from these perceptions. Instead, they were more likely to be punished if they deviated from gender-role stereotypes, such as being too aggressive. Second, men and women were equally likely to be told that they took charge, but men were more likely to be rewarded for doing so with higher performance ratings. Third, no differences emerged in the extent to which men and women's feedback highlight the need for improvements in the future. Women, however, were more likely to receive negative evaluations if they received such feedback. Fourth, women were less likely to be described using exceptional terms such as "genius" or "visionary." Even when they were, they were less likely to receive better evaluations as a result. Taking all this together, Correll et al. conclude, "The fact that, with the same feedback, women receive lower ratings than men means that women have to clear a higher scrutiny bar to get the next level" (1045). Importantly, the researchers advise that establishing clear, deliberate, and transparent evaluation processes would largely remove gender considerations from the feedback process.

Gender biases also exist in how feedback is given and received. Data taken from a large McKinsey survey of thirty-four thousand men and women across 130 companies showed that, although females ask for feedback more than males, they receive less.[92] Compounding the problem, gender biases also exist in the quality of feedback given to men and women.[93] In Lily Jampol and Vivian Zayas' first experimental study, 185 participants were randomly divided into six groups. Each group was presented with the same scenario of an employee who was clearly underperforming; however, the performance reviews participants read differed significantly, ranging from truthful and harsh through to much less truthful but "nice." As the feedback became less honest but kinder, participants were twice as likely to believe that the person receiving the review was a woman. In their second experiment, sixty-nine participants read and evaluated identical work, but were led to believe that the work had been done either by a woman ("Sarah") or a man ("Andrew"). Participants upwardly distorted their feedback to "Sarah" and judged her work more positively, effectively telling "white lies" to "Sarah" in her performance reviews. When questioned later, participants were unaware that their responses had been biased toward "Sarah." These discrepancies have enormous practical implications: accurate feedback is necessary for improvements in task performance, and denying women such feedback could hurt opportunities for advancement.

Men and women also differ in how they process or respond to negative feedback. Contrary to gender stereotypes about men being more agentic and "strong," men respond more negatively when faced with negative performance feedback.[94] As anyone who has delivered negative performance feedback will know, one manifestation of a negative response is crying, which is equally uncomfortable for both parties involved. But would this influence evaluations? One study in the United States had 169 adults view a professionally produced video in which either a male or female actor (named "Pat" in both instances) received negative performance feedback. The video ended with "Pat" being told that there would have to be a serious discussion about continued employment in the organization.[95] Half of the participants in each of these two groups watched Pat visibly cry in response to the negative feedback. Crying during the performance interview exerted indirect negative effects on overall evaluations of Pat's performance over the past year, and resulted in more negative recommendation about Pat for a different job. Moreover, crying led to more negative ratings as to whether Pat had the capabilities to be a leader—but in all cases, only when "Pat" was a male! Thus, women receive both less feedback and less honest feedback than men. However, when men exhibit traits frequently stereotyped as feminine, they too receive negative performance feedback.

Might exposure to female role models benefit women in the workforce too? We see in Chapter 2 how prolonged exposure to a female role model in India influenced young girls' career aspirations and motivation to stay in school longer.[96] Clarissa Cortland and Zoe Kinias investigated whether exposure to role models could minimize women's stereotype threat—the fear that your behaviors will confirm negative stereotypes about your gender.[97] This is important, as stereotype threat hampers women in many ways, such as in inhibiting leadership aspirations.[98] Using a sample of 1,286 women in Europe, Asia, and the United States, having a role model in their career (e.g., "seeing people like [me] succeed in senior management positions" [84]) was associated with significantly lower levels of stereotype threat. What makes these findings compelling is that the researchers also investigated the effects of formal and informal mentors or sponsors, and supportive supervisors and peers—none of whom reduced stereotype threat.

Culture, growth, and development

Differences in the level of growth and development

It might seem to some that training initiatives aimed at cultural awareness and sensitivity is just another fad in organizations. Not so! Programs of this nature have existed for at least half a century, and Fred Fiedler and colleagues' "culture assimilator" training program was probably one of the first.[99] Deliberately designed as a self-administered program to expand its international reach, the culture assimilator presented participants with a series of incidents taken from actual situations in a particular culture or country. Participants were then asked specific questions as to why people involved in the incident had behaved the way they did. The appendix attached to the program provided copious feedback relevant to each possible answer. Fiedler et al. pointed to initial data supporting the usefulness of the culture assimilator.

Organizational training has come a long way since then. Training is now a global phenomenon, and one lesson learned is that while organizational needs and managerial beliefs influence investments in training and development, so too do national and cultural factors. Hilla Peretz and Zehava Rosenblatt studied this issue in 5,991 organizations from twenty-one countries.[§§§§] They focused on three cultural characteristics that might influence investments in training, namely the extent to which obedience is expected (i.e., power distance), whether the norm is to plan for the future (i.e., a future orientation), and a preference for structure and predictability (i.e., uncertainty avoidance).[100] The effects of these cultural characteristics were measured by the proportion of employees in the company receiving training, the percentage of the HR budget spent on training, and whether the company had a formal training policy. Higher levels of future orientation and uncertainty avoidance predicted all three indicators of investment in training. In addition, lower power distance was related to a greater percentage of the HR budget spent on training, and whether the company had a formal training policy.

Deciding whether to invest in mentoring would depend at least in part on its expected return on investment, and Aarti Ramaswami and colleagues showed that such investment decisions are influenced by culture and country.[101] Individualism is higher in the United States than in Taiwan and, as expected, people in the United States were more likely to have mentors than those in Taiwan. The researchers also expected that gender and marital status would send different signals to management in the two countries. In the United States, being a married female often means having one's commitment to work and the organization questioned, raising the question of whether investing in mentoring was a wise decision. Based on 242 employees in Taiwan and 225 in the United States, married women in the United States were indeed less likely to have an organizational mentor. Taken together, one lesson for organizations is the need to be aware that cultural beliefs and characteristics could influence decisions about investments in developmental opportunities for employees, whether training, mentoring, or any of the other developmental practices.

[§§§§] Australia, Austria, Canada, Denmark, Finland, Germany, Greece, Hungary, Ireland, Israel, Italy, the Netherlands, New Zealand, the Philippines, Portugal, Slovenia, Sweden, Switzerland, Turkey, the United States, and the United Kingdom.

Differences in the function of growth and development

Few management practices are as widespread as multisource feedback systems, and one question is whether there are differences in why and how multisource feedback is used in different countries.[102] For example, we can use feedback for administrative or developmental purposes, the process could be mandatory or optional, and employees could choose or be assigned to raters.

Treena Gillespie conducted an intriguing study in which an organization headquartered in the United States had designed their own 360-degree feedback instrument.[103] The organization had branches in several countries, including the United States, Great Britain, Hong Kong, and Japan, and Gillespie analyzed data from 214 direct reports in each of the four countries. Significant differences emerged between these countries in the way in which employees interpreted the items in the same 360-degree feedback survey. Thus, to increase the utility of the feedback offered, Gillespie points to the need to benchmark individuals' feedback against country-specific norms, rather than norms based in where the company is headquartered.

Kok-Yee Ng and her colleagues investigated the effects of power distance on halo[*****] and leniency biases in multisource feedback.[104] As a part of this study, 172 military officers who were attending a nine-month leadership-development program in Singapore received developmental feedback from at least one supervisor, three peers, and three subordinates. As anyone who has given or received 360-degree feedback would appreciate, status and power differentials between subordinates, self, peers, and supervisors can complicate the feedback. As might be expected, subordinates and peers were more lenient in their feedback than supervisors. In addition, subordinates were more susceptible to halo bias than peers or supervisors. Both these inaccuracies were exaggerated among subordinates who scored higher on power distance (e.g., "I believe it is important to respect the decisions made by those who have more power"), possibly because these subordinates view providing upward feedback as inconsistent with supervisors' higher status.

Instead of focusing intensively within one country, Ellen Kossek and colleagues investigated the effects of cultural distance on leadership ratings between expatriate managers and raters in thirty-six countries.[105,†††††] As might be expected, cultural distance resulted in lower peer and subordinate ratings of leadership effectiveness. Similar to Ng et al.'s study, this effect was somewhat stronger for peers in countries characterized as being higher in power distance.

Thus, the functioning of multisource feedback systems is affected by national and cultural characteristics, and several practical implications emerge. First, those

***** A halo bias would reflect the inability by raters to distinguish between different aspects of the ratee's behaviors.

††††† Unlike many studies that examine specific cultural aspects such as power distance, individualism, and so forth, cultural distance in this study reflects the combined or overall difference on all the major cultural values between an expatriate manager and local workers.

involved in multisource feedback need to know that any discrepancies in information might not be a function of the parties and could instead reflect cultural values. Second, errors and biases in multisource feedback are not inevitable. The accuracy and utility of these systems could be enhanced by training those involved before any ratings occur, for example, in how to avoid different rating biases.

TMGT: Can we have too much growth and development?

It seems almost odd to ask this question, but can organizations invest too much in their employees' growth and development? Could there be situations in which the outcomes of programs simply do not justify the costs involved?

While there is very little research on these questions, one study provides some useful insights. Nai-Wen Chi and Carol Yeh-Yun Lin investigated the effects of high-performance work systems (HPWS) on financial performance in seventy-four high-tech and eighty-six traditional manufacturing companies in Taiwan.[106] HPWS are a set of integrated human resource practices (rather than individual best practices) that together increase employees' skills, abilities, and motivations. The HPWS in Chi and Lin's study included selective staffing, extensive training, results-oriented appraisal, competitive compensation, performance-contingent pay, employee participation, teamwork, internal promotion, and a formal complaint system. Selective staffing seeks to attract highly skilled employees, and extensive training develops broad skills among employees. Other elements such as internal promotions and competitive compensation seek to retain and motivate skilled and knowledgeable employees.

Two interesting findings emerged from this study. First, HPWS yielded an inverted-U relationship with return on equity, return on assets, net-profit margin, and productivity and personnel costs. As might be expected, financial performance was lowest when HPWS was lowest. Counterintuitively, financial performance was also low when HPWS was high. The authors invoke the notion of a cost-benefit analysis in explaining these findings. They speculate that the higher costs involved in implementing higher levels of HPWS may not be justified in terms of the financial outcomes they produced.

Second, and unexpectedly, no benefits from HPWS emerged among traditional manufacturing firms. One explanation for this is that knowledge development and retaining more highly qualified skilled staff is less important in working environments that demand fewer skills. As a result, the investments required by the HPWS would not be justified in the financial outcomes in this particular context. An important implication of these findings is that organizations need to tie their developmental initiatives to the needs of both the organization and employees.

Interventions to enhance growth and development

So many different developmental interventions exist that it is almost difficult to know where to begin. However, the mentoring program developed by Paul Lester and colleagues to increase leaders' self-efficacy beliefs stand out from all the others for two reasons.[107] First, leaders were randomly assigned to the different interventions or treatments. This is difficult to do in real organizations, but essential for enhancing the credibility of any findings. Second, their mentorship program did not exist in isolation but was one part of an unusually intensive leadership-development initiative.

All participants in this study were cadets in the four-year program at West Point, the US military academy that trains cadets to assume leadership positions upon graduation. Aside from the classroom and athletic programs that occur each year, all cadets participate in a structured and immersive leadership-development program. This involves participants rotating through different leadership experiences and receiving frequent structured feedback from multiple different sources.

During the fourth and final year, all 193 cadets continued in the leadership program, but seventy-six were assigned randomly to take part in the six-month mentorship initiative. Cadets selected their mentor from a senior staff or faculty member, and were required to attend at least six meetings together over this period. They jointly established roles and expectations (session 1), diagnosed and learned from past leadership challenges (session 2), and focused on the cadet's personal developmental goals (session 3) and leadership during ambiguous ethical situations (session 4). In the final two sessions, they discussed any topics the mentor or cadet thought was relevant to the cadet's leader development. Cadets also interviewed two different military officers to receive additional feedback. Each session ended with a writing exercise relevant to both the session topic and the mentoring experience. To ensure that any differences between the two groups were a function of the mentorship experience (and not, for example, other factors such as feeling deflated that you were not part of the mentorship group), the other 117 cadets also took part in six classroom sessions. To ensure these sessions differed from the mentorship experience, the student/teacher ratio was about 16:1. The mentorship program concluded with cadets writing an essay about their mentorship experience, which they discussed with their mentors. In contrast, cadets who were not in the mentoring program wrote a general essay on leadership character.

The intervention was successful. Leader self-efficacy beliefs were much higher among the cadets who had participated in the six-month mentorship. Higher leadership self-efficacy beliefs were then associated with better leadership ratings from tactical officers approximately one month after the program ended. The effects of this mentorship program should not be underestimated, as they emerged over and above an intensive, lengthy, and rigorous leadership-development program. Taken together, this again emphasizes the benefits of simultaneously implementing different developmental activities.

A special case: Are training and development cost-effective?

As we have seen throughout this chapter, developmental initiatives do indeed influence work attitudes, performance, and worker well-being. Despite this, researchers are often surprised when management remains skeptical about the benefits of these initiatives. But perhaps we shouldn't be surprised? Just because developmental initiatives are effective does not necessarily mean that they are also cost-effective—as we saw in Chi and Lin's study on HPWS,[108] and it is possible that information about cost-effectiveness might be most persuasive. One study investigating the cost-effectiveness of leadership-development initiatives is instructive.

Before examining that research, recall that leadership development has been shown to be effective (see Chapter 2). In one meta-analysis of no fewer than 132 interventions involving 11,552 participants, Bruce Avolio and colleagues noted that on average, participants who received leader training were about 30 percent more likely to achieve significantly better outcomes. A more recent meta-analysis by Christina Lacerenza and colleagues that included 335 interventions involving 26,573 participants concluded that not only is leadership development effective, it "is substantially more effective than previously thought" (1686).[109]

Just because these interventions are effective does not mean they are cost effective as well. Again, pointing to Chi and Lin's findings, it is possible that the investments required for training exceed any benefits gained. Avolio and his team provided an estimate of the costs of leadership training on which they base their calculations of the return-on-*development* investment (the RODI).[110] These costs included participant salaries while they were in the program, instructor-support staff salaries, and productivity losses (e.g., sales) while participants were in training. Other expenditures associated with the intervention include instructor salary, materials expenses, and costs incurred if the program was delivered off-site, such as travel, room rentals, accommodation, and meals. The researchers even accounted for differential expenditures incurred in delivering leadership training to senior vs mid-level leaders, assuming that interventions for senior leaders would be targeted to smaller groups than those directed at mid-level leaders (30 vs 100 participants respectively), and more likely to be conducted off-site. A full accounting of their estimates appears in Table 6.1.

Their findings offer important lessons about the RODI of leadership interventions. On average, the RODI for a 1.5-day intervention ranged between 44–72 percent, and between 50–87 percent for a three-day intervention. Whatever the length, the RODI was higher for mid-level than senior level leaders given the greater costs associated with interventions for senior leaders, and also greater for off-site rather than on-site (with senior leaders more like to enjoy smaller groups and the perks of

Table 6.1 Estimated costs involved in leader-development initiatives

Cost of training	On-site [a]	Off-site	On-line local
Time in participant salary [a]	$1200	$1600	$1200
Lost production time [a]	$2400	$3200	$2400
Instructor	$5000	$5000	$1500
Instructor support staff	$1000	$1000	$5000
Technology [a]	$500	$500	$10,000
Materials-up	$250	$275	$250
Materials-mid	$750	$750	$750
Trainer traveling expenses	$2000	$2000	$0
Travel costs for participants-up [a]	$0	$3000	$0
Travel costs for participants-mid [a]	$0	$10,000	$0
Meals-up	$3600	$3600	$0
Meals-mid	$10,000	$10,000	$0
Hotel conference room for training-up	$400	$500	$0
Hotel conference room for training-mid	$800	$1000	$0
Hotel stay for participants-up	$0	$4500	$0
Hotel stay for participants-mid	$0	$15,000	$0
Total	$27,900	$61,900	$21,100

[a] On-site is the location of the leadership-development program which helps determine costs. These analyses were intended to show the cost structure and effect of outside providers (e.g., academics/practitioners using a validated leadership model as the base of their intervention). On-site in this case does not insinuate internal (e.g., HR) personnel delivering the program. We use the same figures here that guided the work of Avolio et al. (2009)

Republished with permission from Elsevier Science &Technology Journals, from Avolio, B.J., Avey, J.B., & Quisenberry, D. (2010). Estimating return on leadership-development investment. *Leadership Quarterly, 21*, 633–644; permission conveyed through Copyright Clearance Center, Inc.

off-site leadership development). Importantly, even these encouraging findings may underestimate the real financial benefits of leadership interventions. As noted earlier, involvement in training has indirect effects on trainees, such as enhanced organizational commitment[111] and retention,[112] none of which is factored into the cost-benefit analyses.

One issue of considerable relevance following the pandemic is the cost-effectiveness, or RODI, of remote or computer-mediated leadership interventions. Any estimates from Avolio et al. might have been overtaken by technological advances achieved in remote leader development during the pandemic. As we move into a postpandemic environment in which more leadership-development initiatives will likely be conducted remotely, any cost savings may themselves come at a cost. Lacerenza et al.'s meta-analysis showed that the amount of learning was the same whether the training was in-person or remote. However, participants were more likely to use what they had learned in the workplace if programs were delivered in-person vs remotely. Thus, while remotely delivered programs may cost less, they may be less cost effective if leaders do not optimize what they learned during the training once they return to the workplace.

Given the lessons learned about the RODI for leadership interventions, can we rest assured that management will now introduce developmental initiatives? Sadly not. Henry Mintzberg established more than twenty years ago that managerial decision-making is not necessarily rational,[113] and management may remain unimpressed by RODI data for at least two reasons. First, many managers cling to the belief that leadership is "born," not made. Second, managers often doubt whether we really can quantify the financial benefits of different developmental initiatives. Third, and ironically, the magnitude of the RODI may be so impressive that it leaves managers questioning the credibility of the organizational researchers.[114] Thus, organizational researchers communicating with management need to remember that RODI data can be overwhelming and do not speak for themselves. Instead, sharing knowledge about the RODI of leadership-development programs needs to be one part of a broader conversation between researchers and managers that takes place only after mutually trusting relationships have been developed.

Conclusion

In case you are still not convinced

"It all starts at the top"! No doubt this is not the first time you have heard comments such as this in organizations, but it really is true when it comes to developmental opportunities in organizations. Someone has to make the strategic decision that employees are assets, not costs, and that their continued development is in everyone's best interests. Aparna Joshi and colleagues have identified what they call a "generative mindset" among CEOs—a strong commitment to the development of the next generation of organizational leaders, with little personal need to control the CEO succession process.[115] Initially, Joshi et al. suggest that the effects of CEOs' generative mindsets would be evident in the developmental opportunities for members of the top management teams. Presumably, when senior executives have seen the benefits of these initiatives firsthand, they will be motivated to see them flow further down the organization.

Second, the widespread positive effects of developmental activities such as training, feedback, mentoring, role-playing, and executive coaching are certainly encouraging. However, one critical question remains unanswered, and that is how long any positive effects last. Being able to show we can maintain newly acquired attitudes, skills, and well-being for a reasonable amount of time is crucial if organizations are to take findings like this seriously. Yet appropriate long-term analyses have not been undertaken. Organizational scientists would do well to learn a lesson from clinical psychology. In that realm, interventions are typically only considered successful if the effects are still evident many months later. To maximize long-term maintenance, short "booster sessions" are not uncommon in the clinical realm. Given the cost of training programs in organizations, short booster sessions that prolong the benefits of the training would probably justify the minimal investment required.

Third, we already saw the hazards of allowing autonomy without the necessary prior training (see Chapter 3). In the same way, providing developmental opportunities without the opportunity to use newly acquired skills is wasteful at best and can have unintended negative effects.[116] As one example, turnover is ever-present in organizations. But in one large-scale study of 9,543 salaried employees in a high-tech company in the United States, turnover accelerated after two years among employees who had received extensive training (in the form of employer-paid tuition reimbursement) but had not received any additional responsibilities in the interim. What would make this a particularly harsh loss for the organization is that the people quitting would be those with the most extensive skills—which had been obtained at the organization's expense.

Last, as evident throughout this chapter, research has mostly treated training, feedback, role-modeling, mentoring, and executive coaching as stand-alone best practices, investigating them in isolation from each other. No doubt, some organizations do the same in administering human capital programs. Far more will be gained from implementing bundles of different developmental initiatives that build on each other rather than discrete best practices.[117] For example, it would make little sense to focus heavily on newcomer socialization if later on companies don't invest equally in developing employees who have chosen to stay with the organization. Equally, it would be of limited value to invest in training if employees are then confronted by poor quality leadership, or for high-quality leaders to find themselves working with employees who have not been adequately trained.

7
Meaning

If it were desired to reduce a man to nothing—to punish him atrociously, to crush him in such a manner that the most hardened murderer would tremble before such a punishment, and take fright beforehand—it would be necessary to give to his work a character of complete uselessness, even to absurdity.[1]

Acclaimed Russian author Fyodor Dostoevsky had already learned people get reduced to nothing during four years of hard labor in a Siberian prison in the mid-19th century—all you had to do what ensure that their work had "a character of complete uselessness, even to absurdity." Although we might now recognize the wisdom in his observation, the expectation "that work sucks" remained true for workers for more than a century.[2] Indeed, the term *meaningful work* was hardly even used until the mid-1970s.[3] But that would soon change. The growing realization that factors such as financial compensation was an inadequate motivator was popularized in Frederick Herzberg's classic 1968 article, "One more time: How do you motivate employees?"[4] This article had managers turning to intrinsic factors such as achievement, responsibility, and the intrinsic nature of work as real motivators. At about the same time, Richard Hackman and Greg Oldham gave a central role to meaningful work in their *Job Characteristics Model*.[5] Hackman and Oldham also developed the *Job Diagnostic Survey*, a questionnaire that enabled the assessment of the core components of meaningful work.[6] Together, this stimulated decades of research that investigated the nature, causes, and consequences of meaningful work.

The nature of meaningful work

In their groundbreaking research, Hackman and Oldham identified several factors involved in meaningful work. One of these factors is "task identity," a deep personal involvement in, or identification with, the work itself. At its most basic level, task identity involves people being involved in the entire job from start to finish, rather than only fragmented parts of the job. Scholars and practitioners alike now recognize the importance of identification with one's work. As examples, Kevin Kelloway and colleagues point to the intense longing that some people have for the work that they do, and include this passion for your work as one of three factors that make up the love of one's job.[7] Along similar lines, Jeffrey Pfeffer concluded in his classic article

Brave New Workplace. Julian Barling, Oxford University Press. © Oxford University Press 2023.
DOI: 10.1093/oso/9780190648107.003.0007

"Six dangerous myths about pay" that organizations are mistaken when they believe that people are mainly motivated by money. Instead, Pfeffer argues, people are primarily motivated by work that is fun.[8]

A second factor contributing to meaningful work is knowing that your work has a significant impact on the lives of others, and Hackman and Oldham called this "task significance." The idea that purpose and meaning in life derive from our impact on others is hardly new. William J. Winslade illustrates this concept in this wonderful story about Auschwitz survivor and author, Viktor Frankl.[9]

> "Frankl was once asked to express in one sentence the meaning of his own life. He wrote the response on paper and asked his students to guess what he had written. After some moments of quiet reflection, a student surprised Frankl by saying, "The meaning of your life is to help others find the meaning of theirs." "That was it, exactly," Frankl said. "Those are the very words I had written." (164, 165)

To Frankl, meaning in life was "the primary motivational force" (99) for humankind. Thus, work would be experienced as meaningful when people appreciate its impact not on themselves but on others inside or outside work or on society as a whole.* The Gallup survey on the factors that make a great workplace also recognizes the importance of meaningful work. One of the twelve items asks "The mission/purpose of my company makes me feel my job is important."[10]

One way of appreciating the unique nature of task significance is by contrasting it with Maslow's notion of self-actualization.[11] Task significance emphasizes that people derive their motivation from what they can do for others. In sharp contrast, the focus of self-actualization is *self*-fulfillment As Maslow famously described the nature of self-actualization, "A musician must make music, an artist must paint, a poet must write, if he is to be ultimately happy. What a man *can* be, he *must* be" (382, italics added).† The implications of this distinction could not be more far-reaching. Are people more motivated to help others or by self-fulfillment? Or, taking a page from Adam Grant's 2014 book, are we more likely to be motivated when we give or when we take?[12] Much of the research discussed in this chapter will help provide answers to this fundamental question.

* They also suggested that being able to use a variety of different skills would contribute to the work being experienced as meaningful. Aspects of skill variety are discussed briefly in Chapter 6.

† In fairness to Maslow, a clarification is warranted. Most people likely believe that Maslow placed self-actualization at the pinnacle of the hierarchy of needs. While this broadly reflects his earlier writings, such as his classic theory paper in 1944, he later suggested that self-transcendence went beyond self-actualization, and reflects "the very highest and most inclusive or holistic needs of... behaving and relating, as ends rather than means, to oneself, to significant others, to human beings in general." Ackerman, C.E. (June 20, 2022). What is self-transendence? https://positivepsychology.com/self-transcendence/

The benefits of meaningful work

Workplace attitudes

Work motivation theories tell us that when people are intrinsically involved in their work, they enjoy better work attitudes, and this was demonstrated in an important study led by James Westaby and his colleagues.[13] They were intrigued why when faced with a diagnosis of amyotrophic lateral sclerosis (ALS)[‡] some people choose to continue working. After all, ALS is a devastating, terminal illness that progressively robs people of muscle strength leading to paralysis while maintaining cognitive functioning. The average prognosis for people diagnosed with ALS is three years. Westaby et al. suggested that several factors might influence their decision to continue working: financial need, access to transportation, disability severity, and intrinsic factors such as interest and involvement in work. They surveyed a representative sample of 102 adults in New York who been diagnosed with ALS. As might be expected, the severity of the illness at diagnosis, and difficulties commuting, limited people's intentions to continue working. In addition, older people were less likely to want to keep working. In an era in which inclusivity is a major issue, these findings remind organizations of the need to make reasonable accommodations to help people who want to continue working in the face of personal obstacles.

Of much greater importance, financial factors such as compensation, benefits, and bonuses had no effect on intentions to continue working. Instead, by far the most significant personal reason why people wanted to continue working was the intrinsic nature of the work itself. These findings are so important, as this is one of the few studies that directly contrasts the motivating effects of intrinsic and extrinsic factors during extraordinary circumstances.

Support for the role of task significance also comes from an extensive meta-analysis by Lauren Wegman and colleagues of thirty-four studies on task identity and thirty-one on task significance between 1975 and 2011,[14] a period during which the nature of work changed considerably. For example, the 1980s saw the introduction of personal computers and the growth in alternative work arrangements (see Chapter 6). Despite this, both task identity and task significance were significantly related to job satisfaction, and this did not change between 1975 and 2011.

Work performance

A core outcome of task identity is that people are absorbed by their work. That being the case, task identity should be negatively associated with absence from work. Joan

‡ Also known as Lou Gehrig's disease.

Rentsch and Robert Steele reported on an unusually long-term study to assess this proposition.[15] They collected data in May 1983 on the extent to which highly specialized civilian research and technology employees in the US Department of Defense identified with their work. Absence data were obtained from organizational records at the end of the year. They repeated this procedure each year until the end of 1988, at which time 399 employees had responded to the questionnaires each year. The effects of task identity could not have been more consistent: every year between 1983 and 1988, employees with higher levels of task identity subsequently missed fewer days of work and had fewer bouts of absence. Similar to the well-known maxim "Teach people to fish, and you feed them for a lifetime," these findings suggest that if we give people a good reason to work, they will keep coming back to do it.

Unlike task identity, task significance involves appreciating that your work positively affects others (i.e., your work has a prosocial impact).[§] Filipa Castanheira's research on 371 customer service agents in three Portuguese retail organizations contrasted the effects of the perceived social impact of work (e.g., "I have a positive impact on my customers in my work on a regular basis") with the perceived social worth that people derive from their work (e.g., "I feel that customers value my contributions at work").[16] Stated somewhat differently, they investigated what your work means to others vs what it does for you. Castanheira's findings are revealing. Perceived social impact on others had a direct effect on how engaged customer service reps were, but perceived social worth did not. In addition, the indirect effects of perceived social impact on engagement through its effects on affective commitment were much stronger than those of perceived social worth. Adding to the importance of perceived social impact, employees who scored higher on engagement were also rated as higher on job performance by their supervisors one month later.

Fascinating research by Adam Grant and David Hofmann further highlights the counterintuitive effects of prosocial impact vs personal benefits. Given that hand-hygiene habits are notoriously difficult to change, they questioned how we can motivate people to wash their hands thoroughly in a hospital setting, where patient, physician, and public safety are at risk. Intuitively, it might seem that appealing to people's own health and safety should work, but Grant and Hofmann's research points us in a different direction.[17]

In their first study, they randomly placed one of three signs encouraging handwashing above each dispenser at sixty-six handwashing stations in a single US hospital. One sign inspired personal motivation, reading "Hand hygiene prevents you from catching diseases." A second sign inspired prosocial motivation, "Hand hygiene prevents patients from catching disease."[**] The only difference between the two signs was one word, but reflects a substantial difference in the nature of the motivation. To assess the effects of the motivational signs, they measured the amount of soap or

[§] To make this more readable, *task significance* and *prosocial impact* are used interchangeably throughout.

[**] The third sign served as the control, and simply stated "Gel in, wash out."

gel used at the different stations before the signs were put up, and for a period of two weeks during which the signs were placed above the dispensers. As can be seen in Figure 7.1 (left panel), health care professionals responded significantly to a message aimed at protecting *patients'* health and safety: there was a remarkable increase of 45 percent in the amount of soap and gel used under the prosocial motivation sign, but no response to the personal motivation sign.

Nine months later, Grant and Hoffman's second study in the same hospital focused more specifically on the extent to which health care professionals adhered to best hand-hygiene practices before or after a patient contact. For this study, nurses were trained to unobtrusively record hand-washing practices. Hand washing increased by 11.5 percent at stations with the prosocial message. Again, however, there was no response to the personal message (see Figure 7.1, right panel). Taken together, the benefits of prosocial vs personal motivation justify the title given to their article, "It's not all about me," and their findings are credible, as researchers give special emphasis to findings from controlled field studies such as these.

Prosocial impact involves an appreciation of how your work affects others. Sometimes, work puts you in personal contact with the beneficiaries of your efforts. As the old adage tell us, "Seeing is believing," and seeing your impact on others should be intrinsically motivating.[18] I was first introduced to how this idea applies at work by a story told to me by a former executive MBA student, who had just been promoted to be the manager of a large pharmaceutical plant. One part of the plant included an assembly line that manufactured intravenous drips for infants. As he toured the plant on this first day as manager, he stopped at this assembly line and asked a young worker what she did. "Oh," she replied without hesitation, "we save babies." It turned out that sometime before he had assumed his new role of plant manager, the supervisor of

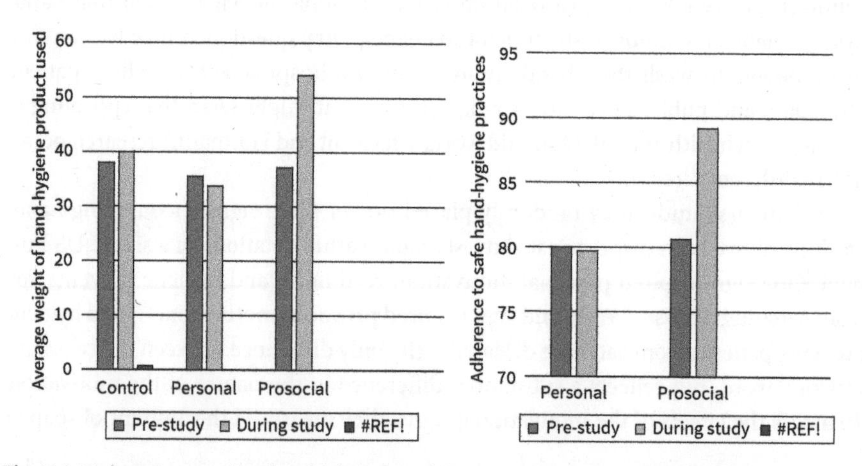

Fig. 7.1 Enhancing motivation for handwashing: prosocial vs personal reasons.
Adapted from Grant, A.M., & Hofmann, D.A. (2011). It's not all about me: Motivating hand hygiene among health care professional by focusing on patients. *Psychological Science, 22*, 1494–1499. Figures created based on data in Grant and Hofmann (2011).

the assembly line had arranged for all the employees to spend a morning at the local children's hospital, seeing that what they did each day saved babies, no doubt having a major impact on how important they viewed their work to be.

Adam Grant's field experiment among thirty-three employees who worked on a US university's fundraising campaign was one of the first studies to directly test this idea of beneficiary contact.[19] Grant randomly assigned each of the thirty-three employees to one of three groups. In the task-significance group, employees read two stories written by scholarship recipients explaining how the scholarship that resulted from the efforts of the employees had affected their lives. In the personal-benefit group, current employees read two stories from previous employees explaining how their work had affected their own lives.[††] The intervention for each group lasted a total of twenty minutes. In each case, ten minutes was spent readings the two stories, with ten minutes allocated for group discussion of the two stories.

The findings from this very brief intervention are compelling! No significant changes emerged in either the personal impact or control groups. Yet in the week following the intervention, employees in the task-significance group enjoyed an increase of 153 percent in the number of pledges made by people they had called, and a 143 percent increase in total value of the pledges. And they achieved these gains from a twenty-minute intervention, in which employees only read and discussed personal stories from grateful recipients of their work, reminding us again that small changes do indeed make a big difference!

To further test the effects of beneficiary contact, Adam Grant and his colleagues conducted a similar study with employees working on another university fundraising initiative. In this case, they again assigned thirty-nine employees to three groups. Employees in two of the groups were called into their manager's office for ten minutes.[20] The managers told them that the organization had received letters from scholarship winners, and that the organization wanted to share these letters with employees so they could see the impact of their work on students for themselves. Employees then spent five minutes reading a letter, at which point the two groups were treated separately. The manager told the "interpersonal contact" group that the scholarship recipient who had written the letter was available, and he met with the group and answered questions for five minutes. Employees in the other group (the "letter" group) were asked to discuss the letter among themselves for five minutes. Employees in the control group simply read the letter.

Grant et al. compared the performance of the three groups on task persistence (amount of time spent on the phone) and work quality (total amount of money donated) in the month following the intervention. Because the interpersonal-contact and letter groups received the exact same information but differed only in terms of direct personal contact, the results of this brief intervention highlight the importance of beneficiary contact. There were no changes in either persistence or quality for the

[††] Employees in the third (control) group spent the equivalent time completing a survey.

letter or control groups. In contrast, beneficiary contact had very significant effects, with increases of 142 percent in the amount of time spent on the phone, and 171 percent in the value of the donations. What makes the role of beneficiary contact even more persuasive is that the increase in persistence and quality lasted for a full month, but resulted from mere a ten-minute intervention!‡‡

Well-being

In addition to its positive effects on work performance, meaningful work also benefits individuals' well-being. For example, research in Germany showed that experiencing meaningful work was associated with lower levels of emotional exhaustion, and in a second study by the same authors, having access to meaningful work predicted fewer depressive symptoms twelve weeks later.[21] And these effects go beyond feelings of well-being. A study among 194 employees in the United States revealed that meaningful work positively affected activities at home up to three months later.[22]

Other studies provide more focused lessons on the advantages of meaningful work. Sabine Sonnentag and Adam Grant were interested in the effects of meaningful work on emotional responses at the end of the day, and they asked forty-four firefighters and twenty-four ambulance drivers from Switzerland, Germany, and Austria to complete questionnaires twice a day for a week.[23] At the end of their shifts, firefighters and ambulance drivers rated how they felt about the prosocial impact of their work, as well as their own positive affect and competence. Each night at bedtime, they completed surveys assessing how they reflected about that day's work and how positively they felt in general. Feelings of prosocial impact had no immediate effect on well-being at the end of the work shift. However, they did have a delayed effect, inasmuch as daily prosocial impact left people feeling better at bedtime.

These findings are interesting for several reasons. First, they again show that the benefits of meaningful work go beyond the workplace. Second, the effects of prosocial impact were not direct. Instead, they were mediated by positive work reflection and feelings of competence about that day's work. In other words, knowing that your work benefitted others left employees feeling more positively about their work, and more competent, and that is what led to increased well-being. Third, these findings have practical implications. To enhance the benefits of meaningful work, supervisors should encourage employees to actively reflect on how their work affects others. Doing so is even more important in demanding contexts, when employees might not spontaneously make the time to do so themselves.

So far, we have seen that that meaningful work benefits the particular job holder. Shiri Lavy and Eman Naama-Ghanayim explored whether any benefits of meaningful work spill over onto others. To do so, they studied 675 fifteen-to-seventeen-year-old

‡‡ Later in this chapter, we will consider how task identity and prosocial impact (or beneficiary contact) work together to effect relevant outcomes.

high school students and their thirty-three homeroom teachers in Israel.[24] Teachers completed surveys assessing the meaning they experienced in their work, and students completed questionnaires asking about (a) the extent to which they believed their teachers cared about them, and (b) their own self-esteem, life satisfaction, and school engagement. The more teachers found meaning in their work, the more students believed that the teachers cared for them. In turn, feeling cared for by their teachers resulted in higher levels of students' self-esteem, life satisfaction, and engagement in their schoolwork. These results have real-world implications for organizations: ensuring that leaders understand how their work benefits others can have a cascading effect on others around them.

When meaningful work goes awry

> *I worked as a museum guard for a global security company in a museum where one exhibition room was left unused. My job was to guard that empty room, ensuring no museum guests touched the, well, nothing in the room and ensure nobody set any fires. To keep my mind sharp and attention undivided, I was forbidden any form of mental stimulation, like books, phones, etc. As nobody was ever there, I sat still and twiddled my thumbs for seven and a half hours, waiting for the fire alarm to sound. If it did, I was to calmly stand up and walk out. That was it.*[25]

What exactly is the opposite of "meaningful" work? This is a difficult question, and even dictionaries provide little help: "meaningless," "minor," "unimportant," "nonessential," "small," "unsubstantial," "trivial," and "worthless"? David Graeber (2018, 2, 3) even talks about "bullshit jobs," which he defines as "so completely pointless that even the person who has to perform is every day cannot convince himself there's a good reason for him to be doing it ... he is convinced the job is pointless."[26] Rather than just substituting any of these words, we will examine the effects of two different ways in which meaningful work goes awry. The first is monotonous work and the ensuing boredom, a problem that William McBain had already recognized in his article "What can be done about job monotony?" more than sixty years ago.[27] In sharp contrast to boring work is "workaholism": the deep-seated desire for an intense involvement in work. The difference between boredom and workaholism goes beyond the *level* of their work involvement or engagement. Work-related boredom is primarily a function of an unstimulating job, whereas workaholism is mostly a function of individual needs and motivation, sometimes even being defined as, or compared to, an addiction.

Work attitudes

Perhaps surprisingly given its prevalence, work-related boredom has not been widely researched. Studies that do exist, however, consistently show that it is associated with negative work attitudes. In an article with a title that leaves little to the imagination ("Watching the paint dry"), Gaby Reijseger and her colleagues investigated the effects of work-related boredom among 6,315 employees from a range of industries in the Netherlands.[28] Their analyses showed that boredom at work is associated with lower levels of job satisfaction and affective commitment. People experiencing higher levels of boredom were also more likely to look to change jobs within the next twelve months. Studies conducted elsewhere show similar effects. As one example, feeling that your work was routine, boring, or monotonous was associated with job dissatisfaction in a sample of 1,278 blue-collar workers in Israel.[29]

Often cited as the first major book on workaholism, William Oates' 1972 book, *Confessions of a workaholic*,[30] stimulated much research in the years that followed. Malissa Clark and colleagues' meta-analysis of twenty-three studies involving 8,831 people showed that workaholism was related to higher levels of job dissatisfaction.[31] This finding is revealing: although both task identity and workaholism involve high levels of job involvement, task identity is positively associated, but workaholism negatively associated, with job satisfaction. Guided by research on the effects of a harmonious and obsessive passion for work respectively,[32] one explanation for this difference is that task identity involves control over your activities and yourself, while workaholism means feeling controlled by external events.

Work performance

One troubling consequence of work-related boredom is that bored employees will be disengaged from their work, and with time on their hands look for other things to do. In *Rivethead: Tales from the assembly line*, Ben Hamper's memoir of life on a General Motors assembly line, he recounts how mind-numbingly monotonous work drove employees to do anything to help make their days feel less dull and time go more quickly. This included continual drinking and overdosing at work, using their riveting guns to shoot at the company mascot—ridiculously named by GM as "Howie Makem," and even torching a mouse running through the factory."[33] Perhaps not surprisingly, research findings confirm Hamper's experiences. In one study of 114 employees in the United States, job-related boredom predicted a range of counterproductive behaviors, including deliberate property damage and theft, working slowly and not following instructions, treating others poorly, and taking extended and unauthorized breaks.[34]

In contrast to boredom, there is some debate as to how workaholism affects work performance. People with higher levels of workaholism do work longer hours and may impose higher standards on themselves, resulting in higher levels of performance. At the same time, the work they do may create little value to the organization,[35] and they may develop problematic relationships with coworkers.[36] Research findings do not paint an encouraging picture of the effects of workaholism on work performance. At best, Clark et al.'s meta-analysis of twelve articles involving 6,726 people yielded no benefits of workaholism for overall job performance.[37] Focusing on more specific behaviors, a study of 175 supervisor-employee dyads in Norway showed that employees who scored higher on workaholism were rated more negatively by their supervisor in terms of cooperative and helpful behaviors.[38] An intensive study by Guido Alessandri and colleagues of eighty-five police officers in Italy over six different time points confirms the negative effects of workaholism on helping behaviors.[39] The authors showed that one reason for this was that workaholism involved people placing greater demands on themselves, and when they did so they were less inclined to help others in the workplace.

Conducting research in lab settings enables researchers to assign truly meaningless work to people. Several studies have done just that, and they provide very valuable insights. In the first of two studies conducted by Dan Ariely and his colleagues, participants were given relatively boring work, and then tasked with finding ten instances of two different letters on a sheet with random letters for which they would receive $0.55.[40] After completing the first page, they were invited to complete a second sheet for $0.50, with the process continuing in decrements of 5 cents per sheet. Participants in one group (the "acknowledged" condition) were asked to place their name at the top of each sheet, with each sheet being examined and kept in a file at the end of the experiment. Participants in the second group (the "ignored" condition) were not asked to write their names on the top of each sheet, their sheets were not examined, and no one placed their names on the sheet. This same procedure was followed by the third group (the "shredded" condition), except that participants were told that their sheets would be put through a shredder at the end of the experiment, and the experimenter did this in front of the participants as they handed in their sheets. In this way, the work of the participants in this "Shredded" condition was deliberately designed to be as meaningless as possible.

As might be expected, productivity was much greater when work was more meaningful. Almost half the participants in the "acknowledged" condition were willing to work until their wage dropped to zero. In contrast, participants in the "ignored" and "shredded" conditions, whose work was ignored, demanded almost twice as much money to complete the same amount of work as those whose work was meaningful. Ariely et al. then replicated these conditions in a second experiment. Work output was 47 percent higher in the meaningful group, but the minimum wage demanded by people who saw the meaning stripped out of their work increased by 39 percent. An important lesson from both these studies is that when work is deprived of meaning, people look for motivation elsewhere, and one source is higher wages. Taken together, these findings provide some indication of the economic costs of meaningless work.

A similar study provides additional insights. Dana Chandler and Adam Kapelner asked 2,471 participants to view and label medical images, but described the task differently to three separate groups.[41] Participants in the "meaningful group" were told that their work would help narrow down images for a research project. They also learned that the images they viewed were of "cancerous tumor cells," heard the word "tumor" or "cells" sixteen times in the introduction, and were thanked for their work. Participants in the remaining two groups were advised that the pictures were only "objects of interest." Those in the "zero-context" group received no recognition or explanation of the purpose of the task, nor were they thanked for their participation. Participants in the "shredded" condition received the same treatment as those in the "zero-context" condition but were also told that none of their responses would be recorded and that they could leave if they wished.

Meaningful work affected helping behaviors. People in the meaningful condition were 4.6 percent more likely to agree to participate in the study, while those in the shredded condition were 4 percent less likely to do so. These results might have practical implications for organizations, as employees might be more willing to engage in discretionary helping behaviors in organizations when they see the tasks as more meaningful. Moreover, people in the meaningful-work condition viewed significantly more slides, though there was no increase in the quality of their work. In contrast, the quality of the work was 7.2 percent lower in the shredded condition, which is perfectly understandable: if you know that your work is unimportant and no one is taking notice, why would you be motivated to achieve high-quality performance?

Well-being

We have probably all heard friends or coworkers bemoan the amount, difficulty, or pace of their work, and wish they just had less to do. Does this imply that people would be better off with boring work, that boring work would promote psychological or physical well-being? That would certainly not be Ben Hamper's experience. After a decade of working on the line, Hamper suffered from chronic panic attacks and was placed on long-term disability. Hamper is by no means alone. Research confirms that work-related boredom is associated with burnout,[42] depressed mood, and sickness absence,[43] and poor health (though in this latter study, only for men).[44]

Several studies refine our understanding of these effects. One study of two hundred employees in the Netherlands by Madelon van Hooff and Edwin van Hooft revealed that the reason job-related boredom negatively affected psychological distress was because it leads people to engage in what they referred to as bored behaviors, such as expressing little emotion at work.[45] In a separate study by these same researchers, 106 people in the Netherlands completed surveys twice a day for three consecutive days. The researchers assessed work-related boredom at the end of each workday, and assessed depressed mood both at the end of the workday and again in the evening.[46] Work-related boredom was associated with depressed mood at the end of the day and later in the evening, but only for people whose work meant a great deal to them, not for those who felt their work was less important. These particular findings give some pause for concern, suggesting that in some cases, meaningful work might be a mixed blessing, an issue we will take up later in this chapter.

Boredom also results in poor concentration and inattention.[47] That being the case, could boredom at work compromise occupational safety?[48] An earlier study by Michael Frone on 319 teenage employees in the United States showed that job boredom predicted injuries at work such as strains or sprains, cuts or lacerations, and fractures and dislocations.[49] Jessica Lang and colleagues' meta-analysis focused more specifically on the effects of work monotony on musculoskeletal injuries at work.[50] Along with high job demands, low control, and low support from supervisor and coworkers, highly monotonous work was associated with neck and/or shoulder problems. Moreover, the negative effects of highly monotonous work on lower back symptoms were stronger than any of the demand, control, or support factors.

There is no ambiguity about the negative effects of workaholism on well-being, and this is clear from Clark et al.'s meta-analysis.[51] First, there are personal consequences related to workaholism. For example, workaholism predicts burnout and its three individual components,[§§] as well as poorer physical and mental health. Workaholism has also been shown to be associated with insomnia.[52] Second, workaholism spills over onto other family members. Given the additional time and emotional energy that workaholics invest in their work, it should not come as a surprise that workaholism promotes family dissatisfaction, marital disaffection, and work-life conflict.[53] Moreover, research by Arnold Bakker and colleagues demonstrated that one partner's workaholism indirectly and negatively effects the other partner's relationship satisfaction, again illustrating how others in the family are inadvertently caught up in the negative effects of workaholism.[54]

How does meaningful work exert its effects?

Meaningful work exerts indirect effects

Blake Allan and colleagues used data from forty-four articles and 23,144 respondents to investigate how meaningful work affects organizational outcomes.[55] Their meta-analysis first confirmed that, as expected, meaningful work is positively associated with work attitudes, job performance, and well-being. More importantly, they then untangled these effects and showed that in the first instance meaningful work affected work attitudes such as job satisfaction and commitment. In turn, these work attitudes positively affected citizenship behaviors, work performance, and intentions to remain with the organization.

[§§] Emotion exhaustion, depersonalization, and a lack of professional effectiveness are often viewed as the three components of burnout.

Adam Grant and colleagues conducted several studies showing the positive effects of task significance and beneficiary contact. In one experiment with 122 participants who were ostensibly required to edit cover letters for a career center, beneficiary contact boosted affective commitment to the beneficiary, and it was this affective commitment that resulted in greater task persistence.[56] In a separate experiment, thirty-two paid lifeguards in the United States were divided into two groups, each of which received thirty minutes of in-service training.[57] The in-service training required that both groups read four stories for the first fifteen minutes. For the task-significance group, the stories portrayed actual rescues by other lifeguards, while the personal-benefit stories told how other lifeguards used the knowledge and skills they had acquired on the job. Thereafter, participants in both groups had fifteen minutes to discuss the stories with each other. Task significance affected both perceived prosocial impact (e.g., "I am very aware of the ways in which my work is benefitting others") and perceived social worth (e.g., "I feel that others appreciate my work"). Over the next month, prosocial impact influenced supervisor ratings of overtime work—an indicator of job dedication. In contrast, perceived social worth had no effect on job dedication.

Workaholism also exerts negative indirect effects on well-being. To test how this process might work, 102 Italian entrepreneurs, self-employed people, managers, and employees completed surveys each day for ten consecutive workdays.[58] Higher levels of workaholism were associated with much greater workloads (perhaps because of the expectations these people placed on themselves), and it was the daily load that led to higher levels of emotional exhaustion. Given these findings, the researchers point to the importance of managers, supervisors and employees being made aware of the health hazards of constantly working at an excessive pace.

So far we have discussed how meaningful work exerts indirect effects on outcomes, but let's change focus. Research has also considered how meaningful work connects other workplace factors such as high-quality leadership with work outcomes. As one example, one goal of transformational leadership is to help followers see beyond daily issues and instill in their work a moral and social purpose that goes beyond self-interest. By doing so, leaders help to provide a sense of meaning in daily work. Consistent with this idea, studies in the health care context in Canada[59] and Denmark[60] show that meaningful work transfers the effects of transformational leadership on followers' psychological well-being. Importantly, the way in which meaningful work links workplace factors and outcomes is not limited to transformational leadership, or even well-being as an outcome. A study of 134 members of twenty-eight teams in private sector organizations in Malaysia, for example, showed that meaningful work also transmitted the effects of empowering leadership on employees' work engagement.[61]

Reinforcing this notion, a lack of meaningful work plays a similar role. To investigate this, Aleksandra Luksyte and colleagues focused on feeling overqualified in your work, in other words, feeling that you have more skills and competencies than your job requires.[62] Feeling overqualified was associated with cynicism about the lack of meaning in your work, which resulted in engaging in behaviors that were detrimental to the organization and other employees.

Meaningful work shapes the way you experience your work

We have already discussed the notion of beneficiary contact—the idea that people gain a real understanding of the value of their work when they come into personal contact with people helped by their work. Adam Grant suggested that beneficiary contact could also help followers appreciate how their own work contributed to their leaders' vision.[63] In a study of seventy-one people in the United States who had just been hired to work in a call-center operation, one group received a brief (fifteen-minute) transformational leadership training session, and a second group a ten-minute visit from a beneficiary of their work. A third group received both the transformational leadership training and the beneficiary contact. Neither the transformational leadership nor the beneficiary contact alone had any effects on sales or revenue over the next seven weeks. However, sales and revenue were both significantly higher among new hires who had received a combination of transformational leadership *and* the beneficiary contact interventions. Grant then conducted a second study that involved 329 public sector employees and their supervisors in the United States. The effect of transformational leadership on supervisor ratings of employee performance was much stronger for employees who interacted with others affected by their work.

A separate study of 138 nurses in Italy who assembled surgical kits for delivery to a former war zone reinforces the notion that beneficiary contact strengthens the effects of transformational leadership.[64] All the nurses first viewed a brief video about the project's goals and how to assemble the kits. Nurses in the transformational leadership group met with the director of nursing for fifteen minutes, during which she explained why the project was meaningful, communicated her enthusiasm, and thanked the nurses. Nurses in the beneficiary contact group met with a former patient from the war zone for fifteen minutes, who explained how similar surgical tools had saved his life. Nurses in the final group met with both the director of nursing and the former patient. Nurses who received both the transformational leadership interaction and beneficiary contact assembled significantly more kits (64.74 kits) in the three-hour period than those who received transformational leadership (42.91) or beneficiary contact (47.04) alone. Those who viewed the video assembled 38 kits in the three-hour period.

Turning our focus to workplace stress, Dong Liu and colleagues studied how meaningful work might affect work stress; their study is especially relevant as it was conducted amid the COVID-19 pandemic in a major hospital in Chengdu, China.[65] COVID-related stress negatively affected work engagement among 258 nurses over a three-week period. In addition, work stress reduced the extent to which nurses took charge in trying to resolve workplace problems. In both cases, however, the negative effects of COVID-19 stress were significantly lower for nurses who experienced more meaning in their work. Similar findings emerged for prosocial impact prepandemic. Adam Grant and Sabine Sonnentag showed that a lack of intrinsic motivation was associated with emotional exhaustion, but this was not the case among the professional fundraisers and sanitation workers in their study who believed their work exerted a positive social impact on others.[66]

Nonetheless, some caution is warranted. Meaningful work might be a mixed blessing if it results in overinvesting in work and being willing to tolerate unduly aversive situations. Kenneth Harris and his colleagues investigated whether this was plausible in a sample of 209 employees and their supervisors in an automotive company in the United States.[67] The effects of meaningful work in their study were opposite to those found in Liu et al.'s research on COVID-19 stress. Specifically, the negative effects of abusive supervision on employee performance and employees' most recent performance appraisals were *greater* when employees experienced meaning at work. In contrast, abusive supervision had no negative effects on performance outcomes for people who experienced little meaning in their work.

Why might this be the case? Harris et al. speculate that people who experience their work as meaningful invest emotionally and physically in the face of abusive supervision, leaving them feeling depleted when they have to deliver high-quality work performance. Nonetheless, these researchers insist that the solution is not to discourage people from experiencing meaning in their work. Instead, organizations should do what they can to ensure people are not subject to abusive supervision in the first instance, so that they can benefit from meaning at work.

Gender and meaningful work

The long-documented stereotype that women tend to favor social relationships whereas men prize personal independence*** suggests that we might find gender differences in prosocial impact in particular and meaningful work more generally. If there is substance to this stereotype, women should be more likely to engage in helping behaviors at work. A meta-analysis involving ninety different studies and no fewer than 30,372 participants corroborates this stereotype. Women were more likely to favor social relationships than men, and this difference was greater in individualistic countries that emphasize the value of independence.[68] The magnitude of this gender difference is evident from the fact that it is about the same as that found for anxiety, depression, self-esteem, guilt, and shame, as well as cooperative behaviors in interactions with mixed-gender groups.

*** What social scientists refer to as *sociotropy*.

However, intriguing research by Selwyn Becker and Alice Eagly on gender differences in heroic behaviors suggests considerable nuance exists in any gender differences in helping others.[69] Becker and Eagly investigated whether gender differences existed within five different groups: (a) Carnegie Hero Medal recipients, with such medals awarded for saving someone else's life at great risk to your own, (b) non-Jewish people who consciously placed themselves in harm's way to save Jews during the Nazi Holocaust, (c) live kidney donors, (d) Peace Corps volunteers in the United States, and (e) medical doctors who volunteer their services in dangerous and unsanitary environments. Their findings are intriguing. Men were substantially more likely to help in dangerous situations that require physical strength, specialist emergency training, and the willingness to respond immediately. In contrast, women were more likely to be live kidney donors, Peace Corps volunteers, and medical volunteers. Women were also more likely than men to help save Jews during the Holocaust and did so on the basis of an ethic of care and compassion and out of an awareness of a shared or common humanity. Underlying these differences is the public nature of the prosocial act. Males were more likely to engage in prosocial behaviors that were visible to others or where the consequences of the behaviors might be visible to others, such as in award ceremonies. In contrast, women were more likely to act prosocially, and especially in more private or personal acts. Thus, women may not routinely be more helpful than men. Instead, any gender differences in prosocial behaviors are nuanced, and may be a function of the type of helping behaviors and the context in which they occur.

The limited evidence available suggests that a similar pattern is manifest in the workplace. Alexandra Beauregard's study of 223 public sector employees in the United Kingdom revealed that women engaged in more helping behaviors than men.[70] While interesting, these findings shed no light on whether men and women engage in different types of helping behaviors at work. Fortunately, Deborah Kidder used data from 251 nurses (86 percent female), and 195 engineers (72 percent male) to investigate whether gender differences emerged in altruistic behaviors (e.g., helping people with excessive workloads), and more instrumental behaviors (e.g., making suggestions to improve productivity).[71] As expected, females engaged in more altruistic helping behaviors and men engaged in more instrumental helping behaviors.

An additional feature of this study warrants attention. Kidder went beyond a binary definition of gender and examined the effects of a masculine or feminine identity on these two helping behaviors. Irrespective of biological sex, masculine identity was associated with instrumental but not altruistic behaviors, while feminine identity was associated with altruistic but not instrumental behaviors. Findings such as these remind researchers that it is now past time to expand their focus beyond biological sex and include gender identity in similar research.

Culture and meaningful work

Differences in the level of meaningful work

Unlike topics such as leadership (see Chapter 2), the possibility of regional or cultural differences in the expression or value of meaningful work has received little attention. As an example, I could find no meta-analyses to guide our understanding of any cultural effects on the level or function of meaningful work. As a result, this discussion is restricted to findings from one large-scale study of 2,283 employees across China, Germany, Holland, Hungary, Israel, Korea, Taiwan, and the United States, all of which provided data on a range of twenty-four distinct work values.[72] Values that reflect intrinsic interest in the job, which included meaningful work, were ranked as significantly more important in Hungary than China. Before puzzling too much over what these differences might mean, the authors themselves caution that they may simply be a function of the different samples used in these countries. The Hungarian sample was made up of employees from a large industrial organization, while those in the Chinese sample were participating in a young-executive program. Thus, the most appropriate conclusion is that we simply don't know whether there are differences in the levels of meaningful work across regions, countries, or cultures. What we can conclude from this single study, however, is that meaningful work was not rated as unimportant in any of these eight countries: "meaningful work" was ranked as anywhere between the third and sixteenth most important of the twenty-four different work values.

Differences in the function of meaningful work

In contrast, some researchers have investigated whether the effects of meaningful work are universal or whether they might be country- or culture-specific. Ting-Pang Huang contrasted the effects of motivating work characteristics (a joint function of task significance, learning, and autonomy) on intentions to leave the organization in blue-collar and knowledge workers in China and Japan.[73] In both countries, meaningful work affected turnover intentions through its direct effects on job satisfaction.

Extending this, Robert Roe and colleagues compared the role of meaningful work and other job characteristics among 565 employees in Bulgaria, 614 in Hungary, and 237 in the Netherlands.[74] The differences between these countries (e.g., sociopolitical history, industrialization) allow for a better assessment of the universality of meaningful work. While differences did exist in the job factors that triggered meaningful work in the three countries, the outcomes of meaningful work were similar: in all three countries, meaningful work was directly associated with job involvement. In turn, job involvement resulted in higher levels of work effort and work satisfaction. Thus, a tentative conclusion is possible. As Roe et al. note, the environments in which we find ourselves motivates us, but the consequences of motivation, in this case meaningful work, tend to be universal.

Thus far, our focus has been on employees' experiences of meaningful work. Similar to the research on organizational commitment by Ted Shore, Lynne Shore, and colleagues (see Chapter 4), Sanford DeVoe and Sheena Iyengar investigated whether managers' perceptions of employees' meaningful work influence how they react to their employees. To do so, they studied 486 employee-manager dyads from Latin America, 251 from Asia, and 1,023 from the United States.[75] Although we might reasonably expect that employees' intrinsic and extrinsic motivation would best predict their own performance, this was not the case. Across all three zones, managers' perceptions of their employees' intrinsic and extrinsic motivations were more closely aligned with their ratings of employee performance than were employees' ratings of their own motivations. This raises very important questions about managerial ratings of employee performance: contrary to organizations' beliefs that managers provide unbiased and objective measures of employee performance, their ratings are influenced by their views of what motivates their employees.

Moreover, important cross-national differences emerged. US managers believed that their employees were more motivated by extrinsic than intrinsic factors, yet US employees rated themselves as more motivated by intrinsic than extrinsic factors.[†††] Asian and Latin American managers were more in step with their employees. Asian managers and employees rated intrinsic and extrinsic motivations as equally important, while Latin American managers and employees rated intrinsic factors as more important. These findings also have important organizational implications. What if managers *incorrectly* believe that their employees are primarily motivated by extrinsic factors, such as pay or benefits, and they act accordingly? Might their motivational attempts be ineffective at best and wasteful at worst? Given that managerial perceptions of employees' intrinsic and extrinsic motivation in the United States are not necessarily accurate, this is a significant practical issue.

TMGT: Can we have too much meaningful work?

Organizational scholars and consultants extol the virtues of meaningful work. But like autonomy or belonging, can too much meaning in our work be harmful? After all, knowing that your work affects whether other people might live, or die, might be enormously motivating, but that could also be an incredible burden. One obstacle in evaluating this issue is the paucity of research that has even asked this question, but a few studies offer some insight.

††† In their study, intrinsic factors were measured with one item, "How motivated do you think this employee is to do his/her job for internal reasons (finding job enjoyable and interesting)?" which closely parallels the task identity component of meaningful work. Extrinsic motivation was also measured with one item, "How motivated do you think this employee is to do his/her job for external reasons (pay/medical benefits)?"

Stuart Bunderson and Jeffery Thompson's research among zookeepers from 157 different institutions‡‡‡ in Canada and the United States provides some initial guidance.[76] As expected, zookeepers who felt a strong calling for their work experienced their work as more meaningful, and the impact of their work to be more significant. At the same time, this also resulted in zookeepers seeing their work as a moral duty, which in their eyes justified accepting lower pay, more dangerous and demanding working conditions, and making a greater personal sacrifice. As a result, Bunderson and Thompson see deeply meaningful work as a "double-edged" sword, and like others[77] caution that it could lead to management exploitation of employees.

Shao-Lung Ti and An-Tien Hsieh took somewhat of a different approach and suggested that work that is too meaningful could be harmful if people become so absorbed that it detracts them from tasks that are viewed as less important.[78] To test this idea, they investigated the link between task identity—the extent to which employees did the entire job—and organizational commitment among 269 lower-level employees in Taiwan. Organizational commitment levels were highest for employees with moderate levels of task identity. In contrast, organizational commitment was lower among employees who had lower or higher levels of task identity. These findings are somewhat similar to those of Harris et al. that we discussed earlier.[79] What these findings suggest is that if tasks become overly central to people doing them, attachment to the organization recedes in importance.

Taking these studies together, some concern can be expressed that very high levels of meaningful work might not necessarily be productive or beneficial for employee well-being. However, we need more research to make robust conclusions about whether higher levels of prosocial impact are counterproductive.

Interventions to enhance meaningful work

There is no shortage of stories about how simple interventions have had huge effects on meaningful work. Classic examples would include how people respond when asked what work they do, such as the janitor at NASA who responded, "Oh, we're putting a man on the moon," or the assembly-line worker manufacturing intravenous drips for infants we met earlier in this chapter who responded "Oh, we save babies." While fascinating and inspiring, organizations need to go beyond stories in developing their policies and practices. Fortunately, studies exist that provide strong evidence that organizations can enhance the experience of meaningful work, and that doing so has positive benefits.

The most stringent tests of interventions would be those conducted in the most unusual or stressful conditions. This was certainly the case with Dong Liu and colleagues' intervention among frontline health care professionals (e.g., doctors, nurses,

‡‡‡ Their sample included people who worked in zoos, aquaria, and other establishments that house and display animals to the public.

phlebotomists, radiologists) in the ICU of a major hospital in Chengdu, China, during the earlier stages of the COVID-19 pandemic.[80] Given the almost unimaginable pandemic-related stress resulting from working in this environment, their overall intervention program had both a COVID-19 crisis component and a meaningful work component.

Sixty-one health care professionals participated and were randomly assigned to one of four groups. Fifteen participants received the crisis-intervention treatment only, sixteen received the meaningful work intervention, fifteen received both interventions, and fifteen received neither intervention. Health care professionals in the COVID-19 crisis intervention attended a one-hour counseling session with a hospital VP who attempted to frame perceptions of COVID-19 as less novel or critical.

The meaningful-work intervention consisted of a written communication that emphasized three aspects of meaningful work from the same VP, delivered via email and letter. It is worth reading the actual message to appreciate the elegance of this intervention. First, the importance of fulfilling the hospital's objective of offering high-quality care to patients was reinforced.

> As a COVID-19 ICU health worker, you are making a significant contribution to the hospital's goal of providing excellent medical services under the current circumstances. Without your unwavering contribution, our hospital would never have received so much appreciation and recognition. Your talent and caring manner are a credit to and pride of our hospital. Undoubtedly, our hospital's future development and success will continue to rely on your hard work and dedication.

Second, the communication from the hospital VP emphasized the critical impact they were having on other people's lives at such a fraught moment.

> You have given your utmost effort to take great care of every patient and have demonstrated your exceptional medical skills. Your compassion and humility are always impressive. Our patients and their families are very grateful for the differences you have made in their lives. They call you and other ICU health workers 'angels sent by God on Earth' because you have saved patients' lives and preserved their health. Human life is so invaluable that your work truly deserves such beautiful praise!

Third, the email/letter mentioned the way in which their own professional growth and development was being positively affected.

> The French writer Sir Thomas Browne once said, "you can't extend the length of your life, but you can grasp its width." Undoubtedly, as a COVID-19 frontline health worker, you are not only providing great assistance to our hospital and patients, but are also enriching your own life. Your work creates meaning and purpose in life and fosters your personal growth and development. Our colleagues who were

involved in the treatment of SARS patients found that they gained valuable experiences and skills, which were extremely beneficial to their later career advancement. We look forward to seeing your continued success and prosperity in the most honorable and esteemed profession in the world!

Both interventions worked (though we are more interested in the meaningful-work intervention)! Perceived-crisis stress decreased significantly for those who received the counseling intervention, but there was no decrease for those who did not. Likewise, work meaningfulness increased considerably in health care professionals who received the email and letter; those who did not receive the email/letter experienced no increase. The researchers then measured the effectiveness of the interventions in two ways. First, they assessed whether there were any changes in employees' reports of work engagement. Second, supervisors provided data on "taking charge at work," proactive behaviors that would be critical for optimal functioning in a COVID-19 ICU environment.

Changes in work meaningfulness resulted in significant increases in both work engagement and "take charge" behaviors. People who received both interventions increased their work engagement by 27.5 percent, and those who only received the work meaningfulness intervention saw a 10 percent increase in work engagement. The effects on supervisors' reports of "take charge" behaviors were even more impressive. Being exposed to both interventions raised supervisor ratings of take-charge behaviors by 57 percent, with the work-meaningfulness intervention alone accounting for a 29 percent increase, and these effects lasted two weeks.

Given that the interventions took place in hospital critical-care units in the confusion and fear of the early stages of the pandemic, the results of Liu et al.'s research are unusually impressive. Especially in the case of the work-meaningfulness intervention, they are an important and timely reminder that small changes in work can have very large outcomes. While it might seem trivial, unnecessary, or even demeaning to remind health care professionals working in a COVID crisis ward just how important their work is, it works!

Nonetheless, even though the effects of Liu et al.'s meaningful work intervention lasted for two weeks, they did not assess whether any effects were maintained later than that. For practical reasons, we need to know whether longer-term maintenance is achievable. Results from other interventions focused on meaningful work are reassuring in this respect. As one example, as part of a major national-organizational initiative in the Netherlands in 2014 and 2015, youth care work was decentralized in Amsterdam and Rotterdam, resulting in frontline youth care professionals being given more responsibility to care for recipients themselves. Doing so placed these professionals closer to those with whom they worked and cared for, and gradually increased the amount of job contact and job impact these professionals experienced.[81] To analyze the effects of this long-term intervention, Joris van der Voet and Bram Steijn collected data just prior to the reorganization in December 2014, in December 2015, and again in January 2017. Both job contact and job impact changed following the reorganization. These changes resulted in higher levels of prosocial impact at the end of the two-year initiative. Interestingly, the effects of job impact on prosocial motivation were somewhat stronger than job contact.

The practical implications of these two interventions are far-reaching. First, if real changes are made to the way people do their work, as happened with the youth professionals, we can indeed expect long-lasting benefits for employees and their organizations. Second, as Liu et al.'s research demonstrated, very small changes can exert huge effects, almost immediately.

A special case: "Dirty work"

If you placed meaningful work at one end of a continuum, what might anchor the opposite extreme? One possibility is "dirty work." Although dirty work has always existed, it made its first appearance in the academic literature about seventy years ago[82] and now includes any work that other people view as physically, socially, or morally disgusting, degrading, or distasteful. Examples of such work are plentiful. Physically disgusting work would include sanitation work, embalming in funeral parlors, and slaughtering animals. Telemarketing is an example of work that is viewed as socially disgusting. Morally disgusting work might include executioners, paparazzi, used-car salespeople, or personal injury lawyers. In all these cases, an indication of society's disgust is that the work is invariably described pejoratively, for example, with personal injury lawyers described as "ambulance chasers."

Several features about dirty work stand out. First, despite some people's moral misgivings, as in the case of sex work, dirty work is almost always both legal and necessary for a functioning society. Second, the physical, social, and moral taint in which the work is held initially resides in the perceptions of others; just imagine how people turn up their noses and roll their eyes when they hear about dirty work. This is amply demonstrated in an anecdote from a mortician:

> A group of funeral directors . . . could sit around in the restaurant talking about the most gory details and it doesn't bother them a bit. It doesn't affect their appetite. But the people around them can't even stay in the restaurant. They have to get up and leave because the thing is so gross.[83]

As a result, people tend to keep their professional and personal distance from others whom they view as engaged in what they think as dirty work, resulting in stigma and dehumanization. Last, some occupations can be viewed as physically, morally, *and* socially tainted, with sex work often given as an example.

Which brings us to what we might call the paradox of dirty work. Even though others view their work with disdain, many of the people involved find real meaning in their "dirty" work. As one example, I was fortunate to supervise a graduate student who interviewed sanitation workers. When asked what he did at work, one employee responded, "Oh we're in public health." Or, as one personal injury lawyer remarked in Ashforth and colleagues' study, "Without personal injury lawyers, manufacturers . . . wouldn't be held accountable for producing defective products" (157).[84] Reinforcing this, more than double the number of people interviewed in this study said that would recommend their current occupation to their children than those who said they would not.

What might explain this? Earlier in this chapter, we discussed research in Canada[85] and Denmark[86] that showed that by enhancing employees' beliefs that their work was meaningful, transformational leadership positively affected employees' well-being. The Canadian researchers did an additional study on dental hygienists and funeral parlor directors, which are invariably viewed as dirty occupations.[87] Despite this, similar findings emerged. When transformational leadership behaviors helped people reframe their work as meaningful, even those engaged in dirty work enjoyed higher levels of well-being.

John Schaubroeck and colleagues took a different approach to this question in their study of 279 people in the United States doing a variety of different jobs.[88] Instead of suggesting that entire occupations involve dirty work, they assumed that anyone could experience aspects of their work as dirty at different times. Once a week for six weeks, participants in their study reported on the extent to which they had been engaged in dirty work. The more people believed they were involved in dirty work, the more embarrassed they were about their work and disengaged while at work. Schaubroeck et al. also showed that the more people felt they were involved in dirty work, the more they were motivated to change the kind of work they did.

Stephen Deery and colleagues were interested in identifying other factors that would help people reframe their dirty work. Their study of 233 employees who cleaned abandoned social or public housing in high-crime areas in the United Kingdom and the United States highlights other ways in which any stigma associated with dirty work can be minimized. Employees who reframed their work and saw it as meaningful—or had the opportunity to do different tasks at work,[§§§] experience a sense of group autonomy, enjoy positive relationships with coworkers, and were satisfied with their work—subsequently felt a sense of pride in their "dirty work."[89] These findings illustrate that the seven work characteristics discussed throughout the book are not "stand-alone best-practices." Instead, meaningful work, autonomy, and belonging even affect the way in which dirty work is experienced.

One additional aspect of dirty work deserves attention, and that is that dirty work is often invisible to others. This should not be surprising given that people shy away from what they see as dirty or disgusting, including work that is viewed as socially, physically, or morally dirty. Feeling that your work is invisible has particular challenges. Verónica Rabelo and Ramaswami Mahalingam surveyed 199 building cleaners, twelve of whom later participated in follow-up interviews to shed more light on

[§§§] Hackman and Oldham identified task variety as one of the factors that contributed to meaningful work.

the experience of invisible dirty work.[90] One immediate lesson was that the workers felt it was not only their work that was invisible ("They really don't care what I am doing. You know, I'll be trying to mop the floor . . . They'll see that, and they'll just go use it anyway"; 108), but that they too were invisible ("You say 'good morning' and they [customers] look right thru you"; 107). As a direct result of this invisibility, many custodians in their study reported that their work made them ashamed, afraid, anxious, and sad. Several even reported relief at not having to engage with others.

The COVID-19 pandemic had many unintended side effects, one of which was to make previously invisible work visible to all. People around the world suddenly realized just how much their lives depended on others whose work had gone unnoticed for so long. Like clockwork, people all around the world started to gather from the safety of their own homes at 7:00 pm each evening during the first wave of the pandemic, enthusiastically banging pots and pans to support their new "heroes"—the many nonphysician health care workers who were becoming infected and dying.[91] Sophie Hennekam and her colleagues were intrigued by what happens when people's work suddenly goes from being invisible to critical, aptly described in the title of their article as "From zero to hero."[92] To understand this, they interviewed 164 nonphysician health care workers in France. The public would likely be surprised to learn that most of the "heroes" they interviewed believed this sudden change would be temporary; in the words of one nurse, "Society is individualistic, once their needs are met, people go back home, and we will be forgotten" (1093). As a result, these health care workers tended to reject their newfound status, believing that they were being manipulated. In the words of a different nurse, "This whole notion of being a hero, of being oh-so-amazing, is just a manipulation. It is to make us work without complaining. It's a trick, and we all got trapped" (1096).

Large retail organizations such as Amazon, Kroger, Stop and Shop, and Albertsons in the United States, and Virgin Media, Danone, Nestlé, and BT in the United Kingdom, inadvertently reinforced the fear that the visibility and recognition suddenly afforded to essential work was temporary and could just as easily be taken away. At the start of the pandemic, these companies abruptly and unexpectedly started paying essential workers a premium.[93] But as the interviewees in Hennekam et al.'s study would have predicted, this did not last. Starting in May 2020, the pandemic pay premiums stopped as abruptly as they had started. Concerns about their newfound visibility being transient, and of being manipulated, were likely confirmed when no pay premiums were offered through later and worse waves of COVID-19 infections and deaths.

The lessons learned from all this are that no matter how dirty or invisible people believe "dirty work" to be, the work remains essential and small changes can help reframe the work as meaningful. However, any initiatives to do so must be authentic. If they are not, such as the temporary increases in pay just discussed, they run the risk of further demoralizing and demeaning the employees involved.

Conclusion

In case you are not yet convinced

First, given the extensive benefits of meaningful work highlighted throughout this chapter, some of the findings from Wegman et al.'s study are concerning.[94] Recall that they were interested in whether changes had taken place in job characteristics between 1975 and 2011. While people enjoyed more autonomy at work since 1975, the news about task identity and task significance is not good. Task identity increased from 1975 until 1991 but has since declined, which the authors attribute to the changing nature of work. They suggest that increasing computer usage from the early 1990s resulted in greater segmentation of work, with fewer people able to participate in all aspects of their jobs.

At the same time, task significance decreased substantially from 1975 to 1985, stabilized until 2000, and continued its decline since then. Wegman et al. blame these declines on a greater emphasis on leaner organizations, and the on-going downsizings resulting in more people being overqualified for their jobs, which limits task significance.[95] Irrespective of the particular reasons for the decline in task identity and task significance, the issue is not that people want less meaning in their work, or that meaning has become less effective. Instead, the way work is currently organized makes it more difficult for people to find meaning in their work.

Second, as Wegman et al. note, changes in the nature of work are invariably gradual rather than abrupt. This notion was turned on its head at the start of the pandemic, perhaps no more so than with the number of people who suddenly found themselves working remotely. This change was soon followed by claims about productivity gains resulting from the move to remote work. However, serious evaluations of the effectiveness of remote work will have to account for lost opportunities for benefiting from beneficiary contact, which may be more difficult in a remote working environment. To ensure these benefits are not lost, organizations offering any form of remote work will need to be creative about deliberately creating opportunities for employees to interact with the beneficiaries of their work.

Third, one longstanding critique of meaningful work is that it is a privilege accessible to the few who occupy the highest rungs of the organization or have coveted skills.[96] Research on 350 full-time employees in the United States by Kelsey Autin and Blake Allan confirms that we need to take this critique seriously.[97] While lower-, middle-, and upper-class employees in their study did not differ in how much they *wanted* meaningful work, upper-class employees *enjoyed* greater access to meaningful work than the others. Coupled with the fact that people from lower socioeconomic backgrounds are more prosocial and care more about others,[98] organizations should ensure that all employees have opportunities to experience their work as meaningful. In an era in which demands for social justice and inclusive workplaces are deservedly front and center, organizations that ensure access to meaningful work for all their members will make it more likely that they can recruit, hire, and retain employees dedicated to helping the organization thrive.

Last, a good place to end this chapter on meaningful work is with a challenging thought. While classic economic theory argues for the primacy of self-interest, the task-significance dimension of meaningful work takes us in a very different direction. Research shows again and again that we are motivated by the positive impact we have on others. Even more importantly, as we have seen, when studies set up a direct competition between the motivating effects of self-interest vs helping others, prosocial motivation wins! For too long, organizations have valued "takers" over "givers," probably to their detriment. It is now time for organizations to incorporate these evidence-based lessons into how they think about employees and structure their motivational strategies and practices accordingly.

8
Safety

Work Safety
When you go to work in the morning
Don't just think of yourself
Whether you have a family or not
Other people do
Safety meetings go on and on don't they
At the time they don't seem important
But they are
Don't disregard them
Listen
One day the information may be important
It may even save a life and a family's despair
You may feel you know your job well
You don't want to waste your time
You go for a shortcut
The shortest isn't always the safest
What if a life is lost?
Could you live with yourself?
Knowing it was your decision
Maybe you don't even think about the consequences
You don't think about everyone affected
By one mistake
Or maybe it's even many mistakes
Safety isn't a joke
But there will always be that one guy
The guy that tries to say the safety meetings are pointless
You can't go back in time
You can't undo mistakes
You can't take away an injury
And you definitely can't give back a life

Alyssa Grocutt[*,1]

[*] Alyssa was only eleven years old when her father, Kevin, was killed in a workplace safety incident, an event that changed her life and the lives of so many others in her family. Five years later, she wrote this poem. Since then, Alyssa has advocated for workplace safety in presentations in schools and organizations. Alyssa is now enrolled as a doctoral student. I am fortunate to serve as her supervisor, and her research is directly focused on workplace safety.

Brave New Workplace. Julian Barling, Oxford University Press. © Oxford University Press 2023.
DOI: 10.1093/oso/9780190648107.003.0008

So far, we have seen how high-quality leadership, autonomy, belonging, fairness, growth and development, and meaningful work are crucial if employees are to enjoy positive workplace attitudes, work performance, and well-being. Workplace safety is equally important. As Alyssa Grocutt reminds us in her very poignant poem, the costs are immeasurable when safety is compromised. As we will see, these costs are felt well beyond the workplace, all too often leaving families, friends, and coworkers in despair. Unfortunately, even while dramatic advances in workplace safety have been achieved over the past century, and work safety has been extensively studied during that same time,[2] one of the most dangerous things you can do at work is take safety for granted.

Each year, the Association of Workers' Compensation Boards of Canada reports on the state of workplace health and safety in Canada.[3] According to their data, 336 workers died as a result of safety incidents and 581 from occupational disease in 2019.[†] During the same year, there were 5,333 fatal work injuries in the United States, an increase of 2 percent over the number of people who died in workplace safety incidents in 2018.[4] In the United Kingdom, 111 workers died in workplace safety incidents between April 2019 and March 2020, the lowest number ever recorded.[5] Of course, the toll of workplace safety is not just seen through occupational fatalities. Most people involved in safety incidents survive, but many are then forced to miss work due to injuries. In 2019, 271,806 claims for lost time injuries were accepted in Canada. In the United States, 888,220 injuries and illnesses resulted in a private sector employee having to miss at least one day of work in 2019, a rate of 2.8 cases per hundred workers.[6] Last, between October 2017 and October 2018, 30.7 million working days were lost in the United Kingdom due to a combination of work-related injuries and illnesses.[7]

We need to keep several issues in mind when evaluating the meaning of statistics like these. Despite the decreasing trend in workplace fatalities over the past century, the number of fatalities has increased in Canada over the past twenty-five years.[8] Moreover, after recording a low of 4,551 fatalities in 2009, the number of workplace fatalities in the United States has increased since then.[9] Yet, as high as the number of injuries and lost work time might seem, they are invariably underestimates for a variety reasons. First, not all occupations (e.g., self-employed) or industries (e.g., agriculture) are included in these data in every jurisdiction. Second, employees are often reluctant to report injuries, either because they fear managerial repercussions in the form of discipline or being fired, or they fear that they will be forced to undergo mandatory drug testing.[10] Thus, injury and illness data are invariably underreported,[11] and a closer inspection of the data points to systematic under- and overreporting of injuries and illnesses. Eisenberg and McDonald report on an OSHA study in which inspectors visited a random sample of about two hundred manufacturing sites with

[†] I have deliberately chosen 2019 even though data are available for 2020 at the time of writing. The reason for this choice is that, as we see later in this chapter, workplace fatality data from injuries and disease are skewed in 2020 (and 2021) as a result of COVID-19.

more than ten employees.[12] At each site, the inspectors conducted interviews with organizational record-keepers and employees, and collected data from workers' compensation reports and medical records when available. Overrecording of injuries occurred among 15 percent of the four thousand injury and illness reports, and underrecording occurred in about 20 percent of the reports. While this reporting issue might seem surprising at first glance, virtually all cases of overrecording involved cases with no lost-time injuries. In contrast, injuries and illnesses that involved lost work time were underrecorded in about 25 percent of the establishments. What these data strongly suggest is that these errors in reporting are systematic—to look good, companies overreport minor incidents but underreport more serious incidents.

Why is all this so important? People go to work each day with the expectation that different needs will be fulfilled at work. These needs include being treated well by their leaders, and that they have a sense of autonomy, belonging, fairness, opportunities for growth and development, and meaningful work, and when these needs are met, employees and their organizations thrive. Equally if not more importantly, people go to work each morning and expect to return home safely each evening, and their families need to feel assured that they will do so. Sadly, for too many employees and families, this is not a realistic expectation. We all know that Maslow recognized safety in general as one of the most basic human needs.[13] When threatened, Maslow claimed that the safety needs become so dominant that, in his terms "we may then describe the whole organism as a safety-seeking mechanism" (376). In practical terms, people at work whose safety is threatened or thwarted would spend most of their time focusing only on their safety. As Maslow asserted, "If it is extreme enough and chronic enough, [they] may be characterized as living almost for safety alone" (376). We spend much of the rest of this chapter determining what happens when the basic need for safety at work is compromised.

The benefits of workplace health and safety

Most organizational researchers live in a world where workplace injuries and fatalities are exceedingly rare. While this is fortunate for those researchers, it does influence whether they choose to study safety or not. In much the same way that reporters don't write articles when airplanes land safely at airports, researchers tend not to investigate the causes of workplace safety incidents and injuries when everything seems to be going well. As a result, there is precious little research on the work attitudes, work performance, and well-being effects on workplace safety. Two studies are especially noteworthy, however, as they remind us that organizational practices do impact work safety. In one study, Michelle Kaminski was intrigued by the possibility that some routine workplace practices may have unintended side effects on safety; one such practice is performance-based pay.[14] In a study of eighty-six manufacturing plants in the US Midwest, those companies that had some form of performance-based (vs hourly rate) pay, did indeed experience more workplace injuries. One possible reason for these unintended negative effects is that performance-based pay signals to employees what is most valued by organizations (in this case, performance) and, by default, what is less important and what can or should be minimized (in this case, safety).

A second study is especially noteworthy as it shows how the different components of the model of productive, healthy, and safe work are interrelated. Based on a sample of 1,077 US employees, Karen Roberts and Karen Markel investigated why people with a repetitive strain injury would choose to file a workers' compensation claim.[15] Over and above the severity of the injury, the decision to submit a claim was much higher among injured workers who reported lower levels of interpersonal unfairness. Tellingly, feeling a sense of distributive unfairness had no effect on the decision to file a compensation claim.

For better or for worse, there is a sizable body of literature on what happens when workplace safety is compromised, and it is to this topic that we now turn our attention.

When workplace safety goes awry

Work attitudes

Several studies have investigated the attitudinal effects of being involved in a safety incident at work. Regina Hechanova-Alampay and Terry Beehr surveyed 531 members of twenty-four teams of a US chemical company that had restructured and eliminated several layers of management two years earlier.[16] They deliberately selected work teams which had either their best or worst safety performance in the prior year. The higher the number of safety incidents involving injuries that required time off work, the lower the level of team empowerment.[‡] A recent study on human resource practices and organizational-injury rates in a sample of forty-nine UK manufacturing companies replicated these findings at the organizational level.[17] Of five human resource practices, namely systematic selection, extensive training, performance appraisal, high relative compensation, and empowerment, only lower levels of empowerment were associated with higher organizational-injury rates.

Together with my colleagues Kevin Kelloway and the late Rick Iverson, I investigated the attitudinal consequences of workplace injuries in a representative sample of just under ten thousand employees in Australia.[18] Being subjected to a workplace injury left people feeling they had less influence in the organization, greater distrust in management, and lower interest in staying with the organization. Like other studies,[19] experiencing a workplace injury also resulted in higher levels of job dissatisfaction. In contrast, no links emerged between the severity of the incident and any of these same

‡ Intriguingly, this study also showed that as the number of employees reporting to a supervisor increased (i.e., the span of control), so to do the number of safety incidents requiring some form of treatment.

attitudes, suggesting that just being involved in a safety incident is enough to affect workplace attitudes.

Because workplace injuries are relatively infrequent, potential problems emerge in how they are analyzed. To overcome this, Anthea Zacharatos, Rick Iverson, and I investigated the effects of near misses and involvement in microaccidents,[20] injuries that require first-aid treatment after which employees can return to their work.[21] Justifying the reason to focus on near misses and microaccidents, the difference between an incident that requires first aid and one that requires a hospital visit, or a near miss and an actual incident, is often arbitrary and just bad luck. In a sample of 196 employees from various petroleum and telecommunications companies in Canada, the higher the number of near misses and incidents requiring first-aid visits, the lower the level of trust in management. In addition, the higher the number of near misses, the less employees believed that management was committed to employee safety.

Physical exposure to workplace hazards would also provide important insights into workplace safety. Michael Ford and Lois Tetrick obtained objective ratings of safety hazards (e.g., exposure to contaminants, hazardous equipment, extremely bright or inadequate lighting, and repetitive motion) among 171 hospital employees in the United States.[22] Greater exposure to occupational hazards was linked with lower levels of empowerment and identification with the organization. The direct implication of these findings is that organizations should do what they can to remove or reduce hazardous conditions. Ironically, those employees exposed to the most hazardous working conditions likely have the most acute insights into what needs to be changed. But because they also experience lower levels of engagement and company identification, they may be less willing to share their ideas with others.

Financial effects

At approximately 1:20 pm on March 23, 2005, a massive blast and fire tore through BP's Texas City Refinery.[§,23] Fifteen people were killed instantly; 180 others were severely injured. The huge explosion burned about nineteen thousand square meters around the blast site, and shattered windows more than a kilometer from the blast site. Two years later, the US Chemical Safety and Hazard Investigation Board (also referred to as the CSB) report into the disaster identified nine organizational factors that played a key role in the disaster. These included cost-cutting and failures to invest in safety, poor oversight by BP's Board of Directors, a reliance on the low personal injury rate as an indicator of the state of safety, certifying safety requirements had been

[§] In the six previous chapters, this section dealt with the effects on work performance of poor leaders, a lack of autonomy and so forth. This was not possible when discussing safety; there is simply not enough research on the effects of safety infractions on work performance. Instead, understanding the financial costs borne by individuals affected by safety incidents and by the companies themselves provides a more-than-adequate picture of what happens when safety is compromised.

met when they had not, ignoring warning signs from numerous surveys and safety audits, and last, tying safety goals, campaigns, and rewards to the wrong outcomes.

The blast at Texas City Refinery caused millions of dollars of damage to equipment at the refinery, and the financial costs did not stop there. OSHA levied a fine of $87 million against BP, and BP paid more than one billion dollars in victim compensation. In the same week as the disaster in Texas City, BP settled a separate case involving major occupational-safety infractions in California by paying a fine of $81 million, suggesting the existence of problems with the organization's overall safety culture.[24]

Short of major disasters, what are the costs of safety infractions? Some research helps to identify financial costs borne by employees, their families, and organizations. A good starting point would be to consider injured employees' experience with workers' compensation authorities. Overwhelmingly, when injured workers are dissatisfied with their contacts with workers' compensation boards, they feel they are treated unfairly, disrespectfully, and stigmatized.[25]** As a result, it is not uncommon for injured or ill employees to choose not to file compensation claims,[26] putting them at an immediate financial disadvantage. Even when employees do file for compensation and the claim is allowed, any income supplements provided are invariably less than the wages or salary lost. Compounding these problems, income supplements often do not start to arrive immediately, creating an acute financial crisis for injured employees. When claims are challenged by organizations, injured workers can wait for months to receive their income supplements, in one case for as long as twenty months.[27]

Xiuwen Sue Dong and colleagues were interested in how safety incidents that require time off work affect annual income and family net worth.[28] To explore this question, they created three different groups from a representative sample of 12,686 US respondents between 1986 and 2008. One group (91.7 percent) had experienced no injuries across the full span of the study, a second group (3 percent) had experienced an injury but took no time off work, while the third group (5.2 percent) took some time off work following an injury. Clear differences emerged regarding annual earnings growth for the ten years following an injury. Annual earnings growth for employees who suffered injuries that required no time off was $1,700 less (in 2015 dollars) than employees who did not experience an injury. For employees who were injured *and* took time off work, the loss in annual earnings growth was $3,700. Importantly, and a point to which we will return later, losses were significantly less for employees who were members of unions.

Using US data from 1985 to 2000, Monica Galizzi and Jay Zagorsky investigated the effects of injuries and illnesses on net-individual worth.[29] For the purposes of their study, wealth included all assets owned by members of the household after subtracting all debts. Their analyses shed further light on the individual costs of workplace injuries and illnesses. Being involved in an injury by itself, either for the first

** This is a different phenomenon from that described by Roberts and Markel earlier in this chapter. In that study, a sense of interpersonal unfairness *in the organization* predicted an increase in filing.

or second time, had no negative effects. However, needing to take time off work, and thus losing wages, resulted in what they called "a large wealth drop" (34), specifically a wealth reduction of up to 20 percent. An additional lesson from their analyses is that receiving workers' compensation benefits did not help prevent financial wealth losses over time.

Nor are the financial costs of safety incidents limited to the injured workers themselves; the financial status of family members is impacted as well. Abay Asfaw and colleagues analyzed workers' compensation data from 2002 to 2005 that produced an enormous database of 15,514 nonseverely and 2,897 severely injured workers who required at least seven days absence from work.[30] The odds of a family member being hospitalized in the nonsevere injury group in the three months following the injury was 31 percent higher than in the corresponding three months before the injury. For the severely injured groups, these odds increased to 56 percent. Because not all employees are covered by workers compensation in the United States, hospitalization would create a significant financial drain for the whole family.

A separate study by Asfaw and colleagues looked at the effects of musculoskeletal injuries on the healthcare costs borne by the family.[31] Using the same basic methodology with data obtained between 2002 and 2005, no differences existed initially in outpatient claims for musculoskeletal injuries between family members of severely and noninjured workers. However, three months after the safety incident, average outpatient costs related to musculoskeletal injuries increased for family members of severely injured workers by 25 percent, and by 3 percent for those of nonseverely injured workers.

Organizations with poor safety records also shoulder large financial costs. One example is the fines levied against BP after the blast at the Texas City refinery and the massive amounts of money paid in compensation to individuals. To investigate these financial costs more broadly, Jonathan Cohn and Malcolm Wardlaw conducted several large-scale studies involving US data.[32] Their analyses enabled them to conclude that a 34 percent increase in the company's injury rate was associated with a 6.1 percent decrease in firm value.[††] While the researchers caution that their specific financial estimates should be taken "with a grain of salt" (2052), they go on to estimate that the average future cost of an individual injury to the organization is $98,924, a figure that includes charges for increased downtime, increases in insurance premiums, and reduced or lost productivity.

Other studies estimate the cost of workplace injuries using different financial measures. In research in the construction industry in Australia, Ryan Allison and colleagues included the many direct and indirect costs accruing from workplace injuries, such as interruptions to production, reductions in employee motivation, medical costs, administrative resources required to deal with investigations, workers' compensation and legal costs, and administering additional benefits.[33] Providing one

[††] As measured by Tobin's Q, which reflects the ratio of the market value of the firm to its replacement cost.

specific value is not possible, given that safety incidents vary in severity. However, Allison et al. estimate that costs vary between $2,040 AUD for an incident that required a short-term absence, to more than $6 million for an incident that resulted in full incapacitation. Taking all this research together, workplace injuries clearly have an enormous impact on the financial well-being of employees, their families, and their organizations.

Last, several observations add to our understanding of the financial burden imposed by workplace injuries. First, the effects of injuries on financial outcomes are not the same for all workers. Workers' Compensation data from California between 2005 and 2011 showed that temporary workers are less likely to find employment after being injured. Moreover, part-time workers earned 9.1 percent less than comparable full-time workers in the three years following an injury. Second, given that post-event investigations invariably implicate organizational factors that resulted in safety events, we might question why injured employees and their families shoulder some, or even any, of the costs of these safety incidents. This predicament is illustrated in the final report by the CSB investigation into the disaster at the Texas City BP refinery. Of the sixteen technical and organizational findings, only one pointed to employees, and that was inadequate operator training—even though safety training remains a legal responsibility for management.[34] Third, the problem is reversed in some cases, with organizations facing financial constraints choosing not to devote their scarce financial resources to safety needs. We see this in the investigation by the CSB, which laid partial blame for the blast at the BP refinery in Texas City on an explicit decision by the company not to replace damaged equipment because of financial pressures.

Well-being

One of the direct consequences of workplace injuries is pain, which can result in personal costs for employees, such as interference with daily activities and disturbed sleep,[35] employee absenteeism,[36] and involvement in licit or illicit drug use at work to reduce pain.[37] Research also points to the effects of workplace injuries on employees' psychological well-being.

Workplace injuries are associated with subsequent depression. In a study of just under 367,900 workers in the United States, Abay Asfaw and Kerry Souza contrasted the incidence and cost of depression among injured and noninjured workers in the three months following the injury.[38] Despite the relatively short time period, injured workers were 45 percent more likely to be treated for depression in an outpatient setting than their noninjured counterparts. Moreover, even though women are more likely to be treated for depression than men, the effects of injuries on subsequent treatment for depression was higher for men than women. What is most notable is that this study assessed whether injured workers were treated for depression, rather than being diagnosed with depression but not receiving treatment. This distinction is important, as research from Australia[39] and Canada[40] shows that, while the incidence of mental illness following injuries is high, the number of people who seek treatment is low.

Let's change focus. Michael Frone investigated the effects of work injuries on well-being among adolescents aged between sixteen and nineteen.[41] Participants in this study recorded the frequency with which they had experienced work-related injuries in the prior nine months, and they provided separate data on their use of alcohol and marijuana both at and away from work. Workplace injuries in the prior nine months were significantly related to the consumption of high levels of on-the-job substances. In contrast, workplace injuries were not related to substance use in general. Findings such as this have important implications for the widespread practice of random testing of employees' substance use away from the workplace and outside normal working hours as an effective strategy for enhancing workplace safety.

Complicating matters, individuals who have suffered workplace injuries have to contend with skepticism and stigma directed at them from others. Even trained professionals, such as nurses and other health professionals who deal with injured workers, tend to minimize the severity of their situation.[42] Focus groups and interviews with injured workers reveal the negative stereotypes, victim blaming, poor treatment, and intrusive surveillance and monitoring that they endure.[43] In turn, injured workers told of how this later affected them ("You know what really hurt ... was my pre-injury circle of friends. I was well respected in the community, well respected as a labour leader ... about a year or so later ... those bridges start to dissolve and you're no longer seeing your old buddies ... you're not getting a call"; 151), their family relationships ("My wife and I, I think we had the most difficult period in our lives when I got hurt ... because ... it goes from a two family income to a one family income, she's ... you know, pulling her weight and, you know it, it was just hard, ... you have no leverage, you don't want to talk ... You go from a breadwinner to a bread eater."; 151), and their mental health (e.g., "You get depressed, ... like the depression is 100% because you feel you need help and then if you can't get the help, you get frustrated, and most of the week is full of depression. You are nothing, just nothing, you are irritated"; 151).

As these quotes reveal, the effects of workplace injuries go beyond the injured person and affect other family members as well. This idea should not be surprising. Because injured workers can have visible injuries, or experience long-term pain or disability, those closest to them physically and interpersonally might be affected as well. One study investigated the mental health effects on 148 people who had a family member killed at work.[44] The average time since the traumatic incident was just over six years, yet 61.5 percent still exceeded the threshold for a diagnosis of PTSD, 44 percent for a diagnosis of major depressive disorder, and 43.2 percent for prolonged grief disorder. These effects were greater if the deceased worker was next of kin, but reduced when the surviving family member received support from a family member and/or from someone who helped them move through the bureaucracy after the fatality. This last finding should be very useful to organizations such as workers' compensation boards, in any efforts to reduce the negative effects on secondary victims.

One of the largest studies in this area looked at the effects on 485,002 children aged two to sixteen who had a military parent injured while on service in Afghanistan or Iraq between 2004 and 2014.[45] The researchers compared data for the two years before and two years following the injury, and their findings uncover a range of negative effects for children of injured parents. Medical visits for injuries to the child increased by 7 percent in the two years following the parental injury, and by a troublesome 41 percent for instances of child maltreatment. Hospital visits for child maltreatment were more likely to increase for boys in the two years following an injury, with mental health care visits increasing more for girls. Medical visits for mental health care increased for just over half the children (55 percent), and the duration for which children of injured parents were taking prescription medication increased by 77 percent. What should be of real concern is that in the face of all these issues, medical visits for preventive care decreased by 22 percent.

But do parents' workplace injuries affect children's mental health outside of non-military contexts? Asfaw and colleagues compared 408 six-to-seventeen-year-old children in the United States who had a parent injured or involved in a poisoning event at work between 2012 and 2016 with 39,201 children whose parents were not injured.[46] Children whose parents had been injured at work were more likely to be worried and depressed, experience emotional and behavioral problems, have a poor attention span, and difficulties in relationships with others.

In a separate study, Nick Turner and colleagues focused on the effects of work injuries among either parent of 4,884 adolescent schoolchildren in Ontario.[47] Parental injuries were related to lower levels of psychological well-being among the adolescents. Moreover, the negative effects of parental injuries were lower for adolescents who believed that work would be more central to their own lives in the future.

Turner at al. offer several interesting recommendations that are also appropriate to the findings from other studies in this section. First, they recommend that injured parents should be made aware of the likelihood that other members of their family, including children, may be adversely affected. Extending this, I would suggest that labor unions and organizations themselves have a role to play in educating employees, and this should be routine for workers' compensation agencies dealing with injured workers. Providing this knowledge could go a long way in mobilizing family members to provide more help and support to the injured person.[48] Second, parents who are injured at work should use it as an opportunity to open a conversation with their children about workplace safety given the role that parents play in the development of children's work attitudes and beliefs.[49] Third, in the same way that families routinely emphasize the importance of road safety with their children, especially before they start driving, they should make workplace safety a routine part of family discussions well before their children enter employment.

How does workplace safety exert its effects?

Workplace health and safety exert indirect effects

Thus, as we have seen, job injuries can affect family functioning, and Ericka Lawrence and colleagues sought to understand why this is the case.[50] Because of the personal financial toll of workplace injuries, Lawrence et al. proposed that the immediate effects of a workplace injury would be a feeling of financial insecurity. In addition, because injured workers can have difficulty regaining employment, or the same level or type of employment they had pre-injury, injured workers would also experience job insecurity. In turn, the resulting financial and job insecurity would disturb family functioning. After all, fear of financial or job loss might place greater financial responsibilities on the noninjured spouse. Using data from 194 US trauma nurses, workplace injuries resulted in higher levels of financial and job insecurity, which predicted work-family problems. Essentially, one partner's injuries affected the other's financial insecurity, which in turn affected the injured spouse's work-family balance. However, any links between workplace injuries and financial and job insecurity were reduced if supervisors were supportive of the injured workers.

At least two practical recommendations can be derived directly from this study. First, helping supervisors appreciate findings like these could expand the positive role they can play in reducing any negative effects of workplace injuries. Second, and more specifically, any negative spillover of workplace injuries onto family functioning might be prevented if organizations are actively engaged in ensuring that injured workers do not suffer financially or do not need to fear for their jobs.

Workplace injuries might result in very different paths forward for injured workers. One option would be to quit an organization that might endanger their safety. But quitting is not always an option given the potential financial costs involved. This is potentially important for organizations, because employees who choose to stay with the organization and face difficult problems do not necessarily remain passive. Instead, they often seek to resolve the problem, in this case, workplace-safety issues. But what do they then do if they fail to resolve the safety issues themselves? One alternative would be to turn to others who have been more successful in resolving similar issues in the past. In this respect, unions could appear to be a viable mechanism for some employees, given that the presence of unions has a major effect on safety.[51] Using data on 9,908 Australian employees, my colleagues and I showed that being involved in an injury left employees with a sense of distrust in management, and the feeling that they lacked influence in the organization, both of which resulted in job dissatisfaction. Ultimately, this job dissatisfaction led some people in this study to want to quit the organization, and others to turn to a union for help in improving their situation.

Workplace safety shapes the way you experience your work

In prior chapters, we have considered how exposure to high-quality leadership, job autonomy, and so forth all shape the way in which people experience their work. We now take a different direction and investigate how one workplace feature, namely the presence or absence of a labor union, markedly influences how people experience safety in their workplace.[52]

Almost immeasurable progress has been made in reducing workplace fatalities over the past century. The earliest recording of workplace fatalities in the United States show that between July 1906 and June 1907, 195 steelworkers were killed at work in Alleghany County, Pennsylvania. Almost a century later, seventeen steelworkers were killed in the whole of the United States in 1997.[53] Similarly, the US National Safety Council reported that between 18,000 and 21,000 workers died from their injuries in 1912. A year later, the US BLS put the number of work-related fatalities at 23,000. To put that number into perspective, the total US workforce in 2013 was 38 million[54]; today it is closer to 185 million, the total number of workplace fatalities in 2019 was 5,333. Two factors are primarily responsible for this change: government legislation and regulations, and the presence of unions.

Securing better working conditions for employees, including workplace safety, has long been a dominant goal for unions. Today, unionized workplaces are safer than nonunionized workplaces. Alison Morantz's study of all operating underground bituminous coal mines in the United States between 1993 and 2010 reveals the magnitude of this effect.[55] Workplace injuries declined between 14 percent and 32 percent following unionization, and the decrease in fatalities ranged between 29 percent and 83 percent. The decreases are especially important because the effects were even greater in larger mines.

Despite findings like these, it is not unusual to read reports in which injuries[56] and illnesses[57] are higher in unionized organizations. Several factors can account for these seemingly counterintuitive findings. First, what social scientists like to call "reverse causality" could be at play. What this means is that it is not that unions cause injuries and fatalities. Instead, higher levels of injuries and illnesses might lead employees to seek union representation. A second major consequence of union membership is that previously unreported incidents and injuries are more likely to be reported when employees have union protection. Third, unionized employees also filed workers' compensation claims earlier than nonunionized, which is critical in preventing longer-term injuries.[58] Last, one of the functions of unions is to monitor management compliance with basic safety requirement—such as reporting injuries to appropriate authorities, which can enhance workplace safety. Examples of this monitoring effect range from Cambodia's garment industry where the presence of unions resulted in a decrease in labor-standard violations,[59] to analyses of 868 US firms that showed that, in the presence of a union, management were less willing to endanger employee safety to meet or beat earnings expectations.[60]

Taken together, the lessons from this research are clear. While management often see unions as adversaries, the presence of unions can enhance workplace safety. Unions likely have little effect on organizations that excel in terms of workplace safety. Instead, employees seek union representation when organizations abdicate their responsibilities for workplace safety, and unions then exert their effect by imposing minimum safety standards and practices on organizations that do not do so of their own initiative. It should not go unsaid that employees are less likely to seek union representation when they believe that management is proactively involved in workplace safety.

Gender and workplace safety

The workplace is unquestionably more dangerous for males than for females. As can be seen from Figure 8.1, more than ten times the number of males than females were killed at work each year in the United States between 2003 and 2019.[61] This pattern is not unique to the United States. Similar gender discrepancies appear in other countries, such as Taiwan[62] and Canada.[63] Perhaps the most frequent explanation offered for this gender disparity is that men occupy more dangerous jobs than females, and this explanation is indeed accurate.[64] Another frequent explanation is that males are more risk-taking than females. Data from self-reports by 12,707 people in fourteen

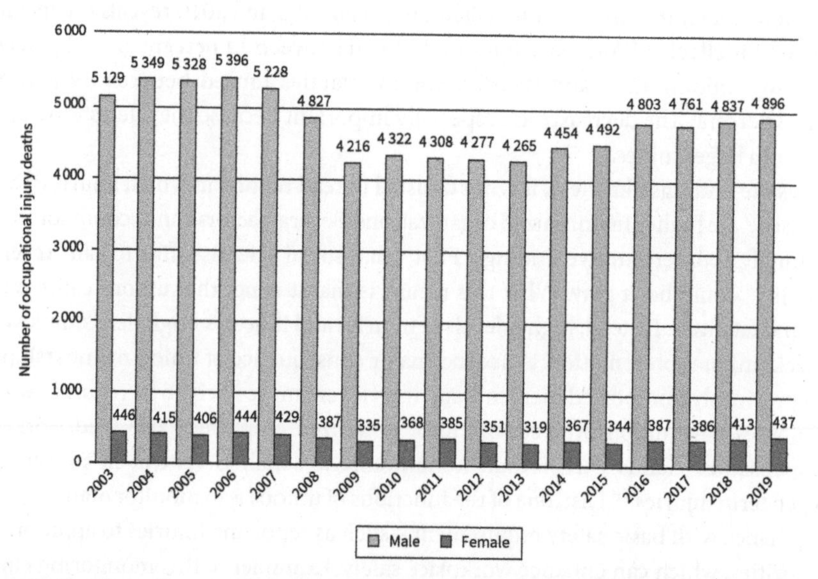

Fig. 8.1 Number of occupational injury deaths in the United States from 2003–2019. https://www.statista.com/statistics/187127/number-of-occupational-injury-deaths-in-the-us-by-gender-since-2003/

Republished with permission.

European, including Nordic, countries support this hypothesis as well.[65] Research investigating actual safety behaviors show similar findings. For example, an experimental study of 147 Chinese construction workers unobtrusively tracked construction workers' safety behaviors: males intruded into dangerous work sites without permission far more frequently than females, and spent more time on those dangerous sites than female construction workers.[66,‡‡]

Yet making sense of these enormous gender differences is more complicated than it seems at first glance. In fact, acclaimed filmmaker Errol Morris reminds us that often at least part of the explanation for any phenomenon lies behind the picture. Morris illustrated this in his probing analysis of the horrific photographs showing the abuses in the Abu Ghraib prison in Iraq. While it seemed as if the situation was one in which a few soldiers had "gone rogue," the actual failures were located higher in the chain of command, a crucial fact that was hidden by what seemed so obvious from the pictures.[67] In the same way, there is more to the link between gender and work safety than meet the eye. One example is that over and above gender, gendered *roles* play a part in occupational fatalities. To understand this dynamic, Timothy Bauerle and colleagues combined data from the 2012 US *Census of Fatal Occupational Injuries* database and the *Women in the Labor Force Databook*.[68] The fatality risk for males compared to females was even greater in traditional feminine occupations, such as those that involve interpersonal interaction as well as interactions with others. The authors speculate that this difference could be because males will be predisposed to take on more physically challenging tasks in feminine jobs to maintain a masculine identity.

Further support for this gender-role explanation emerges from semistructured interviews with twelve workers who were injured in an electrical incident and twelve employer representatives.[69] Strong identification with an agentic masculine-worker role, which involved being viewed as strong, resilient, and responsible, was associated with deciding not to report safety incidents and injuries, and being willing to return to work before you are ready to do so. As "Walter," a skilled tradesperson, said, "I wanted to return to work on my terms. I didn't want to go in there shallow, doubting, looking over my shoulder, nervous. I wanted to return to work as Walter, or as close to Walter as I could be" (726). Likewise, even management decisions about return-to-work might be driven by gender-role perceptions. This can be seen in the metaphors used in an interaction Walter had with his supervisor. "I remember talking to my supervisor, the owner of the company.... [H]e was coming up my street and he was saying to me 'Oh you got to get back on the horse.' And I looked at him and I said, "horse'? I can't even walk to the barn yet" (728).

‡‡ As more women take on jobs that have traditionally been viewed as "men's work" (such as the skilled trades), these gender differences will probably start to change. However, the safety ramifications of structural changes like this cannot be underestimated. As one female millwright in Canada said upon starting her job, "I needed a respirator, I needed gloves and I needed a harness, none of which they had in size small." Gordon, J. (July 29, 2021). Women are the answer to Canada's skilled-trades shortage, but many roadbloacks still exist. *Globe and Mail*. https://www.theglobeandmail.com/business/article-canada-looks-to-women-to-bolster-trades-amid-post-pandemic-labor/

Complicating the challenge of understanding gender and workplace safety, women face far more violence at work than men. Practitioners generally place workplace violence into four categories.[70] The first three occur as a result of criminal intent (e.g., during robberies), customer aggression directed against staff, and worker against worker (or supervisor) violence, respectively. A hallmark of these types of violence is that within each category, the relationship between the perpetrator and victim becomes increasingly more personal. This is most evident in the fourth category, which occurs when domestic violence spills over into the workplace. Invariably in these situations, abused women have taken shelter away from the family home, and their partners do not know where they have taken refuge. However, they do know where they work, and show up at the workplace and harass their former partners, interfering with their work. And in some cases, they kill their former partners in the workplace or nearby carparks. While this form of violence might not be top of mind for many people, 22 percent of the 648 females who were killed at work in the United States between 2003 and 2008 died this way, second only to fatalities involving criminal intent such as burglaries, which accounted for 39 percent of all female fatalities.[71] Last, as we see later in this chapter, the public nature of these incidents alerts us to the reality that coworkers who witness these events could be traumatized by viewing or learning about the violence, and in need of organizational support themselves.

Several important lessons can be learned about family violence spilling into the workplace. Organizations are not hostage to violent former partners; there are preventive measures that can be put in place. As examples, even though organizations are not directly responsible for these fatalities that occur *at* work but not as result *of* work, policies that protect employees who have restraining orders, and require all visitors to sign in before entering the premises, could make a difference.[72] Similarly, though training supervisors and coworkers on what to do in such situations could have widespread benefits, a mere 4 percent of US organizations do so.[73] Given that 22 percent of all workplace fatalities that occur in parking lots involve women murdered by a former partner, ensuring adequate lighting, line of sight, and the presence of security guards could again make a difference.[74] More generally, given the different nature and causes of workplace fatalities for males and females, organizations may well need different policies, practices, and procedures for preventing workplace fatalities among males and females.

Culture and workplace safety

Differences in the level of workplace safety

Comparing workplace safety between countries is probably more difficult than any of the other characteristics we have considered in the previous six chapters. The reason for this difficulty is not an absence of data. Nor is the problem caused by the complexity of the data. Superficially at least, the data on workplace safety are relatively easy to understand. Instead, the problem is a result of widespread underreporting, meaningful differences in recording and notification systems between countries, and vast differences in workers' compensation systems across countries. As examples, some but not all countries include commuting incidents (e.g., traveling to or from work, or between two worksites) while some others include incidents in agriculture as workplace safety issues. As a result, what is recorded as a workplace injury or fatality will differ markedly across countries.[75] Despite these reporting issues, there is some value to an analysis of regional and country differences in workplace safety because of potential lessons that can be learned, but we proceed with due caution.

In an extensive analysis of global trends in workplace fatalities and injuries, Päivi Hämäläinen and colleagues estimated that 360,000 people were killed and approximately 350 million injured in workplace incidents in 2003.[§§] Viewed daily, that would mean that 1,020 workers were killed, and 960,000 workers were injured at work each day.[76] As dire as these numbers are, and recognizing as most authors do that they are based on underreporting, numbers like these alone do not necessarily paint an accurate picture of workplace safety for several reasons.

First, ignoring population size provides misleading estimates of fatalities or injuries. For that reason, the fatality (or injury) rate, i.e., the number of fatalities per hundred thousand workers, is a more useful index. Countries with lower fatality rates in 2003 would include the United Kingdom (0.8), the Netherlands and Sweden (1.3), Switzerland (1.4), Denmark (1.9), Australia (2.0), and Luxembourg (2.4). In stark contrast, countries with some of the worst fatality rates are Thailand (20.3), Bangladesh (21.8), Senegal (24.8), Angola (24.9), Myanmar (26.2), and Nepal (28.8). For comparison, the fatality rates in large industrialized countries such as Germany (3.2), the United States (5.0), Canada (7.6), and Russia (8.7) are more similar to those countries with the lowest workplace fatality rates. Thus, the fatality rate between different countries reveals remarkable differences between countries and regions.

Second, the difference in fatality rate between regions masks differences between countries within those regions. As one example, the average fatality rate for all EU countries in 2018 was 1.77.[77] This average does a disservice to the Netherlands (0.6), and potentially masks safety problems in Romania (4.33).

Third, even while the number of global workplace fatalities increased between 1990 and 2016 by 16 percent, the most plausible explanation for this is the growth in global employment since 2003. Over the same time period, fatality rates decreased by 31 percent.[78] While this is clearly encouraging, the rate of decline is uneven across regions. The largest decreases occurred in European and Middle Eastern regions. Fatality rates in most other regions remained relatively stable, but some African countries saw increases in fatality rates.[79] This overall trend could be misleading. As increasing numbers of production jobs flow from countries better equipped to

[§§] Although we are focusing on workplace safety, it is important to note that Hämäläinen et al. place the number of people who died from workplace-related diseases at just less than 2 million.

enhance safety to those in which workplace fatalities and injuries remain stubbornly stable, overall improvements in global workplace safety will be difficult to achieve.

Fourth, huge gender differences exist in global workplace fatalities and injuries requiring time off work. Based on the Global Burden of Disease data, 94.7 percent of workplace fatalities were suffered by males in 2016. At the same time, males suffered 87.8 percent of all workplace injuries.

Last, any consideration of global trends in workplace safety must include some focus on migrant workers. By 2015, there were approximately 120 million migrant workers, a number that has likely increased since then. Most migrant workers are employed under the most precarious of circumstances. They may lack formal authorization to be in the country in which they are working, and may not be fluent in the host country's language. As well, they are unlikely to hold permanent contracts, and are often engaged in jobs described as dirty, dangerous, demanding, and demeaning.[80] They typically work long hours for low pay, usually in the service sector, manufacturing, or agriculture, doing the hazardous work declined by local citizens. Migrant work is also often invisible, and all too often beyond the reach of safety regulators and enforcement. As a result, while accurate statistics are difficult to obtain because of pressures on migrant workers not to report safety infractions or injuries, Sally Moyce and Marc Schenker note that the disproportionate share of workplace fatalities and injuries among migrant workers compared to local workers has been increasing.[81]

As a result, searching for the reasons for differences in workplace fatality and injury rates is complicated, but remains important. Two factors are often offered for the national differences. First, because of their access to resources, greater knowledge, skills and flexibility, management in developed countries can respond to daily safety challenges and take proactive actions that enhance safety. In contrast, developing countries lack those same resources or level of knowledge and flexibility. Second, legislation protecting workers' safety is critical, and over time, most developed countries are likely to have implemented regulations, and ensured some level of enforcement, often as a result of pressure from labor unions.

Interventions to enhance of workplace safety

Most formal initiatives targeting workplace safety involve safety training of one sort or another; some programs now even use virtual reality as a delivery mechanism.[82] Based on a large body of research and experience, we now know that training improves safety knowledge and safety performance. Even the mere presence of safety training signals to employees that management is committed to their well-being,[83] and that the more engaging the training, the better.[84] Despite the multitude of safety-training programs, I will discuss an intervention to enhance workplace safety that is more basic, and less costly, but decidedly more controversial.

Announcing that government inspectors have arrived for a random safety inspection is unlikely to be met with much enthusiasm by many business owners. Objections are likely to include the intrusion in areas of management discretion, disruption with ongoing operations, the impeding of financial growth, and even the threatening of the survival of the organization. But what if random safety inspections actually enhance safety and have none of the feared side effects?

David Levine and his colleagues studied this issue using a randomized experiment, the type of experiment that many health regulators around the world would demand before allowing new medications onto the market.[85] Between 1996 and 2006, 409 workplaces with at least ten employees in high-injury industries in California were randomly selected for safety inspections by the state's Division of Occupational Safety and Health.*** The researchers constructed a control group of the same number of companies from comparable organizations that were in the same industry and region of California, none of which had experienced a random safety inspection. Procedures like these ensure that any differences between the two groups can be credibly ascribed to the presence of the random safety inspection.

The results of this study provide solid support for random safety inspections from two different perspectives. First, there was strong evidence of a reduction in injuries and their financial consequences. Randomized inspections reduced injuries by 9.4 percent, and this effect lasted for five years following the inspection. Moreover, this effect was achieved for injuries that resulted in compensation claims both less and more than $2,000 US, suggesting that safety inspections reduce minor and major injuries. Using a different metric, the results showed that companies that went through a mandatory safety inspection enjoyed a 26 percent decline in injury costs, with some evidence pointing to consistent reductions in injury costs for the next five years.

Second, there was no support at all for the concern that random safety inspections harm the targeted establishment. There was no statistical difference between the two groups in terms of company survival. However, company "deaths" are relatively rare, and other more nuanced metrics may be better equipped to pick up any harmful effects from random safety inspections. Despite this, there were no differences between the companies in the two groups in terms of creditworthiness, assessed via Dun and Bradstreet's Composite Credit Appraisal and PAYDEX scores. Nor were there any negative effects on employment numbers, total earnings, or sales. In contrast to these concerns, the reduction in injuries over the five-year period following the safety inspection was associated with a reduction of about $355,000 in medical costs, equal to approximately 14 percent of annual payroll.

As impressive as the benefits of randomized safety inspections were shown to be in Levine at al.'s analyses, the positive effects may even be underestimated. For various reasons, 7 percent of the companies selected to receive a safety inspection never received it. However, these companies remained in the analyses, artificially reducing the real impact of randomized safety inspections in these analyses. Thus, perhaps the

*** It is important to differentiate randomized safety inspections vs targeted inspections that occur as a result of injuries or employee complaints. The lessons from Levine et al.'s study would not necessarily hold for targeted inspections.

best way to summarize the findings from this research, and the effects of random safety inspections in general, is to quote from testimony given by the OSHA Director David Michaels to a US Congress subcommittee: "The truth is that OSHA standards don't kill jobs. They stop jobs from killing workers. OSHA standards don't just prevent worker injuries and illnesses. They also drive technological innovation, making industries more competitive."[86]

A special case: Foreign correspondents and workplace safety

When you ask people to name the most dangerous occupations in the world—something I do often both in and out of classrooms—the answers are predictable. Construction and mining almost always get mentioned. Other jobs that are somehow less visible but just as dangerous tend not to earn a mention. A case in point is the work of journalists. The Reporters Without Borders[87] organization estimates that in the ten-year period from 2011 to 2020, 937 journalists[†††] were killed while doing their work.[88] While many if not most were local journalists working to expose corruption or expressing an unpopular political perspective, journalists covering war and conflict on foreign soil still make up a large number of these fatalities. As disturbing as these fatalities are, our focus in this section is not on fatalities but on the *mental health* consequences of this work, as this will provide new insight into an additional and largely unrecognized consequence of workplace safety incidents.

Psychiatrist Anthony Feinstein has studied the mental health of journalists working in conflict zones for much of the past two decades, and some of this research is summarized in his early book *Journalists under fire: The psychological hazards of war reporting*.[89] In one of his largest studies, Feinstein and his colleagues contacted war journalists who either worked for one of six major international news organizations or worked as freelance journalists; 140 eventually participated in this survey.[90] Because local journalism can also be stressful, Feinstein et al. created a comparison group of 107 domestic journalists who may have covered distressing local incidents such as plane crashes, but had never been involved in war journalism. In addition, the two groups were of the same age and had been involved in journalism for the same amount of time. As a result, any differences between these two groups would be a function of the experience of reporting on wars. Providing an initial indication of the dangers of war journalism, one of the war journalists in the initial sample was murdered before the surveys even arrived.

The differences in mental health between the two groups were enormous. War journalists consumed more than twice as much alcohol as local journalists (with the differences being even greater for females). War journalists also suffered significantly

[†††] This number includes people working directly to assist journalists, such as drivers and interpreters.

higher levels of three dimensions of PTSD, namely the extent to which they re-experience traumatic events, consciously try and avoid thoughts or feelings about the event, or become hyperaroused emotionally. Importantly, the lifetime prevalence of PTSD among war journalists was 28.6 percent, which is more than double the prevalence rate for police officers, and approximately the same as that experienced by combat veterans. War journalists also scored much higher on clinical depression, with 21.4 percent of the war journalists rated as suffering from major depression. What makes the elevated rates of substance use, PTSD, and major depression among war journalists even more concerning is that they were no more likely than domestic journalists to be seeking or receiving any form of medication or psychiatric help.

A separate study by Feinstein and a different set of colleagues sheds some light on why war journalists suffer in this way.[91] When we think of journalists, I suspect the image that comes to mind is of people on the frontlines—whether covering wars, plane crashes, or perhaps even political press conferences. But in an era when many news organizations have downsized journalists, news organizations have created a new form of journalism involving user-generated content (UGC). This involves news organizations reaching out to the public and inviting people who are on the scene to submit videos and pictures. This approach requires the establishment of a new group of journalists, whose job it is to sift through all the content submitted, selecting only the material that can be safely shown to the public. As a result, the public is spared from seeing the more horrific submissions, but this group of journalists literally spend their days exposed to horrific events and violence.

Feinstein et al. surveyed 116 journalists involved in UGC who provided information about the frequency (whether daily, weekly, monthly) and duration (number of hours per shift) of their exposure to violent images and videos. This group then completed surveys about their mental health. Greater frequency of exposure to violent images and videos was associated with higher levels of clinical depression, anxiety, and psychosomatic symptoms, and all three dimensions of PTSD. In addition, more time spent viewing violent material per shift was associated with the intrusive or re-experiencing dimension of PTSD.

Findings from this research have crucial implications for managing workplace safety. We have already established that the harm caused by workplace safety incidents affects other family members. What Feinstein's research teaches us is that watching others getting injured or killed at work can have serious psychological consequences. Thus, from a practical perspective, we need to be more concerned about the psychological well-being of employees who witness serious workplace injuries or worse. Would it be realistic to expect these workers to focus on work, let alone to be motivated to perform at the high levels organizations demand, after watching peers, coworkers, or the targets (e.g., combatants) being injured or killed?

A special case: COVID-19 and workplace health and safety

In the fullness of time we will realize just how much the COVID-19 pandemic taught us, but one stark lesson already learned is how unprepared organizations were to maintain workplace safety in the face of a global pandemic. While it will be a while before all the data are available, the number of COVID-related workplace deaths is already staggering. As but one example, the *Guardian* newspaper in the United Kingdom painstakingly tracked the number of health care workers in the United States who died from COVID-19.[92] As of April 2021, they put the toll at 3,607 healthcare workers. To put this number into perspective, the number of US health care workers who died in the first fourteen months of the pandemic exceeds the total number of people killed in the attacks in the United States on 9/11. In addition, based only on the number of workplace fatalities among healthcare workers, we can predict that the total number of workplace fatalities for the United States in 2020 and 2021 will likely increase by about 50 percent, with increases probable for 2022 as well. Importantly, this would exclude employees in other essential industries such as meatpacking, with a congressional committee in the United States estimating that fifty-nine thousand workers contracted COVID-19 between March 1, 2020, and February 1, 2021.[93] When *all* worker-related COVID-19 deaths are accounted for, it is not unreasonable to predict that the annual number of workplace deaths as a function of injuries and illnesses will more than double. Making this picture even darker, members of minority, racialized, and indigenous groups are disproportionately represented among these numbers.

Any effects of the pandemic on workplace health and safety go beyond fatalities. Infections also wreaked havoc on workplaces. As of June 21, 2021, 34,410,000 Americans had been infected with the virus. With approximately 56 percent of the population employed in 2020,[94] this statistic means that just shy of 20 million employees likely contracted the virus by mid-June 2021. Why is this number relevant? If all employees who contracted the virus were required to quarantine for ten *work* days (fourteen in total) as they were at the time, the economy would have suffered 200 million lost days of work due to COVID-19 alone.

So what have we learned? Early in the pandemic, organizations were literally bidding against each other to get hand-sanitizer and masks.[‡‡‡] If you went into organizations at that stage, you would have been confronted with hand-sanitizers and masked people, some of whom would be scrubbing every surface. Go into most organizations or restaurants a year or two later and you will be confronted with hand-sanitizers at the entrance and plexiglass shields between customers and service workers, but far fewer masks or people scrubbing surfaces. Given what we now know about how the

‡‡‡ And surely no one forgets the scramble for toilet paper.

virus spreads, this tells a story of how we still base our safety practices on myth and misinformation, rather than the best of evidence. Derek Thompson called this "hygiene theatre" in July 2020, and it still predominates some time later—safety protocols "that make us feel safer, but don't actually do much to reduce risk, even as more dangerous activities are still allowed."[95] For example, even though we know that the virus is airborne, and that hand sanitizers and plexiglass shields offer very little protection, these practices still predominate, perhaps because they now serve as a symbols (albeit, ineffective ones) of organizations mounting a defense against the virus, and they are less costly than changing ventilation systems in organizations.

What you will see or hear about less, are techniques most likely to limit the virus and enhance workplace safety in the face of this pandemic. The pandemic has exposed the value of personal protective equipment (PPE), primarily face masks, which effectively limit the spread of COVID-19. Similarly, maintaining a distance of at least six feet between people is a critical preventive strategy. Yet neither facemasks nor physical distances were enforced in many businesses in America. This reality is especially egregious in environments most vulnerable to viral spread, such as meatpacking plants and large distribution sites, where management implicitly or explicitly favored production over safety. As a result, large-scale outbreaks occurred, such as those at the Cargill slaughterhouse in Alberta, Canada, where one outbreak early in the pandemic resulted in nine hundred cases and three deaths in one plant.[96]

All these attempts at prevention should be compared with two initiatives that could prevent the spread of COVID-19 in workplaces. First, paid sickness-absence programs enable sick or quarantining employees to stay away from work with no income loss, and this is as important for infectious diseases other than COVID-19. Without such programs, employees who are dependent on their daily wages will feel compelled to go to work. In one study in Peel, Ontario, at the end of the first year of the pandemic, 25 percent of the eight thousand employees surveyed reported going to work when they were symptomatic. Eighty employees even admitted going to work after being diagnosed with COVID-19 because they could not afford to lose any pay.[97] Second, medical and engineering scientists now emphasize that COVID-19 is transmitted via aerosols, and that high-quality ventilation systems (and N95 facemasks) could help stem the spread of viral infections.[98] To date, however, businesses were slow to install high-quality ventilation systems.[99,§§§]

It is not only organizations that missed opportunities to implement practices to mitigate health risks from COVID-19. As have already seen, random government safety inspections reduce workplace injuries,[100] and coupled with enforcement, they

[§§§] Soon after vaccinations were approved, a growing list of major US companies, including Google, Facebook, Netflix, Walmart, Disney, Blackrock, Morgan Stanley, Saks Fifth Avenue, the *Washington Post*, Union Square Hospitality, Ascension Health, Lyft, Uber, and Twitter have all announced that they will require proof of vaccinations—the most effective public health measure available against COVID-19—before employees can return to the workplace. Benveniste, A. (August 4, 2021). From offices to restuarants, companies are requiring proof of vaccination. *CNN Business*. https://www.cnn.com/2021/07/28/business/companies-vaccine-mandate/index.html

could have reduced the enormous numbers of COVID-related infections and fatalities. However, governments did not seize this opportunity. In the United States, for example, OSHA largely retreated from its legislated responsibilities in 2020. After decades of retrenchment, the agency had fewer safety inspectors during the pandemic than any time in the previous forty-two years. One former OSHA official even told of colleagues "being pulled off a COVID-19 fatality inspection at a Walmart where two employees died" and instructed to move on to "do a roofing inspection instead."

The safety lessons from the pandemic for workplace health and safety are both unique and straightforward, and could serve organizations and their employees beyond the COVID-19 pandemic. You cannot mitigate workplace safety threats, whether posed by COVID-19 or other hazards, by stubbornly enforcing practices (such as handwashing and cleaning surfaces) shown to have very little benefit against the specific threat. What is required is encouraging and enforcing evidence-based best practices that would have a positive effect. From a pandemic perspective, that would mean providing PPE and opportunities for physical distancing, paid leave, installing high-quality ventilation systems, and encouraging vaccinations—including paid time off to be vaccinated. Certainly, providing PPE is a relatively low-cost initiative and easy to implement. Physical distancing in most workplaces is achievable. Implementing paid sick leave policies, giving paid time off to be vaccinated, and installing high-quality ventilation systems are more costly. However, each of these evidence-based strategies would provide better protection for employees and reduce the likelihood of enormously expensive and lengthy government-imposed shutdowns that disrupt and threaten businesses.

A special case: Young workers and workplace safety

When we think of demographic groups that are most vulnerable to workplace injuries and fatalities, we likely think about males and marginalized workers. One demographic group that probably goes unnoticed but appears prominently in workplace safety incidents is young workers.[****] Allowing young workers to escape our attention would be a huge mistake. Until we appreciate the extent to which young workers are disproportionately exposed to workplace hazards, change is unlikely. As the adage goes, "Out of sight, out of mind." Just as importantly, an appreciation of *why* young workers experience higher rates of workplace injuries will show that change is well within the grasp of most organizations.

While there are national and cultural differences in young worker injury and fatality rates, the picture painted by US data provides a fair reflection of the situation. In the twenty years between 1994 and 2013, BLS data identified 942 workplace fatalities of youth aged 18 or less. As a comparison, this translates into a rate of 2.9 deaths per

[****] In many jurisdictions, young workers include anyone aged twenty-four or less, and we will follow that tradition for this discussion.

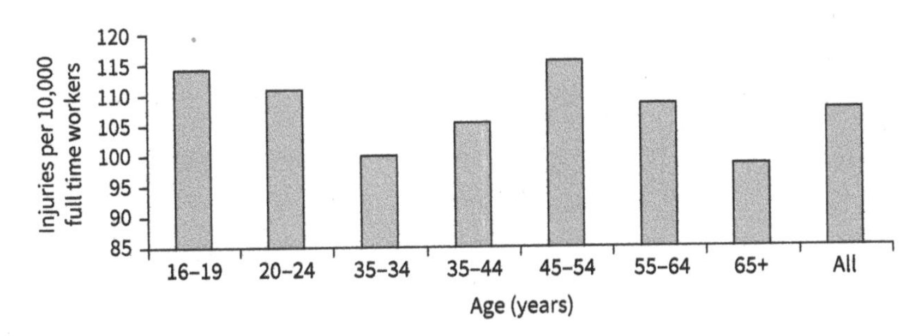

Fig. 8.2 Estimated incidence rates of nonfatal occupational injuries and illness involving days away from work by age group, United States, private sector, 2010.
Source: Survey of Occupational Injuries and Illnesses available at www.bls.gov/news.release/archives/osh2_11092011.pdf Date accessed July 17, 2012

one hundred full-time equivalent employees.[101] Remarkably, 21 percent of the young worker fatalities occurred in children aged 14 and 15, an age at which adolescents are still protected by child labor legislation.[102] Almost half the fatalities occurred in transportation incidents, with 20 percent involving objects and equipment, and 20 percent involving some form of workplace violence. Given that many young workers are employed on a seasonal basis, almost half the fatalities occurred in the three summer months. Young male and white employees were overwhelmingly more likely to suffer workplace fatalities. Last, an important point is that the number of fatalities have decreased over the last twenty years. However, the decrease was much slower for females and young workers of all other races.

How young workers fare with respect to workplace injuries can be gleaned from several different statistics. One traditional metric is the number of injuries that resulted in time away from work. Davis and Vautin showed that younger workers aged sixteen to nineteen experience about the same number of incidents requiring time away from work as those aged forty-five to fifty-four (see Figure 8.2), but more than all other age groups. In addition, young workers aged twenty to twenty-four suffered more lost time incidents than employees aged twenty-five to forty-four and fifty-five years and older.[103] Still, not all young workers report their injuries within the organization; some seek medical help from emergency rooms. Davis and Vautin's analyses again show that young workers visit emergency rooms workplace injuries more than any other age group (see Figure 8.3).[104] Even these numbers do not paint a full picture because employees also experience injuries that do not require time off work. Nick Turner and his colleagues analyzed data on injuries among 19,547 young workers in Canada that did not require time away from work. 25.5 percent of their sample experienced one or two injuries in the past four weeks that did not require time off work, with 8 percent experiencing three or more such incidents over the same time period.[105]

As troubling as this is, the extent to which young workers experience workplace injuries is likely underestimated. One large-scale analysis showed that 21.3 percent of 21,345 Canadian workers between the ages of fifteen and twenty-five reported

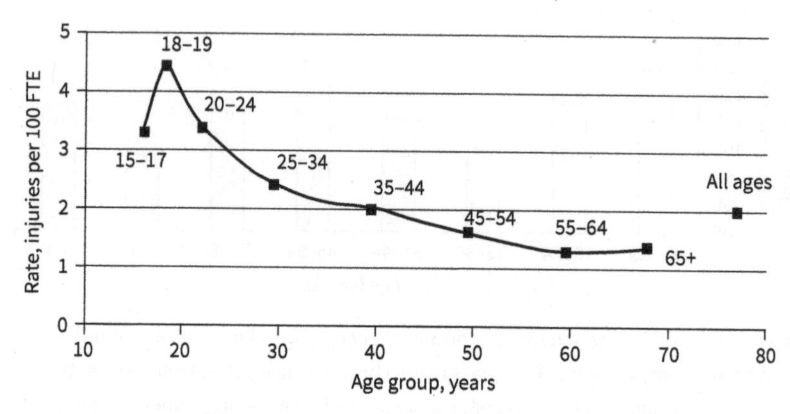

Fig. 8.3 Estimated rates* of work-related nonfatal injuries and illnesses treated in hospital emergency departments, by age group, 2009.

Source: National Electronic Injury Surveillance System—Occupational Supplement

*Numbers of injuries and illnesses per 100 full time workers; standard errors range from 10–15% (not shown).

taking time off work because of a work-related injury. Fully 27 percent of these young workers did not report their injury to their employer or a doctor.[106] By far, the most frequent reason offered for not reporting the injury was that it was believed to be of low severity (e.g., "it was only a burn"; 71). Concerns about how others would respond (e.g., "afraid to tell my employer ... might get fired"; 71) and self-identity (e.g., "It wasn't that serious and I don't want to be a pain/whiney baby"; 71) were also raised. Focus group interviews with thirty-nine teenagers in Canada (aged fifteen to eighteen years old) produced very similar results.[107]

A question with enormous implications is why adolescents and young workers are more likely to experience workplace injuries. One possibility that can be discounted based on recent research is that genetic factors are responsible. In researching genetic factors, social scientists place considerable confidence in comparisons of monozygotic (or identical) and dizygotic twins. The reason for this is that monozygotic twins share the same DNA, while dizygotic twins only share 50 percent of the genetic material. In a study of Finnish twins,[108] Simo Salminen and colleagues showed that irrespective of where the injury took place (e.g., work, sports, home, traffic), genetic factors played no part in the injury. However, environmental factors did play a role.[††††] The obvious implication of these findings is that injury prevention efforts among young workers need to be targeted at environmental, i.e., workplace, factors.

Several credible, evidence-based reports highlight initiatives that organizations can take to enhance young workers' safety. First, we saw in Chapter 6 how early informal socialization affected workplace attitudes a year later.[109] Given that many young workers are still in high school when they take on their first job, schools, teachers, and families

[††††] Salminen et al. also analyzed monozygotic and dizygotic twins aged thirty-three to sixty years old from the Finnish Twin Cohort database. In this older group, both genetic and environmental factors predicted injury involvement.

could play a critical role in influencing students' attitudes to safety before they even assume their first jobs. Second, a report by the ILO draws attention to the need for improved data on young workers' injuries.[110] This is imperative, given the enormous difficulties in managing any issue in the absence of an accurate understanding of the magnitude and scope of the problem. Given that more than 25 percent of young workers do not report their injuries,[111] the absence of high-quality information becomes even more apparent. Third, a feature of all-too-many workplace injuries and fatalities among young workers is the absence of any safety training, as evidenced by extensive analyses of US data ranging from 1982 to 2010,[112] and a wide-ranging review of prior research.[113] One probable reason is that many workers in this age group are temporary, and organizations are reluctant to devote scarce training resources to employees who are not a part of their future plans. Nonetheless, the best available evidence shows that safety training has a large effect on safety behaviors.[114] Fourth, the ILO report recommends that young people be more empowered to take the kinds of steps that will protect themselves and their coworkers. This is consistent with other research showing the importance of empowerment in reducing adult workers' injury rates.[115] Last, the absence of any supervision has frequently been noted in retrospective examinations of young worker injuries and fatalities,[116] yet transformational leadership focusing on safety is indirectly associated with fewer injuries among young workers.[117]

None of these initiatives (i.e., socialization, training, autonomy, leadership) are new. Enhancing young workers' safety is not an issue of developing novel interventions. Instead, organizations need to ensure that young workers have access to the same initiatives that all employees do, regardless of their age or temporary status in the organization.

Conclusion

In case you are not yet convinced

First, let's assume you are convinced, and want to improve workplace safety in your own organization, where would you start? Sean Tucker and colleagues provide an entirely unsurprising answer—at the top.[118] Based on a massive study involving fifty-four Canadian organizations, 224 members of top management teams, 1,398 supervisors and 2,714 frontline employees, their findings strongly suggest starting with the top management team.[‡‡‡‡] CEOs' words and actions that prioritize safety trickled down through the organization. Further down the line, supervisors who are committed to safety then motivate their employees to work safely.

Second, we saw the effects of workplace fatalities and injuries on family members earlier in this chapter. But family members are not the only secondary victims we need to consider. There are also indications that workplace safety infractions can harm the

‡‡‡‡ As we saw in Chapter 6, the notion that it all starts at the top also applied to whether organizations choose to implement human capital initiatives throughout the organization.

public at large. As one example, 111 workplace fatalities were reported in the United Kingdom in 2019–20, a fatality rate of 0.34, and the country's the lowest annual fatality rate ever.[119] Yet, the same incidents that claimed the lives of 111 workers also took the lives of fifty-one members of the public.

A different group of secondary victims that cries out for greater attention from management are the peers and work friends of employees who were killed or hurt at work. Witnessing a colleague being treated unfairly (see Chapter 5), or as we just saw from journalists and foreign correspondents, even witnessing strangers getting injured or killed has pervasive negative effects on work attitudes, work performance, and well-being. The effects of seeing a colleague or friend being injured or even killed at work remain to be investigated, but the outcomes of such research would not be difficult to predict. As a result, current estimates of the costs of safety injuries and fatalities that do not take secondary victims into account surely underestimate the real costs of workplace injuries and fatalities.

Third, the effects of workplace safety disasters are even more widespread. Earlier, we read about the March 23, 2005, explosion at the Texas City Refinery. The formal investigation laid the blame for this tragedy on a series of management failures. The environmental damage was so extensive that the Texas state government sued BP, seeking $25,000 for each day that six different toxic fumes polluted the atmosphere. Eventually, BP agreed to pay a measly $15,000 fine because of its violations to the federal Clean Air Act.[120] Taken together, we see that the harm caused by workplace safety infractions goes well beyond the organization and affects the public, work peers and colleagues, and potentially the environment, too, all of which deserve much greater attention from regulators, management, employees, and the public.

Finally, given the multitude and range of challenges that management face daily, perhaps we should not be too surprised if they do not prioritize safety. After all, as awful as 360,000 workplace fatalities per year is, the truth is that most organizations will never suffer a workplace fatality. How can we better help managers and organizations to understand the scope of the safety problem in a way that leads to greater action? Perhaps think of just how much change occurred following the tragic loss of life on 9/11, an event that is seared in the memory of so many people. Yet in terms of loss of life, the global number of workplace fatalities is so much worse, equivalent to 120 9/11's happening each year. Three each week. We would certainly draw together to do whatever we could to prevent that from happening. Now is the time for management around the world to take action to ensure that a workplace fatality never occurs on their watch. To end where we started, a reminder from the poem by Alyssa Grocutt could not be more appropriate:

You can't go back in time
You can't undo mistakes
You can't take away an injury
And you definitely can't give back a life.

9
Toward productive, healthy, and safe workplaces

As I write the conclusion to this book in the first half of 2022, we are in a unique time and place. There isn't a country in the world that has not faced extraordinary difficulties and choices over the past two years, and for most countries they have had to do so more than once. Even countries that were so successful in initially keeping COVID-19 off their shores were imposing tough restrictions by early 2022.[1] We have seen an unprecedented scale of devastation in deaths and long-term illness, not to mention massive job losses, family disruption, school closures, and supply chain disruptions. Many people now want to, or maybe need to, believe that the worst of the pandemic is over, but many countries still have difficult days ahead.

Despite the uncertainty, I believe that the time is ripe to move forward. As noted in Chapter 1, history teaches us that our worst societal crises have invariably resulted in major social innovations.[2] The Great Depression in the United States resulted in FDR's New Deal, and World War II saw an influx of women into the workplace.[3] We have already seen evidence of change during the COVID-19 pandemic. At the beginning of March 2020, *zoom* was just an onomatopoeia. By the end of March 2020, Zoom was a platform allowing millions of people around the world to connect with others anywhere in the world. Indeed, while there was a total of 2 billion annualized webinar minutes on the Zoom platform in the second quarter of 2020, that number reached 42 billion a year later.[4] Transformations like this set the stage for meaningful longer-term change, no more evident in the debate about and demand for hybrid work. While we cannot yet know all the ways in which work will change in the long term, I remain optimistic about the path forward for three reasons.

First, there is no doubt that we have to build back from the enormous disruption caused by the pandemic. The scale of the task will be enormous. The question is not whether we are going to build back, but *how* we are going to build back. Are we just going to do what we can to return as close as possible to what was? Or maybe "build back better," which implies a return to the status quo ante but with a few improvements? Or instead, can we rise to the challenge set before us by Sir Michael Marmot and colleagues (2020), and avoid the "tragic mistake to attempt to re-establish the status quo," and strive to "build back fairer" (4)?[5] I believe we have a once-in-a-generation opportunity to shape the type of workplaces we want for ourselves, our children, and our grandchildren.

Brave New Workplace. Julian Barling, Oxford University Press. © Oxford University Press 2023.
DOI: 10.1093/oso/9780190648107.003.0009

Second, one of the most inspiring lessons I have learned working with organizational leaders is that no matter the obstacles they face personally, whether it be overwork, limited resources, or a lack of information and training, they somehow rise to the challenge. The challenges now are surely greater than those faced beforehand. But most leaders I have encountered during the pandemic want to see their workplaces become not only better but also more productive, healthier, and safer as we move into a postpandemic era.

Third, organizations and their leaders now have the means to seize this opportunity. Yes, as cartoonists like Scott Adams and his character Dilbert[6] have been pointing out for decades, there are times when management gets it all wrong, sometimes horribly wrong. But what cannot be ignored is the overwhelming number of times management gets it right, often in the face of seemingly insurmountable obstacles. Add to that the fact that we now know what it takes to proactively build productive, healthy, and safe workplaces: high-quality leadership; a sense of autonomy, belonging, and fairness; opportunities for growth and development; meaningful work; and safe work. The task ahead is not to implement all seven characteristics at once—that would likely overwhelm you, and result in inaction. Instead, driven by many examples in each of the chapters, leaders intent on change should ask themselves, What are the smallest changes I can make to have to the most significant effects in the long term?

Questions for the future

Fully appreciating the old adage that "predictions are hazardous, especially about the future,"[7] I am guided by the words of the late Chinese Premier Zhou Enlai in choosing to steer clear of any specific predictions of what the world of work *will* look like in the future. When asked in 1972 what he thought of the French Revolution, Zhou Enlai is reputed to have remarked, "I don't know, it is too soon to tell."* But I will share some thoughts on one idea about the future of work that has captured public attention, so much so that it is presented as a fait accompli. I am talking, of course, about remote (or hybrid) work, or working from home (WFH). Guided by our understanding of the importance of leadership, autonomy, belonging, fairness, growth and development, and meaningful and safe work, my primary goal is to raise questions that might help organizations decide whether and how they should move toward remote work, rather than offer specific predictions about the likelihood that remote work will occur or not.

* The fact that Zhou Enlai was talking about the turmoil in France in 1968, and not the French Revolution of 1789, does not detract from what he meant. It is unwise to predict what the world will look like after a major crisis while you are still struggling amid the crisis. "Too early to say": Zhou was speaking about 1968, not 1789. (June 14, 2011). *Media Myth Alert*. https://mediamythalert.com/2011/06/14/too-early-to-say-zhou-was-speaking-about-1968-not-1789/

Remote work

Much has been written about remote work throughout the pandemic, creating the perception that remote work is the new normal. But is it? This is an incredibly important issue with very significant implications, calling for data-driven answers. So, what do the data tell us?

Yes, there was a substantial increase in remote working during the pandemic, and data from different countries bear this out. In Canada, for example, only 4 percent of employees aged fifteen to sixty-nine worked most of their hours from home in 2016. By January 2021, at the height of the pandemic, 32 percent did so.[8] Two surveys estimate the rates to be lower in the United States than in Canada, with between 22 and 25 percent of US workers involved in remote work during the pandemic.[9] In the United Kingdom, 25.9 percent of people surveyed in 2020 indicated that they had worked from home, up from 12.4 percent in 2019.[10] These data provide more of a realistic baseline of the prevalence of remote working that media reports might have you believe. Going one step further puts the prevalence of remote working arrangements into an even sharper perspective. As the report of remote work in the United Kingdom notes, the 25.9 percent they identified did not necessarily work remotely all the time but had worked from home "at some point before they responded to" the survey.

What might be the situation in the future? Mehdi and Morisette used their data to estimate worker *preferences* for remote working after the pandemic. Instead of focusing on the *number* of people who say they would want to do so, they estimated the total number of *hours* people would prefer to work from home, information that is more nuanced and would be much more useful for organizational planning. On average, Canadian employees aged fifteen to sixty-nine would prefer to spend 24 percent of their working hours at home. As with so many averages, however, the range tells a more interesting story. Employees with a high school diploma or less, would prefer to spend 9 percent of their working hours at home. Yet those with at least an undergraduate degree would prefer to work from home for 44 percent of their total hours. Therefore, we need to be cautious about our future predictions for several reasons.

First, the number of people who actually get to work from home may be much less than either idealists or the prophets of doom about the future of work would have us believe. Second, and more troubling, if these preferences turned into actual remote-work patterns, access to remote work will become a new status symbol at work. Employees with advanced education, specialized skills, and more lucrative compensation would again have the privilege of working from the safety of their own homes, with the accompanying time and financial savings from less commuting. In contrast, employees with less education, fewer skills, and less compensation, would be forced to work in their traditional workplaces where the chances for viral spread during a pandemic is greater, and spend more time and money on commuting. Taken together, what we would see are workplaces with yet one more status division between employees, when organizations could be focused on rising to Marmot's challenge to build back fairer. This is critical given our understanding of the extensive negative consequences when fairness goes awry.

Irrespective of the number of people who do actually end up working from home in the future, substantial questions will need to be answered by organizations, if this model is to be implemented successfully. Clearly, the best time to ask these questions is before any implementation decisions are made. To understand the scope of the challenges and changes that may well emerge, will the term *workplace* even be appropriate if increasing numbers of people work remotely. We have raised questions throughout the book, such as what high-quality leadership entails when leaders and followers no longer work in the same place at the same time, or how multiplex working relationships are developed and maintained when people no longer physically work together. Many more questions will emerge. What happens to the many benefits from the sense of autonomy when large scale corporations *tell* staff that they have to work from home for at least a part of the week, or introduce electronic monitoring of remote employees? What does informal socialization of newcomers look like in an environment of remote work? In addition, how will organizations support remote employees who simultaneously care for children (or elderly parents or relatives)? After all, the R/GA survey of employees in the middle of the pandemic showed that balancing work and family was the most difficult issue for employees with children, so much so that, as one employee reminded us, "for a stressed-out parent, W.F.H can quickly turn into *W.T.F.!*"[11] With regard to safety, management in many jurisdictions is required to inspect the workplace on a monthly or annual basis for safety reasons—in a remote-work model, does management have the right to enter employees' homes for routine safety inspections? Relatedly, we saw in Chapter 8 that randomly selected government safety inspections reduce workplace injuries—does the government have the right to enter employees' homes for random safety inspections? Who pays for the IT equipment and furniture people use at home—does this mean that organizations will double their equipment budgets for remote workers? How will supporting two workplaces factor into productivity analyses? At a very different level, even challenges to taxation systems will emerge. Remote work means you can live in one country but work in a different one. Where do you pay your taxes? At this stage, you will almost certainly be taxed in the jurisdiction in which you work. Is this fair, when you receive all your public goods in a different jurisdiction? These are just some of the questions and issues that will emerge, and they provide some indication of the questions that organizations will need to confront if they are to successfully embrace remote work.

Societal pressures shaping the workplace of the future

Ask many employees, and they will tell you that organizational leaders and managers have considerable control over the nature of the workplace. In that sense, employees see high-quality leadership, autonomy, belonging, fairness, growth and development, meaningful work, and safe work as "simple," explicit choices made by management. Doing so, however, would dismiss the role of external forces. After all, in their "open systems" perspective, Daniel Katz and Robert had argued as early as 1966 that organizations functioned within, and were influenced by, the larger social context.[12] We saw this earlier in Mike Frone's research (Chapter 4), which showed a decline in organizational commitment in US workers after the Great Recession in 2008.[13] As organizations move forward, social forces beyond their control will continue to shape the decisions management make about the nature of the workplace. While countries all over the world were absorbed by the COVID-19 pandemic, social movements focused on equality, exemplified by Black Lives Matter (BLM), and environmental justice, increased in strength. As we move into the future, inequality and environmental justice will also impact the nature and direction of changes organizations make.

Gender

Throughout the book, we have seen all-too-many illustrations of discrimination against women in organizations. Notable examples include the number of women who hold executive positions in organizations, their treatment once they do attain leadership positions (Chapter 2), the disproportionate penalty women face for enacting interpersonal unfairness (Chapter 5), or the fact they are less likely to receive accurate or useful feedback (Chapter 6). Add to this the fact that investors generally respond negatively to the appointment of female CEOs, even though they are no less successful than male CEOs.[14] Beyond being unacceptable, this pattern of discrimination is also a paradox with deep implications for organizations. After decades of research across many different countries, we now know that women as a group are somewhat more likely than men as a group,[†] to enact transformational and participative leadership[15]—the very leadership behaviors that are linked with more positive outcomes. In addition, women leaders also receive more favorable 360-degree feedback ratings.[16] Perhaps most notably, elected female leaders across the world,[17] and governors in the United States,[18] were more effective reducing the impact of COVID-19 in their jurisdictions during the first wave of the pandemic.

There are so many prescriptions for change, from "leaning in" to legislation. So what initiatives are we likely to see in the future? I believe that in the developed world, we are most likely to see companies opt for initiatives that revolve around the notion of voluntary compliance, given a strong negative reaction to the notion of what is often portrayed as government "interference." One example of this compliance approach is "30 percent clubs," which exist in numerous countries,[19] with their goal being to pressure organizations to ensure that 30 percent of all board members are

† There would of course be many exceptions in both groups.

women. Yet there are other more forceful models. As one example, many countries (e.g., Norway, Finland, Iceland, Spain, France, Italy, and the Netherlands) have legislation mandating female representation on governance boards.[20] The mandated targets differ across countries, as do the rewards or penalties for achieving or missing the target, though the outcomes are similar—remarkably higher levels of female representation on governance boards.[21] Other options include countries requiring that privately held organizations publicly disclose the gender composition of their boards, or that they have specific, public targets for greater gender diversity (e.g., Australia, Germany). Irrespective of the particular program, the effect remains the same: countries that introduced legislation mandating targets across a five-year period were effective in getting companies to reach them.[22] This is important, as having more gender diversity on the board is associated with having more female leaders at all levels of the organization.[23] Regardless, if changes continue to be made at the same slow pace, the decision on what strategies to use to improve gender diversity may be taken out of managements' hands, and given to governments, shareholder pressure, and/or external social movements.

Prejudice against women in organizations goes beyond the issue of access to leadership positions. In a fascinating but disturbing analysis, Alicia Grandey and her team documented how the natural experience of what they refer to as the three "M's," namely menstruation, maternity, and menopause, remain taboo topics in most organizations because their discussion would create discomfort for male organizational leaders.[24] But these are issues that most women deal with when they are work, and failure to be able to do so successfully could subtly limit women's work and career advancement.

Discrimination against women is likely just the tip of the iceberg. While this form of discrimination has been widely studied within organizations, there is substantially less understanding on workplace discrimination against people within the LGBTQ community. One perspective is from the top of organizations. We do know that among the Fortune 500 companies, Tim Cook, Jim Fitterling, and Beth Ford, CEOs of Apple, Dow Chemical, and Land O'Lakes respectively, openly identify as gay. The courage of doing so should not be underestimated. In his book *The glass closet: Why coming out is good for business*, former BP CEO John Brown tells how contrary to what he once believed, the decision to come out as gay became increasingly more difficult as he rose up the organizational hierarchy.[25]

Some research explains why coming out is so difficult. In interviews with thirty-six LGBTQ employees in the United States, Sara Baker and Kristen Lucas identified four specific threats to workplace dignity associated with coming out.[26] The major threat was to their careers, which could include denial of opportunities to engage in regular organizational activities, through to fear of, and actual, dismissal from the organization. Almost all respondents also experienced threats to social dignity, inflicted, for example, through slurs, name-calling, ostracism, and off-color jokes by others. Participants also pointed to autonomy violations, which occurred when others in the organization challenged their right to privacy and in turn their personal identity.

Last, participants in the study reported fears of physical harm. One gay police officer reported how "people were afraid to ride with me. People didn't respond and back up.... Or if I was calling out information with the radio ... people would cut into the radio transmission so all of my call would not be brought through" (140).

Research with transsexual employees illustrates the benefits of supportive organizational climates, not just for LGBTQ employees but for their organizations as well. A survey of 114 trans employees in the United States showed that the more supportive the organizations, the more likely employees were to disclose as transmen or transwomen.[27] Separate research showed that this was true for gay men and lesbians as well.[28] Disclosing their transsexual identity was positively associated with higher levels of organizational commitment and job satisfaction, and with lower levels of job anxiety. Taking together, these results highlight important practical implications for organizations. In the extent to which organizations seek to recruit, hire, and retain LGBTQ employees, an appropriate place to start would be to ensure that policies and practices already in place support LGBTQ applicants and employees.

Black Lives Matter!

As profound as it was, the COVID-19 pandemic was not the only major challenge confronting the status quo in so many countries in 2020. Protests inspired by the Black Lives Matter (BLM) movement erupted across the United States after the murder of George Floyd in May 2020. BLM also organized significant protests against racial discrimination in many other countries. Katz and Kahn's "open systems" framework explains why racial discrimination in society makes its way into organizations. Indeed, we even have racial discrimination at the very top of organizations with the miniscule number of Black, indigenous, and other people of color (BIPOC) who are CEOs of US Fortune 500 companies. In 2019, there were seven BIPOC CEOs, with that number going down to three (0.6 percent) in 2020. The highest number in any year since 2007, when there was one, was in 2015, when there were ten BIPOC CEOs—which is 2 percent of the total sample of Fortune 500 CEOs. Yet census data show that in 2020, 22 percent of the US workforce were Black, indigenous, and other people of color.[29]

Research shows how this racial discrimination plays out more subtly. For example, in three different studies, Elizabeth Deitch and her team documented how Black employees in the United States experience everyday mistreatment and discrimination. This discrimination included not receiving assignments needed for promotion, having their work performance evaluated unfairly, and not receiving the information needed to do the job properly.[30] Lincoln Quillian and Arnfinn Midtbøem reached seventeen conclusions about discriminatory hiring practices based on ninety-seven studies.[31] The most important of the conclusions from our perspective, is that discrimination against non-White job applicants was present in every country in Europe, Australia, and North America, with members of White groups receiving 20 percent to 80 percent more callbacks after submitting job applications. In addition, members of White minority ethnic groups are on the receiving end of less discrimination than non-White groups in the same country. Perhaps Quillian and Midtbøem's most discouraging conclusion is that there has been no decrease in racial discrimination in hiring in the United States or the United Kingdom over the last twenty-five years. The effects of racial discrimination within organizations have very real consequences. A large body of research points to the negative effects of racial discrimination on workplace attitudes, citizenship behaviors, and both physical and psychological well-being—all of which harm any progress toward productive, healthy, and safe work.[32]

Religion

Religious discrimination in society also spills over into the workplace. As one example, Aasim Padela and colleagues conducted a survey of Muslim physicians in the United States, most of whom were deeply religious: 89 percent considered religion a central part of their life, and 63 percent prayed five times a day.[33] A quarter of the sample had experienced religious discrimination at some point in their careers, with 14 percent currently experiencing religious discrimination. Moreover, the odds of suffering religious discrimination at work were more than three times greater for survey respondents who strongly identified with their religion. Last, 8.9 percent even reported that patients had refused treatment from them because of their religious identity.

Complicating matters is the fact that gender, race, and religion do not act in isolation, and research points to the existence of a "double jeopardy" effect. As examples, while women experience more workplace harassment at work than men, and members of minority groups experience more harassment than White employees, women members of minority groups experience more harassment than White or minority men, or White women.[34] Similarly, gender and religion can also create double jeopardy. Sonia Ghumman and Anne Marie Ryan conducted an ingenious study on discrimination against religious women wearing a hijab that covered their hair, ears, neck, and chest.[35] Women volunteers entered local retail stores and restaurants near shopping malls in the US Midwest. In some situations, the volunteers wore the full hijab, in others not. In all other respects, they were dressed identically. Formal discrimination existed, inasmuch as women wearing hijabs received fewer requests to complete job applications and fewer calls back. But there was also evidence of informal discrimination, as women wearing hijabs perceived a greater level of negativity and lower level of interest.

Indigeneity

As we have seen so far, sex, race, and religion are markers for workplace discrimination that hurt both organizations and their employees. Indigenous people, who make up 5 percent of the world's population,[36] are not immune from workplace discrimination. One survey of Indigenous peoples living in Canada estimates that about half the people sampled felt the need to be on guard against discrimination when at work, with this number much higher for Indigenous women.[37] A series of qualitative interviews by Mark Julien and his colleagues with fifteen Indigenous leaders in Canada shows how much organizations and their members lose by marginalizing Indigenous peoples at work.[38] Eleven of the Aboriginal leaders they interviewed worked in conventional Canadian organizations, with the remaining four employed in Aboriginal organizations. Consistent with the holistic nature of Aboriginal culture, leadership was viewed not as a role, title, or opportunity to advance the needs of the leader, but as a calling to enhance the good of the community. As one leader said, "We may be out at the pointy end of the spear, but the big weight of the spear, the broad part of the spear, is behind us and that's the people" (121). In a similar vein, another leader reminds us that "your ego will defeat whatever your vision is about" (121). Leadership among these Aboriginal leaders was centered in spirituality. As a result, leaders were focused on the long-term future, from a position of being deeply rooted in the wisdom handed down through stories and symbols over generations. As one leader commented, "Let's make sure we have the wisdom of all those elders that passed before us ... we make our decisions on how this choice will impact children seven generations from now ... and if a decision isn't a good thing five hundred years from now, then it's not a good decision" (120). In addition, leadership was viewed as embedded in an egalitarian and nonhierarchical system, and in the unity of the physical, mental, spiritual, and emotional spheres, which are reflected in importance of the circle in Aboriginal culture. As a result, seeking input from others is an integral part of leadership. One respondent reflected that "you have to respect where everybody is coming from and respect everybody's contribution in an equal way ... leading in such a way that people were able to move themselves forward" (121).

Taken together, these findings point to the possible costs of workplace discrimination against Aboriginal employees and leaders. What organizations might be missing out on is an approach that epitomizes high-quality leadership and would be ideally suited to enhancing belonging, autonomy, fairness, growth and development, meaningful work, and safe work.

Climate crisis

The focus on the future by Aboriginal leaders, and the world we will hand down to our children, may be especially relevant right now. The effects of the climate crisis were thrust into public attention yet again by an extensive heat wave that covered large parts of the US Pacific northwest and south-western Canada in summer, 2021, breaking all-time heat records in Oregon,[39] British Columbia, Alberta, the Yukon, and Northwest Territories.[40] Estimates of the number of people who died in Canada from this one episode vary, but probably exceed seven hundred. A disproportionate share of those who died were elderly, but employees and organizations are not immune from the effects of excessive heat events. In an ingenious study, Jisung Park and colleagues combined data from several sources. They used workplace injuries from California's workers' compensation system, as well as the postal code and date of each injury indicating where and when the injury occurred, which enabled them to get the maximum temperature recorded in the specific location of the day of the injury.[41] When temperatures ranged between 85 and 90°F (29.4–32.2°C), workplace injuries increased between 5 and 7 percent. When temperatures exceeded 100°F (37.8°C), the risk of workplace injuries increased by 10–15 percent.[‡] The scope of this problem is evident from data showing that currently US crop workers face excessive heat conditions on twenty-one days per year.[42]

Two additional findings from Park's research warrant attention. First, the additional injury risk was not borne equally across the workforce, with workers in the bottom 20 percent of all earners suffering five times as many injuries as their counterparts in the top 20 percent of all earners. Second, many of these injuries are preventable: the effects of excessive heat on injuries decreased by one-third after California implemented regulations requiring employers to protect workers by mandating water, shade, and rest during periods of excessive heat,[§] demonstrating again that small changes in working conditions can have very significant effects.

Excessive heat is not the only major symptom of the climate emergency. During the same summer that part of the United States and Canada were struggling with heat in 2021, flash floods devastated whole towns in Belgium, China, Germany, and India, parts of the New York City subway were flooded, and wildfires were ranging in Siberia.[43] Later that year, tornadoes ripping through warehouses in the US Midwest killed workers, demonstrating how external events will shape organizations' efforts as they move toward productive, healthy, and safe work.[44]

Organizations are entangled in global change, being both affected by and a major contributor to the climate crisis. Leaders can play a significant role in helping their organizations to be more environmentally conscious. Research I conducted with my colleague, Jennifer Robertson, documented that when leaders' own behaviors emphasize environmental issues, employees' passion for both the environment and environmentally sustainable behaviors increase.[45] A holistic, Aboriginal understanding of the responsibilities that leaders have to future generations and the earth would likely ensure that organizations head in a socially responsible direction.

Organizations need to be proactive. Failure to be proactive right now will likely have devastating consequences not only for the environment but for organizations as well. A majority of people in most countries surveyed by the Pew organization in 2019 agreed that the climate crisis is a major threat to their country, in fact the most significant threat to the country in half the countries surveyed.[46] The Pew survey also

[‡] As a reference point, the temperature in Multnomah County in Portland, Oregon, reached 116°F (46.6°C) during the recent heatwave in July 2021.

[§] Greater than 95°F (35°C).

reported that anxiety about the climate crisis has increased since 2013, and may well have increased even more since the extreme heat, fires, floods, and tornadoes in North America and Europe in the summer of 2021.[47] The days when CEOs had the luxury of debating whether environmental sustainability was good for business are long gone. This is reinforced by Michelle Lee and colleagues' recent research involving all CEOs from Standard and Poor's 1,500 US companies during the twelve-year period spanning 2006–2016.[48] CSR-based shareholder unrest, as indicated by resolutions focused on social interests such as environmental issues and human rights, predicted subsequent decreases in CEO pay and a greater likelihood of the CEO being fired. Importantly, wealth-oriented shareholder unrest had no effects on CEO pay or the likelihood of being fired.

Moving forward, employees will be watching to see what their organizations do in response to social inequalities and environmental injustice in their workplaces. They will respond favorably when they see their management acting proactively and prosocially as they move toward productive, healthy, and safe work, not because management they have to but because they want to. Failure to act now will likely result in problems hiring and retaining the best available talent. Failure to act now will almost certainly also result in additional regulations imposed by shareholders and legislators—often managements' worst nightmare.

A concluding challenge

Legendary investor Warren Buffett is credited with the observation that "only when the tide goes out do you discover who's been swimming naked." Well, the tide went out at the start of the pandemic, and we learned that our organizations have been swimming naked for some time. The COVID-19 pandemic exposed just how extensively inequality, unfairness, and a lack of opportunities for growth and development, and for safety, pervade our organizations and our work. The challenge before us is not whether we simply dream of "a return to normal" at work, which really was a less-than-perfect "normal."

Instead, the opportunities before us are immense. Successful organizations in the future will be those which choose to "build back fairer," and develop productive, healthy, and safe workplaces for all their members. We now know what those organizations will look like—employees will enjoy high-quality leadership, a sense of autonomy, belonging, and fairness, opportunities for growth and development, meaningful work, and safe work. This will be true for all employees, not just for privileged members of high-status groups. Employees in those organizations will be proud to tell others that they are members of the organization. In an era when the search for talent has become more competitive,[49] these are the organizations that will be able to attract and recruit the most talented people from a larger and more qualified pool of diverse individuals, and then retain those employees who help the organization thrive.

Notes

Chapter 1

1. Huxley, A. (1932). *Brave new world.* NY: HarperPerennial.
2. Jackson, T. (n.d.). About leadership. Accessed September 10, 2022. https://aboutleaders.com/leadership-the-discipline-of-doing/
3. Kessler, S. (July 3, 2017). We've been worrying about the end of work for 500 years. *Quartz.* https://qz.com/1019145/weve-been-worrying-about-the-end-of-work-for-500-years/
4. Zakaria, F. (2020). *Ten lessons for a post-pandemic world.* NY: Norton.
5. Goleman, D. (2006). *Working with emotional intelligence.* NY: Bantam Books.
6. Dweck, C. (2016). *Mindset: The new psychology of success.* NY: Ballantine Books.
7. Sandberg, S. (2013). *Lean in: Women, work, and the will to lead.* NY. Alfred A. Knopf.
8. Chapman-Clarke, M. (2016). *Mindfulness in the workplace: An evidence-based approach to improving wellbeing and maximizing performance.* PA: Kogan Page.
9. McEwen, K. (2011). *Building resilience at work.* Australia: Australian Academic Press.
10. Oher, J.M. (1999). *Employee assistance handbook.* NY: Wiley.
11. Marmot, M. (2015). *The health gap: The challenge of an unequal world.* NY: Bloomsbury.
12. Hsu, T., & Hirsch, L. (September 6, 2021). We'll give you a week off. Please don't quit. *New York Times.* https://www.nytimes.com/2021/09/06/business/media/burn-out-companies-pandemic.html
13. Grabo, A., Spisak, B.R., & van Vugt, M. (2017). Charisma as signal: An evolutionary perspective on charismatic leadership. *Leadership Quarterly, 28,* 473–485.
14. Wall, T.D. et al. (1990). Advanced manufacturing technology, work design, and performance: A change study. *Journal of Applied Psychology, 75,* 691–697.
15. Tannenbaum, S.I. et al. (1991). Meeting trainees' expectations: The influence of training fulfillment on the development of commitment, self-efficacy, and motivation. *Journal of Applied Psychology, 76,* 759–769.
16. Kaminski, M. (2001). Unintended consequences: Organizational practices and their impact on workplace safety and productivity. *Journal of Occupational Health Psychology, 6,* 127–138.
17. Pfeffer, J., & Sutton, R.I. (January 2006). Evidence-based management. *Harvard Business Review, 87*(1), 62–73.
18. Sackett, D.L., Rosenberg, W.M.C., Gray, J.A.M., Haynes, R.B., & Richardson, W.C. (1996). Evidence based medicine: What it is and what it isn't. *British Medical Journal, 312,* 71–72.
19. Sherman, L.W. (July 1988). Ideas in American policing. https://www.policefoundation.org/wp-content/uploads/2015/06/Sherman-1998-Evidence-Based-Policing.pdf
20. Davies, P. (1999). What is evidence-based education? *British Journal of Educational Studies, 47*(2), 108–121.
21. Craig, A.M. et al. (2010). Evidence-based optimization of urban firefighter first response to emergency medical services 9-1-1 incidents. *Prehospital Emergency Care, 14,* 109–117.

22. Rousseau, D.M. (2006). Is there such a thing as "evidence-based management"? *Academy of Management Journal, 31*, 256–269.
23. Pfeffer, J., & Sutton, R.I. (2006). *Hard facts, dangerous half-truths and total nonsense: Profiting from evidence-based management*. MA: Harvard Business School Press.; Pfeffer, J., & Sutton, R.I. (January 2006). Evidence-based management.
24. Pfeffer, J., & Sutton, R.I. (2006). Evidence-based management.
25. Grant, A. (September 13, 2018). Goodbye to the MBTI, the fad that won't die. *Psychology Today*. https://www.psychologytoday.com/ca/blog/give-and-take/201309/goodbye-mbti-the-fad-won-t-die
26. Rudolph, C.W., Rauvola, N.S., Costanza, D.P., & Zacher, H. (2021). Generations and generational differences: Debunking myths in organizational science and practice and paving new paths forward. *Journal of Business and Psychology, 34*, 945–967.
27. Pfeffer, J. (May–June 1998). Six dangerous myths about pay. *Harvard Business Review*, 109–119.
28. Lawler, E.E. III (1996). *From the ground up: Six principles for building the new logic corporation*. CA: Jossey-Bass.
29. Christie, A., & Barling, J. (2011). A short history of occupational health psychology: A biographical approach. In A.S. Antoniou & C. Cooper (Eds.), *New directions in organizational psychology and behavioral medicine* (pp. 7–24). UK: Gower Publishing.
30. Jahoda, M. (1982). *Employment and unemployment: A social psychological analysis*. Cambridge: Cambridge University Press.
31. Jahoda, M. (1988). Economic recession and mental health: Some conceptual issues. *Journal of Social Issues, 44*, 13–24.
32. Nojahoda: Jahoda Witness. Tower Records. Accessed September 10, 2022. https://towerrecords.com/products/nojahoda-jahoda-witness
33. Maslow, A.H. (1943). A theory of human motivation. *Psychological Review, 50*, 370–396.
34. Maslow, A.H. (1965). *Eupsychian management: A journal*. IL: Irwin-Dorsey.
35. Petzinger, T. (April 25, 1997). Leadership guru's work takes thirty years to come to flower. *Wall Street Journal*. https://www.wsj.com/articles/SB861916799663888000
36. Bridgman, T. et al. (2019). Who built Maslow's pyramid? A history of the creation of management studies' most famous symbol and its implications for management education. *Academy of Management Learning and Educations, 18*, 81–98.
37. Business hotel in Sandton. Accessed September 10, 2022. https://www.suninternational.com/maslow/
38. Trist, E.L., & Bamforth, K.W. (1951). Some social and psychological consequences of the Longwall method of coal-getting. *Human Relations, 14*, 3–38.
39. Herzberg, F. (January–February 1968). One more time: How do you motivate employees? *Harvard Business Review, 46*(1), 53–62.
40. Hackman, J.R., & Oldham, G.R. (1976). Motivation through the design of work: Test of a theory. *Organizational Behavior and Human Performance, 16*, 250–279.
41. Karasek, R., & Theorell, T. (1990). *Healthy work: Stress, productivity and the reconstruction of work life*. NY: Basic Books.
42. Marmot, M. (2004). *The status syndrome: How social standing affects our health and longevity*. UK: Bloomsbury.

43. Kaprio, J. et al. (1996). Total and occupationally active life expectancies in relation to social class and marital status in men classified as healthy at 20 in Finland. *Journal of Epidemiology and Community Health, 50*, 653–660.
44. Warr, P.B. (1987). *Work, unemployment and mental health*. NY: Oxford University Press.

Chapter 2

1. Judge, T.A., & Bono, J.E. (2000). Five factor model of personality and transformational leadership. *Journal of Applied Psychology, 85*, 751–756.
2. Barling, J. (2014). *The science of leadership: Lessons from research for organizational leaders*. NY: Oxford University Press.
3. Burns, J.M. (1978). *Leadership*. NY: Harper Collins.
4. Bass, B.M. (1985). *Leadership and performance beyond expectations*. NY: Free Press.
5. Judge, T.A., & Kammeyer-Mueller, J.D. (2012). Job attitudes. *Annual Review of Psychology, 63*, 341–367.
6. Yucel, I. et al. (2014). Does CEO transformational leadership influence top executive normative commitment? *Journal of Business Research, 67*, 1170–1177.
7. Barling, J. et al. (1996). Effects of transformational leadership training on attitudinal and financial outcomes: A field experiment. *Journal of Applied Psychology, 81*, 827–832.
8. Eisenberger, R. et al. (2010). Leader-member exchange and affective organizational commitment: The contribution of supervisor's organizational embodiment. *Journal of Applied Psychology, 95*, 1085–1103.
9. Lambert, L.S. et al. (2012). Forgotten but not gone: An examination of fit between leader consideration and initiating structure needed and received. *Journal of Applied Psychology, 97*, 913–930.
10. Djibo, I.J.A. et al. (2010). Examining the role of perceived leader behaviour on temporary employees' organizational commitment and citizenship behaviour. *Human Resource Development Quarterly, 21*, 321–342.
11. Lin, H-C. et al. (2016). CEO transformational leadership and firm performance: A moderated mediation model of TMT trust climate and environmental dynamism. *Asia Pacific Journal of Management, 33*, 981–1008.
12. Kelloway, E.K. et al. (2012). Transformational leadership and employee psychological well-being: The mediating role of employee trust in leadership. *Work and Stress, 26*, 39–55.
13. Covey, S. (2018). *The speed of trust: The one thing that changes everything*. NY: Free Press.
14. Antonakis, J. et al. (2022). "Just words? Just speeches"? On the economic value of charismatic leadership. *Management Science*. https://doi.org/10.1287/mnsc.2021.4219
15. Resick, C.J. (2009). The bright-side and the dark-side of CEO personality: Examining core self-evaluations, narcissism, transformational leadership, and strategic influence. *Journal of Applied Psychology, 94*, 1365–1381.
16. Jensen, M. et al. (2020). A mixed-methods study of CEO transformational leadership and firm performance. *European Management Journal, 38*, 836–845.
17. Waldman, D.A. et al. (2006). Components of CEO transformational leadership and corporate social responsibility. *Journal of Management Studies, 43*, 1703–1725.
18. Merberg, B. (n.d.). Wellbeing—what is it good for? Accessed September 11, 2022. https://www.jozito.com/wellbeing-what-is-it-good-for/

19. Arnold, K.A. et al. (2007). Transformational leadership and psychological well-being: The mediating role of meaningful work. *Journal of Occupational Health Psychology, 12*, 193–203.
20. Kelloway, E.K. et al. (2012). Transformational leadership.
21. Nielsen, K., & Munir, F. (2009). How do transformational leaders influence followers' affective well-being? Exploring the mediating role of self-efficacy. *Work and Stress, 23*, 313–329.
22. Nielsen, K. et al. (2008). The effects of transformational leadership on followers' perceived work characteristics and psychological well-being: A longitudinal study. *Work and Stress, 22*, 16–32.
23. Parr, A.D. (2013). Questioning universal applicability of transformational leadership: Examining employees with autism spectrum disorder. *Leadership Quarterly, 24*, 608–622.
24. Barling, J., & Cloutier, A. (2017). Leaders' mental health at work: Empirical, methodological and policy directions. *Journal of Occupational Health Psychology, 22*, 394–406
25. Lanaj, K. et al. (2016). Benefits of transformational leadership for followers: A daily investigation of leader behaviors and need fulfillment. *Journal of Applied Psychology, 101*, 237–251.
26. Johnson, R.E. et al. (2014). The good and bad of being fair: Effects of procedural and interpersonal justice behaviors on regulatory resources. *Journal of Applied Psychology, 99*, 635–650.
27. Graen, G.B., & Uhl-Bien, M. (1995). Relationship-based approach to leadership: Development ofleader-member exchange theory ofleadership over 25 years: Applying a multilevel multi-domain perspective. *Leadership Quarterly, 6*, 219–247.
28. Lin, J. et al. (2019). The dark side of transformational leader behaviors for leaders themselves: A conservation of resources perspective. *Academy of Management Journal, 62*, 1556–1582.
29. Tepper, B. (2000). Consequences of abusive supervision. *Academy of Management Journal, 43*, 178–190; and Tepper, B.J. (2007). Abusive supervision in work organizations: Review, synthesis, and research agenda. *Journal of Management, 33*, 261–289.
30. Blake, R.R., & Mouton, J.S. (1964). *The managerial grid*. Houston, TX: Gulf Publishing Company.
31. Bass, B.M. (1985). *Leadership and performance*.
32. Mackay, J.D. et al. (2017). Abusive supervision: A meta-analysis and empirical review. *Journal of Management, 43*, 1940–1965.
33. Yu, K. et al. (2016). The role of affective commitment and future work self salience in the abusive supervision–job performance relationship. *Journal of Occupational and Organizational Psychology, 89*, 28–45.
34. Lyu, Y. et al. (2016). Abusive supervision and customer-oriented organizational citizenship behavior: The roles of hostile attribution bias and work engagement. *International Journal of Hospitality Management, 53*, 69–80.
35. Wu, T-Y. et al. (2019). Role ambiguity and economic hardship as the moderators of the relation between abusive supervision and job burnout: An application of uncertainty management theory. *Journal of General Psychology, 146*, 365–390.

36. Hinkin, T.R., & Schriesheim, C.A. (2008). An examination of "nonleadership": From laissez-faire leadership to leader reward omission and punishment omission. *Journal of Applied Psychology, 93*, 1234–1248.
37. Judge, T.A., & Piccolo, R.F. (2004). Transformational and transactional leadership: A meta-analytic test of their relative validity. *Journal of Applied Psychology, 89*, 755–768.
38. Jackson, T.A. et al. (2013). Leadership, commitment and culture: A meta-analysis. *Journal of Organizational and Leadership Studies, 20*, 84–106.
39. Buch, R. et al. (2015). The destructiveness of laissez-faire leadership behavior: The mediating role of economic leader-member exchange relationships. *Journal of Leadership and Organizational Studies, 22*, 115–124.
40. Barling, J., & Frone, M.R. (2017). If only my leader would just do *something*! Passive leadership undermines employee well-being through role stressors and psychological resource depletion. *Stress and Health, 33*, 211–222.
41. Sutton, R.I. (2010). *Good boss, bad boss: How to be the best ... and learn from the worst.* NY: Business Plus.
42. Zhang, Y., & Liao, Z. (2015). Consequences of abusive supervision: A meta-analytic review. *Asia Pacific Journal of Management, 32*, 959–987.
43. Mitchell, M.S., & Ambrose, M.L. (2007). Abusive supervision and workplace deviance and the moderating effects of negative reciprocity beliefs. *Journal of Applied Psychology, 92*, 1159–1168.
44. Flood, P.C. et al (2000). Chief executive leadership style, consensus decision making, and top management team effectiveness. *European Journal of Work and Organizational Psychology, 9*, 401–420.
45. Hetland, H. et al. (2011). Leadership and learning climate in a work setting. *European Psychologist, 16*(3), 163–173.
46. Kelloway, E.K. et al. (2006). Divergent effects of transformational and passive leadership on employee safety. *Journal of Occupational Health Psychology, 11*, 76–86.
47. Skogstad, A. et al. (2007). The destructiveness of laissez-faire leadership behavior. *Journal of Occupational Health* Psychology, *12*, 80–92.
48. McTernan, W.P. et al. (2013). Depression in the workplace: An economic cost analysis of depression-related productivity loss attributable to job strain and bullying. *Work and Stress, 27*, 321–338.
49. Fosse, T.Z.F. (2019). Active and passive forms of destructive leadership in a military context: A systematic review and meta-analysis. *European Journal of Work and Organizational Psychology, 28*, 708–722.
50. Zhang, Y., & Liao, Z. (2015). Consequences of abusive supervision.
51. Allen, D.G. et al. (2016). When "embedded" means "stuck": Moderating effects of job embeddedness in adverse work environments. *Journal of Applied Psychology, 101*, 1670–1686.
52. Deng, H. et al. (2021). My fault or yours? Leaders' dual reactions to abusive supervision via rumination depend on their independent self-construal. *Personnel Psychology, 74*, 773–798.
53. Querstret, D., & Cropley, M. (2012). Exploring the relationship between work-related rumination, sleep quality, and work-related fatigue. *Journal of Occupational Health Psychology, 17*, 341–353.

54. Turgeman-Lupo, K., & Biron, M. (2017). Make it to work (and back home) safely: The effect of psychological work stressors on employee behavior while commuting by car. *Work & Stress, 26*, 161–170.
55. Caplan, R.D., & Jones, K.W. (1975). Effects of work load, role ambiguity, and Type A personality on anxiety, depression and heart rate. *Journal of Applied Psychology, 60*, 713–719.
56. Schmidt, S. et al. (2014). Uncertainty in the workplace: Examining role ambiguity and role conflict, and their link to depression—a meta-analysis. *European Journal of Work and Organizational Psychology, 23*, 91–106.
57. Barling, J., & Frone, M.R. (2017). If only my leader.
58. Barling, J. (2014). *Science of leadership*.
59. Strauss, K. et al. (2009). Proactivity directed toward the team and organization: The role of leadership, commitment and role-breadth self-efficacy. *British Journal of Management, 20*, 279–291.
60. Walumbwa, F.O., Cropanzano, R., & Goldman, B.M. (2011). How leader-member exchange influences effective work behaviors: Social exchange and internal-external efficacy perspectives. *Personnel Psychology, 64*, 739–770.
61. Ahearne, M. et al. (2005). To empower or not empower your sales force? An empirical examination of the influence of leadership empowerment behavior on customer satisfaction and performance. *Journal of Applied Psychology, 90*, 945–955.
62. Walumbwa, F.O. et al. (2011). Linking ethical leadership to employee performance: The roles of leader-member exchange, self-efficacy, and organizational identification. *Organizational Behavior and Human Decision Processes, 115*, 204–213.
63. Griffin, M.A. et al. (2010). Leader vision and the development of adaptive and proactive performance: A longitudinal study. *Journal of Applied Psychology*, 95, 174–182.
64. Salanova, M. et al. (2011). Linking transformational leadership to nurses' extra-role performance: The mediating role of self-efficacy and work engagement. *Journal of Advanced Nursing, 67*, 2256–2266.
65. Mayer, R.C. et al. (1995). An integrative model of organizational trust. *Academy of Management Review, 20*, 709–734.
66. Srivastava, A. et al. (2006). Empowering leadership in management teams: Effects of knowledge sharing, efficacy, and performance. *Academy of Management Journal, 49*, 1239–1251.
67. Kelloway, E.K., & Barling, J. (2000). Knowledge work as organizational behavior. *International Journal of Management Reviews*, 2, 287–304.
68. Chen, Z-x., & Wang, H-y. (2017). Abusive supervision and employees' job performance: A multiple mediation model. *Social Behavior and Personality: An International Journal, 45*, 845–858.
69. Wang, P., & Walumbwa, F.O. (2007). Family-friendly programs, organizational commitment, and work withdrawal: The moderating role of transformational leadership. *Personnel Psychology, 60*, 397–427.
70. Jansen, J.J.P. et al. (2008). Senior team attributes and organizational ambidexterity: The moderating role of transformational leadership. *Journal of Management Studies, 45*, 982–1007.
71. Parr, A.D. (2013). Questioning universal applicability.
72. American Presidents (February 17, 2014). https://charlierose.com/videos/17978_September%2011,%202022

73. McGregor, J. (February 5, 2014). A thank you note from Mark Zuckerberg. *Washington Post.* https://www.washingtonpost.com/news/on-leadership/wp/2014/02/05/a-thank-you-note-from-mark-zuckerberg/
74. Grant, A.M., & Gino, F. (2010). A little thanks goes a long way: Explaining why gratitude expressions motivate prosocial behavior. *Journal of Personality and Social Psychology, 98,* 946–955.
75. Kumar, A., & Epley, N. (2018). Undervaluing gratitude: Expressers misunderstand the consequences of showing appreciation. *Psychological Science, 29,* 1423–1435.
76. Boothby, E.J., & Bohns, V.K. (2021). Why a simple act of kindness is not as a simple as it seems: Underestimating the positive impact of our compliments on others. *Personality and Social Psychology Bulletin, 47,* 826–840.
77. Porath, C.L., & Erez, A. (2007). Does rudeness really matter? The effects of rudeness on task performance and helpfulness. *Academy of Management Journal, 50,* 1181–1197.
78. Porath, C.L et al. (2015). How incivility hijacks performance: It robs cognitive resources, increases dysfunctional behavior, and infects team dynamics and functioning. *Organizational Dynamics, 44,* 258–269.
79. Porath, C.L., & Erez, A. (2009). Overlooked but not untouched: How rudeness reduces onlookers' performance on routine and creative tasks. *Organizational Behavior and Human Performance, 109,* 29–44.
80. Ditchburn, J. (November 6, 2015). "Because it's 2015": Trudeau forms Canada's 1st gender-balanced Cabinet. https://www.cbc.ca/news/politics/canada-trudeau-liberal-government-cabinet-1.3304590
81. Hinchliffe, E. (2020). The number of female CEOs in the Fortune 500 hits an all-time record. *Fortune.* https://fortune.com/2020/05/18/women-ceos-fortune-500-2020/
82. Georgeac, O., & Rattan, A. (2019). Progress in women's representation in top leadership weakens people's disturbance with gender inequality in other domains. *Journal of Experimental Psychology: Applied, 148,* 1435–1453.
83. Dezső, C. L., Li, Y., & Ross, D. G. (2022). Female CEOs and the Compensation of Other Top Managers. *Journal of Applied Psychology.* http://dx.doi.org/10.1037/apl0000988.
84. Graham, M.E. (2019). Women executives and off-the-job misconduct by high profile employees: A study of National Football League team organizations. *Journal of Organizational Behavior, 41,* 815–829.
85. Lyness, K.S., & Thompson, D.E. (1997). Above the glass ceiling? A comparison of matched samples of female and male executives. *Journal of Applied Psychology, 82,* 359–375.
86. Gupta, V.K. et al. (2018). Do women CEOs face greater threat of shareholder activism compared to male CEOs? A role congruity perspective. *Journal of Applied Psychology, 103,* 228–236.
87. Gupta, V.K. et al. (2020). You're fired! Gender disparities in CEO dismissal. *Journal of Management, 46,* 560–582.
88. Beaman, L. et al. (2012). Female leadership raises aspirations and educational attainment for girls: a policy experiment in India. *Science, 335,* 582–586.
89. Eagly, A.H., Johannesen-Schmidt, M.C., & van Engen, M.L. (2003). Transformational, transactional, and laissez-faire leadership styles: A meta-analysis comparing women and men. *Psychological Bulletin, 129,* 569–591.

90. Zenger, J., & Folkman, J. (June 25, 2019). Women score higher than men in most leadership skills. *Harvard Business Review*. https://hbr.org/2019/06/research-women-score-higher-than-men-in-most-leadership-skills
91. Garikipati, S., & Kambhampati, U. (2021). Leading the fight against the pandemic: Does gender "really" matter. *Feminist Economics, 27*(1–2), 401–418.
92. Sergent, K., & Stajkovic, A.D. (2020). Women's leadership is associated with fewer deaths during the COVID-19 crisis: Quantitative and qualitative analyses of United States governors. *Journal of Applied Psychology, 105*, 771–783.
93. Kakkar, H., & Sivanathan, N. (2017). When the appeal of a dominant leader is greater than a prestige leader. *PNAS, 114*, 6734–6739.
94. Bass, B.M. (1990). Does the transactional-transformational leadership paradigm transcend organizational and national boundaries? *American Psychologist, 52*, 130–139.
95. Leong, L.Y.C., & Fischer, R. (2011). Is transformational leadership universal? A meta-analytic investigation of Multifactor Leadership Questionnaire means across countries. *Journal of Leadership and Organizational Studies, 18*, 164–174.
96. Mackay, J.D. et al. (2017). Abusive supervision.
97. Gelfand, M.J. et al. (2011). Differences between tight and loose cultures: A 33-nation study. *Science, 332*, 1100–1104.
98. Aktas, M. et al. (2016). Cultural tightness-looseness and perceptions of effective leadership. *Journal of Cross-Cultural Psychology, 47*, 294–309.
99. Crede, M. et al. (2019). The generalizability of transformational leadership across cultures: A meta-analysis. *Journal of Managerial Psychology, 34*(3), 139–155.
100. Skinner, B.F. (1972), *Beyond freedom and dignity*. NY: Bantam Books.
101. Barling, J. (2014). *Science of leadership*.
102. Lacerenza, C.N. et al. (2017). Leadership training design, delivery, and implementation: A meta-analysis. *Journal of Applied Psychology, 102*, 1686–1718.
103. Avolio, B.J. et al. (2010). Estimating return on leadership development investment. *Leadership Quarterly, 21*, 633–644.
104. Antonakis, J. et al. (June 2012). Learning charisma: Transform yourself into the person others want to follow. *Harvard Business Review*, 127–130.
105. Antonakis, J. et al. (2011). Can charisma be taught? Tests of two interventions. *Academy of Management Learning and Education, 10*, 374–396.
106. Lacerenza, C.N. (2010). Leadership training design.
107. Ernst, B.A. et al. (2021). Virtual charismatic leadership and signaling theory: A prospective analysis in five countries. *Leadership Quarterly*. https://doi.org/10.1016/j.leaqua.2021.101541
108. Barling, J. (2014). *Science of leadership*.
109. Pfeffer, J. (1998). *The human equation: Building profits by putting people first*. MA: Harvard Business School Press..
110. Barling, J. (2014). *Science of leadership*.
111. Cohen, F. et al. (2004). Fatal attraction: The effects of mortality salience on evaluations of charismatic, task-oriented, and relationship-oriented leaders. *Psychological Science, 15*, 846–851.
112. Rendell, S. (May–June 2007). The media's mayor: Mythologizing Giuliani and 9/11. FAIR: Fairness and Accuracy in Reporting. https://fair.org/home/the-medias-mayor/

113. Waldman, D.A. et al. (2001). Does leadership matter? CEO leadership attributes and profitability under conditions of perceived environmental uncertainty. *Academy of Management Journal, 44*, 134–143.
114. De Hoogh, A.H.N. et al. (2004). Charismatic leadership, environmental dynamism, and performance. *European Journal of Work and Organizational Psychology, 13*, 447–471.
115. Waldman, D.A. et al. (2004). Charismatic leadership at the strategic level: A new application of upper echelons theory. *Leadership Quarterly, 15*, 355–380.
116. Avolio, B.J. (2008). Bernard (Bernie) M. Bass (1925–2007). *American Psychologist, 63*, 620.
117. Bass, B.M. (1990). *Bass and Stogdill's handbook of leadership: Theory, research and managerial implications* (3rd ed). NY: Free Press.
118. Ackermann, E. (April 2, 2020). There is an antidote to our fear: It's called leadership. *New York Times*. https://www.nytimes.com/2020/04/02/opinion/sunday/coronavirus-trump-leadership.html
119. Ricks, T.E. (2017). *Churchill & Orwell: The fight for freedom*. NY: Penguin Books.
120. Dreisbach, T. (November 11, 2020). Pfizer CEO sold millions in stock after coronovirus vaccine news, raising questions. https://www.npr.org/2020/11/11/933957580/pfizer-ceo-sold-millions-in-stock-after-coronavirus-vaccine-news-raising-questio
121. Kreps, T.A. et al. (2017). Hypocritical flip-flop, or courageous evolution? When leaders change their moral minds. *Journal of Personality and Social Psychology, 113*, 730–752.
122. Air Canada CEO's compensation cut by more than half to $5.8 million due to COVID-19. (May 25, 2020). https://www.theglobeandmail.com/business/article-air-canada-ceos-compensation-cut-by-more-than-half-to-58-million/
123. Milstead, D. (June 7, 2021). Air Canada's senior executives to return 2020 bonuses over "public disappointment." *Globe and Mail*. https://www.theglobeandmail.com/canada/article-air-canadas-senior-executives-to-return-2020-bonuses-over-public/
124. Tomkins, L. (2020). Where is Boris Johnson? When and why it matters that leaders show up in a crisis. *Leadership, 16*, 331–342.
125. Görlich, Y., & Stadelmann, D. (2020). Mental health of flying cabin crews: depression, anxiety, and stress before and during the COVID-19 pandemic. *Frontiers in Psychology, 11*, 1–8.
126. Yu, L. (2005). The great communicator: How FDR's radio speeches shaped American History. *History Teacher, 39*, 89–106.
127. "My day" column (1935–1962). https://www2.gwu.edu/~erpapers/mep/displaydoc.cfm?docid=erpo-myday
128. Uxorial advice. (June 2020). International Churchill Society. https://winstonchurchill.org/publications/churchill-bulletin/bulletin-144-jun-2020/uxorial-advice/
129. Yu., L. (2005). Great communicator.
130. Meacham, J. (March 24, 2020). Great leadership in a time of crisis. *New York Times*. https://www.nytimes.com/2020/03/24/books/review/great-leadership-in-a-time-of-cri sis.html
131. Porter, C. (June 5, 2020). The top doctor who aced the coronovirus test. *New York Times*. https://www.nytimes.com/2020/06/05/world/canada/bonnie-henry-british-columbia-coronavirus.html
132. Judge, T.A. et al. (2002). Personality and leadership: A qualitative and quantitate review. *Journal of Applied Psychology, 87*, 765–780.

133. MacLaren, N.G. et al. (2020). Testing the babble hypothesis: Speaking time predicts leader emergence in small groups. *Leadership Quarterly, 31*, 1–16.
134. Cohn, J., & Moran, J. (2011). *Why are we bad at picking good leaders?* CA: Jossey-Bass.
135. Barling, J. (2014). *Science of leadership.*
136. Grant, A.M. et al. (2011). Reversing the extraverted leadership advantage: The role of employee proactivity. *Academy of Management Journal, 54*, 528–550.
137. Grant, A. (September 18, 2013). Goodbye to MBTI, the fad that won't die. *Psychology Today.* https://www.psychologytoday.com/ca/blog/give-and-take/201309/goodbye-mbti-the-fad-won-t-die
138. Antonakis, J. (2009). Predictors of leadership: The usual suspects and the suspect traits. In A. Bryman et al. (Eds.), *Sage Handbook of Leadership.* CA: Sage Publications.
139. Brown, F.W., & Reilly, M.D. (2009). The Myers-Briggs type indicator and transformational leadership. *Journal of Management Development, 28*, 916–932.
140. Fine, S. et al. (2016). Beware those left behind: Counterproductive work behaviors among nonpromoted employees and the moderating effect of integrity. *Journal of Applied Psychology, 101*, 1721–1729.
141. Lacerenza, C.N. (2017). Leadership training design.
142. Meindl, J.R. et al. (1985). The romance of leadership. *Administrative Science Quarterly, 30*, 78–102.

Chapter 3

1. Lauletta, T. (February 13, 2018). Steve Kerr the Warriors players coach themselves because they were tired of his voice—and they won by 46. *Insider.* https://www.businessinsider.com/steve-kerr-warriors-coach-themselves-they-won-by-46-2018-2
2. Lammers, J. et al. (2016). To have control over others or to be free from others? The desire for power reflects a need for autonomy. *Personality and Social Psychology Bulletin, 42*, 498–512.
3. Herzberg, F. et al. (1959). *The motivation to work* (2nd ed.). NY: John Wiley.
4. Herzberg, F. (1969). One more time: How do you motivate employees? *Harvard Business Review, 47*(1), 53–62.
5. Hackman, J.R., & Oldham, G.R. (1976). Motivation through the design of work: Test of a theory. *Organizational Behavior and Human Performance, 16*, 250–279.
6. Wegman, L.A. et al. (2018). Placing job characteristics in context: Cross-temporal meta-analyses of changes in job characteristics since 1975. *Journal of Management, 44*, 352–386.
7. Stafford, I. (1984). Relation of attitudes toward women's roles and occupational behavior to women's self-esteem. *Journal of Counselling Psychology, 31*, 332–338.
8. Hock, E., & DeMeis, D.K. (1990). Depression in mothers of infants: The role of maternal employment. *Developmental Psychology, 25*, 285–291.
9. Barling, J. et al. (1988). Employment commitment as a moderator of the maternal employment status/child behavior relationship. *Journal of Organizational Behavior, 9*, 113–122.
10. Kelly, J. (May 24, 2020). Here are the companies leading the work-from-home revolution. *Forbes.* https://www.forbes.com/sites/jackkelly/2020/05/24/the-work-from-home-revolution-is-quickly-gaining-momentum/?sh=15fbd4c31848
11. Breaugh, J.A. (1985). The measurement of work autonomy. *Human Relations, 38*, 551–570.

12. Spector, P.E. (1986). Perceived control by employees: A meta-analysis of studies concerning autonomy and participation at work. *Human Relations, 39*, 1005–1016.
13. Gajendran, R.S., & Harrison, D.A. (2007). The good, the bad, and the unknown about telecommuting: Meta-analysis of psychological mediators and individual consequences. *Journal of Applied Psychology, 92*, 1524–1541.
14. Barling, J. (1990). *Employment, stress and family functioning*. London: Wiley.
15. Baltes, B.B. et al. (1999). Flexible and compressed workweek schedules: A meta-analysis of their effects on work-related criteria. *Journal of Applied Psychology, 84*, 496–513.
16. Spector, P.E. (1986). Perceived control.
17. Chen, Z.X., & Francesco, A.M. (2003). The relationship between the three components of commitment and employee performance in China. *Journal of Vocational Behavior, 62*, 490–510.
18. Barling, J., & Frone, M.R. (Eds.). (2004). *The psychology of workplace safety*. Washington, DC: American Psychological Association.
19. Barling, J. et al. (2003). High quality work, members' employee morale and occupational injuries. *Journal of Applied Psychology*, 88, 276–283.
20. Parker, S.K. et al. (2001). Designing a safer workplace: Importance of job autonomy, communication quality, and supportive supervisors. *Journal of Occupational Health Psychology*, 6, 211–228.
21. Chugtai, A.A. (2015). Creating safer workplaces: The role of ethical leadership. *Safety Science*, 73, 92–98.
22. Turner, N. et al. (2005). Railing for safety: Job demands, job control, and safety citizenship role definition. *Journal of Occupational Health Psychology, 10*, 504–512.
23. Fischer, R., & Boer, D. (2011). What is more important for national well-being: Money or autonomy? A meta-analysis of well-being, burnout, and anxiety across 63 societies. *Journal of Personality and Social Psychology, 101*, 164–184.
24. Wheatley, D. (2017). Autonomy in paid work and employee subjective well-being. *Work and Occupations, 44*, 296–328.
25. Breaugh, J.A. (1985). The measurement of work autonomy. *Human Relations, 38*, 551–570.
26. Scott, B.A., & Barnes, C.M. (2011). A multilevel field investigation of emotional labor, affect, work withdrawal, and gender. *Academy of Management Journal, 54*, 116–136.
27. Hülsheger, U., & Schewe, A.F. (2011). On the costs and benefits of emotional labor: A meta-analysis of three decades of research. *Journal of Occupational Health Psychology, 16*, 361–389.
28. Parker, S.K. (2003). Longitudinal effects of lean production on employee outcomes and the mediating role of work characteristics. *Journal of Applied Psychology, 88*, 620–634.
29. De Croon, E.M. et al. (2004). Stressful work, psychological job strain, and turnover: A 2-year prospective cohort study of truck drivers. *Journal of Applied Psychology, 89*, 442–454.
30. Hamper, B. (1991). *Rivethead: Tales from the assembly line*. NY: Warner Books.
31. Väänänen, A. et al. (2003). Job characteristics, physical and psychological symptoms, and social support as antecedents of sickness absence among men and women in the private industrial sector. *Social Science and Medicine, 57*, 807–824.
32. Vahtera, J., Kivimäki, M., Pentti, J., & Theorell, T. (2000). Effect of change on the psychosocial work environment on sickness absence: A seven year follow up of initially healthy employees. Journal of Epidemiology and Community Health, 54, 484–493

33. Johns, G., & Miraglia, M. (2015). The reliability, validity and accuracy of self-report absenteeism from work: A meta-analysis. *Journal of Occupational Health Psychology, 20*, 1–14.
34. Barling, J. et al. (1992). *The union and its members: A psychological perspective.* NY: Oxford University Press.
35. Schriesheim, C.A. (1978). Job satisfaction, attitudes toward unions, and voting in a union representation election. *Journal of Applied Psychology, 63*, 548–552.
36. Hammer, T.H., & Berman, M. (1981). The role of noneconomic factors in faculty union voting. *Journal of Applied Psychology, 66*, 415–421.
37. Koul, P., & Shaw, C. (January 4, 2021). We built Google. This is not the company we want to work for. *New York Times.* https://www.nytimes.com/2021/01/04/opinion/google-union.html?action=click&module=Opinion&pgtype=Homepage
38. Allen, R.E., & Keaveny, T.J. (1985). Factors differentiating grievants and nongrievants. *Human Relations, 38*, 519–534.
39. Bluen, D.D. (1994). The psychology of strikes. In C.L. Cooper & I.T. Robertson (Eds.), *International review of industrial and organizational psychology* (Vol. 9) (pp. 113–145). UK: John Wiley & Sons.
40. Talgam, I. (2015). *The ignorant maestro: How great leaders inspire unpredictable brilliance.* NY: Portfolio/Penguin.
41. Day, R., & Hamblin, R. (1964). Some effects of close and punitive styles of supervision. *American Journal of Sociology, 69*, 499–510.
42. Oldham, G.R., & Cummings, A. (1996). Employee creativity: Personal and contextual factors at work. *Academy of Management Journal, 39*, 607–634.
43. Dupré, K.E., & Barling, J. (2006). Predicting and preventing supervisory workplace aggression. *Journal of Occupational Health Psychology*, 11, 13–26.
44. Barling, J. et al. (2018). The impact of positive and negative intraoperative surgeons' leadership behaviors on surgical team performance. *American Journal of Surgery, 215*, 14–18.
45. Bosma, H. et al. (1997). Low job control and risk of coronary heart disease in Whitehall II (prospective cohort) study. *British Medical Journal, 314*, 558–564.
46. Bosma, H. et al. (1998b). Job control, personal characteristics, and heart disease. *Journal of Occupational Health Psychology, 3*, 402–409.
47. Bishop, G.D. et al. (2003). Job demands, decisional control, and cardiovascular responses. *Journal of Occupational Health Psychology, 8*, 146–156.
48. Cooklin, A.R. et al. (2011). Employment conditions and maternal postpartum mental health: results from the Longitudinal Study of Australian Children. *Archives of Women's Mental Health, 14*, 217–225.
49. De Jonge, J. et al. (2000). Linear and nonlinear relations between psychosocial job characteristics, subjective outcomes, and sickness absence: Baseline results from SMASH. *Journal of Occupational and Health Psychology, 5*, 256–268.
50. Mausner-Dorsch, H., & Eaton, W.W. (2000). Psychosocial work environment and depression: Epidemiologic assessment of the demand-control model. *American Journal of Public Health, 90*, 1765–1770.
51. Wang, B. et al. (2020). Achieving effective remote working during the COVID-19 pandemic: A work design perspective. *Applied Psychology: An International Review, 70*, 16–59.
52. Barling, J. (2014). *The science of leadership: Lessons from research for organizational leaders.* NY: Oxford University Press.

53. Bakker, A.B. et al. (2003). Job demands and job resources as predictors of absence duration and frequency. *Journal of Vocational Behavior*, *62*, 341–356.
54. Thompson, C.A., & Prottas, D.J. (2005). Relationships among organizational family support, job autonomy, perceived control, and employee well-being. *Journal of Occupational Health Psychology*, *10*, 100–118.
55. Xanthopoulou, D. et al. (2007). The role of personal resources in the job demands-resources model. *International Journal of Stress Management*, *14*, 121–141.
56. Spell, C.S., & Arnold, T. (2007). An appraisal perspective of justice, structure and job control as antecedents of psychological distress. *Journal of Organizational Behavior*, *28*, 729–751.
57. Bakker, A.B. et al. (2005). Job resources buffer the impact of job demands on burnout. *Journal of Occupational Health Psychology*, *10*, 170–180.
58. Trougakos, J.P. et al. (2014). Lunch breaks unpacked: The role of autonomy as a moderator of recovery during lunch. *Academy of Management Journal*, *57*, 405–421.
59. Park, Y., & Kim, S. (2019). Customer mistreatment harms nightly sleep and next-morning recovery: Job control and recovery self-efficacy as cross-level moderators. *Journal of Occupational Health Psychology*, *24*, 256–269.
60. Cendales-Ayala, B. et al. (2016). Bus drivers' responses to job strain: An experimental test of the job demand-control model. *Journal of Occupational Health Psychology*, 22, 518–527.
61. Volmer, J. et al. (2012). Leader-member exchange (LMX), job autonomy, and creative work involvement. *Leadership Quarterly*, *23*, 456–465.
62. Tepper, B. (2002). Consequences of abusive supervision. *Academy of Management Journal*, *43*, 178–200.
63. Mackey, J.D. et al. (2017). Abusive supervision: A meta-analysis and empirical review. *Journal of Management*, *43*, 1940–1965.
64. Velez, M.J., & Neves, P. (2016). Abusive supervision, psychosomatic symptoms, and deviance: Can job autonomy make a difference? *Journal of Occupational Health Psychology*, *21*, 322–333.
65. Chandola, T. et al. (2004). The effect of control at home on CHD events in the Whitehall II study: Gender differences in psychosocial domestic pathways to social inequalities in CHD. *Social Science and Medicine*, *58*, 1501–1509.
66. Kim, H. et al. (2016). Gender differences in the effects of job control and demands on the health of Korean manual workers. *Health Care for Women International*, *37*, 290–302.
67. Ding, H. et al. (2020). Is self-employment a good option? Gender, parents and the work-family interface. *Sex Roles*, *84*, 731–746.
68. Bellman, S. (2003). Gender differences in the use of social support as a moderator of occupational differences. *Stress and Health*, *19*, 45–58.
69. Theorell, T. et al. (2015). A systematic review including meta-analysis of work environment and depressive symptoms. *BMC Public Health*, *15*, 2–14.
70. Grandey, A.A. et al.. (2005). Must "service with a smile" be stressful? The moderating role of personal control for American and French employees. *Journal of Applied Psychology*, *90*, 893–904.
71. Man, D.C., & Lam, S.S.K. (2003). The effects of job complexity and autonomy on cohesiveness in collectivistic and individualistic work groups: A cross-cultural analysis. *Journal of Organizational Behavior*, *24*, 979–1001.

72. Liu, C. et al. (2011). The interaction of job autonomy and conflict with supervisor in China and the United States: A qualitative and quantitative comparison. *International Journal of Stress Management, 18*, 222–245.
73. Spector, P.E. et al. (2002). A comparative study of perceived job stressor sources and job strain in American and Iranian managers. *Applied Psychology: An International Review, 51*, 446–457.
74. Narayanan, L. et al. (1999). A cross-cultural comparison of job stressors and reactions among employees holding comparable jobs in two countries. *International Journal of Stress Management, 6*, 197–211.
75. Mueller, C.W., & Wynn, T. (2000). The degree to which justice is valued in the workplace. *Social Justice Research, 13*, 1–23.
76. Spector, P.E. et al. (2002). Locus of control and well-being at work: How generalizable are Western findings? *Academy of Management Journal, 45*, 453–466.
77. Fock, H. et al. (2013). Moderating effects of power distance on the relationship between types of empowerment and employee satisfaction. *Journal of Cross-Cultural Psychology, 44*, 281–298.
78. Liu, C. et al (2011). Interaction of job autonomy..
79. Cendales, B.E., & Ortiz, V.G. (2019). Cultural values and the job-demands-control model of stress: A moderation analysis. *International Journal of Stress Management, 26*, 223–237.
80. Wu, C-H. et al. (2015). Overqualification and subjective well-being at work: The moderating role of job autonomy and culture. *Social Indicators Research, 121*, 917–937.
81. Man, D.C., & Lam, S.S.K. (2003). Effects of job complexity.
82. Warr, P.B. (1987). *Work, unemployment, and mental health*. Oxford: Oxford University Press.
83. De Jonge, J. et al. (2000). Linear and nonlinear relations.
84. Kubicek, B. et al. (2014). Too much job control? Two studies on curvilinear relations between job control and eldercare workers' well-being. *International Journal of Nursing Studies, 51*, 1644–1653.
85. Stiglbauer, B., & Kovacs, C. (2018). The more, the better? Curvilinear effects of job autonomy on well-being from Vitamin Model and PE-Fit theory perspectives. *Journal of Occupational Health Psychology, 23*, 520–536.
86. Lu, J.G. et al. (2017). The dark side of experiencing job autonomy: Unethical behavior. *Journal of Experimental Social Psychology, 73*, 222–234.
87. Wall, T.D. et al. (1990). Advanced manufacturing technology, work design, and performance: A change study. *Journal of Applied Psychology, 75*, 691–697.
88. Parker, S.K. (2003). Longitudinal effects.
89. Parker, S.K. (2003). Longitudinal effects.
90. Modern Times Synopsis. https://www.charliechaplin.com/en/films/6-modern-times/articles/11-Modern-Times-Synopsis
91. Orwell, G. (1949). *Nineteen eight-four: A novel.* London: Secker & Warburg.
92. Garson, B. (1988). *The electronic sweatshop: How computers are transforming the office of the future into the factory of the past.* NY: Penguin Books.
93. Bibby, A. What the new BLS report about the size of the gig economy leaves out. https://www.flexjobs.com/blog/post/new-bls-report-size-gig-economy-leaves/

94. Dubal, V., & Schor, J.B. (Jan 18, 2021). Gig workers are employees: Start treating them that way. *New York Times*. https://www.nytimes.com/2021/01/18/opinion/proposition-22-california-biden.html?action=click&module=Opinion&pgtype=Homepage
95. Heavy and tractor-trailer truck drivers. https://www.bls.gov/ooh/transportation-and-material-moving/heavy-and-tractor-trailer-truck-drivers.htm
96. Murphy, F. (2017). *The long haul: A trucker's talks of life on the road*. NY: W.W. Norton & Co.
97. Levy, K.E.C. (2015). The contexts of control: Information, power, and truck-driving work. *Information Society*, *31*, 160–175.
98. Aiello, J.R., & Kolb, K.B. (1995). Electronic performance monitoring and social context: Impact on productivity and stress. *Journal of Applied Psychology*, *80*, 339–353.
99. Smith, M.J. et al. (1992). Employee stress and health complaints in jobs with and without electronic performance monitoring. *Applied Ergonomics*, *23*, 17–28.
100. Stanton, J.M. (2000). Traditional and electronic monitoring from an organizational justice perspective. *Journal of Business and Psychology*, *15*, 129–147.
101. Stanton, J.M., & Barnes-Farrell, J.L. (1996). Effects of electronic performance monitoring on personal control, task satisfaction, and task performance. *Journal of Applied Psychology*, *81*, 738–745.
102. McNall, L.A., & Roch, S.G. (2007). Effects of electronic monitoring types on perceptions of procedural justice, interpersonal justice, and privacy. *Journal of Applied Social Psychology*, *37*, 658–682.
103. Wheatley, D. (2017). Autonomy in paid work.
104. Raveendhran, R., & Wakslak, C. (2017). Telltale signs: Micromanagement signals insecurity and low-levels of leadership. https://doi.org/10.5465/ambpp.2014.10845abstract
105. Canadian Survey on Business Conditions: Impact of COVID-19 on business in Canada, May 2020. *Daily*. https://www150.statcan.gc.ca/n1/daily-quotidien/200714/dq200714a-eng.htm?CMP=mstatcan
106. Partington, R. (May 17, 2021). Most people in the UK did not work from home in 2020, says ONS. *Guardian*. https://www.theguardian.com/world/2021/may/17/home-working-doubled-during-uk-covid-pandemic-last-year-mostly-in-london
107. Meakin, L. (February 2, 2021). Remote working's longer hours are new normal for many. *Bloomberg*. https://www.bloomberg.com/news/articles/2021-02-02/remote-working-s-longer-hours-are-new-normal-for-many-chart
108. Pfeffer, J. (May 18, 2020). Learning corner with Jeffrey Pfeffer: To build trust, cut down on surveillance—even for employees working at home. https://www.cornerstoneondemand.com/resources/article/learning-corner-jeffrey-pfeffer-build-trust-cut-down-surveillance-even-employees-working-home/
109. Hern, A. (December 2, 2020). Microsoft apologises for feature criticized as workplace surveillance. *Guardian*. https://www.theguardian.com/technology/2020/dec/02/microsoft-apologises-productivity-score-critics-derided-workplace-surveillance
110. Pfeffer, J. (May 18, 2020). Learning corner.
111. Jackson, S.E. (1983). Participation in decision-making as a strategy for reducing job-related strain. *Journal of Applied Psychology*, *68*, 3–19.
112. Crouter, A.C. (1984). Participative work as an influence on human development. *Journal of Applied Developmental Psychology*, *5*, 71–90.
113. Perry-Jenkins, M. et al. (2019). Parents' work and children's development: A longitudinal investigation of working-class families. *Journal of Family Psychology*, *34*, 257–268.

114. Abraham, K.G. et al. (2019). The rise of the gig economy: Fact or fiction? *AEA Papers and Proceedings, 109*, 357–361.
115. Kessler, S. (2018). *Gigged: The end of the job and the future of work*. NY: St. Martin's Press..
116. Kessler, S. (March 18, 2014). Pixel and dimed on (not) getting by in the gig economy. *Fast Company*. https://www.fastcompany.com/3027355/pixel-and-dimed-on-not-getting-by-in-the-gig-economy

Chapter 4

1. tompeters! Writing. https://tompeters.com/writing/books/
2. Maslow, A.H. (1943). A theory of human motivation. *Psychological Review, 50*, 370–396.
3. Based on Gallup research: What makes a great workplace. https://thepeoplegroup.com/wp-content/uploads/2008/04/article-gallup-research-what-makes-a-great-workplace1.pdf
4. "Item 10: I have a best friend at work." *Workplace* (May 26, 1999). https://www.gallup.com/workplace/237530/item-best-friend-work.aspx
5. Grant, A. (September 4, 2015). Friends at work? Not so much. *New York Times*. https://www.nytimes.com/2015/09/06/opinion/sunday/adam-grant-friends-at-work-not-so-much.html
6. Kelloway, E.K. et al. (2010). Loving one's job: Construct development and implications for well-being. In P.L. Perrewe & D.C. Ganster (Eds.), *Research in occupational stress and well being* (Vol. 8). UK: Emerald Publishing.
7. Meyer, J.P., & Allen, N. (1997). *Commitment in the workplace: Theory, research, and application*. CA: SAGE Publications.
8. Kelloway, E.K. et al. (2010). Loving one's job.
9. Sohn, H. (2015). Health insurance and risk of divorce: Does having your own insurance matter? *Journal of Marriage and the Family, 77*, 982–995.
10. Cialdini, R. (2021). *Influence, new and expanded: The psychology of persuasion*. NY: Harper Business.
11. Ehrhardt, K., & Ragins, B.R. (2019). Relational attachment at work: A complementary fit perspective on the role of relationships in organizational life. *Academy of Management Journal, 62*, 248–282.
12. Meyer, J.P. et al. (2002). Affective, continuance, and normative commitment to the organization: A meta-analysis of antecedents, correlates, and consequences. *Journal of Vocational Behavior, 61*, 20–52.
13. Hardin, A.E. et al. (2020). Show me the … family: How photos of meaningful relationships reduce unethical behavior at work. *Organizational Behavior and Human Decision Processes, 161*, 93–108.
14. Yudkin, D.A. et al. (2021). Binding moral values gain importance in the presence of close others. *Nature Communication, 12*. https://doi.org/10.1038/s41467-021-22566-6
15. Ehrhardt, J., & Ragins, B.R. (2019). Relational attachment.
16. Meyer, J.P. et al. (1989). Organizational commitment and job performance: It's the nature of the commitment that counts. *Journal of Applied Psychology, 74*, 152–156.
17. Wei, L-Q. et al. (2019). Founder need to belong, *tertius iungens* orientation and new venture performance. *Journal of Organizational Behavior, 42*, 48–67.

18. Schermuly, C.C., & Meyer, B. (2016). Good relationships at work: The effects of leader-member exchange and team-member exchange on psychological empowerment, emotional exhaustion and depression. *Journal of Organizational Behavior*, 37, 673–691.
19. Puranik, D. et al. (2021). Excuse me, do you have a minute? An exploration of the dark- and bright-side effects of daily work interruptions for employee well-being. *Journal of Applied Psychology, 106*, 1867–1884.
20. Methot, J.R. et al. (2021). Office chit-chat as a social ritual: The uplifting yet distracting effects of daily small talk at work. *Academy of Management Journal, 64*, 1445–1471.
21. Seabrook, J. (February 1, 2021). Has the pandemic transformed the office forever? *NewYorker*. https://www.newyorker.com/magazine/2021/02/01/has-the-pandemic-transformed-the-office-forever
22. Coissard, F. et al. (2017). Relationships at work and psychosocial risk: The feeling of belonging as indicator and mediator. *Revue européenne de psychologie appliquée, 67*, 317–325.
23. Currie, S.L. et al. (2011). Bringing the troops back home: Modeling the postdeployment reintegration experience. *Journal of Occupational Health Psychology, 16*, 38–47.
24. Bennett, A.A. et al. (2021). Videoconference fatigue? Exploring changes in fatigue after videoconference meetings during COVID-19. *Journal of Applied Psychology, 106*, 330–344.
25. Meyer, J.P., & Allen, N. (1997). *Commitment in the workplace.*
26. Bureau of Transportation Statistics. (2003). *Omnibus household survey results (August)*.Washington, DC: Government Printing Office.
27. Golden, T.D., & Veiga, J.F. (2005). The impact of extent of telecommuting on job satisfaction: Resolving inconsistent findings. *Journal of Management, 31*, 301–318.
28. Gajendran, R.S., & Harrison, D.A. (2007). The good, the bad, and the unknown about telecommuting: Meta-analysis of psychological mediators and individual consequences). *Journal of Applied Psychology, 92*, 1524–1541.
29. Howard, M.C. et al. (2020). The antecedents and outcomes of workplace ostracism: A meta-analysis. *Journal of Applied Psychology, 105*, 577–596.
30. Ozcelik, H., & Barsade, S.G. (2018). No employee an island: Worker loneliness and job performance. Acad*emy of Management Journal, 61*, 2343–2366.
31. Howard, M.C. et al. (2020). Antecedents and outcomes.
32. Meyer, J.P. (2002). Affective, continuance.
33. Twenge, J.M. et al. (2001). If you can't join them, beat them: Effects of social exclusion on aggressive behavior. *Journal of Personality and Social Psychology, 81*, 1058–1069.
34. Thau, S. et al. (2007). Self-defeating behaviors in organizations: The relationship between thwarted belonging and interpersonal work behaviors. *Journal of Applied Psychology, 92*, 840–847.
35. O'Reilly, J. et al. (2015). Is negative attention better than no attention? The comparative effects of ostracism and harassment at work? *Organization Science, 26*, 774–793.
36. Hogh, A. et al. (2011). Bullying and employee turnover among healthcare workers: A three-wave prospective study. *Journal of Nursing Management, 19*, 742–751.
37. Yang, L. et al. (2022). The effects of remote work on collaboration among remote workers. *Nature Human Behavior*, 6, 43–54.
38. Peterson, A. (undated). Why return to the workplace? https://www.linkedin.com/news/story/why-return-to-the-workplace-5478642/

39. Yang, L-Q. et al. (2020). Abusive supervision, thwarted belongingness, and workplace safety: A group engagement perspective. *Journal of Applied Psychology, 105*, 230–244.
40. Meyer, J.P. et al. (1989). Organizational commitment and job performance.
41. Stillman, T.F. et al. (2009). Alone and without purpose: Life loses meaning following social exclusion. *Journal of Experimental Social Psychology, 45*, 686–694.
42. Hershcovis, M.S. et al. (2017). Targeted workplace incivility: The roles of belongingness, embarrassment, and power. *Journal of Organizational Behavior, 38*, 1057–1075.
43. Chen, Y., & Li, S. (2019). The relationship between workplace ostracism and sleep quality: A mediated moderation model. *Frontiers in Psychology, 10*(319), 1–13.
44. Harris, G.E., & Cameron, J.E. (2005). Multiple dimensions of organizational identification and commitment as predictors of turnover intentions and psychological well-being. *Canadian Journal of Behavioral Sciences, 37*(3), 159–169.
45. Glazer, S., & Beehr, T.A. (2005). Consistency of implications of three role stressors across four countries. *Journal of Organizational Behavior, 26*, 467–487.
46. Meyer, J.P. et al. (2012). Employee commitment in context: The nature and implication of commitment profiles. *Journal of Vocational Behavior, 80*, 1–16.
47. Andel, S.A. et al (2021). Depending on your own kindness: The moderating role of self-compassion on the within-person consequences of work loneliness during the COVID-19 pandemic. *Journal of Occupational Health Psychology 26*, 276–290.
48. Ozcelik, J., & Barsade, S.G. (2018). No employee is an island: Workplace loneliness and job performance. *Academy of Management Journal, 61*, 2343–2366.
49. Turkle, S. (March 21, 2021). Sherry Turkle: "The pandemic has shown us that people need relationships." https://www.theguardian.com/science/2021/mar/21/sherry-turkle-the-pandemic-has-shown-us-that-people-need-relationships?CMP=Share_iOSApp_Other
50. Chiniara, M., & Bentein, K. (2016). Linking servant leadership to individual performance: Differentiating the mediating role of autonomy, competence and relatedness need satisfaction. *Leadership Quarterly, 27*, 124–141.
51. Hershcovis, M.S. et al. (2017). Targeted workplace incivility.
52. Gong, Y. et al. (2009). Human resource management and firm performance: The differential role of managerial affective and continuance commitment. *Journal of Applied Psychology, 94*, 263–275.
53. Kwan, H.K. et al. (2018). Workplace ostracism and employee creativity: An integrative approach incorporating pragmatic and engagement roles. *Journal of Applied Psychology, 103*, 1358–1366.
54. Junger, S. (May 7, 2015). How PTSD became a problem beyond the battlefield. *Vanity Fair*. https://www.vanityfair.com/news/2015/05/ptsd-war-home-sebastian-junger
55. Currie, S.L. et al. (2011). Bringing the troops.
56. Rivkin, W. et al. (2015). Affective commitment as a moderator of the adverse relationships between day-specific self-control demands and psychological well-being. *Journal of Vocational Behavior, 88*, 185–194.
57. Birdi, K. et al. (2008). The impact of human resource and operational management practices on company productivity: A longitudinal study. *Personnel Psychology, 61*, 467–501.
58. Raineri, A. (2017). Linking human resource practices with performance: The simultaneous mediation of collective affective commitment and human capital. *International Journal of Human Resource Management, 28*, 3149–3178.

59. Taylor, S.E. (2006). Tend and befriend: Biobehavioral bases of affiliation under stress. *Current Directions in Psychological Science, 15*, 273–277.
60. Turton, S., & Campbell, C. (2005). Tend and befriend versus fight or flight: Gender differences in behavioral responses to stress among university students. *Journal of Applied Biobehavioral Research, 10*, 209–232.
61. Marsden, P.V. et al. (1993). Gender differences in organizational commitment: Influences of work positions and family roles. *Work and Occupations, 20*, 368–390.
62. Dalgiç, G. (2014). A meta-analysis: Exploring the effects of gender on organizational commitment of teachers. *Issues in Educational Research, 24*(2), 133–151.
63. Thien, L.M., & Adams, D. (2021). Distributed leadership and teachers' affective commitment to change in Malaysian primary schools: The contextual influence of gender and teacher experience. *Educational Studies, 47(2)*, 179–199.
64. Jayasingam, S. et al. (2016). Instilling affective commitment: Insights on what makes knowledge workers want to stay. *Management Research Review, 39*, 266–288.
65. Shin, D. et al. (2020). HRM systems and employee affective commitment: The role of employee gender. *Gender in Management: An International Journal, 35*, 189–210
66. Meyer, J.P. et al. (2012). Affective, normative, and continuance commitment levels across cultures: A meta-analysis. *Journal of Vocational Behavior, 80*, 225–245.
67. Schwartz, S. (2006). A theory of cultural value orientations: Explication and applications. *Comparative Sociology, 5(2–3)*, 137–182.
68. Yang, L.Q. et al. (2020). Abusive supervision.
69. Haldorai, K. et al. (2020). Left out of the office "tribe": The influence of workplace ostracism on employee work engagement. *International Journal of Contemporary Hospitality Management, 32*, 2717–2735.
70. Gill, H. et al. (2011). Affective and continuance commitment and their relations with deviant workplace behaviors in Korea. *Asia Pacific Journal of Management, 28*, 595–607.
71. Liu, J. et al. (2013). Work-to-family spillover effects of workplace ostracism: The role of work-home segmentation preferences. *Human Resource Management, 52*, 75–94.
72. Zhao, H. et al. (2013). Workplace ostracism and hospitality employees' counterproductive work behaviors: The joint moderating effects of proactive personality and political skill. *International Journal of Hospitality Management, 33*, 219–227.
73. Meyer, J.P. et al. (2002). Affective, continuance.
74. Bedi, A. (2019). No herd for black sheep: A meta-analytic review of the predictors and outcomes of workplace ostracism. *Applied Psychology: An International Review, 70*, 861–904.
75. MacEwen, K.E., & Barling, J. (1988). Interrole conflict, family support and marital adjustment of employed mothers: A short term, longitudinal study. *Journal of Organizational Behavior, 1988*, 9, 241–250.
76. Ehrhardt, J., & Raggins, B.R. (2019). Relational attachment.
77. Ehrhardt, J., & Raggins, B.R. (2019). Relational attachment.
78. MacEwen, K.E., & Barling, J. (1988). Interrole conflict.
79. Nahum-Shani, I., & Bamberger, P. (2011). Explaining the variable effects of social support on work-based stressor-strain relationships: The role of perceived pattern of social exchange. *Organizational Behavior and Human Decision Processes, 114*, 49–63.
80. Brockner, J. et al. (1987). Survivors' reactions to layoffs: We get by with a little help from our friends. *Administrative Science Quarterly, 32*, 526–541.

81. Grunberg, L. et al. (2000). Surviving layoffs: The effects on organizational commitment and job performance. *Work and Occupations*, *27*, 7–31.
82. Liu, W. et al. (2018). Effect of workplace incivility on OCB through burnout: The moderating effect of affective commitment. *Journal of Business and Psychology*, *34*, 657–669.
83. Kabat-Farr, D. et al. (2018). The emotional aftermath of incivility: Anger, guilt, and the role of organizational commitment. *International Journal of Stress Management*, *25*, 109–128.
84. Ingram, P., & Zou X. (2008). Business friendships. *Research in Organizational Behavior*, *28*, 167–184
85. Peterson, A. (undated). *Why return*.
86. Methot, J.R. et al. (2016). Are workplace friendships a mixed blessing? Exploring tradeoffs of multiplex relationships and their associations with job performance. *Personnel Psychology*, *69*, 311–355.
87. Shah, N.P. et al. (2017). Examining the overlap: Individual performance benefits of multiplex relationships. *Management Communication Quarterly*, *31*, 5–38.
88. Peterson, L-E., & Dietz, J. (2008). Employment discrimination: Authority figures' demographic preferences and followers' affective organizational commitment. *Journal of Applied Psychology*, *93*, 1289–1300.
89. Berry, Z. et al. (2021). The double-edged sword of loyalty. *Current Directions in Psychology*, *30*, 321–326.
90. Kenigsberg, B. (July 20, 2020). "John Lewis: Good trouble" review: Past progress and more to come. https://www.nytimes.com/2020/07/02/movies/john-lewis-good-trouble-review.html
91. Hoch, J.E. et al. (2018). Do ethical, authentic and servant leadership explain variance above and beyond transformational leadership? A meta-analysis. *Journal of Management*, *44*, 501–529.
92. Jackson, T.A. et al. (2013). Leadership, commitment, and culture: A meta-analysis. *Journal of Leadership and Organizational Studies*, *20*, 84–106.
93. Barling, J. et al. (1996). Effects of transformational leadership training on attitudinal and financial outcomes: A field experiment. *Journal of Applied Psychology*, 81, 827–832.
94. Kelloway, E.K., & Barling, J. (2000). What we have learned about developing transformational leaders. *Leadership and Organization Development Journal*, 21, 355–362.
95. Barling, J. (2014). *The science of leadership: Lessons from research for organizational practitioners*. NY: Oxford University Press.
96. Gong, Y. et al. (2009). Human resource management.
97. Shore, L.M. et al. (1995). Managerial perceptions of employee commitment to the organization. *Academy of Management Journal*, *38*, 1593–1615.
98. Meyer, J.P. et al. (2002). Affective, continuance.
99. Shore, T.H. et al. (2008). An integrative model of managerial perceptions of employee commitment: Antecedents and influences on employee treatment. *Journal of Organizational Behavior*, *29*, 635–655.
100. Frone, M.R. (2018). What happened to the employed during the Great Recession? A U.S. population study of net change in employee insecurity, health, and organizational commitment. *Journal of Vocational Behavior*, *107*, 246–260.
101. Shah, N.P. et al. (2017). Examining the overlap.
102. How many gig workers are there? https://www.gigeconomydata.org/basics/how-many-gig-workers-are-there

103. Henderson, R. (December 10, 2020). How COVID-19 has transformed the gig economy. https://www.forbes.com/sites/rebeccahenderson/2020/12/10/how-covid-19-has-transformed-the-gig-economy/?sh=64f1fd86c99f
104. Wood, A. et al. (2018). Good gig, bad gig: Autonomy and algorithmic control in the global gig economy. *Work, Employment and Society, 33*, 56–75.
105. Cortina, L.M. et al. (2021). The embodiment of insult: A theory of biobehavioral response to workplace incivility. *Journal of Management*. https://doi.org/10.1177/0149206321989798
106. Mitchell, J. (January 7, 1970). Big Yellow Taxi. https://jonimitchell.com/music/song.cfm?id=13
107. Mutz, D.C., & Mondak, J.J. (2006). The workplace as a context for cross-cutting political discourse. *Journal of Politics, 68*, 140–155.
108. Seabrook, J. (January 25, 2021). Has the pandemic transformed the office forever? *New Yorker*. https://www.newyorker.com/magazine/2021/02/01/has-the-pandemic-transformed-the-office-forever

Chapter 5

1. Kivimäki, M. et al. (2005). Justice at work and reduced risk of coronary heart disease among employees. *Archives of Internal Medicine, 165*, 2245–2251.
2. Ziv, T. et al. (2021). Toddlers' interventions toward fair and unfair individuals. *Cognition, 214*, 1–14
3. Brosnan, S.F., & de Waal, F.B.M. (September 18, 2003). Monkeys reject unequal pay. *Nature, 425*, 297–299.
4. Goldman, B., & Cropanzano, R. (2015). "Justice" and "fairness" are not the same thing. *Journal of Organizational Behavior, 36*, 313–318.
5. Editorial (December 16, 2020). The Guardian view on shameless CEOs: Because they're worth it? https://www.theguardian.com/commentisfree/2020/dec/16/the-guardian-view-on-shameless-ceos-because-theyre-worth-it
6. Steffens, N.K. et al. (2020). Identity economics meets identity leadership: Exploring the role of elevated CEO pay. *Leadership Quarterly, 31*, 1–15.
7. Claypool, R. (November 25, 2020). Amazon and Walmart halted hazard pay for workers despite making $30 billion. *PublicCitizen*. https://www.citizen.org/article/amazon-and-walmart-halted-hazard-pay-for-workers-despite-making-30-billion/
8. Leventhal, G.S. et al. (1980). Beyond fairness: A theory of allocation preferences. In G. Mikula (Ed.), *Justice and social interaction* (pp. 167–218). NY: Springer.
9. Greenberg, J. (1990). Employee theft as a reaction to underpayment inequity: The hidden cost of pay cuts. *Journal of Applied Psychology, 75*, 561–568.
10. Colquitt, J.A. (2001). On the dimensionality of organizational justice: A construct validation of a measure. *Journal of Applied Psychology, 86*, 386–400.
11. Ambrose, M.L., & Schminke, M. (2009). The role of overall justice judgments in organizational justice research: A test of mediation. *Journal of Applied Psychology, 94*, 491–500.
12. Brockner, J. (March 1, 2006). It's so hard to be fair. *Harvard Business Review, 51*, 122–128.
13. Belogolovsky, E., & Bamberger, P. (2014). Signaling in secret: Pay for performance and the incentive and sorting effects of pay secrecy. *Academy of Management Journal, 57*, 1706–1733.

14. Colquitt, J.A. et al. (2001). Justice and the millennium: A meta-analytic review of 25 years of organizational justice research. *Journal of Applied Psychology, 86*, 425–445.
15. Brockner, J. et al. (1994). Interactive effects of procedural justice on outcome negativity on victims and survivors of job loss. *Academy of Management Journal, 37*, 397–409.
16. Brockner, J. et al. (1992). The influence of prior commitment to an institution on reactions to perceived unfairness: The higher they are, the harder they fall. *Administrative Science Quarterly, 37*, 241–261.
17. Schaubroeck, J. et al. (1994). Procedural justice explanations and employee reactions to economic hardship: A field experiment. *Journal of Applied Psychology, 79*, 455–460.
18. Konovsky, M.A., & Cropanzano, R. (1991). Perceived fairness of employee drug testing as a predictor of employee attitudes and job performance. *Journal of Applied Psychology, 76*, 698–707.
19. Kessler, S. (2018). *Gigged: The end of the job and the future of work*. NY: St. Martin's Press.
20. Wang, H-j., Lu, C-q., & Siu, O-l. (2015). Job insecurity and organizational performance: The moderating role of organizational justice and the mediating role of work engagement. *Journal of Applied Psychology, 100*, 1249–1258.
21. Kivimäki, M. et al. (2005). Justice at work.
22. Whitehall II (also known as the Stress and Health Study). http://www.ucl.ac.uk/whitehalllII.
23. Greenberg, J. (2011). Organizational justice: The dynamics of fairness in the workplace. In S. Zedeck (Ed.), *APA handbook of industrial and organizational psychology, Vol. 3. Maintaining, expanding, and contracting the organization* (pp. 271–327). DC: American Psychological Association.
24. Johnson, R.E. et al. (2014). The good and bad of being fair: Effects of procedural and interpersonal justice behaviors on regulatory resources. *Journal of Applied Psychology, 99*, 635–650.
25. Schlosser, E. (2001). *Fast food nation: The dark side of the all-American meal*. NY: Houghton Mifflin.
26. Murphy, F. (2017). *The long haul: A trucker's tales of life on the road*. NY: W.W. Norton & Co.
27. Jones, D.A. (2009). Getting even with one's supervisor and one's organization: Relationships among types of justice, desires for revenge, and counterproductive work behaviors. *Journal of Organizational Behavior, 30*, 525–542.
28. Inness, M. et al. (2005). Understanding supervisor-targeted aggression: A within-person, between-jobs design. *Journal of Applied Psychology, 90*, 731–739.
29. Jones, D.A. (2009). Getting even.
30. Rubenstein, A.L. et al. (2018). Surveying the forest: A meta-analysis, moderator investigation, and future-oriented discussion of the antecedents of voluntary employee turnover. *Personnel Psychology*, 71, 23–65.
31. Greenberg, L., & Barling, J. (1996). Employee theft. In C.L. Cooper and D.L. Rousseau (Eds.), *Trends in organizational behaviour* (pp. 49–64) (Vol. 3.). London: Wiley and Sons.
32. Greenberg, J. (1990). Employee theft.
33. Greenberg, J. (1993). Stealing in the name of justice: Informational and interpersonal moderators of theft reactions to underpayment inequity. *Organizational Behavior and Human Decision Processes, 54*, 81–103.

34. Roberts, K., & Markel, K.S. (2001). Claiming in the name of justice: Organizational justice and the decision to file for Workplace Injury Compensation. *Journal of Occupational Health Psychology, 6*, 332–347.
35. Ryan, A. (January 12, 2010). Conan rejects the NBC shuffle, hints he's poised to take a hike. *Globe and Mail.* http://www.theglobeandmail.com/arts/conan-rejects-the-nbc-shuffle-hints-hes-poised-to-take-a-hike/article1207227/
36. Elovainio, M. et al. (2006). Organisational injustice and impaired cardiovascular regulation among female employees. *Occupational and Environmental Medicine, 63*, 141–144.
37. Kouvenen, A. et al. (2008). Low organizational injustice and heavy drinking: A prospective cohort study. *Organizational and Environmental Medicine, 65*, 44–50.
38. Ylipaavalniemi, J. et al. (2005). Psychosocial work characteristics and incidence of newly diagnosed depression: A prospective cohort study of three different models. *Social Science and Medicine, 61*, 111–122.
39. Andel, S.A. et al (2021). Depending on your own kindness: The moderating role of self-compassion on the within-person consequences of work loneliness during the COVID-19 pandemic. *Journal of Occupational Health Psychology, 26*, 276–290.
40. Greenberg, J. (1990). Employee theft.
41. Eib, C. et al. (2015). Don't let it get to you! A moderated mediated approach to the (in) justice-health relationship. *Journal of Occupational Health Psychology, 20*, 434–445.
42. Barclay, L.J., & Skarlicki, D.P. (2009). Healing the wounds of organizational injustice: Examining the benefits of expressive writing. *Journal of Applied Psychology, 94*, 511–523.
43. Yuan, Z. et al. (2018). Bad behavior keeps you up at night: Counterproductive work behaviors and insomnia. *Journal of Applied Psychology, 103*, 383–398.
44. Jacobs, G. et al. (2014). (Un)ethical behavior and performance appraisal: The role of affect, support and organizational justice. *Journal of Business Ethics, 121*, 63–76.
45. Yang, L-Q. et al. (2014). Physiological mechanisms that underlie the effects of interactional unfairness on deviant behavior: The role of cortisol activity. *Journal of Applied Psychology, 99*, 310–321.
46. Kelloway, E.K., & Barling, J. (2000). Knowledge work as organizational behavior. *International Journal of Management Reviews*, 2, 287–304.
47. Tangirala, S., & Ramanujam, R. (2008). Employee silence on critical work issues: The cross level effects of procedural justice climate. *Personnel Psychology, 61*, 37–68.
48. Cohen-Charash, Y., & Mueller, J.S. (2007). Does perceived unfairness exacerbate or mitigate interpersonal counterproductive work behaviors related to envy. *Journal of Applied Psychology, 92*, 666–680.
49. Eagly, A.H., & Karau, S.J. (2002). Role congruity theory of prejudice toward female leaders. *Psychological Review, 109*, 573–598; Heilman, M.E. (2001). Description and prescription: How gender stereotypes prevent women's ascent up the organizational ladder. *Journal of Social Issues, 57*, 657–674.
50. Caleo, S. (2016). Are organizational justice rules gendered? Reactions to men's and women's justice violations. *Journal of Applied Psychology, 101*, 1422–1435.
51. Shäfer, M. et al. (2015). Fair is not fair everywhere. *Psychological Science, 26*, 1252–1260.
52. Mueller, C.W., & Wynn, T. (2000). The degree to which justice is valued in the workplace. *Social Justice Research, 13*, 1–23.

53. Jiang, Z. et al. (2017). Relationships between organizational justice, organizational trust and organizational commitment: A cross-cultural study of China, South Korea and Australia. *International Journal of Human Resource Management, 28*, 973–1004.
54. Rahim, M.A. et al. (2001). Do justice relationships with organization-directed reactions differ across U.S. and Bangladesh employees? *International Journal of Conflict Management, 12*, 333–349.
55. Shao, R. et al. (2013). Employee justice across cultures: A meta-analytic perspective. *Journal of Management, 39*, 263–310.
56. Robbins, J.M. et al. (2012). Perceived unfairness and employee health: A meta-analytic integration. *Journal of Applied Psychology, 97*, 235–272.
57. Adams, J.S. (1963). Toward an understanding of inequity. *Journal of Abnormal and Social Psychology, 67*, 422–436.
58. Lawler, E.E. et al. (1968). Inequity reduction over time in an induced overpayment situation. *Organizational Behavior and Human Performance, 3*, 253–268.
59. Greenberg, J. (1988). Equity and workplace status: A field experiment. *Journal of Applied Psychology, 73*, 606–613.
60. Baumeister, R.R. et al. (2001). Bad is stronger than good. *Review of General Psychology, 5*, 323–370.
61. Harder, J.W. (1992). Play for pay: Effects of inequity in a pay-for-play performance context. *Administrative Science Quarterly, 37*, 321–335.
62. Pennebaker, J.W., & Smyth, J.M. (2016). *Opening up by writing it down*. NY: Guilford Press.
63. Barclay, L.J., & Skarlicki, D.P. (2009). Healing the wounds..
64. Skarlicki, D.P., & Latham, G.P. (1996). Increasing citizenship behavior within a labor union: A test of organizational justice theory. *Journal of Applied Psychology, 81*, 161–169.
65. Burke, M.J., & Day, R.R. (1986). A cumulative study of the effectiveness of managerial training. *Journal of Applied Psychology, 71*, 232–246.
66. Leventhal, G.S. et al. (1980). Beyond fairness.
67. Greenberg, J. (2006). Losing sleep over organizational injustice: Attenuating insomniac reactions to underpayment inequity with supervisory training in interactional justice. *Journal of Applied Psychology, 91*, 58–69.
68. Johnson, M.D. et al. (2014). Outcomes of absence control initiatives: A quasi-experimental investigation into the effects of policy and perceptions. *Journal of Management, 40*, 1075–1097.
69. Johns, G. (1994). Absenteeism estimates by employees and managers: Divergent perspectives and self-serving perceptions. *Journal of Applied Psychology, 79*, 229–239.
70. Colquitt, J.A. (2001). On the dimensionality of organizational justice: A construct validation of a measure. Journal of Applied Psychology, 86, 386–400.
71. Kivimäki, M. et al. (2004). Organizational justice and change in justice as predictors of employee health: The Whitehall II study. *Journal of Epidemiology and Community Health, 58*, 931–937.
72. Hausknecht, J.P. et al. (2011). Justice as a dynamic construct: Effects of individual trajectories on distal work outcomes. *Journal of Applied Psychology, 96*, 872–880.
73. Rubenstein, A.L. et al. (2017). What's past (and present) is prologue: Interactions between justice levels and trajectories predicting behavioral reciprocity. *Journal of Management, 45*, 1569–1594.

74. Matta, F.K. (2020). Exchanging one uncertainty for another: Justice variability negative the benefits of justice. *Journal of Applied Psychology, 105*, 97–110.
75. Barling, J. (1996). The prediction, psychological experience and consequences of workplace violence. In G. VandenBos & E.G. Bulatao (Eds.), *Violence on the job: Identifying risks and developing solutions* (pp. 29–49). DC: American Psychological Association.
76. Bandura, A. (1976). *Social learning theory*. NY: Prentice-Hall.
77. Totterdell, P. et al. (2012). Can employees be emotionally drained by witnessing interactions between coworkers? A diary study of induced emotion regulation. *Work and Stress, 26*, 112–129.
78. Reich, T.C., & Hershcovis, M.S. (2015). Observing workplace incivility. *Journal of Applied Psychology, 100*, 203–215.
79. Hershcovis, M.S., & Bhatnagar, N. (2017). When fellow customers behave badly: Witness reactions to employee mistreatment by customers. *Journal of Applied Psychology, 102*, 1528–1544.
80. Hershcovis, M.S. et al. (2017). Witnessing wrongdoing: The effects of observer power on incivility intervention in the workplace. *Organizational Behavior and Human Decision processes, 142*, 45–57.
81. Bandura, A. (1965). Influence of models' reinforcement contingencies on the acquisition of imitative responses. *Journal of Personality and Social Psychology, 1*, 589–595.
82. Dekker, I., & Barling, J. (1998). Personal and organizational predictors of workplace sexual harassment of women by men. *Journal of Occupational Health Psychology*, 3, 7–18.
83. Dupré, K., & Barling, J. (2006). Predicting and preventing supervisory workplace aggression. *Journal of Occupational Health Psychology*, 11, 13–26.
84. Collins, B.J., & Mossholder, K.W. (2017). Fairness means more to some than others: Interactional fairness, job embeddedness, and discretionary work behaviors. *Journal of Management, 43*, 293–318.
85. Liu, F. et al. (2017). How do leaders react when treated unfairly? Leader narcissism and self-interested behavior in response to unfair treatment. *Journal of Applied Psychology, 102*, 1590–1599.
86. Bobocel, D.R. (2013). Coping with unfair events constructively or destructively: The effects of overall justice and self-other orientation. *Journal of Applied Psychology, 98*, 720–731.
87. Barling, J. et al. (1992). *The union and its members: A psychological perspective*. New York: Oxford University Press.
88. Koul, P., & Shaw, C. (January 4, 2021). We built Google: This is not the company we want to work for. *New York Times*. https://www.nytimes.com/2021/01/04/opinion/google-union.html?action=click&module=Opinion&pgtype=Homepage
89. Qureshi, Z. (November 17, 2020). Tackling the inequality pandemic: Is there a cure? *Brookings*. https://www.brookings.edu/research/tackling-the-inequality-pandemic-is-there-a-cure/
90. Fisher, R. (2013). Belonging, status, or self-protection? Examining justice motives in a three-level cultural meta-analyses of organizational justice effects. *Cross-Cultural Research, 47*, 3–41.
91. Diehl, M-R. et al. (2018). Variations in employee performance in response to organizational justice: The sensitizing of socioeconomic conditions. *Journal of Management, 44*, 2375–2404.
92. Greenberg, J. (1990). Employee theft.

Chapter 6

1. Hyacinth, B. (undated). Train people well enough so they can leave: Treat them well enough so they don't want to. *Thrive*. https://thriveglobal.com/stories/train-people-well-enough-so-they-can-leave-treat-them-well-enough-so-they-dont-want-to-richard-branson/
2. Alderfer, C.P. (1973). *Existence, relatedness, and growth: Human needs in organizational settings*. NY: Free Press.
3. Hackman, J.R., & Oldham, G.R. (1980). *Work redesign*. MA: Addison Wesley.
4. Beaman, L. et al. (2012). Female leadership raises aspirations and educational attainment for girls: A policy experiment in India. *Science, 335*, 582–586.
5. Volpe, C.E. et al. (1996). The impact of cross-training on team functioning: An empirical investigation. *Human Factors, 38*, 87–100.
6. Benson, G.S. et al. (2004). You paid for the skills, now keep them: Tuition reimbursement and voluntary turnover. *Academy of Management Journal, 47*, 315–331.
7. Life at Deloitte: Top 10 reasons to join the firm. https://www2.deloitte.com/ca/en/pages/careers/articles/top-10-reasons-to-join-our-firm.html
8. Joshi, A. et al. (2021). The generativity mindsets of chief executive officers: A new perspective on succession outcomes. *Academy of Management Review, 46*, 385–405.
9. Fullagar, C.J.A. et al. (1995). Impact of early socialization on union commitment and participation: A longitudinal study. *Journal of Applied Psychology, 80*, 147–157.
10. Bell, B.S. et al. (2017). 100 years of training and development research: What we know and where we should go. *Journal of Applied Psychology, 102*, 305–323.
11. Freifeild, L. (November 6, 2019). *2019 Training Industry Report*. https://trainingmag.com/2019-training-industry-report/
12. Kooij, D.T.A.M. et al. (2010). The influence of age on the associations between HR practices and both affective commitment and job satisfaction: A meta-analysis. *Journal of Organizational Behavior, 31*, 1111–1136.
13. Hosie, P. et al. (2013). The effect of autonomy, training opportunities, age and salaries on job satisfaction on the South East Asian retail petroleum industry. *The International Journal of Human Resource Management, 24*, 3980–4007.
14. Axtell, C.M., & Parker, S.K. (2003). Promoting role breadth self-efficacy through involvement, work redesign and training. *Human Relations, 56*, 113–131.
15. Tannenbaum, S.I. et al. (1991). Meeting trainees' expectations: The influence of training fulfillment on the development of commitment, self-efficacy, and motivation. *Journal of Applied Psychology, 76*, 759–769.
16. Steffens, N.K. et al. (2018). How feedback about leadership potential impacts ambition, organizational commitment, and performance. *Leadership Quarterly, 29*, 636–647.
17. Allen, T.D. et al. (2017). Taking stock of two relational aspects of organizational life: Tracing the history and shaping the future of socialization and mentoring research. *Journal of Applied Psychology, 102*, 324–337.
18. Eby, L.T., & Robertson, M.M. (2020). The psychology of workplace mentoring relationships. *Annual Review of Organizational Psychology and Organizational Behavior, 7*, 75–100.
19. Hartmann, N.N. et al. (2013). The effects of mentoring on salesperson commitment. *Journal of Business Research, 66*, 2294–2300.

20. Richard, O.C. et al. (2009). Mentoring in supervisor-subordinate dyads: Antecedents, consequences, and test of a mediation model of mentorship. *Journal of Business Research, 62*, 1110–1118.
21. *2016 ICF Global Coaching Study* (2016). International Coach Federation. California. https://coachfederation.org/app/uploads/2017/12/2016ICFGlobalCoachingStudy_ExecutiveSummary-2.pdf
22. Theebom, T. et al. (2013). Does coaching work? A meta-analysis of the effects of coaching on individual level outcomes in an organizational context. *Journal of Positive Psychology, 9*, 1–18.
23. Jones, R.J. et al. (2016). The effectiveness of workplace coaching: A meta-analysis of learning and performance outcomes from coaching. *Journal of Occupational and Organizational Psychology, 89*, 249–277.
24. Kraimer, M.L. et al. (2011). Antecedents and outcomes of organizational support for development: The critical role of career opportunities. *Journal of Applied Psychology, 96*, 485–500.
25. Benson, G.S. et al. (2004). You paid for the skills.
26. Burke, M.J., & Day, R.D. (1986). A cumulative study of the effectiveness of managerial training. *Journal of Applied Psychology, 71*, 232–245.
27. Burke, M.J. et al. (2011). The dread factor: How hazards and safety training influence learning and performance. *Journal of Applied Psychology, 96*, 46–70.
28. Hughes, A.M. et al. (2016). Saving lives: A meta-analysis of team training in health care. *Journal of Applied Psychology, 101*, 1266–1304
29. Fried, Y., & Ferris, G.R. (1987). The validity of the job characteristics model: A review and meta-analysis. *Personnel Psychology, 40*, 287–322.
30. Smither, J.W. et al. (2005). Does performance improve following multisource feedback? A theoretical model, meta-analysis, and review of empirical findings. *Personnel Psychology, 58*, 33–66.
31. Kluger, A.N., & DeNisi, A. (1996). The effects of feedback interventions on performance: A historical review, a meta-analysis, and a preliminary feedback intervention theory. *Journal of Applied Psychology, 119*, 254–284.
32. Brett, J.F., & Atwater, L.E. (2001). 360^0 feedback: Accuracy, reactions and perceptions of usefulness. *Journal of Applied Psychology, 86*, 930–942.
33. Tannenbaum, S.I., & Cerasoli, C.P. (2013). Do team and individual debriefs enhance performance? A meta-analysis. *Human Factors, 55*, 231–245.
34. Luthans, F., & Peterson, S.J. (2003). 360-degree feedback with systematic coaching: Empirical analysis suggests a winning combination. *Human Resource Management, 42*, 243–256.
35. Jones, R.J. et al. (2016). Effectiveness of workplace coaching.
36. Theeboom, T. et al. (2013). Does coaching work?
37. Thach, E.C. (2002). The impact of executive coaching and 360 feedback on leadership effectiveness. *Leadership and Organization Development Journal, 23*(4), 205–214.
38. Lacerenza, C.N. et al. (2017). Leadership training design, delivery, and implementation: A meta-analysis. *Journal of Applied Psychology, 102*, 1686–1718.
39. Kelloway, E.K., & Barling, J. (2010). Leadership development as an intervention in occupational health psychology. *Work & Stress, 24*, 260–279.

40. Mohr, C.D. et al. (2021). Can supervisor support improve daily employee well-being? Evidence of supervisor training effectiveness in a study of veteran employee emotions. *Journal of Occupational and Organizational Psychology, 94*, 400–426.
41. Brady, J.M. et al. (2021). Supportive supervisor training improves family relationships among employee and spouse dyads. *Journal of Occupational Health Psychology, 26*, 31–48.
42. Holman, D.J. et al. (2010). The mediating role of job characteristics in job redesign interventions: A serendipitous quasi-experiment. *Journal of Organizational Behavior, 31*, 84–105.
43. Chun, J.U. et al. (2012). A longitudinal study of mentor and protégé outcomes in formal mentoring relationships. *Journal of Organizational Behavior, 33*, 1071–1094.
44. Grant, A.M. et al. (2009). Executive coaching enhances goal attainment, resilience and workplace well-being: A randomized controlled study. *Journal of Positive Psychology, 4*, 396–407.
45. Kessler, S. (July 3, 2017). We've been worrying about the end of work for 500 years. *Quartz*. https://qz.com/1019145/weve-been-worrying-about-the-end-of-work-for-500-years/.
46. Fenwick, R., & Tansig, M. (2001). Scheduling stress: Family and health outcomes of shift work and schedule control. *American Behavioral Scientist, 44*, 1179–1198.
47. Barling, J. et al. (2002). Alternative work arrangements and employee-well-being. In P. Perrewe and D.C. Ganster (Eds.), *Research in occupational stress and well-being* (pp. 183–216). NY: JAI Press.
48. Haraldsson, G.D., & Kellam, J. (July 4, 2021). Going public: Iceland's journey to a shorter working week. https://autonomy.work/portfolio/icelandsww/
49. Katz, L.A., & Krueger, A.B. (2019). The rise and nature of alternative work arrangements in the United States, 1995–2015. *Industrial and Labor Relations Review, 72*, 382–416.
50. Grekou, D. (January 27, 2021). How did the COVID-19 pandemic affect the hours worked in Canada? An analysis by industry, province and firm size. https://www150.statcan.gc.ca/n1/pub/36-28-0001/2021001/article/00005-eng.htm
51. Falk, G. et al. (June 15, 2021). Unemployment rates during the COVID-19 pandemic. Congressional Research Service. R46554. https://crsreports.congress.gov
52. Benson, G.S. et al. (2004). You paid for the skills.
53. Kauhanen, M., & Nätti, J. (2015). Involuntary temporary and part-time work, job quality and well-being at work. *Social Indicators Research, 120*, 783–799.
54. McCallum. J.K. (2020). *Worked over: How round-the-clock work is killing the American dream*. NY: Basic Books.
55. Kooij, D.T.A.M. et al. (2010). Influence of age.
56. Van Dyne, L., & Ang, S. (1998). Organizational citizenship behavior of contingent workers in Singapore. *Academy of Management Journal, 41*, 692–703.
57. Wilkin, C.L. (2013). I can't get no job satisfaction: Meta-analysis comparing permanent and contingent workers. *Journal of Organizational Behavior, 34*, 47–64.
58. Buddelmeyer, H. et al. (2014). Non-standard "contingent" employment and job satisfaction: A panel data analysis. *Industrial Relations, 54*, 256–275.
59. Barling, J., & Gallagher, D.G. (1996). Part-time employment. In C.L. Cooper and I.T. Robertson (Eds.), *International review of industrial and organizational psychology* (pp. 243–277) (Vol. II). London: Wiley and Sons.
60. Barling, J. et al. (2002). Alternative work arrangements.
61. Barling, J., & Gallagher, D.G. (1996). Part-time employment.

62. Katz, L.A., & Krueger, A.B. (2019). Rise and nature.
63. Haines, V.Y. et al. (2018). Good, bad, and no so sad part-time employment. *Journal of Vocational Behavior, 104*, 128–140.
64. Liden, R.C. et al. (2003). The dual commitments of contingent workers: An examination of contingents' commitment to the agency and the organization. *Journal of Organizational Behavior, 24*, 609–625.
65. Shore, L.M., Barksdale, K., & Shore, T.H. (1995). Managerial perceptions of employee commitment to the organization. *Academy of Management Journal, 38*, 1593–1615.
66. Shore, T.H., Bommer, W.H., & Shore, L.M. (2008). An integrative model of managerial perceptions of employee commitment: Antecedents and influences on employee treatment. *Journal of Organizational Behavior, 29*, 635–655.
67. De Cuyper, N. et al. (2014). A multiple-group analyses of associations between emotional exhaustion and supervisor-rated individual performance: Temporary versus permanent call-center workers. *Human Resource Management, 53*, 623–633.
68. Chadwick, C., & Flinchbaugh, C. (2016). The effects of part-time workers on establishment financial performance. *Journal of Management, 42*, 1635–1662.
69. Eldor, L., & Cappelli, P. (2021). The use of agency workers hurts business performance: An integrated indirect model. *Academy of Management Journal, 64*, 824–850.
70. Jonsson, K.I. et al. (2018). Precarious employment and occupational accidents and injuries: A systematic review. *Scandinavian Journal of Work, Environment and Health, 44*, 341–350.
71. Anyfantis, I.D., & Boustras, G. (2020). The effects of part-time employment and employment in rotating periods on occupational accidents: The case of Greece. *Safety Science, 121*, 1–4.
72. Collinson, D.L. (1999). "Surviving the rigs": Safety and surveillance on North Sea oil installations. *Organization Studies, 20*, 579–600.
73. Jahoda, M. (1982). *Employment and unemployment: A social psychological analysis.* NY: Cambridge University Press.
74. Kachi, Y. et al. (2014). Precarious employment and the risk of serious psychological distress: A population-based cohort study in Japan. *Scandinavian Journal of Work, Environment and Health, 40*, 465–472.
75. Jang, S-Y. et al. (2015). Precarious employment and new onset severe depression symptoms: A population-based prospective study in South Korea. *Scandinavian Journal of Work, Environment and Health, 41*, 329–337.
76. Rönnblad, T. et al. (2019). Precarious employment and mental health: A systematic review and meta-analysis of longitudinal studies. *Scandinavian Journal of Work, Environment and Health, 45*, 429–443.
77. Kauhanen, M., & Nätti, J. (2015). Involuntary temporary.
78. Hock, E., & DeMeis, D.K. (1990). Depression in mothers of infants: The role of maternal employment. *Developmental Psychology, 26*, 285–291.
79. Barling J. et al. (1988). Employment commitment as a moderator of the maternal employment/child behaviour relationship. *Journal of Organizational Behavior, 9*, 113–122.
80. Guan, X., & Frenkel, S. (2019). How perceptions of training impact employee performance: Evidence from two Chinese manufacturing firms. *Personnel Review, 48*, 163–183.
81. Hughes, A.M. et al. (2016). Saving lives.

82. Belschak, F.D., & Den Hartog, D. (2009). Consequences of positive and negative feedback: The impact of emotions and extra-role behaviors. *Applied Psychology: An International Review, 58*, 274–303.
83. Sparr, J.L., & Sonnentag, S. (2008). Fairness perceptions of supervisor feedback, LMX, and employee well-being at work. *European Journal of Work and Organizational Psychology, 17*, 198–225.
84. Ogunfowora, B. et al. (2020). How do leaders foster morally courageous behavior in employees? Leader role modeling, moral ownership, and felt obligation. *Journal of Organizational Behavior, 42*, 483–503.
85. Baranik, L.E. et al. (2010). Why does mentoring work? The role of perceived organizational support. *Journal of Vocational Behavior, 76*, 366–373.
86. Carlisle, J. et al. (2019). Enhancing task performance through effective training: The mediating role of work environment and the moderating role effect of non-mandatory training. *Journal of Business Research, 104*, 340–349.
87. Baldwin, T.T., & Magjuke, R.J. (1991). Organizational training and signals of importance: Linking pretraining perceptions to intentions to transfer. *Human Resource Development Quarterly, 2*, 25–36.
88. Ragins, B.R. et al. (2017). Anchoring relationships at work: High-quality mentors and other supportive work relationships as buffers to ambient racial discrimination. *Personnel Psychology, 70*, 211–256.
89. Van Oosten, E.B. et al. (2019). Investing in what matters: The social impact of emotional and social competency development and executive coaching on leader outcomes. *Consulting Psychology Journal: Practice and Research, 71*, 249–269.
90. Albelda, R. et al. (2020). Gender and precarious work in the United States: Evidence from the Contingent Work Supplement 1995–2017. *Review of Radical Political Economics, 52*, 542–563.
91. Correll, S.J. et al. (2020). Inside the black box of organizational life: The gendered language of performance assessment. *American Sociological Review, 85*, 1022–1050.
92. Coury, S. et al. (September 30, 2020). Women in the workplace 2020. https://www.mckinsey.com/featured-insights/diversity-and-inclusion/women-in-the-workplace#
93. Jampol, L., & Zayas, V. (2021). Gendered white lies: Women are given inflated performance feedback compared with men. *Personality and Social Psychological Bulletin, 47*, 57–69.
94. Ciancetta, L.M., & Roch, S.G. (2021). Backlash in performance feedback: Deepening the understanding of the role of gender in performance appraisal. *Human Resource Management, 60*, 641–657.
95. Motro, D., & Ellis, A.P.J. (2017). Boys, don't cry: Gender and reactions to negative performance feedback. *Journal of Applied Psychology*, 102, 227–235.
96. Beaman, L. et al. (2012). Female leadership.
97. Cortland, C.I., & Kinias, Z. (2019). Stereotype threat and women's work satisfaction: The importance of role models. *Archives of Scientific Psychology, 7*, 81–89.
98. Davies, P. et al. (2005). Clearing the air: Identity safety moderates the effects of stereotype threat on women's leadership aspirations. *Journal of Personality and Social Psychology, 88*, 276–287.
99. Fiedler, F.E. et al. (1971). The culture assimilator: An approach to cross-cultural training. *Journal of Applied Psychology, 55*, 95–102.

100. Peretz, H., & Rosenblatt, Z. (2011). The role of societal cultural practices in organizational investment in training: A comparative study in 21 countries. *Journal of Cross-Cultural Psychology, 42*, 817–831.
101. Ramaswami, A. et al. (2014). Mentoring across cultures: The role of gender and marital status in Taiwan and the U.S. *Journal of Business Research, 67*, 2542–2549.
102. Brutus, S. et al. (2006). Internationalization of multi-source feedback systems: A six-country exploratory analysis of 360-degree feedback. *International Journal of Human Resource Management, 17*, 1888–1906.
103. Gillespie, T.L. (2005). Internationalizing 360-feedback: Are subordinate ratings comparable? *Journal of Business and Psychology, 19*, 361–382.
104. Ng, K-Y. et al. (2011). Rating leniency and halo in multisource feedback ratings: Testing cultural assumptions of power distance and individualism-collectivism. *Journal of Applied Psychology, 96*, 1033–1044.
105. Kossek, E.E. et al. (2017). Rating expatriate leader effectiveness in multisource feedback systems: Cultural distance and hierarchical fit. *Human Resource Management, 56*, 151–172.
106. Chi. N-W., & Lin, C.Y-Y. (2011). Beyond the high-performance paradigm: Exploring the curvilinear relationship between high-performance work systems and organizational performance in Taiwanese manufacturing firms. *British Journal of Industrial Relations, 49*, 486–514.
107. Lester, P.S. et al. (2011). Mentoring impact on leader efficacy and development: A field experiment. *Academy of Management Learning and Education, 10*, 409–429.
108. Chi. N-W., & Lin, C.Y-Y. (2011). Beyond the high-performance.
109. Lacerenza, C.N. et al. (2017). Leadership training design.
110. Avolio, B.J., Avey, J.B., & Quisenberry, D. (2010). Estimating return on leadership development investment. *Leadership Quarterly, 21*, 633–644.
111. Tannenbaum, S.I. et al. (1991). Meeting trainees' expectations.
112. Benson, G.S. et al. (2004). You paid for the skills.
113. Mintzberg H. (1989). *Mintzberg on management: Inside our strange world of organizations*. NY: Free Press.
114. Latham, G.P., & Whyte, G. (1994). The futility of utility analysis. *Personnel Psychology, 47*, 31–46.
115. Joshi, A. et al. (2021). Generativity mindsets.
116. Benson, G.S. et al. (2004). You paid for the skills.
117. Lepak, D.P. et al. (2012). Strategic HRM moving forward: What can we learn from micro perspectives. In G.P. Hodgkinson & J.K. Ford (Eds.), *International review of industrial and organizational psychology* (pp. 231–259). NY: Wiley.

Chapter 7

1. Dostoevsky, F. (2015). *The house of the dead; or, prison life in Siberia*. NY: Yurita Press.
2. Jaffe, S. (2021). *Work won't love you back: How devotion to our jobs keeps us exploited, exhausted, and alone*. NY: Hachette Book Group.
3. Lepore, J. (January 18, 2021). What's wrong with the way we work? *New Yorker*. https://www.newyorker.com/magazine/2021/01/18/whats-wrong-with-the-way-we-work

4. Herzberg, F. (January 1968). One more time, how do you motivate employees? *Harvard Business Review, 46*(1), 53–62.
5. Hackman, J.R., & Oldham, G.R. (1980). *Work redesign*. MA: Addison Wesley.
6. Hackman, J.R., & Oldham, G.R. (1975). Development of the Job Diagnostic Survey. *Journal of Applied Psychology, 60*, 159–170.
7. Kelloway, E.K. et al. (2010). Loving one's job: Construct development and implications for well-being. In P.L. Perrewe & D.C. Ganster (Eds.), *Research in occupational stress and well being* (Vol. 8). UK: Emerald Publishing.
8. Pfeffer, J. (1998). Six dangerous myths about pay. *Harvard Business Review, 76*(3), 109–119.
9. Frankl, V.E. (2006). *Man's search for meaning*. Boston: Beacon Press.
10. Based on Gallup research: What makes a great workplace? https://thepeoplegroup.com/wp-content/uploads/2008/04/article-gallup-research-what-makes-a-great-workplace1.pdf
11. Maslow, A.H. (1943). A theory of human motivation. *Psychological Review, 50*, 370–396.
12. Grant, A. (2014). *Give and take: A revolutionary approach to success*. NY: Penguin Books.
13. Westaby, J.D. et al. (2005). Intentions to work during terminal illness: An exploratory study of antecedent conditions. *Journal of Applied Psychology, 90*, 1297–1305.
14. Wegman, L.A. et al. (2018). Placing job characteristics in context: Cross-temporal meta-analyses of changes in job characteristics since 1975. *Journal of Management, 44*, 352–386.
15. Rentsch, J.R., & Steel, R.P. (1998). Testing the durability of job characteristics as predictors of absenteeism over a six-year period. *Personnel Psychology, 51*, 165–190.
16. Castanheira, F. (2016). Perceived social impact, social worth, and job performance: Mediation by motivation. *Journal of Organizational Behavior, 37*, 789–803.
17. Grant, A.M., & Hofmann, D.A. (2011). It's not all about me: Motivating hand hygiene among health care professional by focusing on patients. *Psychological Science, 22*, 1494–1499.
18. Bandura, A. (1977). *Social learning theory*. NJ: Prentice Hall.
19. Grant, A. (2008). The significance of task significance: Job performance effects, relational mechanisms, and boundary conditions. *Journal of Applied Psychology, 93*, 108–124.
20. Grant, A.M. et al. (2007). Impact and the art of motivation maintenance: The effects of contact with beneficiaries on persistence behavior. *Organizational Behavior and Human Decision Processes, 103*, 53–67.
21. Schermuly, C.C., & Meyer, B. (2016). Good relationships at work: The effects of leader-member exchange and team-member exchange on psychological empowerment, emotional exhaustion and depression. *Journal of Organizational Behavior, 37*, 673–691.
22. Johnson, M.J., & Jiang, L. (2017). Reaping the benefits of meaningful work: The mediating versus moderating role of work engagement. *Stress and Health, 33*, 288–297.
23. Sonnentag, S., & Grant, A.M. (2012). Doing good at work feels good at home, but not right away: When and why perceived prosocial impact predicts positive affect. *Personnel Psychology, 65*, 495–530.
24. Lavy, S., & Naama-Ghanayim, E. (2020). Why care about caring? Linking teachers' caring and sense of meaning at work with students' self-esteem, well-being, and school engagement. *Teaching and Teacher Education, 91*, 1–12.
25. Graeber, D. (May 4, 2018). "I had to guard an empty room": The rise of the pointless job. https://www.theguardian.com/money/2018/may/04/i-had-to-guard-an-empty-room-the-rise-of-the-pointless-job?CMP=Share_iOSApp_Other

26. Graeber, D. (2018). *Bullshit jobs: A theory*. NY: Simon & Schuster.
27. McBain, W.N. (1963). What can be done about job monotony? *Personnel Administration, 26*(3), 24–30.
28. Reijseger, G. et al. (2013). Watching the paint dry at work: Psychometric evaluation of the Dutch Boredom Scale. *Anxiety, Stress and Coping, 26*, 508–525.
29. Melamed, S. et al. (1995). Objective and subjective work monotony: Effects on job satisfaction, psychological distress, and absenteeism in blue collar workers. *Journal of Applied Psychology, 80*, 29–42.
30. Oates, W. (1972). *Confessions of a workaholic: The facts about work addiction*. NY: World Publishing.
31. Clark, M.A. et al. (2016). All work and no play? A meta-analytic examination of the correlates and outcomes of workaholism. *Journal of Management, 42*, 1836–1873.
32. Pollack, J.M. et al. (2020). Passion at work: A meta-analysis of individual work outcomes. *Journal of Organizational Behavior, 41*, 311–331.
33. Hamper, B. (1992). *Rivethead: Tales from the assembly line*. NY: Grand Central Publishing.
34. Bruursema, K. et al. (2011). Bored employees misbehaving: The relationship between boredom and counterproductive work behavior. *Work & Stress, 25*, 93–107.
35. Clark, M.A. (2016). All work and no play.
36. Ng, T.W.H. et al. (2007). Dimensions, antecedents, and consequences of workaholism: A conceptual integration and extension. *Journal of Organizational Behavior, 28*, 111–136.
37. Clark, M.A. (2016). All work and no play.
38. Birkeland, I.K., & Buch, R. (2015). The dualistic model of passion for work: Discriminate and predictive validity with work engagement and boredom. *Motivation and Emotion, 39*, 392–408.
39. Alessandri, G. et al. (2020). The costs of working too hard: Relationships between workaholism, job demands, and prosocial organizational citizenship behaviors. *Journal of Personnel Psychology, 19*, 24–32.
40. Ariely, D. et al. (2008). Man's search for meaning: The case of Legos. *Journal of Economic Behavior and Organization, 67*, 671–677.
41. Chandler, D., & Kapelner, A. (2013). Breaking monotony with meaning: Motivation in crowdsourcing markets. *Journal of Economic Behavior and Organization, 90*, 123–133.
42. Reijseger, G. et al. (2013). Watching the paint dry.
43. Melamed, S. et al. (1995). Objective and subjective monotony at work: Effects on job satisfaction, psychological distress, and absenteeism in blue-collar workers. *Journal of Applied Psychology, 80*, 29–42.
44. Bauer, G.F. et al. (2009). Socioeconomic status, working conditions and self-rated health in Switzerland: Explaining the gradient in men and women. *International Journal of Public Health, 54*, 23–30.
45. Van Hooff, M.L.M., & van Hooft, E.A.K. (2014). Boredom at work: Proximal and distal causes of affective work-related boredom. *Journal of Occupational Health Psychology, 19*, 348–359.
46. Van Hooff, M.L.M., & van Hooft, E.A.K. (2016). Work-related boredom and depressed mood from a daily perspective: The moderating roles of work centrality and need satisfaction. *Work & Stress, 30*, 209–227.
47. Tam, K.Y.Y. et al. (2021). Attention drifting in and out: The boredom feedback model. *Personality and Social Psychology Review, 25*, 251–272.

48. Wallace, J.C., & Chen, G. (2005). Development and validation of a work-specific measure of cognitive failure: Implications for occupational safety. *Journal of Occupational and Organizational Psychology, 78*, 615–632.
49. Frone, M.R. (1998). Predictors of work injuries among employed adolescents. *Journal of Applied Psychology, 83*, 565–576.
50. Lang, J. et al. (2012). Psychosocial work stressors as antecedents of musculoskeletal problems: A systematic review and meta-analysis of stability-adjusted longitudinal studies. *Social Science and Medicine, 75*, 1163–1174.
51. Clark, M.A. (2016). All work and no play.
52. Andreassen, C.S. et al. (2011). "Workaholism" and potential outcomes in well-being and health in a cross-occupational sample. *Stress and Health, 27*, e209–e214.
53. Clark, M.A. et al. (2016). All work and no play.
54. Bakker, A.B. et al. (2009). Workaholism and relationship quality: A spillover-crossover perspective. *Journal of Occupational Health Psychology, 14*, 23–33.
55. Allan, B.A. et al. (2019). Outcomes of meaningful work: A meta-analysis. *Journal of Management Studies, 56*, 500–528.
56. Grant, A.M. et al. (2007). Impact and the art.
57. Grant, A.M. (2008). The significance of task significance: Job performance effects, relational mechanisms, and boundary conditions. *Journal of Applied Psychology, 93*, 108–124.
58. Balducci, C. et al. (2021). The impact of workaholism on day-level workload and emotional exhaustion, and on longer-term job performance. *Work & Stress, 35*, 6–26.
59. Arnold, K.A. et al. (2007). Transformational leadership and psychological well-being: The mediating role of meaningful work. *Journal of Occupational Health Psychology, 12*, 193–203.
60. Nielsen, K. et al. (2008). The effects of transformational leadership on followers' perceived work characteristics and psychological well-being: A longitudinal study. *Work & Stress, 22*, 16–32.
61. Lee, M.C.C. et al. (2017). The linkages between hierarchical culture and empowering leadership and their effects on employees' work engagement: Work meaningfulness as a mediator. *International Journal of Stress Management, 24*, 392–415
62. Luksyte, A. et al. (2011). Why do overqualified incumbents deviate? Examining multiple mediators. *Journal of Occupational Health Psychology, 16*, 279–296.
63. Grant, A. (2012). Leading with meaning: Beneficiary contact, prosocial impact, and the performance effects of transformational leadership. *Academy of Management Journal, 55*, 458–476.
64. Bellé, N. (2013). Leading to make a difference: A field experiment on the performance effects of transformational leadership, perceived social impact, and public service motivation. *Journal of Public Administration Research and Theory, 24*, 109–136.
65. Liu, D. et al. (2021). Tackling the negative impact of COVID-19 on work engagement and taking charge: A multi-study investigation of frontline health care workers. *Journal of Applied Psychology, 106*, 185–198.
66. Grant, A.M., & Sonnentag, S. (2010). Doing good buffers against feeling bad: Prosocial impact compensates for negative task and self-evaluations. *Organizational Behavior and Human Decision Processes, 111*, 13–22.

67. Harris, K.J. et al. (2007). An investigation of abusive supervision as a predictor of performance and the meaning of work as a moderator of the relationship. *Leadership Quarterly, 18*, 252–263.
68. Yang, K., & Girgis, J.S. (2019). Are women more likely than men are to care excessively about maintaining positive social relationships? A meta-analytic review of gender differences in sociotropy. *Sex Roles, 81*, 157–172.
69. Becker, S.W., & Eagly, E.H. (2004). The heroism of women and men. *American Psychologist, 59*, 163–178.
70. Beauregard, T.A. (2012). Perfectionism, self-efficacy and OCB: The moderating role of gender. *Personnel Review, 41*, 590–608.
71. Kidder, D.L. (2002). The influence of gender on the performance of organizational citizenship behaviors. *Journal of Management, 28*, 629–648.
72. Elizur, D. et al. (1991). The structure of work values: A cross cultural comparison. *Journal of Organizational Behavior, 12*, 21–38.
73. Huang, T-P. (2011). Comparing motivating work characteristics, job satisfaction and turnover intention of knowledge workers and blue-collar workers, and testing a structural model of the variables' relationships in China and Japan. *International Journal of Human Resource Management, 22*, 924–944.
74. Roe, R.A. et al. (2000). A comparison of work motivation in Bulgaria, Hungary, and the Netherlands: Test of a model. *Applied Psychology: An International Review, 49*, 658–687.
75. DeVoe, S.E., & Iyengar, S.S. (2004). Managers' theories of subordinates: A cross-cultural comparison of managers' perceptions of motivation and appraisal of performance. *Organizational Behavior and Human Decision Processes, 93*, 47–61.
76. Bunderson, J.S., & Thompson, J.A. (2009). The call of the wild: Zookeepers, callings, and the double-edged sword of deeply meaningful work. *Administrative Science Quarterly, 54*, 32–57.
77. Lepore, J. (2021). *What's wrong with the way.*
78. Lin, S-L., & Hsieh, A-T. (2002). Constraints on task identity on organizational commitment. *International Journal of Manpower, 23*(2), 151–165.
79. Harris, K.J. et al. (2007). Investigation of abusive supervision.
80. Liu, D. et al. (2021). Tackling the negative impact.
81. Van der Voet, J., & Steijn, B. (2021). Relational job characteristics and prosocial motivation: A longitudinal study of youth care professionals. *Review of Public Personnel Administration, 41*, 57–77.
82. Hughes, E.C. (1951). Work and the self. In J.J. Rohrer & M. Sherif (Eds.), *Social psychology at the crossroads: The University of Oklahoma lectures in social psychology* (pp. 313–323). NY: Harper & Row.
83. Ashforth, B.E. et al. (2007). Normalizing dirty work: managerial tactics for countering occupational taint. *Academy of Management Journal, 50*, 149–174.
84. Ashforth, B.E. et al. (2007). Normalizing dirty work.
85. Arnold, K.A. et al. (2007). Transformational leadership.
86. Nielsen, K. et al. (2008). Effects of transformational leadership.
87. Arnold, K.A. et al. (2007). Transformational leadership.
88. Schaubroech, J. et al. (2018). Changing experiences of work dirtiness, occupational disidentification, and employee withdrawal. *Journal of Applied Psychology, 103*, 1086–1100.

89. Deery, S. et al. (2019). Can dirty work be satisfying? A mixed method study of workers doing dirty jobs? *Work, Employment and Society, 33*, 631–647.
90. Rabelo, V.C., & Mahalingam, R. (2019). "The really don't want to see us": How cleaners experience invisible "dirty" work. *Journal of Vocational Behavior, 113*, 103–114.
91. Newman, A. (April 10, 2020). *What N.Y.C. sounds like every night at 7.* https://www.nytimes.com/interactive/2020/04/10/nyregion/nyc-7pm-cheer-thank-you-coronavirus.html
92. Hennekam, S. et al. (2020). From zero to hero: An exploratory study examining sudden hero status among nonphysician health care workers during the COVID-19 pandemic. *Journal of Applied Psychology, 105*, 1088–1100.
93. Saigol, L., & Mitchell, A. (April 7, 2020). Companies hike pay to support the frontline heroes of the U.K.'s coronavirus pandemic. https://www.marketwatch.com/story/dozens-of-companies-hike-pay-to-support-the-frontline-heroes-of-the-uks-coronavirus-pandemic-2020-04-07
94. Wegman, L.A. et al. (2018). Placing job characteristics.
95. Luksyte, A. et al. (2011). Why do overqualified incumbents.
96. Lepore, J. (2021). *What's wrong with the way.*
97. Autin, K.L., & Allan, B.A. (2020). Socioeconomic privilege and meaningful work: A psychology of working perspective. *Journal of Career Assessment, 28*, 241–256.
98. Piff, P.J. et al. (2010). Having less, giving more: The influence of social class on prosocial behavior. *Journal of Personality and Social Psychology, 99*, 771–784.

Chapter 8

1. Grocutt, A. (2014). Work safety. *WCB-Alberta Worksight, 8*(1), 4.
2. Hoffman, D.A. et al. (2017). 100 years of occupational safety research: From basic protections and work analysis to a multilevel view of workplace safety and risk. *Journal of Applied Psychology, 102*, 375–388.
3. Statistics. Association of Workers' Compensation Boards of Canada. https://awcbc.org/en/statistics/#nwisp
4. Injuries, illnesses, and fatalities. U.S. Bureau of Labor Statistics. https://www.bls.gov/iif/oshcfoi1.htm
5. https://press.hse.gov.uk/2020/07/01/hse-releases-annual-workplace-fatality-figures-for-2019-20/
6. HSE fatal accident statistics—a decrease in workplace fatalities for 2019/20. (July 6, 2020). https://www.dacbeachcroft.com/es/es/articles/2020/july/hse-fatal-accident-statistics-a-decrease-in-workplace-fatalities-for-201920/#:~:text=A%20total%20of%20111%20workers,lowest%20annual%20number%20on%20record
7. Over 30 million working days lost due to illness and injury in the past year. (September 11, 2020). https://www.phrsolicitors.co.uk/news/over-30-million-working-days-lost-due-to-illness-and-injury-in-the-past-year
8. *2017–2019 National work injury, disease and fatality statistics.* (2017–2019). Association of Workers' Compensation Boards of Canada.
9. Brown, J. (2020). Nearly 50 years of occupational safety and health data. *Beyond the Numbers, 9*(9). https://www.bls.gov/opub/btn/volume-9/nearly-50-years-of-occupational-safety-and-health-data.htm

10. Greenhouse, D. (November 16, 2009). Work-related injuries underreported. *New York Times*. https://www.nytimes.com/2009/11/17/us/17osha.html
11. *Death on the job: The toll of neglect. A national and state-by-state profile of worker safety and health in the United States* (29th ed.). (2020). DC: AFL-CIO.
12. Eisenberg, W.M., & McDonald, H. (1988). Evaluating workplace injury and illness records: Testing a procedure. *Monthly Labor Review, 111*, 58–60.
13. Maslow, A.H. (1943). A theory of human motivation. *Psychological Review, 50*, 370–396.
14. Kaminski, M. (2001). Unintended consequences: Organizational practices and their impact on workplace safety and productivity. *Journal of Occupational Health Psychology*, 6, 127–138.
15. Roberts, K., & Markel, K.S. (2001). Claiming in the name of fairness: Organizational justice and the decision to file for workplace injury compensation. *Journal of Occupational Health Psychology, 6*, 332–347.
16. Regina Hechanova-Alampay, R., & Beehr, T.A. (2001). Empowerment, span of control, and safety performance in work teams after workforce reduction. *Journal of Occupational Health Psychology, 6*, 275–282.
17. Turner, N. et al. (2021). Human resource management practices and organizational injury rates. *Journal of Safety Research, 78*, 69–79.
18. Barling, J. et al. (2003). Accidental outcomes: Attitudinal consequences of workplace injuries. *Journal of Occupational Health Psychology, 8*, 74–85.
19. Ready, A.E. et al. (1993). Fitness and lifestyle parameters fail to predict back injuries in nurses. *Canadian Journal of Applied Physiology, 18*, 80–90.
20. Zohar, D. (2000). A group-level model of safety climate: Testing the effect of group climate on microaccidents in manufacturing jobs. *Journal of Applied Psychology, 85*, 587–596.
21. Zacharatos, A. et al. (2005). High performance work systems and occupational safety. *Journal of Applied Psychology*, 90, 77–93.
22. Ford, M.T., & Tetrick, L.E. (2011). Relations among occupational hazards, attitudes, and safety performance. *Journal of Occupational Health Psychology, 16*, 48–66.
23. BP American refinery explosion. *CSB*. https://www.csb.gov/bp-america-refinery-explosion/
24. Cummins, C., & Gold, R. (July 27, 2005). An oil giant faces questions about a deadly blast in Texas. *Wall Street Journal*. https://www.wsj.com/articles/SB112241614288796636
25. Dembe, A.E. (2001). The social consequences of occupational injuries and illnesses. *American Journal of Industrial Medicine, 40*, 403–417.
26. Biddle, J. et al. (1998). What percentage of workers with work-related illnesses receive workers' compensation benefits? *Journal of Occupational & Environmental Medicine, 40*, 325–331.
27. Dawson SE. 1994.Workers' compensation in Pennsylvania: The effects of delayed contested cases. *Journal of Health Social Policy, 6*, 87–100.
28. Dong, X.S. (2016) Economic consequences of workplace injuries in the United States: Findings from the National Longitudinal Survey of Youth (NLSY79). *American Journal of Industrial Medicine, 59*, 106–118.
29. Galizzi, M., & Zagorsky, J. (2009). How do on-the-job injuries and illnesses impact wealth? *Labour Economics, 16*, 26–36.

30. Asfaw, A. et al. (2012). Incidence and costs of family member hospitalization following injuries of Workers' Compensation claims. *American Journal of Industrial Medicine, 55,* 1028–1036.
31. Afsaw, A. et al. (2015). Musculoskeletal disorders and associated healthcare costs among family members of injured workers. *American Journal of Industrial Medicine, 58,* 1205–1216.
32. Cohn, J.B., & Wardlaw, M.I. (2016). Financing constraints and workplace safety. *Journal of Finance, 71,* 2017–2057.
33. Allison, R.W. et al. (2019). Construction accidents in Australia: Evaluating the true costs. *Safety Science, 120,* 886–896.
34. BP American refinery explosion.
35. Keogh, J. et al. (2000). The impact of occupational injury on injured worker and family: Outcomes of upper extremity cumulative trauma disorders in Maryland workers. *American Journal of Industrial Medicine, 38,* 498–506.
36. Van Eerd, D. et al. (2011). The course of absenteeism involving neck pain: A cohort study of Ontario lost-time claimants. *Spine, 36,* 977–982.
37. Frone, M.R. (2013). *Alcohol and illicit drug use in the workforce and workplace.* DC: American Psychological Association.
38. Asfaw, A., & Souza, K. (2012). Incidence and cost of depression after occupational injury. *Journal of Occupational and Environmental Medicine, 54,* 1086–1091.
39. Orchard, C. et al. (2020). Prevalence of serious mental illness and mental health service use after a workplace injury: A longitudinal study of workers' compensation claimants in Victoria, Australia. *Occupational and Environmental Medicine, 77,* 185–187.
40. Carnide, N. et al. (2016). Course of depressive symptoms following a workplace injury: A 12-month follow-up update. *Journal of Occupational Rehabilitation, 26,* 204–215.
41. Frone, M.R. (1998). Predictors of work injuries among employed adolescents. *Journal of Applied Psychology, 83,* 565–576.
42. Dembe, A.E. (2001). Social consequences.
43. Kirsh, B. et al. (2012). The nature and impact of stigma towards injured workers. *Journal of Occupational Rehabilitation, 22,* 143–154.
44. Matthews, L.R. et al. (2019). Posttraumatic stress disorder, depression, and prolonged grief in families bereaved by a traumatic workplace death: The need for satisfactory information and support. *Frontiers in Psychiatry, 10,* 1–10.
45. Hisle-Gorman, E. et al. (2019). The impact of military parents' injuries on the health and well-being of their children. *Health Affairs, 38,* 1358–1365.
46. Asfaw, A. et al. (2021). Association of parent workplace injury with emotional and behavioral problem in children. *Journal of Occupational and Environment Medicine.* https://europepmc.org/article/med/33929401
47. Turner, N. et al. (2021). Parents' work injuries and children's mental health: The moderating role of children's work centrality. *Journal of Safety Research, 77,* 61–66.
48. Kosny, A et al. (2018). Family matters: Compensable injury and the effect on family. *Disability and Rehabilitation, 40,* 935–944.
49. Barling, J. et al. (1991). Preemployment predictors of union attitudes: The role of family socialization and work beliefs. *Journal of Applied Psychology, 76,* 725–731.

50. Lawrence, E.R. et al. (2013). The influence of workplace injuries on work-family-conflict: Job and financial insecurity as mechanisms. *Journal of Occupational Health Psychology, 18*, 371–383.
51. Barling, J. et al. (1992). *The union and its members: A psychological approach.* NY: Oxford University Press.
52. Barling, J. et al. (1992). *Union and its members.*
53. (June 11, 1999). Achievements in Public Health, 1900–1999: Improvements in workplace safety—United States, 1900–1999. *Morbidity and Mortality Weekly Report Weekly, 48*(22), 461–469. https://www.cdc.gov/mmwr/preview/mmwrhtml/mm4822a1.htm
54. Achievements in Public Health, 1900–1999.
55. Morantz, A.D. (2013). Coal mine safety: Do unions make a difference? *Industrial and Labor Relations Review, 66*, 88–116.
56. Fenn, P., & Ashby, S. (2004). Workplace risk, establishment size and union density. *British Journal of Industrial Relations, 42*, 461–480.
57. Mastekaasa, A. (2013). Unionization and certified sickness absence: Norwegian evidence. *Industrial and labor Relations Review, 66*, 117–141.
58. Morse, T. et al. (2003). The relationship of unions to prevalence and claim filing for work-related upper-extremity musculoskeletal disorders. *American Journal of Industrial Medicine, 44*, 83–93.
59. Oka, C. (2015). Improving working conditions in garment supply chains: The role of unions in Cambodia. *British Journal of Industrial Relations, 53*, 1–26.
60. Caskey, J., & Ozel, N.B. (2017). Earnings expectations and employee safety. *Journal of Accounting and Economics, 63*, 121–147.
61. Number of occupational injury deaths in the U.S. from 2003 to 2020, by gender. *Statista.* https://www.statista.com/statistics/187127/number-of-occupational-injury-deaths-in-the-us-by-gender-since-2003/
62. Lin, Y-H. et al. (2008). Gender and age distribution of occupational fatalities in Taiwan. *Accident Analysis and Prevention, 40*, 1604–1610.
63. Todd, D. (April 28, 2012). Nine of 10 workplace deaths are men: Day of mourning. *Vancouver Sun.* https://vancouversun.com/news/staff-blogs/nine-of-10-workplace-deaths-men-day-of-mourning
64. Bauerle, T.J. et al. (2016). Mere overrepresentation: Using cross-occupational injury and job analysis data to explain men's risk for workplace fatalities. *Safety Science, 83*, 102–113.
65. Hauret, L., & Williams, D.R. (2017). Cross-national analysis of gender differences in job satisfaction. *Industrial Relations, 56*, 203–235.
66. Shuang, D. et al. (2019). An experimental study of intrusion behaviors on construction sites: The role of age and gender. *Safety Science, 115*, 425–434.
67. Morris, E. (September 2008). Making sense of ambiguous evidence. *Harvard Business Review*, 53–57. https://hbr.org/2008/09/making-sense-of-ambiguous-evidence
68. Bauerle, T.J. et al. (2016). Mere overrepresentation? Using cross-occupational injiury and job analysis data to explain men's risk for workplace fatalities. *Safety Science, 83*, 102–113.
69. Stergiou-Kita, M. et al. (2016). What's gender got to do with it? Examining masculinities, health and safety and return to work in male dominated skilled trades. *Work, 54*, 721–733.
70. Turner, B. (April 29, 2021). Workplace violence is broken down into 4 categories. *Loss Prevention Magazine..*

71. Tiesman, H.M. et al. (2012). Workplace homicides among U.S. women: The role of intimate partner violence. *Annals of Epidemiology, 22*, 277–284.
72. When domestic violence intersects with your workplace. (September 9, 2016). *Crisis Prevention Institute.* https://www.crisisprevention.com/en-CA/Blog/September-2016/When-Domestic-Violence-Intersects-With-Your-Workpl
73. Bureau of Labor Statistics. (May 12, 2011). *Survey of workplace violence prevention.* http://www.bls.gov/iif/osh_wpvs.htm
74. Fayard, G.M. (2008). Work-related fatal injuries in parking lots, 1993–2002. *Journal of Safety Research, 39*, 9–18.
75. Takala, J. (1999). Global estimates of fatal occupational accidents. *Epidemiology, 10*, 640–646.
76. Hämäläinen, P. et al. (2009). Global trend according to estimated number of occupational accidents and fatal work-related diseases at region and country level. *Journal of Safety Research, 40*, 125–139.
77. Accidents at work statitsics. (January 2022). *Eurostat Statistics Explained.* https://ec.europa.eu/eurostat/statistics-explained/index.php?title=Accidents_at_work_statistics
78. Driscoll, T. (2020). Global and regional burden of disease and injury in 2016 arising from occupational exposures: A systematic analysis for the Global Burden of Disease study 2016. *Occupational and Environmental Medicine, 77*, 133–141.
79. Hämäläinen, P. et al. (2009). Global trend.
80. Moyce, S.C., & Schenker, M. (2018). Migrant workers and their occupational health and safety. *Annual Review of Public Health, 39*, 351–365.
81. Moyce, S.C., & Schenker, M. (2018). Migrant workers.
82. Joshi, S. et al. (2021). Implementing virtual reality technology for safety training in the precast/prestressed concrete industry. *Applied Ergonomics, 90*, 1–11.
83. Granger, S. et al. (2021). The next best safety dollar: Using evidence to decide how to invest in workplace safety. *Organizational Dynamics, 50*, 1–9.
84. Burke, M.J. et al. (2011). The dread factor: How hazards and safety training influence learning and performance. *Journal of Applied Psychology, 96*, 46–70.
85. Levine, D.I. et al. (2012). Randomized government safety inspections reduce worker injuries with no detectable job loss. *Science, 336*, 907–911.
86. Smith, S. (February 17, 2011). OSHA's Michaels responds to criticism his agency is a job killer. https://www.ehstoday.com/standards/osha/article/21908012/oshas-michaels-responds-to-criticism-his-agency-is-a-job-killer
87. Reporters without borders. https://rsf.org/en
88. RSF's 2020 round-up: 50 journalists killed, two-thirds in countries "at peace." https://rsf.org/en/news/rsfs-2020-round-50-journalists-killed-two-thirds-countries-peace
89. Feinstein A. (2006). *Journalists under fire: The psychological hazards of war reporting.* Baltimore: Johns Hopkins University Press.
90. Feinstein, A. et al. (2002). A hazardous profession: War, journalists, and psychopathology. *American Journal of Psychiatry,* 159, 1570–1575.
91. Feinstein, A. (2013). Witnessing images of extreme violence: A psychological study of journalists in the newsroom. *Journal of the Royal Society of Medicine Open, 5*(8), 1–7.
92. 3607 US healthcare worker deaths. *Guardian.* https://www.theguardian.com/us-news/ng-interactive/2020/aug/11/lost-on-the-frontline-covid-19-coronavirus-us-healthcare-workers-deaths-database

93. Hassan, A. (October 28, 2021). Coronavirus cases and deaths were vastly underestimated in U.S. meatpacking plants, a House report says. *New York Times*. https://www.nytimes.com/2021/10/28/world/meatpacking-workers-covid-cases-deaths.html
94. Employment rate in the United States from 1990 to 2021. *Statistica*. https://www.statista.com/statistics/192398/employment-rate-in-the-us-since-1990/
95. Thompson, D. (July 27, 2021). Hygiene theatre is a huge waste of time. *Atlantic*. https://www.theatlantic.com/ideas/archive/2020/07/scourge-hygiene-theater/614599/
96. Baum, K.B. et al. (May 3, 2020). How Cargill became the suite of Canada's largest single outbreak of COVID-19. *Globe and Mail*. https://www.theglobeandmail.com/business/article-how-cargill-became-the-site-of-canadas-largest-single-outbreak-of/
97. (January 27, 2021). New study shows some people with COVID-19 symptoms still go to work in Peel Region. *City News*. https://toronto.citynews.ca/2021/01/27/new-data-shows-some-people-with-covid-19-symptoms-still-go-to-work-in-peel-region/
98. Addleman, S. et al. (2021). Mitigating airborne transmission of SARS-CoV-2. *Canadian Medical Association Journal*, *193*(26), e1010–e1011. https://www.cmaj.ca/content/193/26/E1010.short
99. Grant, T. (June 17, 2021). How to keep workers safe from COVID-19: Focus on the air they breathe. *Globe and Mail*. https://www.theglobeandmail.com/canada/article-how-to-keep-workers-safe-from-covid-19-focus-on-the-air-they-breathe/
100. Levine, D.I. et al. (2012). Randomized government.
101. Perritt, K.R. et al. (2017). *Young worker injury deaths: A historical summary of surveillance and investigated findings*. WV: U.S. Department of Health and Human Services, Centers for Disease Control and Prevention, National Institute for Occupational Safety and Health. DHHS (NIOSH) Publication No. 2017–168.
102. Geurin, R.J. et al. (September 4, 2020). Nonfatal occupational injuries to younger workers—United States, 2012–2018. *Morbidity and Mortality Weekly Report*, 69(35), 1204–1209. https://www.cdc.gov/mmwr/volumes/69/wr/mm6935a3.htm#F1_down
103. Davis, L., & Vautin, B.P. (2013). Tracking work-related injuries among young workers: An overview of surveillance in the United States. In C.W. Runyan et al. (Eds.), *Health and safety of young workers: Proceedings of a U.S. and Canadian series of symposia* (pp. 105–125). WV: U.S. Department of Health and Human Services, Centers for Disease Control and Prevention, National Institute for Occupational Safety and Health. DHHS (NIOSH) Publication No. 2013-144.
104. Davis, L., & Vautin, B.P. (2013). Tracking work-related injuries.
105. Turner, N. et al. (2015). Prevalence and demographic correlates of microaccidents and reactions to dangerous work among young workers in Canada. *Journal of Safety Research*, *53*, 39–43.
106. Tucker, S. et al. (2014). Work-related injury underreporting among young workers: Prevalence, gender differences, and explanations for underreporting. *Journal of Safety Research*, *50*, 67–73.
107. Tucker, S., & Turner, N. (2013). Waiting for safety: Responses by young Canadians workers to unsafe work. *Journal of Safety Research*, *45*, 103–110.
108. Salminen, S. et al. (2021). Age, sex, and genetic and environmental effects on unintentional injuries in youth and adult twins. *Twin Research and Human Genetics*, *21*, 502–506.
109. Fullagar, C.J.A. et al. (1995). Impact of early socialization on union commitment and participation: A longitudinal study. *Journal of Applied Psychology*, *80*, 147–157.

110. (April 2018). Safety and health at work: Why are youth at risk? *International Labor Organization: InfoStories*. https://www.ilo.org/infostories/en-GB/Stories/safety-health/youth#how-do-we-solve-the-problem
111. Tucker, S. et al. (2014). Work-related injury.
112. Perritt, K.R. et al. (2017). *Young worker*.
113. Rauscher, K.J., & Runyan, C.W. (2013). Prevalence of working conditions associated with adolescent occupational injury in the U.S.: A review of the literature. In C.W. Runyan et al. (Eds.), *Health and safety of young workers: Proceedings of a U.S. and Canadian series of symposia* (pp. 126–136). WV: U.S. Department of Health and Human Services, Centers for Disease Control and Prevention, National Institute for Occupational Safety and Health. DHHS (NIOSH) Publication No. 2013-144..
114. Robson, L.S. et al. (2012). A systematic review of the effectiveness of occupational health and safety training. *Scandinavian Journal of Work, Environment and Health, 38*, 193–208.
115. Turner, N. et al. (2021). Human resource.
116. Rauscher, K.J., & Runyan, C.W. (2013). Prevalence of working conditions.
117. Barling, J. et al. (2002). Development and test of a model linking safety-specific transformational leadership and occupational safety. *Journal of Applied Psychology*, 87, 488–496.
118. Tucker, S. et al. (2016). Safety in the C-suite: How chief executive officers influence organizational safety climate and employee injuries. *Journal of Applied Psychology, 101*, 1228–1239.
119. HSE fatal accident statistics—a decrease in workplace fatalities for 2019/20. (July 6, 2020). https://www.dacbeachcroft.com/es/gb/articles/2020/july/hse-fatal-accident-statistics-a-decrease-in-workplace-fatalities-for-201920/
120. Texas City aftermath. (October 1, 2010). *ENN: Environmental News Network*. https://www.enn.com/articles/41839-bp-texas-city-aftermath

Chapter 9

1. Corlett, E. (February 21, 2022). *Guardian*. https://www.theguardian.com/world/2022/feb/21/new-zealand-will-lift-covid-restrictions-only-when-well-beyond-peak-jacinda-ardern-says
2. Zakaria, F. (2020). *Ten lessons for a post-pandemic world*. NY: Norton.
3. Barling, J. (1990). *Employment, stress and family functioning*. NY: Wiley.
4. Dean, B. (January 6, 2022). Zoom under stats: How many people used zoom in 2022? *Backlinko*. https://backlinko.com/zoom-users
5. Marmot, M. et al. (2020). *Build back fairer: The COVID-19 Marmot Review. The Pandemic, Socioeconomic and Health Inequalities in England*. London: Institute of Health Equity
6. Adams, S. (September 18, 2022). *Dilbert*. https://dilbert.com/
7. https://quoteinvestigator.com/2013/10/20/no-predict/
8. Mehdi, T., & Morisette, R. (May 26, 2021). Working from home after the COVID-19 pandemic: An estimate of worker preferences. https://doi.org/10.25318/36280001202100500001-eng
9. Dey, M. et al. (June 2020). Ability to work from home: Evidence from two surveys and implications for the labor market in the COVID-19 pandemic. *Monthly Labor Review, 1–19*.

10. Partington, R. (May 17, 2021). Most people in the UK did not work from home in 2020, says ONS. *Guardian*. https://www.theguardian.com/world/2021/may/17/home-working-doubled-during-uk-covid-pandemic-last-year-mostly-in-london
11. Seabrook, J. (January 25, 2021). Has the pandemic transformed the office forever? *New Yorker*. https://www.newyorker.com/magazine/2021/02/01/has-the-pandemic-transformed-the-office-forever
12. Katz, D., & Kahn, R.L. (1966). *The social psychology of organizations*. NY: Wiley.
13. Frone, M.R. (2018). What happened to the employed during the Great Recession? A U.S. population study of net change in employee insecurity, health, and organizational commitment. *Journal of Vocational Behavior, 107*, 246–260.
14. Smith, E.B. et al. (2021). Better in the shadows? Public attention, media coverage, and market reactions to female CEO announcements. *Sociological Science, 8*, 119–149.
15. Barling, J. (2014). *The science of leadership: Lessons from research for organizational leaders*. NY: Oxford University Press.
16. Zenger, J., & Folkman, J. (2019). Women score higher than men in most leadership skills. *Harvard Business Review*, June 25, 2019. https://hbr.org/2019/06/research-women-score-higher-than-men-in-most-leadership-skills
17. Garikipati, S., & Kambhampati, U. (2021). Leading the fight against the pandemic: Does gender "really" matter. *Feminist Economics, 27*(1–2), 401–418.
18. Sergent, K., & Stajkovic, A.D. (2020). Women's leadership is associated with fewer deaths during the COVID-19 crisis: Quantitative and qualitative analyses of United States Governors. *Journal of Applied Psychology, 105*, 771–783.
19. Welcome to the 30% club. (2021). https://30percentclub.org/
20. McFarland, J. (November 26, 2012). Glacial progress of women on Canada's boards prompts calls for reform. *Globe and Mail*. http://www.theglobeandmail.com/report-on-business/careers/management/board-games-2012/glacial-progress-of-women-on-canadas-boards-prompts-calls-for-reform/article5644350/
21. Barling, J. (2014). *Science of leadership*.
22. Barling, J. (2014). *Science of leadership*.
23. Terjesen, S., Sealy, R., & Singh, V. (2009). Women directors on corporate boards: A review and research agenda. *Corporate Governance: An International Review, 17*, 320–337.
24. Grandey, A.A. et al. (2020). Tackling taboo topics: A review of the three *M*s in working women's lives. *Journal of Management, 46*, 7–35.
25. Browne, J. (2014). *The glass closet: Why coming out is good for business*. NY: Harper.
26. Baker, S.J., & Lucas, K. (2017). Is it safe to bring myself to work? Understanding LGBTQ experiences of workplace indignity. *Canadian Journal of Administrative Sciences, 34*, 133–148.
27. Law, C.L. et al. (2011). Trans-parency in the workplace: How the experiences of transsexual employees can be improved. *Journal of Vocational Behavior, 79*, 710–723.
28. Griffith, K.H., & Hebl, M.R. (2002). The disclosure dilemma for gay men and lesbians: "Coming out" at work. *Journal of Applied Psychology, 87*, 1191–1199.
29. Labor force statistics from the Current Population Survey. https://www.bls.gov/cps/cpsaat11.htm
30. Deitch, E.A., Barsky, A., Butz, R.M., Chan, S., Brief, A.P., & Bradley, J.C. (2003). Subtle yet significant: The existence and impact of everyday racial discrimination in the workplace. *Human Relations, 56*, 1299–1324.

31. Quillian, L., & Midtbøem, A.H. (2021). Comparative perspectives on racial discrimination in hiring: The rise of field experiments. *Annual Review of Sociology, 47*, 391–415.
32. Triana, M.D.L. et al. (2015). Perceived workplace racial discrimination and its correlates: A meta-analysis. *Journal of Organizational Behavior*, 36, 491–513.
33. Padela, A.I. et al. (2016). Religious identity and workplace discrimination: A national survey of American Muslim physicians. *AJOB Empirical Bioethics, 7*(3), 149–159.
34. Berdahl, J.L., & Moore, C. (2006). Workplace harassment: Double jeopardy for minority women. *Journal of Applied Psychology, 91*, 426–436.
35. Ghumman, S., & Ryan, A.M. (2013). Not welcome here: Discrimination towards women who wear the Muslim headscarf. *Human Relations, 66*, 671–698.
36. Indigenous peoples. https://www.worldbank.org/en/topic/indigenouspeoples
37. Thorpe-Moscon, J., & Ohm, J. (2021). *Building inclusion for Indigenous peoples in Canadian workplaces*. Catalyst.org.
38. Julien, M. et al. (2010). Stories from the circle: Leadership lessons learned from aboriginal leaders. *Leadership Quarterly, 21*, 114–126.
39. Gardner, J.R. (October 11, 2021). Seventy-two hours under the heat dome. *New Yorker*. https://www.newyorker.com/magazine/2021/10/18/seventy-two-hours-under-the-heat-dome
40. Cecco, L. (July 3, 2020). Record heatwave may have killed 500 people in western Canada. *Guardian*. https://www.theguardian.com/world/2021/jul/02/canada-heatwave-500-deaths
41. Flavelle, C. (July 15, 2021). Work injuries tied to heat are vastly undercounted, study finds. *New York Times*. https://www.nytimes.com/2021/07/15/climate/heat-injuries.html
42. Tigchelaar, M. et al. (2020). Work adaptations insufficient to address growing heat risk for U.S. agricultural workers. *Environmental Research Letters, 15*. https://doi.org/10.1088/1748-9326/ab86f4
43. Sengupta, S. (July 17, 2021). "No one is safe": Extreme weather batters the wealthy world. *New York Times*. https://www.nytimes.com/2021/07/17/climate/heatwave-weather-hot.html
44. Paul, K. (December 15, 2021). Amazon faces scrutiny over worker safety after tornado strikes warehouse. *Guardian*. https://www.theguardian.com/technology/2021/dec/13/amazon-warehouse-collapse-safety-illinois
45. Robertson, J., & Barling, J. (2013). Greening organizations through leaders' influence on employees' pro-environmental behaviors. *Journal of Organizational Behavior, 34*, 176–194.
46. *In most countries surveyed, majorities see climate change as a major threat*. (April 18, 2019). Pew Research Centre. https://www.pewresearch.org/fact-tank/2019/04/18/a-look-at-how-people-around-the-world-view-climate-change/ft_19-04-18_climatechangeglobal_inmostsurveyedcountries_edited_2/
47. Dewan, A. (July 20, 2021). Scientists are worried by how fast the climate crisis has amplified extreme weather. https://www.cnn.com/2021/07/20/world/climate-change-extreme-weather-speed-cmd-intl/index.html
48. Lee, M. (2022). The distinct effects of wealth- and CSR-oriented shareholder unrest on CEO career outcomes: A new lens on settling up and executive job demands. *Academy of Management Journal*. https://doi.org/10.5465/amj.2019.1346
49. Cook, I. (September 15, 2021). Who is driving the Great Resignation? *Harvard Business Review*. https://hbr.org/2021/09/who-is-driving-the-great-resignation

Index

For the benefit of digital users, indexed terms that span two pages (e.g., 52–53) may, on occasion, appear on only one of those pages.

Tables and figures are indicated by *t* and *f* following the page number. Numbers followed by n indicate footnotes.